MEMOIRS
OF THE
REVIVAL
IN THE SOUTH PACIFIC

MEMOIRS
OF THE
REVIVAL
IN THE SOUTH PACIFIC

HOW GOD LIT A FIRE AND CHANGED NATIONS

REV. J.S. PASTERKAMP

Copyright © 2023 by Rev. J.S. Pasterkamp.

Library of Congress Control Number:		2022916100
ISBN:	Hardcover	978-1-6698-3161-7
	Softcover	978-1-6698-3160-0
	eBook	978-1-6698-3159-4

All rights reserved. No part of this book may be reproduced or transmitted in any form or by any means, electronic or mechanical, including photocopying, recording, or by any information storage and retrieval system, without permission in writing from the copyright owner.

Any people depicted in stock imagery provided by Getty Images are models, and such images are being used for illustrative purposes only.
Certain stock imagery © Getty Images.

Print information available on the last page.

Rev. date: 01/27/2023

To order additional copies of this book, contact:
Xlibris
AU TFN: 1 800 844 927 (Toll Free inside Australia)
AU Local: (02) 8310 8187 (+61 2 8310 8187 from outside Australia)
www.Xlibris.com.au
Orders@Xlibris.com.au
826202

CONTENTS

Chapter 1   'Pray for that Boy with The Red Hair!' 1

Chapter 2   Tell Me Your Company, and I will
Tell You Who You Are 8

Chapter 3   A Horse Named Reus (Giant)
and a Horse Named Ico 17

Chapter 4   Coby 27

Chapter 5   Going 'Down Under' 37

Chapter 6   Thursday Island 46

Chapter 7   Daru 59

Chapter 8   A Few Months in Australia 74

Chapter 9   Rabaul 91

Chapter 10 Siwai 106

Chapter 11 Rabaul – We Start! 114

Chapter 12 The Plantations 129

Chapter 13 Siwai 143

Chapter 14 Coby's First Trip into Siwai, and
Her Very Special Experience 155

Chapter 15 The Story of David Pookaro 168

Chapter 16 Kavieng and . . . Back to Siwai 178

Chapter 17 Australia – The Lord Turns Our Lives
Upside Down 190

Chapter 18 Tari in The Highlands 204

Chapter 19 The Solomon Islands 214

Chapter 20 A Few More Months in Rabaul and Then 234

Chapter 21	Kiwai Island	245
Chapter 22	David Wallis	260
Chapter 23	Kavieng	268
Chapter 24	'Yu Mas Tanim Bel!'	290
Chapter 25	Two Very Precious People	302
Chapter 26	We Are Moving to Bougainville!	320
Chapter 27	The Capital – Port Moresby	341
Chapter 28	'In My Name shall They Cast Out Evil Spirits'	361
Chapter 29	Rascals	376
Chapter 30	The Bible School	383
Chapter 31	Much Blessing, Many Miracles, and Breakthroughs	394

CHAPTER 1

'Pray for that Boy with The Red Hair!'

FILLED WITH EXPECTATIONS, I sat down to listen to my brother's new gramophone recording. What I heard on that Sunday evening in 1961 would change my life, and the course of my life, completely.

I received my love for popular classical music from my mother and my elder brother Klaas. Sometimes he took me to concerts which I really enjoyed. Klaas was married and lived in close proximity to my parents. Whenever he bought a new gramophone recording, he would come by to let us hear it. When I came home that Sunday evening during the 1961 summer, Klaas told us that he had bought this recording and that we should really listen to it. I expected beautiful classical music, but that was not what I heard at all. It was something completely different.

Klaas worked in a city some sixty kilometres north from where he lived. A young man at his work had given his life to Jesus in an evangelistic service at a Pentecostal church. He shared his testimony with my brother, who was greatly impacted by it. He also took my brother to other evangelistic services, and he was so impressed by it all that he had bought the recording. On that recording were testimonies of people who had found Jesus or had been healed by Him. It also contained a short message: 'Jesus is the way to God.' I did not understand it all, but it grabbed me. I had never heard anything like this, but it was real. I felt it. I knew it!

My parents had five children. I was the fourth. My father was born and bred on Urk, a little island, which later became part of the mainland after it was reclaimed from the sea, Dutch style.

As a young man, he had moved from the island to the town of Zaandam, not far from Amsterdam. Having been raised as a nominal Christian, he was quite legalistic and conservative, as most people on the island were. He brought a fair share of this into our family. As a young boy, I absolutely believed in God, but many aspects of the church were meaningless to me. I had observed quite a few people who went to church on Sunday but did not behave like Christians during the week. I thought it was all very hypocritical. Nevertheless, there were some aspects of church life that I felt attracted to. Like a youth pastor, who originally came from Indonesia, he really made an impression on me. When he spoke about Jesus, it was like he knew Him. Years later, I visited him. He had become a minister in a Dutch Reformed church. At that time, I realised again that this pastor knew Jesus intimately. Somehow I had felt this when I was young.

Every Sunday we had to go to church. Obeying caused less trouble than refusing, so I would go. When Klaas got married, he almost immediately stopped this weekly church visit. In a way, I was jealous, and I was looking forward to leaving my parental home and to be able to decide for myself whether or not I would go to church. Actually I had already made my decision: I would no longer go.

Then came that Sunday evening and the gramophone recording that would change everything. Klaas had not made a personal decision for Jesus yet, but he had been greatly impacted by what he had seen and heard. There would be a service in Amsterdam the following Friday. He asked me if I wanted to come with him, and I did. The service was conducted by the Pentecostal movement called Streams of Power led mainly by the Hoekendijk family. It was held in a Lutheran church building in the south of Amsterdam. I remember a few things very well: the joy, the enthusiasm, the happy and beautiful singing, and the organ playing. It was impressive. Communion was celebrated that evening. I had experienced communion in our church but had not understood much of it. Usually it was a very serious business, but here it was different.

The preacher handed everyone the bread personally, which was new for me. I sat and watched. When he came to someone he did not know, he would ask that person if he or she was a child of God. When that person said no, a short conversation followed in the middle of the service, while everyone could hear what was being said. If that person wanted to become a child of God, the preacher would pray, and that person was asked to repeat his words in prayer, audible to everyone. I was getting tense. He did not know me, so the chance of him asking me if I was a child of God was high, and I did not know whether I was. Or rather, I knew for sure that I was not, for I had experienced this quite strongly some weeks before.

I was an enthusiastic member of the lifeguard rescue team, and I was in training to be a youth instructor. During an exercise, I nearly drowned. While I was stuck underwater, the thought flashed through my mind: *Now I have to appear before God, and I am not ready at all.* I was terrified. Luckily, it ended well, and I am still here, but the fact that things were not right between God and me had become very clear.

And here was the possibility looming that the preacher would ask me if I was a child of God. I quickly figured out what my options were. I could not leave because Klaas was with me, and he clearly had no desire to leave. If I were to leave, I had to get out of my seat, and there were people on both sides of me. Everyone would see, and what would happen then? Suppose someone spoke to me. So leaving was not an option, but I had never participated in a communion service because I had not publicly professed my faith in the church, which is a prerequisite for celebrating communion in our denomination, the Dutch Reformed Church. Why this was a prerequisite was unclear to me. The speaker came closer. I had to quickly choose an option. I chose one and hoped it would go well. He gave the bread to Klaas and obviously knew that he had accepted Jesus, which he had done the week before.

Then it was my turn. I broke out in a sweat. The speaker looked at me intently and asked, 'Are you a child of God?' I had my answer ready and said, 'I think so!' Then he gave me the bread and put his hand on my head and began to speak. I will never forget this one line: 'At a young age I will call you, and at a young age you will serve Me.' I now understand that this was a prophecy, but at the time I had no idea what that meant. However, I did know that these were words from God to me. They touched something very deep inside me, because even as a child, I did have the thought: *I want to be a missionary.* I was ashamed of that thought, however, because I did not really know what it meant and did not understand how that thought came to me. The only thing I vaguely remember is that at Sunday school, two women had shared something about missions. The story was about dark-skinned people and a tropical warm country. I also knew that the Reformed Church had a college to train missionaries. I also knew the words of Jesus, that the gospel should be preached in all the world. But when I had to choose my further education at high school, I did not dare to say that I wanted to be a missionary, so I chose a profession which I thought was similar, namely that of a teacher. In that same month, September, I would go to college to become a teacher. It was my intention to become a high school teacher. So when the preacher told me that God would call me at a young age to stand in His service, it touched the right spot in my heart. Actually, I made my decision for Jesus that evening, late August 1961; but I did it deep within my heart and not openly *as* yet. I did not dare!

Klaas and I continued to go to the Friday night services at Streams of Power. I enjoyed it. Then came the first Friday in October. The evangelist who preached on the gramophone recording, Ben Hoekendijk, preached that night.

Then came the altar call to really, radically, and openly make a decision for Jesus. I think the word 'repentance' was even mentioned. I could no longer restrain myself and went forward, together with three or four others. We knelt down; and that night, the sixth of October 1961, I gave my life to Jesus and made a total commitment to Him. I was thrilled. What I will always remember from that night is the deep peace that entered my heart. A peace that has never left forty-six years now.

On my way back on the train from Amsterdam to Zaandam, where my parents' home was, something happened. Two elderly ladies who had been to the service as well were on the same train. We sat opposite each other. I was so happy that I had openly made my decision for Jesus that I wanted to celebrate this with a cigarette. I was seventeen years old and already smoked quite a bit!

The ladies were shocked when they saw the cigarette. They had heard my name, and one of them said, 'John, a child of God does not smoke!' I was greatly surprised and replied, 'Where is that in the Bible?' I did not know! She could not answer the question, and I made a decision in my heart that I would show all these Christians that you could smoke and be a child of God. I stuck to this decision for a few months. I never doubted the good intentions of these ladies; but the first thing that fellow Christians told me, after I had chosen for Jesus, was that I should not smoke. So I received their judgment and disapproval instead of them leaving it to the Holy Spirit, who convicts of sin. What they achieved was a negative inner reaction. I was already prophesying in services and testifying about Jesus in open-air street services, while I was still smoking. But the moment came when the Holy Spirit convicted me, and I stopped smoking and never smoked again.

At home I went to my bedroom as quickly as possible. I smoked another cigarette and knelt down. I was so happy. I did not know how to pray, but I tried. The next moment my small bedroom was filled with the presence of the Lord. It was as if everything was light. I tried to pray in Dutch, but the only thing that came out of my mouth was a different language, and I could not seem to stop it, nor did I want to. I was in heaven. The Lord was with me, everywhere around me and in me. And I felt so close, so very close to Him. I had no idea what that language was, but it was of God; there was no doubt about it. I had heard people in the meeting speak in a strange language. I knew that in the Roman Catholic Church they spoke Latin, so it had to be good. I now understand that I was filled with the Holy Spirit at that moment and that I spoke in new tongues, just like the disciples on the day of Pentecost. I still speak in tongues, and there have been very few days that I haven't.

I made a joke about it later: after two cigarettes to celebrate my conversion, I was filled with the Holy Spirit. Don't misunderstand me, smoking is really not good for you! And I still think that children of God should not smoke. However, there are also other things that children of God should not do . . .

While the glory of the Lord filled my bedroom and the language of the Holy Spirit kept flowing out of my mouth, God spoke to me. Whether I really heard the audible voice of God, or whether I heard the voice of God clearly in my heart, I do not know, but God said, 'I am calling you to be a missionary!' The word 'missionary' meant other countries and maybe even the farthest corners of the world – that was clear to me. I was not going to be a teacher but a missionary. I knew it and made sure everyone around me knew it as well.

After the first service, in which the preacher prophesied over me, I knew for certain that I should not go to college and study to become a teacher, because I was going to become a missionary. So I cancelled teachers college. My father was furious, but I was certain. Sadly, he was going to get angry a few more times. My relationship with my father was not good for quite some time after my conversion.

I took a job at the head office of a chain of supermarkets. I did not stay for more than a year because I did not enjoy the job at all.

A few days later, while my mother was cooking in the kitchen, I told her that I had made a decision for Jesus and that I now knew I was a child of God. My mother listened very quietly and looked at me with tears in her eyes. She said, 'As a little girl, I also gave my life to Jesus in the Salvation Army, and I was dedicated to the Lord. But as a teenager and a young adult, I lost it.' I had never realised that my mother came out of a Salvation Army family. I knew that my grandmother on my mother's side went to the Salvation Army, but I had never realised that this was how my mother was raised.

I was filled with passion. I had come to know Jesus, and I was going to be a missionary. I even thought I might never marry because of it. I was burning with the desire to tell other people about Jesus and to lead them to Him.

A year or two later, a woman who always came to the services told me that the Lord had given her the ministry of intercession. She spent a lot of time in prayer. One day, while she was praying, she received a vision. She saw the Lutheran church building where the Pentecostal church met. The service was about to start. Then a boy with red hair entered. She knew most people in the service but did not know that boy. She asked the Lord about it, and He told her that this boy did not know Him yet. The Lord gave her the assignment of praying for this boy with the red hair.

A while after that, a boy with red hair entered. 'That is not him,' spoke the Lord to her heart. 'Keep praying.' A few weeks later, I entered with my brother Klaas. Her heart leapt when she saw a young man with red hair. 'That is him,' spoke the Lord in her heart. 'Keep praying for him because he will serve Me.' Apparently, she kept praying for me for a long time. How very special is that!

When I gave my life to Jesus, I had just turned seventeen; 'At a young age I will call you, and at a young age you will serve Me.' I was twenty when I started to serve the Lord full-time. And now, forty-two years later, I am still serving Him full-time. But then I still had very, very much to learn.

CHAPTER 2

Tell Me Your Company, and I will Tell You Who You Are

IN HOLLAND, THERE is a saying which, roughly translated, says, 'The people you mix with [hang out with] will sooner or later affect you and make you better or worse.'

These words are mainly used in a negative sense, but the positive is absolutely true too!

Streams of Power, the Pentecostal movement in which I came to Jesus, owed its existence to two great, powerful movements of God. The first was the healing movement of the fifties and sixties in the twentieth century. God used men like Oral Roberts, T. L. Osborn, A. A. Allen, and William Branham in a special way in healing. Their books, records, tapes, and films were well known within Streams of Power, and I read the books eagerly and also listened and watched the tapes and films. The names I just mentioned are of men who were used powerfully and extraordinarily by God. They were a sheer inspiration to me.

The second, and maybe the strongest connection, was the unique outpouring of the Holy Spirit in 1948 in Canada. That outpouring became known as the Latter Rain Revival. In it the teaching about the nine gifts of the Holy Spirit was central, as the apostle Paul described them in his first letter to the Corinthians. In the Pentecostal movement that had begun in 1906 in Azusa Street, Los Angeles, the focus was more on speaking in tongues as a sign and proof of receiving the baptism in the Holy Spirit. Concerning the other gifts of the Spirit, people took the attitude that you had to wait for God to give them to you.

In the Latter Rain Revival, it was taught that when a believer receives the baptism in the Holy Spirit, the nine gifts of the Spirit are in the believer and that it is a matter of faith to see them function. Especially the gift of prophecy was very central. This movement brought a rediscovered truth back to God's children.

A leader from that movement, a brother Leonard, came to the Netherlands and conducted courses about the gifts of the Holy Spirit. Streams of Power was a result of his coming and his teaching. Consequently there was a lot of attention given to the gifts of the Holy Spirit, especially the prophetic.

A few weeks after my conversion, followed by the baptism in the Holy Spirit, I prophesied in a service for the first time. After we had sung for some time, there was a time to prophesy or share what the Lord gave you. I sensed very deeply that God had given me a message for the church. It was a simple prophecy, and the preacher that night even referred to it in his sermon. In the atmosphere and spiritual environment of the gifts of the Holy Spirit, it was not difficult to enter that dimension.

There was also a lot of attention given to healing. The sick were prayed for in nearly every service, and as a new Christian, I saw miracles happen.

A few months after my conversion, there was a baptismal service. A swimming pool was rented, and a Bible study was given about baptism in water by immersion. I really wanted to obey the Lord and get baptised. Baptism was, after all, one of the first signs of being someone who wanted to be a disciple of Jesus. But if I were to ask my father for permission, I knew what the answer would be! A very big *no*. So I decided to say nothing and to be baptised.

The baptismal service was in January 1962. Nearly eighty people were baptised. I was one of the last ones to be baptised. I was extremely nervous, but I did what the Lord asked of me. That evening I came home with a bundle of wet clothes. 'Where have you been, and what have you done?' was my father's stern question. When I told him that I was baptised, the atmosphere at home changed. It was almost war.

A few days later, our Dutch Reformed minister came to talk with me. What had I done, and how could I have done such a thing? I had kicked God in the face by my baptism. I testified and shared about my love for the Lord. The minister went home with many things to think about. Shortly afterwards, he asked me if I wanted to share about my conversion and the experience with the Holy Spirit on Pentecost Sunday in a Reformed church service. But I was not to talk about baptism. That Sunday evening, the minister gave an introduction, and I shared my testimony for about fifteen minutes. It went very well, and I sensed that the Lord helped me enormously. Shortly thereafter, I heard that this matter had been discussed in the church council and that this Pasterkamp boy was not allowed to share about his experience in a service ever again. The minister was very disappointed. He was clearly searching for the truth himself. As a result, I then left that church and became totally involved in the Pentecostal movement. Years later, after I had become a missionary, I received a letter from this minister. He had heard that I had become a missionary and was very happy about that. He had retired and was studying the life and ministry of Thomas à Kempis, the author of the famous book *The Imitation of Christ*.

Not long after my conversion, I was in a meeting in Amsterdam. After the message came the invitation for people to come forward and accept Jesus. An older man who sat near me obviously wanted to get up and go forward. He looked around but saw that no one else stood up, so he remained seated. The speaker gave another invitation for people to come to repentance. Again, he wanted to get up and go forward but, looking around, saw that he probably would be the only one; so he remained seated. *I will go and talk to him later, and maybe I can lead him to Jesus*, I thought. Immediately after the service, the man walked to the exit. I went after him to talk to him, but someone else reached him before me. Unfortunately, it was a man who often came to disrupt the meetings. He also regularly showed up at street services to cause trouble and to ridicule us. He said to the old man, 'What a circus, isn't it? So this is what they call Christianity. It looks like a show, all these hypocrites!'

The old man listened, bewildered. I felt so angry that I whispered in the ear of the old man, 'You must not listen to the devil.' I might have been right, but it was a very foolish thing to say. The man heard it and called out, 'Did you call me a devil?' He started cursing and shouting and got into a rage, even when some of the leaders tried to get him out of the building. He made so much noise that people living next to the church came to see what was happening. Peter Vlug, who was responsible for the service, eventually called the police. The man continued to rant and rave outside. It was around 10.30pm. Then the police came and took the man with them. Peter Vlug came to me and had a stern conversation with me, as only he could. I knew that his serious rebuke was completely deserved. I felt so small. I had tried to do something for the Lord, and the police had to come to clean up the mess. Pasterkamp in action! When I got home, my father asked if the service had been good. 'Yes, it was okay,' I replied and went straight to my bedroom. I knelt down and poured out my heart before the Lord. I would always follow Him, but I would never do anything again. I was a complete failure. For once I had the courage to do something and the police needed to be called to sort it out. On top of that, Peter Vlug had rebuked me quite firmly. After my rage had subdued, I heard the voice of the Lord deep within my heart, 'Are you finished?' 'Yes, I am finished and I think that I made myself very clear!' I replied. Then I heard the voice of the Lord again. 'I still love you so very much.' I could not argue with that and realised that I would go on and serve the Lord.

I have always felt a little bit like David, who wanted to bring the Ark of the Covenant back to Jerusalem. Someone had died, and the celebration stopped. But David did not stop. He sought God intensely, and a great revival followed.

Peter Vlug Sr. and I became very good friends, and to this day there is a deep bond between us. He and his dear wife, Els, were witnesses at our wedding. They are two special people. Their book *I Have Kept the Faith* is a gripping account of their walk with God.

The first great healing I experienced myself was my grandmother's healing. She was a sweet woman, but I never saw her in any other dress than her traditional attire that was customarily worn by women from Urk. But Grandmother was ill, and in the hospital, on the point of death. Although my relationship with my father was complicated, he called me at work and asked, 'You believe that God heals, don't you?' He already knew my answer. 'Can you come to the hospital and pray for Grandma?' My father was the eldest of ten children, though only seven were still alive. My boss allowed me to go and see my grandmother. When I arrived at the hospital, my grandmother, who was unconscious, lay in a separate room; and my aunts and uncles were all there, surrounding her, making sure they were close to her when she died. They were all there, even the aunt who had migrated to Canada.

To walk in and say that I was going to pray for Grandma now and that God would heal her was not an option! I joked about it once saying that if I did that, then there would be two people in the hospital. I knew one uncle all too well, and he wasn't a nice man. So in my heart I prayed. Soon a nurse arrived. She asked the family to move to a waiting room on the opposite side of the corridor, because she had to make the bed. Suddenly I realised that I might have ten or twenty seconds alone with Grandma. The nurse was ready, and she walked over to the family to say they could return. Grandma was alone for a few moments! I went in, put my hands on her, and prayed, 'Lord, heal Grandma, amen.' Then I left quickly. I was leaning innocently against the door when my aunts and uncles re-entered the room, and as before, they sat in a circle around her. My father whispered when he passed me, 'Have you been able to pray?' I nodded. The family waited, but on the third day, Grandma was eating again. A week later she was home, and she lived for several more years. I was able to speak with her later. With her church background, she had never accepted Jesus. I explained it to her, and I know that she consciously made a decision for Jesus. I will see my dear grandma again in heaven.

Another miracle was the healing of Mrs. Van Leeuwen. I had faithfully attended the Friday night services at Streams of Power in Amsterdam for a few months when I discovered that a few other people from my hometown, Zaandam, also attended. I got in touch with them and visited them. They were lovely people. I offered to conduct a Bible study, and they were eager for me to do that. I read every pamphlet and book that I could get my hands on, and those were the first Bible studies I gave!

One of the first nights was about healing. In the middle of the Bible study, Mrs. Van Leeuwen's face showed that she was in pain. She went to the kitchen, and it was obvious that she took some medication. She came back, but the pain was still evident on her face. I was nervous. I had never prayed for a sick person while others were watching. Mrs. Van Leeuwen went to the kitchen again. Clearly she was in a lot of pain. I really wanted to pray for her, but I just did not dare. Finally I could do nothing else; and deadly nervous, I said, 'Shall I pray for you?' Her answer was clear: 'I was hoping all the time you would say that.' My knees were shaking while I prayed. The Bible study group of about ten people watched, and some prayed with me. It was certainly not a long prayer, but she was healed that evening. Later she told me that she suffered from gallstones. When I was 'home' in the years to come, I visited her a few times. She has never had gallstone attacks again. I was eighteen when I saw the first healing miracles happen through my own hands, and it was an awesome experience.

In Streams of Power, Bible courses lasting two weeks were given every year. You gave up your summer holidays to attend. One summer, after my conversion, I went to such a Bible course. Over a hundred people participated and were together at a beautiful conference centre in the forests. A Bible study was held every morning and afternoon by Elisabeth Hoekendijk, the wife of the founder of Streams of Power, who was affectionately called Mother Bep. The six fundamental principles from Hebrews were covered with a strong emphasis on the baptism in the Holy Spirit, and the nine gifts of the Spirit, as Brother Leonard from Canada had taught. Much of the course content was actually taken from his study material. Anyone who had not yet received the baptism in the Holy Spirit received it during such a course. Or if you had never spoken in new tongues or prophesied, they prayed for you, and you were encouraged to step out in faith and use these gifts. Many people prophesied for the first time in their lives during these courses.

In the evenings, it was usually Karel Hoekendijk who spoke. Everyone called him Father Karel. I never forgot one of his sermons.

'Christ in you, the hope of glory,' the words of the apostle Paul in Colossians 1:27. It was a revelation to him, but it became a revelation to me as well that evening.

At the end of the two weeks, a prophetic word from the Lord was given over each one who had followed the course. I still have mine as I copied it from the tape recording forty-four years ago. Right up till today, this prophecy has been literally fulfilled. They were unforgettable weeks that gave one a major spiritual boost.

In Streams of Power, the emphasis was on the power of God, but there was little emphasis on spiritual character. This would cause problems later, but I received a foundation in that movement that I am very, very thankful for.

A few months after my conversion, I became involved with the youth. On Sunday afternoons, the youth conducted their own meeting in a nice little hall at the Keizersgracht, along one of the beautiful and famous old canals in Amsterdam. Afterwards, we had a meal together; and in the evening, we evangelised in the centre of Amsterdam. We sang and then shared our testimonies one by one out in the open, often with many people listening. Very soon I had to share my testimony before a crowd as well. I learned to preach in the infamous red-light district of Amsterdam – a good place to learn preaching!

Evangelising in the red-light district sometimes led to major confrontations with pimps, prostitutes, and the like. We often prayed with people in the street, for them to accept Jesus. Follow-up care consisted of an invitation to come to a service or to make an arrangement to meet them personally. From time to time we heard from people who came out of that lifestyle.

If the weather was not too good, a covered shopping mall was a good place to evangelise. One Sunday evening, a young man shared his testimony. A man from the crowd became angry, walked up to him, and was about to hit him in his face. Suddenly his arm stiffened, and he could not do anything. His arm was fixed in the position to attack! The guy panicked and tried with all his might to pull his arm back, but he couldn't. The one who had shared his testimony went up to the man, and he prayed a simple prayer, and the arm was released and became normal again. That open-air service lasted a long time. We had a very, very attentive crowd after that event.

In another open-air meeting, there were a lot of people listening, but it looked as if a downpour was about to begin. The first people began to leave. They did not want to get wet. One of our youth leaders was preaching and shouted that the people had to wait, because he was going to pray that it would not rain. That is something the people wanted to see. He prayed. It rained around the square, but it was dry where we stood! Everyone saw it and was amazed.

Despite imperfections in the movement, this was the atmosphere in which I came to the Lord, and a strong foundation was laid in my life. Indeed, *the people you mix with (hang out with) will sooner or later affect you and deeply influence your life.*

Still, I sometimes felt that there was something in me that I did not understand. One evening in the last days of summer, I was home alone. I did not feel well at all. I tried to read the Bible, but I just could not. I tried to pray, but I could not do that either. My head began spinning. I went to bed around nine o'clock because I felt so miserable, but then it really started. Suddenly, I heard nails scratching my pillow next to my ear. I was terribly frightened, got dressed, and went to our new youth leaders in Amsterdam. I had heard of demons and that people sometimes had to be delivered from them, and this appeared to be the case. A little after ten, I plopped down on this lovely couple's couch and told them what was going on. I asked them if they could pray for me. The youth leader, named Harry, laid his hands on me and commanded the demons to leave me. Very clearly I felt twice that something from inside come up and left me. I, indeed, needed deliverance. What a relief! What I was delivered of I do not know. I always suspected it had something to do with the family and previous generations, but what I had felt for quite a while has never returned. I came home late and slept wonderfully, and the next day I could read the Bible without any trouble. My Bible reading even improved, and it was as if I understood God's Word better and that it entered my heart even more strongly. It all started with a powerful repentance, and now there was deliverance. Both aspects, repentance and deliverance, would become a major emphasis of the ministry the Lord would give us in the years to come.

Precisely one year after I had come to the Lord, I preached for the first time, together with Martin van der Mooren, another young man from the youth group. We had to fill the time slot for preaching: Martin fifteen minutes and I fifteen minutes. Martin went first, and then it was my turn. I preached about the parable of the talents that Jesus told in Matthew 25. The talents were and are to me the fullness of the Holy Spirit and the gifts, fruit, and abilities of the Holy Spirit. What do we do with these gifts? Perhaps I was preaching mostly to myself. Afterwards, I walked past two of the leaders. They were talking, and I overheard them saying, 'That boy just has it. He is surely going to be a preacher.' If there is something that I never, never thought I would do, it was to stand very often before people to preach. Preaching and teaching are to me very precious gifts that God has given. After that first time, I preached again, and then again, until I regularly spoke at youth and outreach activities.

In the autumn of 1962, there was a youth weekend, and we went with all the youth in rented Volkswagen vans to a lovely place in the forest about an hour-and-a-half drive from Amsterdam. There was a request to pick up two girls at a boarding school for children of skippers, in Amsterdam West. So we did. The two girls were waiting. They were smoking. Their clothes were different. It looked as if they were rebelling against what was considered normal. They did not give the impression of being hungry for God. They were looking for adventure and wanted to experience what these 'crazy' Pentecostal people were all about. But after the first service of the youth weekend, they both came forward, crying and wanting to accept Jesus. The next morning they were both filled with the Holy Spirit. It was amazing. One of them cried and cried. Within twenty-four hours, she had come to Jesus and had been filled with the Holy Spirit. In the following week, she stopped smoking once and for all. From that youth weekend onward, she would follow Jesus radically. That girl was Coby!

CHAPTER 3

A Horse Named Reus (Giant) and a Horse Named Ico

A BURNING PASSION TO evangelise and win people for Jesus, seeing lots of possibilities, but having no money to do it – that was a good description of our youth group. But even without money, there are possibilities. God is the God of the impossible!

Two leaders in our youth group had a plan: to go from small town to small town and from village to village, with a horse and cart during spring and summer, that is, from May to September, to evangelise. The cart would be their home – a kind of caravan. The meetings would all be in the open air. The horse needed only grass and water, and the Lord would provide for the young leaders' daily needs. The ravens brought food to Elijah, didn't they?

A farmer friend gave the two youth leaders a flat cart used to carry hay. A steel frame was built onto it and covered with a canopy. On the inside was a cabinet with a cooking stove, a place for a bottle of gas, an old desk, a piece of carpet on the floor, and a settee for two. They slept on inflatable beds on the floor. On one side of the white canopy was painted in big letters 'Jesus Christ the same yesterday and today.' There was no room for the words 'and forever'. On the other side were the words of an old Negro spiritual: 'That old time religion is good enough for me!' On the back was a map of the Netherlands with all the places the horse and cart would visit. Above the map was written 'Evangelistic Crusade'. On the front, a lifebuoy, on which was painted 'Jesus saves'.

Another farmer was willing to lend a horse for four months, which was already destined to be slaughtered. The young men planned the route, applied for permits to conduct open-air services, and contacted related and well-known congregations, mostly Pentecostal, to ask for help.

The leaders of Streams of Power raised their eyebrows, but it became a big success. During four months in 1962, the two youth leaders, who were also brothers, and everyone who helped them, were able to lead many people, young and old, to Jesus.

Whenever I could, I would visit them. The outreach mainly took place in the east of the country. Hitch-hiking was a popular way to travel for all members of our youth fellowship. Often, I would persuade my brother Klaas to go together in his car and join the team in the evening, for the open-air meetings. It was a huge success. A leading Dutch secular weekly magazine published a large article with pictures and gave it very positive exposure. I was very enthusiastic about it and was involved as much as possible. The following year, one of the brothers did the horse-and-cart tour again with another young man from the youth group. That year I used my two weeks' holiday to be with them. We were in the north-east of our country; and we even went to Ameland, one of the islands in the north of the Netherlands, to evangelise. After the summer, one of the team intended to go to Switzerland while the other team member was planning something else. That meant that the horse-and-cart tours would end. That could not be! I prayed and prayed and prayed; and the following two years, Martin, a friend from the Amsterdam youth group, and I did the tour together. Though it was originally the two brothers' idea, I was the one who became well known because of it. In the Netherlands, many elderly people and others of my age still know me as 'John of the horse and cart'.

In the winter of 1963–1964, I began dating Coby, the girl who cried so much when she came to the Lord at a youth weekend. In this book, I am devoting an entire chapter to Coby! In May 1964, Martin and I started the third horse-and-cart tour. We began in the area which is world famous for its flowers, mainly tulips, then to the southern part of the province, and from there to the centre of Holland. We arrived there in the beginning of September with a rally which drew quite a crowd.

In this tulip bulb region, we received help from a new Pentecostal congregation that had a very active youth group. Night after night people came to the open-air service, where we had the opportunity to pray with many people.

How did we organise it? During the day we travelled with the horse and cart to the next village or small town. That was never far away, no more than three hours. On the cart, behind the horse on the driver's seat, over the back roads, through the Netherlands, it was lovely. When we arrived in the village, we would ask a farmer if we could camp for the night on his property, and if the horse could spend the night in the pasture. We almost always found a farmer who would allow it. In the afternoon, we rode through the village with a small sound system powered by a battery. We announced the service, and in the evening around seven o'clock, we were in the town square or another suitable open place. We could always find some grass for the horse. A young woman, who helped us tremendously, held a children's meeting first. She did that very well. Hundreds of children prayed to accept Jesus. Afterwards, we sang together with the Christians who came to help us, and one by one we testified. When possible, we ended with a short message (usually by Martin or me), and we always made a call for repentance. After the service, there was time to testify one on one; we handed out literature and talked with people. Often, we met Christians, and we had the opportunity to pray for them to receive the baptism in the Holy Spirit. After the service, the horse was hooked up to the cart, to go to the farmer and spend the night there. I still have many fond memories of this period, and it helped me learn to preach in open-air meetings. It is also interesting to realise that our Lord Jesus preached most of His sermons in the open air! We were in good company.

Sometimes we were invited by Christians to come over for dinner, at times even to overnight at their place. But most of the time we cooked for ourselves, or something which looked and tasted like cooking. Once a greengrocer gave us a cardboard box filled with damaged tins of carrots and peas. He could not sell them anymore, but they were still good to eat. For weeks I ate carrots for one day and Martin peas, and the other day I ate peas and Martin ate carrots. I could not stand carrots and peas for many years after that. My attitude became a little less critical towards the Israelites who had to eat manna for forty years and who could no longer stand it. It is surprising how quickly we can become discontented.

Often, when we came back to the cart, we found someone had put a box full of groceries or fruit in the cart. Usually we were back home on Sunday and Monday and then hitch-hiked back to the cart on Tuesday morning.

Never before in my life had I handled a horse. As a child, I had actually been afraid of horses. Despite this fact, I did quite well, but Martin had a natural talent. Our horse's name was Reus, which is Dutch for Giant. Reus was a big horse. I could stand under his neck. He was also a very likeable animal. After the summer, he was going to be slaughtered, and I went to the market to see him once more. There was Reus, with a big mark on his hindquarters. That was his last day. I should never have gone to see Reus that last time. I could not eat any product containing horse meat for months! The thought that it could be from Reus was just too much. Every once in a while, when I get a sandwich with horse's smoked beef (which is a Dutch speciality), it makes me think of Reus.

When Coby had a day off and was free, she came to help with the open-air services, so we saw each other regularly. That was very nice. Meanwhile, Martin was dating Ina. Day after day he would continually talk about Ina until I once shouted, 'Please shut your mouth about Ina! It is so tiring!' The thought that Martin might be tired of all my talk about Coby never crossed my mind.

If Youth with a Mission had existed in those years, I would certainly have joined them. I think it would have suited me perfectly. Years later, on the mission field, we came to know Youth with a Mission very well.

One experience during our first tour is etched in our memories. We were in the small township of Culemborg and held two or three open-air meetings. Christians from the area came to help. A policeman from Culemborg was a born-again Christian, and he came every few hours to check if everything was going okay. We camped with a few young people just outside the town, on a farmer's field. It happened after our second evening service. We had just arrived back at our camping spot. It was late and dark. Adjacent to the field where we camped was a narrow road, but the nearest house or farm was far away. We were outside with our oil lamp, having a coffee, when the police came by. They told us they had heard a rumour that a group of boys wanted to beat us up and take the two girls from our team and abuse them. There were only a few police on duty that night, but they would try to drop by as often as they could.

The police drove off, and I said to the others, 'The Lord will protect us!' Soon after, we heard shouting and screaming in the dark. It came from the direction of the narrow road adjacent to the field. I was not afraid for myself, but I was quite worried about the two girls. The shouting came closer. Suddenly, we saw three angels. On both sides of the narrow road, an angel stood still, and one walked up and down the road. They were shining white, and each of them had a sword in his hand. They were about as tall as we were. I stood as if nailed to the ground. I could not utter a word, and felt that I was on holy ground. The thought crossed my mind, *Should I take off my shoes?* They were there for about fifteen minutes, then they disappeared. We did not sleep much that night. I was completely dazed by it. I believed in angels, I read about them in the Bible, and suddenly I had seen them with my own eyes. It was indescribable. I have not seen angels again as I had seen them that night, but I have experienced their presence often.

What happened to the group of vandals who were on their way to us, we don't know. We never heard them run away. What did they see or experience? We never found out. After midnight, the police dropped by again. They too had heard that the group was on their way to us. When we told them what had happened, they were quiet for a long time. We were all deeply touched by this visit from heaven.

The next morning I phoned Coby and told her what had happened. I heard nothing at the other end of the line. 'Are you still there?' I asked. 'Yes' was the answer, but Coby could not say a word.

Four months of full-time evangelising, praying with people, and leading people to Jesus as well as praying for healing or the baptism in the Holy Spirit for others – I was enjoying it immensely. When the trip was over, I felt quite lost. I took a temporary job, but my heart was not in it. My boss rebuked me once because I was not putting my heart and attention into the job. It was not pleasant to receive that rebuke, but he was right.

I held a weekly Bible study for youth, which was the result of our contact with them through the horse-and-cart tour. I also began to conduct another weekly Bible study with youth in a little township north of where my parents lived, and I started speaking more and more in churches. I was, and still am, head over heels in love with Coby; and meeting with her required time as well. At Christmas 1964, we became engaged. My attention and focus was set on the summer of 1965. Martin and I would arrange another horse-and-cart tour. We only needed a new cart and another horse, because Reus was no longer there. The Lord provided both. We could again borrow a horse, but it had no name. This horse was also quite big, but we did not want to use the name Reus again. Martin was engaged to Ina and I to Coby. Therefore, we named the horse Ico.

When I did the first horse-and-cart tour, I was nineteen years old. Many people thought I was too young, but I certainly did not share their opinion. God had called me, and I did what God asked me to do, and that was the end of that. In May 1965, the next horse-and-cart tour started. Filled with joy, I quit my temporary job and went back to evangelising. I would never have a secular job again. Starting in May 1965, I began to serve the Lord full-time.

After much prayer, Martin and I decided to have an evangelism crusade with the horse and cart in the north of Brabant, a province in the south of the Netherlands. As far as we knew, there had never been any evangelistic activity initiated by Pentecostal or Evangelical groups in these southern provinces, because this province was almost entirely Roman Catholic.

It was evident that in the north of Brabant, we could count on much less support from Evangelical or Pentecostal believers. Also, Martin and

I would see less of Ina and Coby than on our first trip, which was a pity. Despite that, this trip was also a success and thoroughly blessed.

Spending the night at farms became more difficult because most farmers were strictly Roman Catholic. More than once we had to tie Ico to a rope on the side of the road and put our cart next to the horse in the grass. But occasionally we were allowed to stay the night on the property of monasteries, and we were invited to eat in the monastery. We had many deep conversations with monks. I once asked a young monk why he had entered the monastery. His answer touched me deeply: 'I want to find God in my life.' What a hunger to know God, and what a sacrifice! We testified that you can find God by accepting Jesus. I learned much from these encounters.

We had just started one evening, when a Roman Catholic priest came to listen. I had spoken briefly and had shared something from the Old Testament. The priest had trouble with that. He could accept the New Testament literally, but to accept the Old Testament literally – no, he could not do that. He was a very kind man, and in my heart I asked the Lord for wisdom. Suddenly I had a thought and asked him, 'Do you believe we should reach the Jews with the gospel of Jesus Christ?'

His answer was surprising. 'Absolutely. In fact, it is my greatest desire to work amongst the Jews.'

'Then you will have a problem, because the Jews take the Old Testament literally, and they reject the New Testament. You believe the New Testament literally but do not accept the Old Testament.'

He thought about it. 'I have never thought about that before' was his honest answer, and he left a little later deeply in thought. This was the first time that I experienced a 'word of wisdom' in a specific situation.

Towards the end of the trip, we made plans for the next trip. We thought of Belgium, the country that shares its border with the south of the Netherlands. Half of the population speaks Flemish, which is like our language, though it is a dialect. We also thought of the possibility of going with a cart which needed two horses to pull it. But shortly afterwards, I had a meeting that changed all our plans. Frans and Yvonne Hoekendijk had returned to the Netherlands, after a few years of missionary work in the Caribbean. Frans was a son of Karel

Hoekendijk, the founder and, to us, the apostle of Streams of Power. Actually we looked up to the Hoekendijk family, and to get a visit from this couple was an honour. They wanted to speak to me privately and told me that they wanted to go to Australia. They were desirous to work amongst Dutch immigrants and to use that as a base for missionary work in the north of Australia, amongst the Aboriginals and maybe even in countries like Indonesia. In the Caribbean, they had helped in a crusade of the famous American evangelist T. L. Osborn; and in a conversation with him, they told him about their desire to go to Australia. T. L. Osborn had been thinking about having crusades in Australia, but he needed people to make preparations for this. There was already one American couple, but he needed a travelling team as well.

Evangelist Osborn offered the Hoekendijks work with his organisation for one or two years, after which he would come and have crusades. Afterwards, they would be free to start their own work. The offer was accepted, but a team was needed because it was quite a job. Osborn asked them to find a young couple in the Netherlands with whom they could work as a team in Australia. The Hoekendijks would be supported by the Osborn organisation, but the young couple would have to be supported by the Netherlands. They immediately thought of Coby and me. They asked if we were prepared to get married as soon as possible and to migrate to Australia in the beginning of 1966, to work together for the Osborn organisation for one or two years. After that we could pioneer together and start a work of Streams of Power in the south of Australia. Then we could go as missionaries from the south of Australia to the north, to do missionary work. What a question! During the conversation, something kept going through my mind. A few months earlier in a meeting, someone had a short prophetic word for me: 'Soon the Lord will send you to a country you have never thought of.' Streams of Power did missionary work in the Caribbean, South America, and South Italy, and logically, we had thought of these areas. We, as it were, saw ourselves already as missionaries in one of these areas in the future; but we had never thought of Australia.

I had much to tell and discuss with Coby when I saw her again. Deep in our hearts, we both had the conviction that this was God's plan for us, but we wanted confirmation and asked the Lord for it. We received that confirmation loud and clear.

Shortly after my meeting with the Hoekendijks, I had to preach in a Pentecostal church in the east of our country, close to the border with Germany. I had preached there before and knew a few of the people, including a certain brother Vos. Brother Vos was a sweet, dedicated, but simple man. Moreover, he stammered, except when he prayed or prophesied. That evening, after we had sung a few songs, there was an open time for the gifts of the Holy Spirit. If someone received something from God, then there was the opportunity to share it. Brother Vos began speaking without stammering. He shared a vision he saw. He saw a very big island, and he described it. It was very dry and arid like a desert, but the small outer edges were green. Then he said something very remarkable. 'I do not know what this means, but the Lord tells me that the island is in the southern hemisphere.' After he had described the vision, he started to prophesy. 'My son and my daughter, this is the country to which I am sending you very shortly.' We do not remember what followed after that, but we were stunned. Quite a clear confirmation. A few weeks later, I spoke to him about this. He really did not know what the southern hemisphere was or that Australia was an island.

More similar confirmations followed. When it became known that we were going to Australia, a woman prophesied that from Australia, we would preach the gospel to many tribes! Papua New Guinea alone has some 800 tribes, and we have reached people from many tribes! In addition, we have often been to other nations to share the gospel. This dear woman has probably never realised the accuracy of her prophecy.

That autumn, T. L. Osborn had a crusade in Düsseldorf, Germany, not far from the Dutch border. Frans Hoekendijk was one of the workers and took some youth with him from the Netherlands, to help in the meetings, as ushers. One evening T. L. Osborn had preached and invited people to come to Jesus and invite Him into their lives. In the large auditorium, many people came forward, among them an older German couple, who were seated near me. The man was blind, and his wife helped him to walk to the front. He was weak and did not walk very well. I quickly arranged a chair for him so that he could sit while all the people were standing in front of the stage. He was still holding on to his wife's arm. I stood behind them to help when needed and to make sure that no one would bump into them. T. L. Osborn explained what he would do. He would lead the people in prayer to invite the Lord Jesus into their hearts and lives.

The evangelist prayed sentence by sentence in English which was then translated into German, and the people who had come to the front repeated it. The old blind man and his wife also started to pray the prayer. Suddenly after having prayed a few sentences, the man shouted loudly, 'Ich kann sehen, Ich kann sehen! Liebe Schatz, Ich kann dich sehen!' ('I can see, I can see! My darling, I can see!') The old man took his wife's face in both hands, and with tears rolling down his cheeks, he kept shouting that he could see his wife. Then they fell into each other's arms crying. They never finished the prayer to accept Jesus, but I think that things worked out fine! There was great excitement everywhere – a blind man was healed while he prayed the sinner's prayer. And it happened right before my eyes! I was right there! I had seen how a blind man had been healed by Jesus in an instant. Years later, I would see a lame man being healed while saying the sinner's prayer. That night I could not sleep, and out of pure excitement and emotion, I walked through Düsseldorf for several hours. It was already morning when I went to sleep.

On the seventh of January 1966, we were married; and in March 1966, we left for Australia by ship. I was twenty-one years of age when I got married and, with my new bride, left for Australia.

'At a young age I will call you, and at a young age you will serve Me.'

CHAPTER 4

Coby

WHEN COBY WAS eight years old, she had a dream. In that dream, she saw herself as a missionary in a warm, tropical country. She saw houses on poles made of bush material, like people make them in the jungle. It was getting dark, and people were coming towards her. She noticed that the people had a very dark skin colour. In that dream, she saw herself with someone else. She had heard somewhere that female missionaries do not marry and usually work together with other unmarried female missionaries. She was therefore convinced that she would not marry but work with another woman. The only missionary area she had heard of as a child was Surinam in South America, so she believed she would end up in Surinam someday. Coby experienced the fulfilment of this dream fifteen years later and literally saw and recognised the picture she had seen in her dream, but it was not in Surinam. More about that later.

A year or two after the dream, something else greatly impacted her. Coby had taken money from her mother, to buy an ice cream. Her mother had discovered it, and when Coby went to bed that night, her mother came to talk with her. She told her to ask the Lord Jesus for forgiveness and ask if He wanted to give her a new heart. Coby did that, and as a child, she experienced the presence of the Lord in a very special way, something she never forgot. She never experienced or felt that presence again until the first evening of the youth weekend that she went to, at eighteen years of age. She recognised the presence of the Lord immediately, just as she had experienced it as a child!

Coby grew up in a strict Reformed (similar to Presbyterian) family in a village near Amsterdam. She is the second of seven children and the eldest daughter. Although her father undoubtedly loved her in his own way, he never communicated that, and he was distant and not emotionally involved as a father. The family on her father's side was strictly Christian Reformed (i.e. legalistic), and that religion controlled the whole family, and the way the children were raised. Her mother, who was a very sweet woman, came from a small township on the coast. She only had one brother, Uncle Cees. However, there was little contact with her family.

As a child, Coby told everyone, after her dream, that she was going to be a missionary; but no one took her seriously. She knew that as a missionary, you had to follow a challenging educational course and also study theology. That, she did not want to, but the thought of becoming a missionary never left her. Instead, she studied child welfare. When I got to know her, she was a group leader at a boarding school for children, whose parents worked and lived on boats that transported cargo along the many canals and rivers in Holland and into Germany.

After a couple of years, there was a small revival amongst church people in her home village, especially amongst members of the Reformed Church. Quite a number of people had been touched by the Pentecostal movement and had received the baptism in the Holy Spirit. People had been healed, and a few believers had been baptised by immersion. Their baptism by immersion caused an uproar. They were forced to leave the traditional church and could not attend their church any longer. As a result, weekly Pentecostal services started in the village, and these were so well attended that these meetings grew into a church of more than 200 members. Coby's father was an elder in the Reformed Church and was strongly opposed to what was happening. At home, he uttered his criticism loud and clear, and the children heard it. So Coby heard many negative things about Pentecostals at home, and this actually made her all the more curious to find out who these people were.

At the boarding school, where she worked as a group leader, she had two colleagues who went to a Pentecostal church and who testified about Jesus everywhere. They invited Coby and another colleague to go to a youth weekend. Coby wanted to experience the whole thing because she had heard so many crazy things about Pentecostals. She accepted the invitation and was ready for some adventure. Our youth group was asked to pick the two up and to take them to the youth weekend.

As soon as the first service started, Coby recognised the presence of the Lord that she had experienced as a child. She cried and cried, and at the invitation to ask Jesus into her life, she went forward. That evening she repented, and the next morning she was filled with the Holy Spirit in a powerful way. From that moment on, the dream came back. 'I will be a missionary,' she told herself and others. For her, there was no doubt about it.

Shortly after her conversion, a two-week winter Bible course was held, similar to those that were held during the summer. Coby and her colleague had registered, and I had also registered because I wanted to do the course again. It became an unforgettable and impressive course. One evening Karel Hoekendijk preached about angels. I did not know angels were mentioned so often in the Bible. When he was halfway through his sermon, a man started to interrupt him. Father Karel paused and asked him what was going on. 'I see an angel to your left and one to your right!' he exclaimed, and he described what the angels looked like. Suddenly more people in the service saw angels. I looked and looked and saw nothing, but I definitely experienced the presence of the Lord all around us. That service went on for a long, long time, but no one was aware of it. The presence of the Lord was awesome.

There was much talk about missions and becoming a missionary. It was a topic that was on people's hearts, especially amongst the youth. Many young people had only one desire: to become a missionary. That included me and Coby. According to Coby, I had asked her during a conversation we were having during the mission course: 'Would you want to be the wife of a missionary?' I cannot remember this, but she was offended. She had been converted and had also repented of relationships she did have with boys, and now it was happening here as well. Coby really thought that I was making her a proposal! Again, I do not remember this, and I asked the question with the purest of motives. Now that she had really found the Lord Jesus, she was convinced that she would never get married but would go into missions working with another woman. However, a little later we started to date; and after two years, we did get married.

From the moment of my conversion, I was burning with a passion to tell people about Jesus. I had an idea: on Saturday, my day off, I was going to have a market stall with Bibles and Christian reading materials. I had no money to buy books or Bibles, so I sold my hobby 'model trains', and with the money that I received, which was not much, I bought Bibles and books. Nearly every Saturday I went to the market in the city of Alkmaar. If I had money, I would carry my heavy suitcase onto the train to Alkmaar. But if I had no money, I prayed and went hitch-hiking. In Alkmaar, I sometimes received help from some local Christians. Coby heard about my activity in the market. She too was burning with a desire to do something for the Lord. Had she not been called to be a missionary? So whenever her shift work at the boarding school allowed her time to come, she would come and help me. We talked a lot in the train as well as at the market stall and were getting along very well. I liked her and soon found out that our thoughts about the things of the Lord were very similar, which captivated me. After a little while, something started growing inside of me. Not only did I like her, but I felt very attracted to her. Then it happened: at the youth service on Sunday afternoon, she very demonstratively took the seat next to me, even while there were many more empty chairs! Was this her way of making something clear?

We had gone to a meeting with a group of young people, and on the way home, Coby and I arrived at Amsterdam Central Station. I had to go further by train, while she was going to her parents for the day. 'Shall I take you home?' I asked nervously. Coby looked at me as only she can look. The expression in her eyes and the tone of her voice were clear. 'No, I can find it just fine on my own.' I do not remember how I replied but went home quite disappointed. Clearly, I had misinterpreted her signals.

Despite this, she came to help me again at the market stall, and when from time to time I was to speak at a youth service, members of the youth would join me, and often she would come along as well. At the open-air evangelism meetings on Sunday evening, she often came with me. My disappointment disappeared. *Maybe she does want to be my girlfriend and be the woman I am going to marry*, I thought. A little later, again being quite nervous, I asked her if I could take her home. Again that look and that tone in her voice. 'No, I can find it perfectly well on my own,' was her very clear answer.

What I didn't know was that Coby was deeply convinced that she would not marry, because she was going to be a missionary. Later she told me that though she liked me very much, she actually thought that I was very unspiritual, because I wanted to date her. Totally beaten, I made for home. It was now very obvious. If I had not understood it the first time, I did now: the answer was a blatant no.

I tried to get Coby out of my mind and my emotions. I prayed about it, but it was a real battle. Somewhere inside, I was deeply convinced that she was the girl the Lord had for me as a life partner. Coby did not go to the market stall for a while, neither did she seek my company. I managed to think less about her, but deep in my heart, I was still very disappointed. Of course there were other girls in the youth group, but they did not have my attention.

Then there was the youth meeting on Sunday afternoon. The service had just begun, and there were some empty seats. Coby came a little late, because she worked varying shifts and could not always be there on time. She looked around at the empty chairs. There was an empty chair next to me, and she very demonstratively sat next to me. I could hardly believe it. Maybe she had repented, I thought. She again joined me at the market stall and was very open towards me. Then one day we had gone with a group of youth to a meeting in Utrecht, and once again we were at Central Station in Amsterdam. I told Coby I wanted to talk with her. At the back of the station, in a dark corner, I told her how I felt about her and that I believed we could serve the Lord together. Coby told me that she really liked me and that after her last no, she had very much missed having contact with me. However, she was not sure if it was right for her to have a boyfriend. Was this really God's plan for her? She was in doubt. But I did not doubt and gave her a first kiss, to which she responded. We agreed to see each other a few days later. She went to her parents' home taking the last bus, and I went to my hometown catching the last train. There was unfortunately no time to take her home, but I cheered! How happy I felt. But I also was in doubt. Is this for real, or is it just temporary?

A few days later, I came to the hall of Amsterdam Central Station where we had arranged to meet. Exactly on time, a very happy-looking Coby walked towards me and gave me a kiss! It was real: I had a girlfriend! I can't remember where we went next, but I was on cloud nine. I think we drank coffee in a restaurant, had a bite to eat, and talked. After dating for one year, being engaged for one year, and married for fifty years, we still talk, often and much. I teased Coby for a long time about the fact that she never said yes to me. But she did say yes in our wedding service! It was not until later that Coby told me about her dream and her conviction that she would not marry. In that dream, she saw herself with someone else. She naturally assumed that it was a woman, because she thought female missionaries did not marry.

We became inseparable and were able to spend a lot of time together. Karel Hoekendijk, the founder and leader of Streams of Power, often saw me with a girl he did not know, and was worried. He asked me to come to his home, because he wanted to talk with me. I thought maybe he wanted to talk with me about missions, because he knew I had a calling for missions on my life. It turned out to be a very serious conversation. He had seen different promising young preachers who began a relationship with the wrong girl, and nothing had become of their calling. He also saw me as a young preacher with potential, but he did not know the girl I was dating. Coby did not appear to attend the meetings very often, or at least he did not see her regularly. I explained that she worked irregular shifts, but he did not believe our friendship was of the Lord, and asked me to end our relationship. I was stunned! End the relationship? I had prayed so much about this.

The train journey back home was not pleasant; and the following days were, to put it mildly, 'not so great'. Karel Hoekendijk was a man of God who was used in special ways by the Lord. He had heard God's voice many times; he could not be wrong, or could he? The next few nights I hardly slept and did not dare to call Coby. I confided in one of the youth leaders and made my decision. I knew the relationship with Coby was right. I had prayed much about it, and I made up my mind. I would tell Karel Hoekendijk that I would not end the relationship. I was very nervous when I called Karel Hoekendijk and told him that I had thought much about what he had said but that I believed that the relationship was right and would therefore not end it. 'Well, I warned you and gave you my opinion. Now the responsibility and consequences are yours to carry,' he said. The phone call came to an end. I had told him that I would not end the relationship. It was not until much later that I told Coby what had happened. For the first time, from a right attitude and with respect for my leader, I had not obeyed but had dared to follow the Lord from my own heart. This became a lesson that would later profit me greatly. There came a time that Coby worked for a while in the office of Streams of Power, and Karel Hoekendijk really came to like her. When we got married, he congratulated me on having such a splendid wife. Even men of God can sometimes get it wrong.

At home, things did not go so well. My father complained that I was never home and felt that he and my mother did not mean anything to me anymore. It was right that I was not home much, but I did love my parents. It was just that my father could be very controlling, and I knew that if I gave in to that, nothing would come of the calling of God upon my life. I also found it hard to know if they liked Coby. Because we usually did not have money to eat out, Coby would come to our home, especially when the weather was bad. However, the atmosphere at home was not always the best. At least, that's how I experienced it.

Conversations with my father became more and more sporadic, and after a while, he stopped speaking to me altogether. When I said, 'Good morning,' his response was a soft mumble; and when I said, 'Good night,' I did not get much of a response either. It became so unpleasant at home that I considered moving out, even though I had no money to do that, having only a low-paying job. One evening Coby was at our home, and the atmosphere was bad. That evening we prayed together about this; things had become unbearable. What was going on? I started to discover that Coby could be very prophetic. The Lord showed her that my father was troubled by a 'spirit of jealousy', so it was a work of the devil! Together we rebuked this spirit and commanded it to leave my father and to stop working against us. The very next morning at breakfast, my father came in and said, 'Good morning, John, how was the meeting last night?' I nearly fell off my chair; my father was talking to me again and has continued to do so.

Later, actually, on the evening before we were departing for Australia, my parents spoke with us until deep into the night. My father had really experienced the Lord in our wedding service and then told us, 'I searched for God. I wanted to know God personally. I went to special Bible courses to know God better, but I did not find Him. Then you came home, seventeen years old, and you told us that you had accepted Jesus and had become a child of God. First I did not believe it, but then I saw in your life that it was true. You had found what I was looking for and which I did not have. I became so jealous that I could not talk to you for quite a while!'

My father used the word 'jealous', the very word that the Lord had given Coby. That jealousy was good, but the devil used it to try to destroy our relationship. A few years later, when on leave, a pastor friend and I were able to pray with my parents. In that prayer, they very consciously accepted Jesus as their Lord and Saviour. Much later, right before my father passed away, I could often talk and pray with him. I was a sort of 'confessor' to him. He shared deep things from his heart with me, and in the last years of his life, I had a very good and strong relationship with him. I will see him again in heaven!

Coby lived at the boarding school, but at her home, things did not go so well. We were engaged and had been encouraged to get married and then to go to Australia. I needed permission from her father to marry his daughter. In that time, parents still had to give their consent, even if the woman was older than twenty-one. Coby's father's answer was plain and clear: 'No, I will not give my consent.' I did not have a good job, no steady income, and no decent education; and besides all that, I belonged to the Pentecostal movement, about which his thoughts were well known to us. Coby was the only one in the family who was converted, and she experienced quite a lot of misunderstanding and resistance.

If Coby's father would not give permission, there was only one option left: to marry before the court, which would give us permission, because Coby was twenty-two years old! I told this to her father. He was clearly not happy with this response and asked for a week's respite. If I would come the following Tuesday, he would give me his decision. I still remember that Tuesday very well!

Around eight o'clock, being somewhat nervous, I came in. Coby's father was reading the newspaper. Coby's mother, who suffered because of all this, handed him his coffee. He remained behind his newspaper until ten o'clock, then he put it down and said, 'I'm going to bed.' I became angry but tried with all my might to remain respectful. I said, 'No, you will not go to bed. You asked me to come, and I came. I want to hear your answer.' He took me to another room, closed the door, and said, 'When you marry before the court, it becomes a great disgrace to the family. I will sign the papers. You can marry my daughter, and we will come to the city hall, and I will sign. We will not come to the wedding ceremony in the church, and not the reception either. I also will forbid the other children to go. If you're ever in trouble, don't bother coming to me, especially if you're in financial trouble. You can have my daughter, but we do not take any responsibility for the two of you. We take our hands off both of you.'

My parents did give their consent. When I told my father that we wanted to get married and that I needed his permission, he said, 'Are you not a little too young to get married? You're only twenty-one.' My reply was short and clear: 'But you were twenty when you married mum. I'm twenty-one!'

'You always have an answer to everything, don't you?' he replied, but of course he gave his consent. My parents visited Coby's father and tried to talk to him, but it did not help.

On the seventh of January 1966, in the middle of winter, we were married. Coby's parents came to the city hall, signed, and went home. We now know that this was very hard on Coby's mother, who was a very sweet woman. None of Coby's family was present at the wedding service. Two of her sisters secretly showed up at the reception; but her father, of course, was not to know about it. Though the contact with her father became better in later years, they even visited us in Papua New Guinea, the relationship with her father was never fully restored. What a pity. Later, Coby was able to share this story many times on the mission field, where children would sometimes be kicked out of the family or persecuted, when they became Christians. Coby had been through this also, and she understood only too well what it was like.

In March 1966, we departed on an Italian migrant ship, the *Flavia*, to Australia. The ship departed from the Rotterdam harbour. Never did we expect that almost thirty years later, we would live and pastor a church very close to the same place from where we left Holland. We are now able to see out of our bedroom windows the same buildings we saw when we left.

Saying goodbye to the family was difficult, especially for Coby's parents. It would take six years before we would see each other again. We left as a team of four adults and two children for the mission field. I was twenty-one, Coby twenty-two.

'At a young age I will call you, and at a young age you will serve me.'

CHAPTER 5

Going 'Down Under'

WE HAD LOOKED forward to the boat trip from Rotterdam to Sydney, Australia. Because the Suez Canal was closed in 1966, our journey took us through the Panama Canal in Central America. The journey would take five weeks. We did not have a honeymoon as there was no money for that, and even less time. I worked temporarily in the office of Streams of Power, where Coby worked as well. There was much to be organised, and the preparations for our journey and emigration to Australia took every spare moment. The Hoekendijk family with their two little children also looked forward to the journey. It would be a sort of holiday for them as well.

At the ship, we were shown our cabin. To our surprise, there was a children's bed in it. One of the Hoekendijk children was to sleep in our cabin. That was an unexpected surprise. We did not enjoy the journey very much. A crowded migrant ship, people everywhere, and no peace and quiet at all. I longed to have a meaningful quiet time with the Lord. So one day I set my alarm for three o'clock in the morning. We were on the Pacific Ocean with lovely tropical weather, so there was a pleasant temperature at night. I looked forward to spending that night on the top deck. But at three o'clock, there were people there having a party! So there was no quiet time with the Lord for me.

On the ship was a hairdresser who cut my hair. When he had cut my hair, I asked him in English, which was not very good as yet, 'Please cut also my backside.' The hairdresser answered without moving a muscle, 'You mean the back of your head, sir!' I just learned a little more English!

We made a stop-over in New Zealand and walked through the city of Auckland for a couple of hours, especially through the famous Queen Street. I still remember the big building, the Town Hall. I could never have thought that years later, I would speak there at the large Assemblies of God Church, Queen Street AOG, which used that building for their services and conferences. And I could never have realised that God would speak to me one night in that building, telling me that our time in Papua New Guinea had ended and that our next mission would be Japan.

When we arrived in Australia, we stayed in Sydney for the first few days. There was a car and a caravan ready and waiting. The Hoekendijks had received these from the Osborn organisation. We then travelled to Brisbane where we would get our equipment. Money had been collected in the Netherlands for a Kombi Van and a caravan. What actually happened never became clear, but the van became a Morris Mini, with a small trailer behind it. We never received a caravan, and from the little money we had, we bought a camping tent which would be our home for the coming year. In Northern Australia, the weather is subtropical and the temperatures moderate; therefore, sleeping in a tent was possible. There were exceptions, when we were invited to spend the night at someone's home. We identified greatly with Abraham, who together with Isaac and Jacob lived in tents and looked forward to the promised city of the Lord.

While we were in Brisbane to arrange and buy our equipment, Coby and I stayed in what was then the Bible School of the Assemblies of God, the largest and oldest Pentecostal movement in Australia. They made us welcome, and the principal asked me to lead a morning service. This would be my first time to preach in English. I remember that I spoke about Gideon. After the message, there was a time of prayer, and then something very unique happened. Someone started singing in new tongues, and immediately all the students joined in, singing in new tongues. We had never experienced this before. The principal of the Bible school was greatly touched and had tears in his eyes. He had not experienced it before either but knew the stories of the outpouring of the Holy Spirit in Los Angeles in 1906, now known as the Azusa Street

Revival. History tells us of times when the people sang in new tongues, the language of the Holy Spirit. It was impressive. Years later, there would be a new movement of the Holy Spirit, first in New Zealand and later in Australia. Singing in new tongues or singing in the Holy Spirit would be a unique characteristic of that movement. We found ourselves in the middle of that movement and were very deeply touched by it, but more about that later.

Australia was very different from the Netherlands. Firstly, the long distances. But also the roads. At that time, there were often unpaved single-lane roads. If you saw an oncoming car, you had to pull off the road to let the other pass. Our windscreen broke four times because of the gravel that was thrown up by passing vehicles. Secondly, the language. Australian English is different from the English we had learned in high school and in further advanced English courses we had completed. Once I asked someone how far the nearest town was, and he replied, 'Not that far, mate, about 180 miles,' so nearly 300 kilometres of unpaved road in a Morris Mini. Not far at all?

After a week or two, we left Brisbane and went further inland, because we had been invited by small churches and congregations. It was our job to promote the ministry of American evangelist T. L. Osborn and to evangelise where it was possible. In the small town of Clermont, we had a little stand with reading matter, at a yearly show – a sort of fair. I drove back to the township and was pulled over by a police officer. 'Are you the bloke that drove the little red Morris Minivan with your wing outside the window? Once more, mate, and I'll fine you!' was his remark. In my poor English, and being very surprised, I asked, 'Sir, what is a bloke, and what is a wing?' His answer was 'Your elbow, stupid!' Those were not words I had learned at home.

In Clermont, the weekly airplane arrived. Our hosts went to meet some people, and we joined them. The plane landed, but also a small single-engine plane. A man got out, picked up a newspaper that had arrived with the other plane, and left again. Collecting your daily newspaper with your plane; that was very different indeed.

We were somewhere inland and were going to show a film at a cattle property. The people were faithful followers of the work of T.

L. Osborn. When we arrived, we introduced ourselves as 'John and Coby Pasterkamp'. The farmer asked for Coby's name again, as he had not heard it before. I repeated it. He again asked for Coby's name, and again I told him that her name was Coby. 'No, never heard of it,' he said. 'But I do know a farmer who has a cow with that name. Welcome to Australia!'

For a few weeks I tried to introduce myself very correctly with my Dutch name: Jan Sjoerd. 'Jan' sounds like 'Jen' in English, but that is a girl's name in Australia. 'Sjoerd' sounds like 'Short' in English, and I am not short with my 1.86 metres, or as it was then in Australia, 6 foot 3 inches. So my name became John, and that stuck. For the people in English-speaking countries, we are John and Coby.

Pasterkamp is an impossible name in English as well. 'Paster' sounds very much like the general title of a church leader, 'Pastor'. So I became 'Pastor Pasterkamp'. Endless confusion. 'Pastor John Kamp' was the name often used, but 'kamp' in Australian slang refers to an unacceptable lifestyle, but we have learned to live with it.

Our name apparently caused more confusion. In our first year, we had to be somewhere to conduct meetings. Coby and I arrived at the house where we had agreed to meet. After sharing a meal, the evangelism and promotion meeting would start. We knocked on the door, and a lady answered it. I introduced ourselves, 'Hello, we are John and Coby Pasterkamp.'

The lady looked at us very surprised and said, 'Are you John and Coby Pasterkamp who are here for the Osborn meetings?'

'Yes, that's us,' we answered.

The surprised look remained. 'Oh,' said the lady, 'we saw the strange name and thought you were Aboriginals, the indigenous people of Australia, and that is how we announced you.' That evening I preached, but unfortunately for them, we were not Aboriginals but Dutchmen.

Preaching in English was quite a job. Although I had learned English for a good many years, it still was not easy. Not long after we had arrived, I was asked to preach one Sunday morning in a small fellowship. I decided to preach on one of my favourite verses: 2 Timothy 1:10 – 'But is now made manifest by the appearing of our Saviour Jesus

Christ, who has abolished death, and has brought life and immortality to light through the gospel.' I preached that Jesus had brought to light 'immorality'. After a few moments, the pastor could no longer restrain himself and stood up and said, 'Pastor John, the word is immortality and not immorality.' I understood what mistake I had made and looked for the emergency escape to disappear. Luckily Australians have a good sense of humour, and they admire a person who tries something new. It remained a joke amongst Pentecostals in that area for a long time!

Sometimes we ministered with the Hoekendijks, but we also accepted other invitations where we ministered as a couple. We had to learn quickly. Though it was not easy, because Australia is so very different from the Netherlands, we enjoyed that first year. We especially liked the north-east of the state of Queensland, the area around the city of Cairns. There were many islanders, dark-skinned people who arrived more than a century earlier, from the Pacific Islands, to work at the sugar plantations. Instead of returning to their country, they stayed and never went back home to their islands. When they finished working on the sugar plantations, they moved to small islands in North Queensland. The most central and well-known island is Thursday Island, named that way by Captain Cook, who actually discovered the whole area and mapped it. Repeatedly the islanders said, 'You must come to Thursday Island.' That request stuck with us. When we were at the Gold Coast in Queensland, and at the point of going down to New South Wales, I was praying in a forest one evening. I felt that the Lord strongly spoke to me about Thursday Island. I knew that someday we would go there.

The Pentecostal churches in Australia were pretty dead and dry; there was not much life. We came from a Pentecostal movement in the Netherlands, which was very alive, when compared to churches and various groups in Australia. We actually became discouraged because we saw so little happening. For the Hoekendijks, this must have been difficult as well. They had worked in the West Indies for a few years. They had seen much blessing, and their work had been successful. Australia, on the other hand, was literally and spiritually dry and barren. One day I expressed my frustration to the Lord. The Lord spoke to my heart with the words from the prophet Ezekiel, 'Son of man, can these bones live?' 'I do not know, Lord,' I replied, but actually I thought, *I don't think so.* In that first year, we attended sometimes prayer meetings with a handful of believers. We heard these people deliver prophecies and heard them speak about visions they had seen. They said the day would come when the largest stadiums in Australia would be filled with young people who would worship the Lord with great passion and enthusiasm. When we looked around, we could not see that ever happening. However, more than thirty years later, we were in Sydney during a Hillsong conference where 28,000 mostly young people had gathered for a week. The praise, singing, and worship were unforgettable. We had heard the prophecies, when nothing looked like anything would ever happen. But during that conference, we saw the fulfilment of those prophetic words, with our own eyes! That has now strengthened our hope and faith for the Netherlands.

We had good and enjoyable moments as a team, but generally speaking, Frans Hoekendijk was not the easiest person to work for. Before he started working as a full-time evangelist, he was an army officer, and I often had the impression that he thought he still was. He regularly treated us as young rookies. A pastor from a rather lively fellowship came to us and advised us to leave the team. He offered me a full-time position as youth pastor with a fixed income. It was very tempting and appealing. I was willing and prayed, but the Lord said, 'Stay where I have positioned you.' I protested, 'But, Lord, You see what is happening and how Hoekendijk is treating us, don't You?' The Lord said only one thing, 'Follow Me and stay where you are.' The Bible gives us several stories of people with the call of God on their lives, like Moses, Joseph, David, and Daniel, who ended up in very difficult situations but then submitted to those circumstances, which other people would call unjust. They knew very well that their situation was not fair, but they chose to submit, and did not grow bitter or become disrespectful.

God used those situations to produce something very beautiful in their lives. In no way do I want to compare us or our situation with these men of God, but we did feel that God used the situation 'Down

Under' to build something into our lives as well. We have no doubt about that now. Many people have heard me preach about the subject of 'submission' and how the Lord uses situations to work something in us of great value, namely 'meekness.' One of the stories I share at times is from our first period 'Down Under'.

We had expected much support in organising crusades with T. L. Osborn, but that support never came. For T. L. Osborn, that was enough reason not to make any further plans for Australia. Although we had been able to win some people for Jesus and had led others into the baptism in the Holy Spirit, the real purpose of our coming was finished after a short year. The Hoekendijks were so discouraged, we think, that they went to Indonesia to help their father, Karel Hoekendijk, with crusades and then returned to the Netherlands.

Looking back on that first year, we realise that this time had been a gift from the Lord. In a little less than a year, we had travelled through three states, a large part of Australia, and came to know it. We also learned much about Australian society and culture. We had become familiar with the spiritual climate of the Pentecostal and Evangelical groups and were convinced that this country badly needed a fresh move of the Holy Spirit. We had made many contacts, and friendships had been born. Especially in the north-east of the state of Queensland, we had become quite well known. It was like a foundation for the time to come. Though we are Dutch, we still feel a bit like Australians! We came to love this dry, barren, but beautiful country and its inhabitants very much.

I was twenty-two, and we were on our own in Australia. In Melbourne, all the way down in the south, we had made good connections with a group of Dutch immigrants who had found the Lord in Australia and formed a Pentecostal group. For years they prayed for us and supported us financially as best as they could. I have dedicated this book to those marvellous people and those in Holland who supported us. One day one of them said to us, 'We had a meeting about your car. You cannot travel all the way back to the north in that little Morris Mini. If you are prepared to trade in the Morris, you will get a Land Rover from us!' Awesome! That is how it happened. We went back to the north in our brand-new Land Rover. After a year of driving in a Morris Mini, the Land Rover felt like a big truck. On our journey to the north, we even slept many times in the back of the Land Rover. We went back to the north, to the islanders, and our goal was Thursday Island. On our journey north, we visited many of our contacts from that first year. We were invited to preach or lead Bible studies in small churches and in small groups. In those meetings, a remarkable number of people were filled with the Holy Spirit and started speaking and singing in new tongues. Also, especially in the north, there were some remarkable healings. The testimonies of what happened at those meetings would go ahead of us and prepare hearts on Thursday Island for what was coming.

In the city of Geelong, in the state of Victoria, we came to know a businessman and his wife: Len and Joan Day. They were true Pentecostal people, loved the Lord dearly, and were excited about evangelism. Len had a license to fly and was the proud owner of an old four-seater biplane. I think it was a Beechcraft 7. Len heard that Coby and I had never flown and asked if we would like to join him on a short flight. Going up in the air for the first time? We said yes, we would love to experience this. Beautiful weather and an amazing landscape. Len told us all about what we saw and where we were, but something happened: the engine suddenly stopped. Len was startled, panicked for a brief moment, and immediately checked all the equipment. I knew that a plane like this would glide for a little while if it had engine trouble, but this was no theory. We were in the plane. I briefly looked at Len and thought, *There is a beautiful hymn, 'Lord, I Am Coming Home'. Should I start singing it now?* Len quickly discovered what was wrong. One fuel tank was empty, and he had not switched to the second tank. After a small dive, the engine started again, and we finished our tour. We never forgot that the engine stopped during our very first-ever flight! We did not know then that our ways would cross in a unique way in Papua New Guinea. God would use Len and Joan and their plane as an answer to our prayer.

Near Cairns, we planned an evangelism outreach, but no money had come in, either from Melbourne or from Brisbane, or from the

Netherlands. For a few days, we only ate porridge and drank coffee. In the morning porridge and coffee, for lunch coffee and porridge, and for dinner coffee mixed with porridge. Then we ran out of everything: food, money, fuel. In the evening, we drove to the place of the outreach; we had no fuel to go back to the camping ground, to our tent. Nobody showed up at the open-air service. I preached anyway. To the houses. But no one came.

When we packed up our things, we were wondering how we would get back to the camping site. Suddenly the door of a little shop opened, and a man came towards us. 'This is amazing. We listened inside and prayed with you. Thanks so much.' He gave me five dollars. We were able to buy a few litres of petrol and drove back to the camping site. When we went to the post office the next day, several letters had arrived. Three of them contained cheques from Melbourne, sent in three successive weeks. The bank was willing to honour the cheques, giving us enough money to travel as the only passengers, with our car, on a cargo vessel to Thursday Island. We did not know what was awaiting us, and what it would be like, but Thursday Island we will never forget. For the first time, we would see God work in a very unique way and experience a small revival.

CHAPTER 6

Thursday Island

THE JOURNEY ON the crowded migrant ship from Rotterdam to Sydney was not something we had really enjoyed, and we would certainly not do that again. But the trip from Cairns to Thursday Island, travelling past the beautiful coast of North Queensland, Cape York, and islands of the Great Barrier Reef, was amazing! The beautiful blue ocean had many gradations of colour. Little islands were everywhere – it was awesome. Sometimes there was a reef just above the waterline with a few palm trees, like you sometimes see in cartoons. Then the dazzling sunrise in the east and the magnificent sunset in the west, above the coastline of Australia. The trip, unfortunately, only lasted three days. I slept in the captain's cabin which had a second single bed. Coby slept in a cabin with a small single bed. My bed was too short, especially when I stretched, so I put a chair at the end, where I could put my legs. But we were happy to put up with that, during such an amazing trip.

Thursday Island is a somewhat small, untidy island. There are a few hills, which you definitely could not call mountains. When we arrived, the vegetation was green, because the rainy season had just finished; but when we left the island, it was brown, dry, and dusty. There were only one or two stretches of beach; the rest of the coast was rocky. The population was about 2,500 people. Besides a few Caucasian and Chinese people, all the island's inhabitants were Melanesians, who originally came from the islands of the South Pacific. There were no Aboriginals, the original inhabitants of Australia. Thursday Island was known because of its pearl divers. When we came, there were still some pearl fishing boats that would go to the reefs to dive for pearls.

There were only four police officers on the island, and they were kept very busy. Fights and drunkenness were the order of the day. Thursday Island is the government administration centre of a group of islands that were all discovered and named by Captain Cook, such as Wednesday Island, Thursday Island, and Friday Island. Together the islands are called the Torres Strait Islands.

The Anglican Church had been working on these islands for years. Undoubtedly there must have been true and faithful Christians in these churches; but what we encountered was usually a blend of pagan practices, traditional customs, and superstitions mixed with elements of Christianity. While we were on the island, during a special ceremony, the grave of a man who had been dead for quite a while was opened. In the grave, they placed especially prepared food. The deceased man was still in purgatory and therefore needed food during his stay! Pure paganism. These people needed Jesus. About three years later, the charismatic movement started in Australia which also affected many Anglican churches. We do not know what influence this movement had on these islands, but we sincerely hope that this movement's influence did come.

There was also a small Pentecostal group on Thursday Island. They had heard about us through family connections in North Queensland. Leaders of the Assemblies of God had encouraged the group to accept us and help us with evangelism efforts. When the boat arrived, some were waiting for us, to give us a very special welcome. They made us feel very welcome during the three and a half months we were there. Also, an Australian couple invited us to stay with them at their place.

We were introduced to this group and almost immediately noticed that hardly anyone was filled with the Holy Spirit and spoke in tongues. Only two had received the baptism in the Holy Spirit. So before we started to evangelise, we held Bible studies about the baptism in the Holy Spirit. After a few nights we prayed, and about ten people received the Holy Spirit and spoke in new tongues. Some had very powerful experiences. The news spread that believers had received the Holy Spirit, and more people came. Actually evangelism had already started. In a very short period, about thirty people had been filled with the Holy Spirit and spoke in tongues.

There was great joy within the group. They told us that there had never been anyone before on the island who had preached so openly about the Holy Spirit. One woman, who also came to the small group, had not yet been filled with the Holy Spirit but had longed for it for years. When she saw how easy it was, she became very angry. She apparently had been taught that one had to wait to become holy. Consequently, nothing had happened to her for years. But a few weeks later, she also very simply received the Holy Spirit.

In the Netherlands, we were part of a movement. There were always others ready and willing to help. Also we had leaders who would back you up and who could give advice or counsel when needed. Now we were on our own. We came from a Pentecostal movement that emphasised the message of divine healing; and in the year we had worked in Australia, I had devoured and studied all the books, articles, tapes, and movies by T. L. Osborn. We were deeply convinced that healing is tied up with missions and evangelism, and it could not be left out. We are still totally convinced of this. So we started preaching about healing on Thursday Island and began praying for the sick. The Lord used this to reach many. Now, years later, when we read the letters, newsletters, and accounts of that period, it strikes us just how many great miracles happened. Healings of rheumatism, asthma, and blood disease are mentioned in our first letter.

A little old man, completely bent over, came to a meeting. When you looked at him, you would think of the event recorded in Luke 13, when the Lord Jesus healed a woman who was totally bent over and could not raise herself up. She was bound by a spirit of infirmity. When the Lord Jesus delivered her of that spirit, the woman stood up straight. Exactly the same thing happened to this little man.

A man with severe abdominal problems asked us to come to his house to pray for him. We heard that he was an important man in the Anglican Church. We prayed for him, and he was healed. He and his wife and children repented and were filled with the Holy Spirit.

Sometime later, they were baptised in water. This man became a pillar in the fellowship that was beginning to form. In the first three months that we were on the island, it did not rain, and water became scarce. The family we lived with was a fair distance away on the other side of the island. To get to the water well was quite a walk, but that well had run dry. They had only one bottle of water left, and prayed. During the Bible studies, we had looked at the gift of miracles, like the account of the widow of Zarephath, whose flour and oil did not run out for a long time. This family prayed, and for days the water in the bottle did not run out. They drank, cooked, even washed themselves; but the bottle remained full until it rained again. This story spread all over the island. We even saw the bottle! In the years to come, we would see a few similar miracles.

Among the first healings was the biggest miracle – the healing of a woman with cancer. She was in a little hospital on the island, in much pain and no longer able to walk. Her family asked us to pray for her. After we prayed for her in Jesus's name, she got out of bed and walked. All the pain was gone. The nurses told us that she kept walking the entire day. Shortly afterwards, she was allowed to go home; the doctor saw no reason to keep her in the hospital. Her healing was the cause of the conversion of nearly the whole family.

A young boy came to the meeting, and when he went home, he prayed and accepted Jesus. At the same moment, he was filled with the Holy Spirit and spoke in tongues. Three days later, he gave a radiant testimony. It was clearly visible: he who is in Christ is a new creation. All these testimonies greatly impacted the inhabitants of the island.

A well-known drunk and troublemaker came to the Lord. Another well-known drunk also repented! A prostitute came to the Lord. It was wonderful!

Most of the people lived close to the small harbour. But on the other side of the island were two villages. Well, villages might be too big a word. Two groups of houses. In one of these lived Sister Sagigi. She was part of the group of Pentecostal believers and one of the first who had been filled with the Holy Spirit. She had six children; but her nine-year-old son, Jacob, had a problem. One leg was normal length; his other leg was too short and deformed. He could put his normal foot on the ground, and with the toes of his other foot, he could just reach the ground. That's how he limped and moved forward, half limping and half jumping. It was obvious that, because he was still growing, he soon would not be able to touch the ground with his toes anymore and would have to walk with crutches. We prayed for him, and six weeks later, his leg was the same length as the other leg. Though he still had a slight limp, he could walk well. That testimony spread throughout the island. Everyone knew this boy. Years later, when I was a pastor in Australia, we met him again. Jacob had now grown up and lived in Australia not far from where we lived. I was delighted to see his progress. As an adult, he still limped slightly but could use his leg just fine.

Then came probably the greatest most visible miracle. One Sunday morning, we were asked to pray for a nine-year-old boy. I understood that something was wrong with his knee. We prayed, and we can still remember the incredible presence of the Lord. Several believers who prayed with us started to cry. That afternoon, some believers came running towards the place where we were staying and shouted, 'Brother John, Brother John, Johnny Fell is playing soccer!' I knew that the boy we had prayed for was named Johnny Fell, but what was so special about the fact that he was playing soccer? Well, it was very special. Johnny had been a cripple, but that morning we had not seen his crutches which stood against the wall. He did have an accident as a little child and had not been able to use his legs since then. Johnny was healed and was playing soccer. We went to see him, and there he was running after a ball! The people who knew him were cheering. Johnny himself was overjoyed. The woman in the hospital who had been healed of cancer was his grandmother. His mother was healed and converted, his sister was healed, and now he was. A few years later when he lived in Australia, we visited Johnny once. He walked normally!

Johnny's mother came from the islands, but his father was an Australian, a rough kind of man. His father, Mr Fell, was the owner of the only petrol station on the island, so I knew him. Cursing was his normal language. A few days after Johnny's healing, I came to fill up the tank of our Land Rover. Mr Fell asked me to come into his messy small office. He took the seat behind his desk covered with clutter and started to cry. 'What have you done to my boy? What have you done to my wife, my daughter, and mother-in-law? They are now well, healed, and everything is different!' I testified about Jesus. Still crying, he listened. Then he offered to finance a small building for the congregation. We heard that in the months after we left the island, he indeed arranged the construction of a small simple building. It was mainly financed by Mr Fell. Whether he ever repented I don't know, but this man could no longer deny the gospel.

There were some Muslims on the island, people who originally came from Malaysia. With the knowledge that we now have, we think that they were quite moderate Muslims. The wife of one of them had converted, and after a while, her husband also came to the meeting – Johnny Majid, who was the manager of the post office. In the middle of the meeting, he fell to the ground, and something happened to him. I walked up to him. He was prophesying! Shortly afterwards, he started speaking in tongues. He had already made a decision for Jesus in his heart, but that night the Holy Spirit came. It was the first time we had seen someone, who was being filled with the Holy Spirit, first prophesied and then spoke in tongues, just like it happened amongst the believers in Ephesus as described in Acts 19.

In one of the villages, we held a film night in the open air. I knew that an elderly couple, the Saylors, lived there. They were nearly always drunk, and their fights were infamous. I had tried to get in touch with them but without success. They kept us at a distance. They were absolutely not open to the gospel. That night I saw in the dark how the man, Cook Saylor, was hiding behind a big tree. Apparently he was listening! When the film started, I saw his head still behind the tree. Cook was watching the film! Cook probably expected that I would, as usual, preach right after the film. But I arranged that one of the men who had come with me would say something. The film had ended, and I walked straight up to Cook. 'What can I do for you, Cook?' I asked. He was stunned and surprised, but after a few moments, he collected himself and showed me his hand. He could not move several fingers because they were stiff. He told me that once, while he was cleaning a fish, the knife had slipped and had cut through some muscles in his hand. Since then he had some stiff fingers on one hand. He had practically no feeling in those fingers. 'God wants to heal you, Cook, because He loves you!' I said. He did not know what to say, and it was obvious that he did not know what to do with himself. I took a step of faith. 'Cook, may I pray for you and ask God to heal your fingers? If He heals you, you must promise to give your life to Him and follow Jesus. If He does not heal you, then you are free, and you can live the rest of your life the way you like.' He agreed, and I prayed. The next moment, he could move his fingers.

Cook's eyes became so big they looked as if they would pop out. He kept looking at his hand and fingers. He tried to speak but could not say a word. He was literally dumbfounded. 'God has healed you,' I said. 'You promised to give your life to Him.' Cook was clearly not ready for that and beat about the bush, but I challenged him. He went home and was caught up in a deep inner battle for three days. Then he gave up and gave his life to Jesus. His wife also repented. What fiery witnesses of Jesus these two became! They testified everywhere. As far as I know, they never again drank a drop of alcohol. This story also spread throughout the island. Cook and his wife have converted. Not long thereafter, they were filled with the Holy Spirit and baptised in water.

Near the tiny village was a small tuberculosis clinic. About ten patients could stay there, until they were well enough to go home again. Some patients came from other islands. Cook was so filled with the Holy Spirit and compassion for people that he would regularly go to the small tuberculosis clinic to pray for the patients. I heard that for a long time there were no patients at all, because Cook Saylor had found Jesus!

A few months after we had left the island, we heard the moving account of how Cook's wife had died. They were both in their late sixties or early seventies. We did not know exactly. Anyway, the people of the island regarded them as old people. One day Cook's wife did not feel well, and she rested. That afternoon, right after lunch, she called her husband. 'Cook,' she said, 'the Lord has just told me that I am going home today. Let us thank God together for the good time He gave us after we repented, and then I will say goodbye and go home.' Cook was stunned and did not know what to do. His wife took his hands, held them, and prayed. She thanked God for the miracle of their conversion and deliverance from alcoholism and everything that came with it. Then she prayed for her husband and committed him to the Lord. Then she looked her husband in the eyes and said, 'Goodbye, Cook, the Lord will be with you.' She closed her eyes, and she was gone. What a way to die! Cook was dazed, but the next day at her funeral, he testified and told what had happened and how his wife had gone to be with the Lord. After that he testified often, and in many places. What a man he was! In heaven I will see Cook and his wife again. We had the privilege of leading them to Jesus.

The Tapau family belonged to the original small Pentecostal group. They were among the first ones who were filled with the Holy Spirit. After that, many miracles happened in their family; but to the outside world, the greatest miracle was the healing of their eight-year-old deaf and dumb daughter. She had never gone to school, but after her healing, she caught up with all she had missed in one or two years and could attend school at the normal level for her age. Truly an amazing miracle of the Lord. Mother Tapau liked to testify about her daughter's healing, especially during open-air meetings. She testified how she had accepted Jesus and that her life had really changed after she had been baptised. After her baptism, she was sure she was saved. Finally she would tell the story of her daughter, who had been deaf and dumb but was now healed and could hear and speak. That healing was of lesser importance to her than her conversion and baptism, which were definitely the most important. I took time during the following days to explain that salvation comes through faith and that we become a child of God when we accept Jesus, as John 1:12 teaches us. She seemed to understand, but the next time she testified, she again shared that she had prayed and accepted Jesus but that her life had only really changed when she was baptised. Again I tried to explain to her that salvation comes through faith and accepting Jesus and that baptism is an outward testimony of that. This time she really seemed to understand, but the next time her testimony was the same: only when I was baptised my life really changed. I became a little desperate and said within myself,

'Lord, she does not understand.' I sensed that the Lord said to me, 'She understands, but you don't understand!' Whoops! Slowly but surely I began to understand that baptism by immersion is important, and much more than an outward testimony. I still believe that salvation comes through faith and accepting Jesus, but also that we Westerners do not understand baptism well enough. There is great, great power of God released in baptism. Years later, we would often experience people being delivered from evil spirits during baptism. Demons would come out screaming, and straight after that the people who had been baptised spoke in new tongues. Then they would be slain in the Spirit, and we had to carry them out of the water and lay them on the grass. Those things happened much later in Papua New Guinea, when there was a breakthrough of the Holy Spirit in the entire country.

In the large Tapau family, more members had been converted. One day a few of them went fishing. Coby and I joined them. Sometimes I like fishing, but it is not my greatest hobby. We caught practically nothing, and I became bored. To brighten things up a bit, I told a few jokes. I like humour, laughing, having fun, telling crazy stories and clean jokes. I told them about a missionary who was walking in the jungle and suddenly stood face to face with a lion. The surrounding trees were high, and they had no low branches. Besides, the missionary knew that lions were able to climb up trees. He saw no way out and panicked. He knelt down and prayed. While he prayed, he actually expected the lion to jump on him, but nothing happened. For a brief moment, he looked up and saw the lion sitting on his hind legs with his front paws in a sort of prayer posture. Then the lion said, 'Lord, bless this food. Amen.' One of the men shouted, 'Praise God, Brother John, the Lord made a lion talk! A miracle!' I had some trouble explaining that it was a joke and therefore not true. When they understood, they were offended because I told jokes about this sort of thing. The island's inhabitants have a great sense of humour and love to laugh and make fun of each other, but their sense of humour is different from ours, and I really had to get used to it. According to everyone, I achieved that pretty well.

A well-known pearl diver, a man of the islands, was a drunk and a troublemaker. He officially belonged to the Anglican Church but obviously did not know Jesus. He had openly uttered his opinion and criticism about these Pentecostal people and the miracles that happened. He ridiculed everything that took place. At Easter, a play was organised, performed by members of the Anglican Church. Of all people, he was asked to play Jesus. The whole island knew what he had said and done. In fact, because of this, the gospel was ridiculed by unbelievers! In the week after Easter, he went to the reefs with his boat and crew to dive for pearls. He was an experienced diver, but he drowned that week. Even though we cannot and should not make a connection in any way and see this as a judgment, it was as if a cold wind blew over the island when it became known. Everybody knew what had happened the week before. The fear of the Lord came over the island's population. People clearly became more careful in what they said about the things God was doing. In our early years in Papua New Guinea, we would several times experience something similar. We have always felt and noticed that when God works powerfully, the fire of God burns on all sides: with supporters as well as with opponents!

Then one evening something happened that would change the course of our lives completely. God planned it, there is no doubt about it. Just before the meeting, I was told that someone from Papua New Guinea had come. I was curious. Someone from Papua New Guinea? What do they look like? I was introduced to a young man who could not have been older than twenty-five years. He looked just like the island's inhabitants: the same skin colour and curly hair. At least I could not see any difference. He spoke reasonably good English, and I introduced myself. He said that he worked as a crew member on a boat that had brought special cargo to Thursday Island. He went on to say that he came from Daru. 'Daru?' I asked. 'Where is that?' He told me that it was an island almost the same size as Thursday Island (in reality it is almost twice the size). It was about a hundred kilometres away from Thursday Island, on the opposite side of Torres Strait, which separates North Queensland and Papua New Guinea. On the island was an

Australian government station for the Western District of Papua New Guinea, which was at that time still governed by Australia.

Daru was easy to reach by ship, and it also had a small airfield. I asked more questions, and he told me that there were a few thousand people (approximately three thousand, I learned later) living there. Because there had been schools for quite some time, many people spoke simple English. There was a church, the London Missionary Society, or the LMS; but according to him, not many people attended church. He had heard about the miracles and conversions on Thursday Island and said that Daru needed this as well. We only spoke briefly, and I never met him again. He told me that he originally came from a village called Mabaduan. I looked on the map that evening; and there it was, Daru, as the crow flies no more than 100 kilometres away, just before the coastline of Papua New Guinea and not very far from the border with West Irian, the former Dutch colony.

I could not let it go. Every time I prayed, there it was, in my heart and mind, Daru, Daru, Daru. Every afternoon I would drive the Land Rover to an isolated place at the coast to pray. I looked out over the beautiful Torres Strait, the water shimmering in the sun in all different shades of blue, depending on the depth of the water. Far away I saw the islands where we would love to go, but according to some government rules we were not allowed, because they were reserves, only for island inhabitants. Every time I prayed, it almost pounded within me: Daru, Daru, Daru. After a few days, I came to the conclusion that the Holy Spirit was trying to make something clear to me. I shared it with Coby, and she too began to pray. I asked around to see if I could get more information. There was no connection from Thursday Island to Daru – no boats, no regular cargo vessel or a plane. If we were to fly, it would mean going back to the mainland of Australia; take a plane to the capital, Port Moresby; and then another plane to Daru. We simply did not have the money to do that. Travelling by plane to and within Papua New Guinea is by comparison still very expensive.

In the meantime, we were giving the believers Bible studies about the works and gifts of the Holy Spirit and also a series of studies about prophecy, as we had learned and practised it in the Pentecostal movement in Holland. The prophet Joel prophesied that in the great outpouring of the Holy Spirit, young men and women would prophesy. Prophecy is therefore a characteristic of an outpouring of the Holy Spirit! In a few studies, I had told the group of believers all I then knew about prophecy. Now we needed to do it! The next study would be a practice session! After a short introduction, I asked, 'Who believes that he or she would be able to prophesy this evening?' Three hands went up, one of them a young woman who was married to a Japanese man. Her name was Hilda Yamashito; but everyone, including ourselves, called her Lalla. I have no idea why, but she was just Lalla. I went up to her and encouraged her to speak in new tongues for a few minutes and then to prophesy. That's how it happened. She spoke in tongues for a few moments and then started to prophesy. I still remember the first sentence, but the rest I do not remember literally, but I do remember what it was about.

'My brother,' she began. 'Not far away from here is an island that you have been praying for, for quite a while, and you're asking yourself if you should go there. The Lord says that it is His will that you do not wait any longer, but go to this island. The Lord will open the door and make it possible. There is a harvest of souls, and it will also open doors for the days to come. I say it again, do not wait any longer but go to that island.' Then she abruptly stopped and looked at me surprised. 'This is not a prophecy. This is gibberish! I must be doing it wrong!' I encouraged her, 'You are absolutely not doing it wrong. I will explain it to you later.' If I ever heard God speak to me through someone else, it was that evening! I was, as it were, nailed to the ground! Lalla knew nothing, absolutely nothing. Only Coby knew about my growing conviction to go to Daru. The other two also prophesied, but I cannot remember any of it. Lalla's prophecy pounded through my whole being. 'Do not wait any longer!'

A few days later, I heard about someone who was going to sail his small cargo vessel to Daru and from there go on to another place in Papua New Guinea. He was towing a beautiful sailing yacht that belonged to a government official who worked somewhere in Papua New Guinea. I looked for him, and indeed he was going to Daru the following week. I could come with him for fifty Australian dollars. He would not go back to Thursday Island but was going on to other places and would stay in Papua New Guinea for some time. However, he would not take women on board under any circumstance. The boat was not designed for that. The toilet did not work properly so you had to do that over the side of the boat. I prayed and prayed, and someone gave me a fifty-dollar bill. Because Papua New Guinea, and therefore Daru, was under the Australian government, I received permission to go. But under no circumstance was I allowed to get off the boat, therefore no going on shore of any other island in the Torres Strait. Together with the other believers, we prayed. Coby would stay on Thursday Island. I had no idea how I would get back. I did not have much money with me, definitely not enough to pay my way back. Someone on Thursday Island had an acquaintance on Daru and gave me two letters of recommendation so that I would have a roof over my head.

The journey lasted almost four days, zigzagging from island to island. We were on the boat with about six men. One day the weather was pretty rough, and we almost lost the cargo, but it ended well. At least, the journey was an adventure. In the evening, we anchored at an island. Everyone stayed on board apart from the captain. I thought that besides other cargoes, we had a load of soft drinks on board but soon realised that the bottles of soft drink contained alcohol. I was absolutely not allowed to enter the hold of the boat. Alcohol was forbidden in Papua New Guinea. This captain was smuggling! I wondered if they would ever believe my story if we got caught by the authorities. However, we were not caught and safely arrived in Daru. I was alone, entirely alone, and knew nobody on the island; neither did I have any idea about what was going to happen. What I had brought was a small generator, a film projector, and some films of T. L. Osborn, as well as a small amplifier, a loudspeaker, and my guitar. I had no idea how or when I would get back. But God had sent me, of that I was sure! Daru would become a turning point in our lives. More than once Daru would leave an imprint in my life.

I was twenty-two years old when I set foot on Daru.

CHAPTER 7

Daru

ALTHOUGH THEY ARE not very far apart, Daru is very different from Thursday Island. Thursday Island has hills, and the coastline is rocky. Most of the year the island is scorched brown and yellow from the sun, and it is withered and dry because there is not much rainfall.

Daru, on the other hand, is very green. The coastline is overgrown with mangroves, and on the island are many palm trees. The island is completely flat, a big pancake in the ocean. You can't see a mountain or hill when you look to the horizon, which is very unusual for Papua New Guinea. More to the north of the district, there are high mountains which are not visible from the coast. I read in an account by people who study languages and culture that in the languages spoken at the coast, the word 'mountain' is unknown. The southern part of the Western District is actually a delta area surrounding the outlets of several rivers, amongst which the most eastern, the Fly River, is by far the largest. The Fly River is perhaps even comparable to the Amazon in South America. At the outlet, the river is about eighty kilometres wide. The entire southern coastline is flat and muddy with mangroves growing in the seawater. When it rains, the whole island is muddy, and that happens quite often! There is also quite a population of mosquitos on the island.

The harbour consisted of a large jetty where ships could moor. Near the end of the jetty was the government station, the small headquarters of the government of the Western Province.

The captain told us to stay on board while he registered at the government office. A while later, he returned with a government official, who also was a customs officer. They obviously knew each other. Our papers were looked at and stamped, and our cargo was briefly checked. Everything was fine, and we were allowed to get off the boat. After almost four days on that small cargo vessel, it was good to have some solid ground beneath my feet. The cargo vessel would stay a few days, and I was allowed to leave my things on board for a while. I left the jetty and walked to the houses and buildings surrounding the government station. There were a few houses, a shop, a small hospital, and a school. Further on there were a few groups of houses, called corners. Actually they were very small villages where people lived together according to their language group. In the centre of those villages was a big grassed open field, which carried the grand title 'sports oval'. There even were a few cars on Daru. The longest drive possible was from the jetty to the small airstrip and then around the airport, to a very small village on the other side of the airstrip, a drive of about 2.5 to 3 kilometres. Walking was the means of transport. A bicycle, like we use in the Netherlands, would fit in well here. Many people would think Daru was a sleepy little island. But this was the island to which the Lord had clearly sent me.

I had a letter with me from a Christian on Thursday Island, who had met someone from Daru, a certain Mr George Tabua. I asked someone, and Mr Tabua was a well-known person. He lived close to the government office. His house was pointed out to me, and praying silently, I went to the house. A woman opened the door, but she spoke little English. I understood that she was his wife. I also understood that her husband was somewhere in the district on the mainland, with a team of carpenters, building a school; and he would be home in two weeks' time. Mrs Tabua obviously did not know what to do with me, even more so when I told her that I was looking for a place to stay. I took the honourable way out, said goodbye, and left. What now? Still praying, I walked around and explored the centre, which did not take me very long. The sports oval in the middle of the island caught my attention. A good place to have meetings, I thought.

If necessary, I could spend another night on the boat; but after that, I really needed a place to stay. I had walked around the sports oval when a young Daru woman walked up to me and addressed me in good English. Was I the missionary who had just arrived from Thursday Island, and was I the person who had knocked on her mother's door and asked for accommodation? Yes, that was me. She told me that she was a daughter of Mr Tabua and that he indeed would not be back for two weeks. He might have lodgings for me, because he had a new house almost finished. Until that time, I could stay with them. She told me she was married to an Australian man who worked for the government. He did technical maintenance on machines. They had met on Daru and had been married there and now lived in one of the government houses. Such houses were actually houses on poles allowing breezes to keep the house cooler in the tropics and providing a shady area underneath the house.

Under their house was also a spare room with a simple toilet and shower and a single bed. I could stay there temporarily. I was also more than welcome to join them for dinner! She had spoken to her husband, and he too welcomed me. This woman, and I later discovered there were others also, had heard of the miracles on Thursday Island. The testimony of the miracles had gone ahead of me. I asked her about my luggage: a small generator, a film projector, sound equipment, and a few other things. No problem, those could simply be put under the house. On Daru, people at that time did not steal! She even arranged for a few boys to help get my things off the boat and to her house. Between their house and the sports oval was one of the few roads on the island. I was surprised and thanked God, who had given me lodgings so quickly. Years later, I heard that they had moved to Australia, and I spoke with them once over the phone. The commission and promise of the Lord Jesus as written in Matthew 10 is true: 'When someone welcomes you, stay in their house.' The room was comfortable, and the food was excellent.

The next day I went to the government office and received permission to use the sports oval. Someone had heard about the miracles on Thursday Island there too! There was a radio station that sent messages throughout the district. Not many people had a radio yet, but the government tried to provide radios to as many places as possible. Over the radio it was announced that there would be meetings at the sports oval the following evening and that the sick would be prayed for. Because not much was happening on Daru, this was big news.

The next day, two days after arrival, I started. I spent much time in prayer. I tried to send Coby, on Thursday Island, a telegram. And sure enough it arrived. They prayed there too.

The evening came. It was dry! My first enthusiastic estimation of the number of people was about a 1,000, and that's what I wrote in my accounts. Later, after looking at the photos which I had taken, it looks like 700 would have been a more accurate number. Anyway, of the approximate 3,000 inhabitants, 700 were present, almost a quarter. A few boys who spoke reasonable English were fascinated by everything I did, they stayed around and helped where possible. The generator was on, and a few lights shone, and the sound equipment was working. In very simple English, I welcomed the people. I told them who I was, why I had come, and what we would do.

Accompanied by my guitar, I sang a simple song and tried to teach it to the people, especially the children: 'He is the Christ of yesterday, today, forever, and He is mine, mine, mine.' I now know that most, if not all, people did have some connection with the gospel and the church. So some things that I shared and sang were not strange to them. After that, I preached briefly about the miracles Jesus did when He was on earth and that He is still the same. That was obviously new to many people. After that came the film. A film with a short simple sermon, prayer for the sick, and testimonies of people who had been healed by the power of the Lord Jesus. After the film, I spoke for a short while and then prayed for the people en masse. I tried to tell people how they could get to know Jesus and how to ask Him to come into their hearts. Some prayed with me, but I was not sure if they understood everything. Then I prayed for the sick. I asked sick people to place their hands on their bodies, and I prayed. I had barely finished praying when a man jumped up and shouted something, and he was very happy. One of the boys who was with me explained that he had been healed during the prayer. They did not know of what he had been healed for the man spoke no English. But he had been healed, and that caused quite some commotion. I spoke for a while longer and then ended the meeting by saying, 'Tomorrow I'll be here again,' and I invited the people to come. A few people, mainly young boys, stayed around and were talking together. I gave them simple English gospel tracts and invited them to come again. All this I had done on my own: singing, preaching, and praying.

The next evening was similar to the first. The same number of people, singing, preaching, a film, and prayer. This time again people were evidently healed. But especially for the older people, the English language was a problem. Despite that, the Lord had touched and healed people. Again the group of young boys came and helped me with setting everything up. They more or less became my crew who maintained order and supervised where necessary.

Then came the third evening: an evening I will never forget. It was an evening that greatly impacted the inhabitants of the island, and the people of the district! I was about to start the meeting, and it looked as if more people had come. A few boys came up to me while I was behind the microphone and was just about to sing. They brought a woman aged about thirty. This woman had fallen out of a palm tree as a little girl and had not been able to speak or hear since – she had been deaf and dumb for all those years. I had said that God heals, and I had prayed for the sick. They asked if I could pray for her too. Everyone who understood English had heard the conversation and the request. At that moment, I realised that I needed a substantial dose of courage, but believed without a doubt that God was able! I could not decline. I prayed for the woman, and the great miracle happened. I prayed a short prayer, and immediately she grabbed her ears. She could hear again! I held the microphone in front of her mouth and asked her in English to say 'Jesus'. 'Iesu,' she said, exactly what Jesus is called in her own language. She said it again and again and tried to repeat after me, when I started counting in English. She spoke and kept grabbing her ears and looked around almost in a panic, but at the same time so happy. She was overjoyed. The people jumped up and down, shouted and cheered, waved their arms, ran around, and very soon started dancing. I had never seen an original dance from Papua New Guinea, but I later understood that they expressed their surprise and joy in their own joyful dancing. In a number of tribes, these kinds of dances can be evil and demonic but in this area are more often folklore and expressions of things that happened in the past. Using the amplifier, I tried to get the people to sit down again so that I could preach, but it was in vain! They were overjoyed. I was not able to continue the meeting, but it was one of the best meetings in my life. After several hours, we stopped and packed up all my gear for the night. The boys helped me again. It was a Saturday night. I had just arrived in my room when I was called by one of the boys. He asked if I wanted to come to one of the corners because there was a feast, so I went with him. I had not yet been in these very small villages, called 'corners'. The healed woman belonged to their group. The people had quickly prepared a large meal to celebrate the miracle, and there was a sort of decorated throne for me. The decoration consisted of branches of palm trees, flowers, and all kinds of beautiful leaves. It was party time. They were dancing here as well, and I was the guest of honour! The three meetings I had held so far had started around six o'clock, when it was still light, and ended around nine. That evening the feast went on until late in the night. The testimony of this healing spread like wildfire through the entire island and the district.

I continued the meetings; and people were healed, though I sometimes had trouble finding out what exactly had happened, because most people spoke little English. A few young people had clearly made decisions for Jesus and came by in the afternoon to talk with me. Soon I was able to have a Bible study with them. Some had a simple English Bible which they apparently received at school or church. We read how you could become a child of God and why the Lord Jesus had come. Then I started to speak about the baptism in the Holy Spirit and how you could receive the Holy Spirit just like on the day of Pentecost, as described in Acts 2. After five or six days, we prayed for the baptism with the Holy Spirit. They received and spoke in tongues. This was possibly the first time that in the Western District believers received the Holy Spirit. You would also hear people, especially the young people, sing songs like 'He is the Christ of yesterday, today, forever, and he is mine, mine, mine' and also the simple song 'I have decided to follow Jesus. No turning back, no turning back.' It was fun to hear those songs being sung so spontaneously.

When I reread the newsletters from that time, we had written about a young man with a broken collarbone. He was healed in front of everyone. An older man whose whole body was shaking, probably with Parkinson's disease, was healed. Another old man who walked with a stick walked normally and waved his stick in the air. A man who took about ten pills a day for some disease in his abdomen was healed and gave a radiant testimony days later.

Very remarkable was the story of a boy who came from a faraway village in the district. One night he dreamed. He saw in the dream how he found Jesus and was baptised. But he also saw how the heavens opened above the district and how the Holy Spirit descended like a dove on the district, firstly on Daru. The boy went to Daru, and when he arrived there, I was just about to start the crusade. He was one of the first ones to accept Jesus, was filled with the Holy Spirit, spoke in new tongues, and was baptised in water.

A few young men prayed for others to receive the Holy Spirit. They laid their hands on people who were filled with the Holy Spirit and started speaking in new tongues. One of these boys came to me excited and enthusiastic after he had received the Holy Spirit. 'Brother John,' he said, 'I have just received your native language, and I can speak it.' He did not know what speaking in tongues was and thought that it was my own language, Dutch. He was beaming with joy. But I had some explaining to do.

The meetings at the sports oval lasted for a week. I don't know how many people accepted Jesus, but it was quite a number. People were healed, and a few spectacular miracles had taken place. The people had seen God's power. I later learned that people from the whole district came to a government station like Daru, for all kinds of reasons: to meet their family, to make certain arrangements, to be in touch with a government official, to seek medical help, or to purchase supplies. Therefore, not all people in the meeting lived on the island. They would go back to the mainland, to their villages. Consequently, I understood later that the news about the meetings and healings had reached many people in the district. In the years that followed, we often met people in different places of the country who had experienced the meetings at the sports oval in Daru. They could remember the meetings and miracles very well.

About four years ago, we visited Daru, and I was again standing with Coby on the sports oval where it all started. A lot went through my mind as I stood there. This was where our mission to Papua New Guinea had started! This is where people came to Jesus, and this is where the deaf and dumb woman was healed! The sports oval had hardly changed, but to me it was holy ground.

The journey from the mainland to Daru almost always happened in big, traditional canoes called 'lakatois'. A lakatoi is a large hollowed-out tree trunk with a little platform for a few people to sit on. There is a floating device on either side to keep the canoe balanced. The boat also has a mast with a sail. We travelled in a lakatoi several times over the years. I even crossed a part of the sea once and sailed on one for a few days. It always remains a challenging undertaking as well as an adventure.

After about a week, someone from the government station came looking for me. He told me they had received a radio message that Mr and Mrs Len and Joan Day were on their way to Daru with their private plane to visit me. Len Day and his wife are coming to visit me? I was quite surprised. They could be in Daru in three or four days' time, depending on the weather. I asked if he could send a message back to Len and Joan and ask them if they could find Coby on Thursday Island and bring her with them to Daru. Len actually received this message, and three days later, a little white plane circled over Daru. I had told the boys, who often were with me, that Len, his wife, and maybe even my wife, Coby, were coming. They ran with me to the airport. There they were, Len; his wife, Joan; and Coby! Len and Joan had landed on an island with an airstrip, near Thursday Island. They had gone to Thursday Island by boat, asked around, and found Coby. After spending the night there, they flew to Daru together! It was the first time that Len had flown over the open sea. Whoever would have thought that this could happen? I had gone to Daru all alone and had no idea when or how I would return. And now there were four of us.

Mr Tabua had come back a little sooner than expected. He had heard everything from his wife and daughter. He had also heard that Len, Joan, and maybe even Coby would come. And indeed he had almost finished a small cottage, and we were allowed to stay there with the four of us. A sheet made two bedrooms out of one. The family gave us a warm welcome and cooked for us. I remember one meal very well. The meat was cockatoo. The meat was tough, hard to eat. But the Lord Jesus had clearly said, 'Eat whatever is set before you.'

The large meetings were over. We continued with Bible study. A large group of people came, especially young people. English was no problem for them as they had learned English at elementary and secondary school. Len spoke explicitly about the baptism in the Holy Spirit and was experienced in praying with people to receive the Holy Spirit. That did not seem to happen very often in Australia at that time when we were there.

But Len had also another motivation in coming to Daru. He had served in the army during the war and had taken part in the famous Kokoda Trail battle, where there had been long and horrible warfare between Japanese and Australian forces. The Kokoda Trail is a path through the jungle from north to south, over mountains and through rivers, on the narrowest part of the mainland of Papua New Guinea. The Japanese landed on the north coast and thought they could reach the south within a few days and occupy the capital, Port Moresby. It became a massive failure. They had hopelessly underestimated the jungle, the difficult terrain, and, last but not least, their tenacious opponents. In the Second World War, it was on the Kokoda Trail that the Japanese for the first time were defeated on land. This battle cost thousands of soldiers their lives. Just outside Port Moresby is a cemetery and a large monument for soldiers killed in that war. Len was eager to see this and wanted to fly from Daru to the capital as soon as possible. We were going with him and Joan, but it would become a very tense and difficult flight. On top of that, God would speak to us in Port

Moresby and unmistakably call us to this country but that we did not know as yet.

One of the boys who attended the Bible studies had actually come to Daru to buy something for his family. He should have gone back already but had stayed behind, because of the meetings. He had come to know Jesus and had been filled with the Holy Spirit. Now he was worried, because the people in the village would miss him. Len had an idea. We would go to his village by plane and fly low over his village and drop the package with his purchases, well wrapped, on the land. The boy had never flown before. We took off and went on our way to the mainland, to his village. After we had followed the river for a while, he recognised his village. He became very excited. 'My village!' he shouted. He recognised his parents' house. Len started to circle lower, and the people of the village stood in an open place, watching the plane and waving at it. Then Len flew very low and shut down the engine for a brief period. We had opened the window, and above the village we threw the package down. A while later, when we were circling higher up, they had found the package and understood that the boy from the village had done his job. It was a great experience, an experience I would go through a few more times in the years to come, dropping packages from a plane.

Len had seen on his aviation maps that the southern part of the Western District was only accessible by water. There were some villages in the swamps and mangrove areas. Len wanted to explore the area by plane, and I joined him. After about an hour, we flew back to Daru, and we saw the airstrip in front of us. We started our descent. Len had informed the control tower in the capital that we would land on Daru, and they had given permission. When the airstrip came very close, and we were going to land in a couple of seconds, I could no longer restrain myself. 'Len, your landing gear is not out!' Len was startled, accelerated, and pulled the plane up. He had been so fascinated by all that he saw and experienced that he had forgotten about lowering the landing gear. The tower in Port Moresby called us, '*Tango Oscar Tango*, did you land?' 'No,' Len said, 'we are making another circle around Daru to look around.' We did indeed circle Daru and looked around, but I thought to myself, *What if we had landed without the landing gear? Would we have survived?* That I did not know but was glad that we had safely landed.

The next day we left for Port Moresby, the capital and final destination of Len and Joan's trip. Straight across the sea, it would take about an hour or two for Len's old plane, but Len had never flown that long over open sea. From Thursday Island to Daru was only a forty-five-minute flight, and there were small islands along the way where you could possibly land on a small strip of grass or gravel. Len decided to fly along the coast so he could see where to go. While we were flying above the Fly River, suddenly the right-hand door flew open. Coby could look down from her seat and see the vast amount of water so far below. The plane had no adapted air pressure possibility, so we had to fly low. We circled around for a while until we could shut the door again. Since then we have always shut the door firmly and secure. In the middle of the Fly River, there is a large island, Kiwai Island. Years later, this island would be part of an important and unforgettable moment in my life. After the Fly River, we followed the coast and began to fly over the Gulf District. Endless mangroves, swamps with some villages here and there. Again, many big and small rivers ran through the swampy area to the sea and coloured the sea brown for kilometres, because of all the mud that the current dragged along.

Slowly but surely the weather grew worse. The clouds were low, and visibility was deteriorating. On the east side of the Gulf Province, the landscape becomes mountainous and joins the mountainous area of the Central Province. Len could not fly high because the air pressure in the cabin did not automatically adjust. We had to stay low, but the clouds also hung lower and lower. To this day, I have never seen a pilot so anxious and sweating so much. Len had a private pilot's license, and though he had flown quite a lot of hours in Australia, this was new territory for him. At a given moment, the mountains became higher and the clouds lower. Len nearly did not dare to go on. We were looking along the coast for a wide, solid beach to make an emergency landing. But there was no beach or flat surface to be found. Finally we saw a small area of sand at the mouth of a river which was actually far too small to land on. We could clearly see a few people who had just killed a crocodile and were skinning it. So we flew on. Then the outside antenna of the cockpit broke off, and we lost radio contact with Port Moresby. There was nothing we could do but pray. Len flew along the coast but needed to fly above land again, because his calculations indicated that we were not far from Port Moresby. A little while later, the clouds broke, and the weather improved. Now we could see the airport of Port Moresby in the distance. What a relief! Not long after that, we landed, without radio contact with Port Moresby. Two men from the control tower came up to us, congratulated us, and told us that they had seriously thought about the possibility that we might have crashed. Whew! They admired the small airplane, an old Beechcraft 7 biplane with canvas wings. It had been years since they had last seen such a plane. They caressed it. Coby heard one of the men of the control tower say, 'Beautiful airplane, but you won't see me in it!' *Thanks*, she thought, *we still have to go back.*

A few months later, we were with the Dutch migrant group in Melbourne. They had a burning question for us. Had anything special happened on the 25th of July? But more particularly, had we been in danger that day? I checked my diary. The 25th of July was the day that we had flown from Daru to Port Moresby and had almost not made it. They told us that on that morning, one of the men of the group woke up, and the Lord had told him to phone the group because John and Coby were in danger. Some prayed at home, and others came together. They prayed all morning. Around twelve o'clock, they sensed that the danger had passed. It was around twelve o'clock that we landed in Port Moresby! With such supporters on the home front, we as missionaries are very glad and extremely thankful.

The antenna was quickly repaired, and the aircraft was parked. Len arranged a rental car, and we went into the city where Len booked us into a guesthouse. That afternoon, we spent time walking around Port Moresby. Compared to Daru, Port Moresby was dry like Thursday Island. Quite a big mountain range surrounds the city, especially on the north side. The wind and rain come from the north for most of the year, so the rain falls on the north side of the mountain range. The south side, where Port Moresby is located, gets little rain.

I could have never imagined that we would live and work in Port Moresby for seven years and experience what might have been one of the best times of our lives, as missionaries in this country. When I saw the city and its people, I was moved. There were some churches, but many people obviously did not know the Lord Jesus. Our visit to Koki market, where the people sell their home-grown fruit and vegetables, made a deep impression on me. I intently looked at many of the people and saw a lot of darkness.

The next day we went to Bomana, just outside Port Moresby; this cemetery is in honour of the soldiers who gave their lives in the Second World War defending Papua New Guinea. Impressive, all those crosses with the soldiers' ages written on them. So many young men had died. For what? Why? This must have been a moving experience for Len. He had also fought here; maybe he even knew some of the men. After visiting the Bomana cemetery, we went to the beginning of the Kokoda Trail. There begins the path, as you could call it, that runs right through the middle of the jungle, over the mountains, and through rivers to the north side of the island. People fought along this path from north to south. Recently I read a book about this part of the war in the Pacific Ocean. They also made a film of the book. In the years to come, we would frequently visit the beginning of the Kokoda Trail and see the small monument.

That evening, back in Port Moresby, I could not sleep. Coby was sleeping; Len and Joan were in their room and were probably sleeping as well. But I could not sleep. I got out of bed and stood in front of the window. The guesthouse was located on a hill, and I looked at the lights of this small city. I had seen so many people who needed Jesus. I knelt down and prayed. After a while, I sensed that God, unmistakably clear, spoke to me. We had to come back to this land, first to Rabaul, then Kavieng, then the island of Bougainville, and eventually the mainland. I had never heard of Rabaul, Kavieng, or Bougainville! The next morning I looked for a map. There, on the eastern point of the large island of New Britain, was Rabaul, the government centre of that province. On the next, slightly smaller island, New Ireland, was Kavieng, the government station of that province. Lower was the large island, Bougainville, so named after the French captain who discovered it. The mainland was where Port Moresby was located. I had heard the voice of the Lord so clearly. I told Coby and also Len and Joan. Coby immediately accepted it, because she prayed about it and felt it was what the Lord wanted us to do. Len and Joan encouraged us and have continued for years to be a great support for the work on Daru.

That morning we flew back to Daru. The weather was great, and the weather forecast was good. Len took no risk; he flew straight across the open sea to Daru. It was an amazing flight! We stayed in Daru for another week and had Bible studies with a group of young people as well as some older folk. We noticed that the church on the island was not very happy with our meetings and our influence on the people. They warned them against us. Regardless, we did baptise some young people in the sea. Len and Joan had to go back to Australia; their so-called holiday was over. We could fly with them to Thursday Island, and sure enough, the boat that I had come to Daru on was in Daru again and would go back to Thursday Island in a few weeks' time. For a small payment, the captain was willing to take back my generator, film projector, and some other things. Len paid! How wonderfully God has used that dear couple in such unique ways in our life during that period. I had gone to Daru on my own, not knowing how I would get back, and now went back by plane together with Coby.

We promised the group on Daru that we would do everything possible to get a missionary couple to come to the island. God was sending us to another place: Rabaul. A year later, a young couple from Melbourne went to Daru. After them, a Dutch couple from the Dutch migrant fellowship group went to Daru, because the young couple had gone to Indonesia. Len Day built a boat in the place where he lived especially for the work on Daru. That boat was used a lot for evangelism in the villages along the rivers. Eventually the boat ended up in Indonesia where it was used for evangelism as well. When the young couple first came to Daru, there was not much left of the meetings we had held, but there was acceptance, and the people understood who they were. They also regularly met people who had been in the meetings and who had seen the miracles or heard about them.

Slowly but surely the work grew; but the substantial, almost spectacular growth came years later, when the Bible school student Jack Laukepe and his wife came to Daru. Jack planted church after church in the entire district – a true Papua New Guinean apostle!

The flight to Thursday Island was also in beautiful weather. To fly over the most northern area of the Great Barrier Reef of Australia is spectacular. The colours of the ocean, the islands, the reefs that you can clearly see below the surface of the water, are all amazing. Len and Joan stayed for a day and then left us on Thursday Island. From Thursday Island, they flew to Cooktown in the north of the state of Queensland. They refuelled in Cooktown, but during take-off, things went wrong. Just when Len wanted to pull his plane up into the air, the landing gear broke. The plane started to get airborne and then came down just past the airstrip, between the bushes and trees. Len and Joan were unharmed; but their airplane *Tango Oscar Tango*, Len's big love, had passed away and never flew again. Joan became fearful of flying for many years, following this crash. Later Len bought another plane, a beautiful Cessna 210. I flew in this new plane a number of times. Under Len's supervision, there were occasions when I even flew myself, and on one occasion even over Sydney.

Coby and I were back on Thursday Island. Here we would enjoy a special, almost funny, and unforgettable goodbye. We were going back to the mainland of Australia in order to prepare for a permanent return to Papua New Guinea. We would live and work in Papua New Guinea for fourteen years; and our three sons, Mark, Stephen, and Daniel, would be born there.

I was twenty-three when we arrived in Rabaul. 'At a young age I will call you, and at a young age you will serve me.' But before that, we would spend several months in Australia and experience some special events.

CHAPTER 8

A Few Months in Australia

THE BELIEVERS ON Thursday Island were glad to see us back again. They had prayed much for us while we were on Daru and thanked God with us for the good report we were able to bring. I had taken photos on Daru, and when we were back on Thursday Island, I showed them to the believers. Lalla, the woman who had spoken that special prophecy about Daru, became very excited when she saw one particular photograph. It was taken from the jetty and showed a part of the coast of Daru. 'This is what I saw when I prophesied!' she exclaimed. What a confirmation for her, but also for us.

We started to announce that soon we would have to say goodbye. We were expected in Brisbane at the beginning of October, to conduct a crusade for four days, in a well-known church. The news about the miracles had reached them. When we returned to Thursday Island, it was the end of August. The ship that could take us and our car, the MV *Malukka*, sailed only once every fourteen days from Cairns to Thursday Island. The ship would then go to the most northern point of Queensland, where the government had built quite a large settlement, named Bamaga, mostly occupied by islanders and Aboriginal people. There were some Christians there who had asked us to come. So we booked our trip that would leave on a Friday from Thursday Island to go to Bamaga. From there we would go to Cairns by car. People had assured us that you could drive from Bamaga, through the northernmost point of Queensland, the Cape York Peninsula, with a four-wheel-drive vehicle. There was no road, but you had to follow the telegraph line from north to south. Sometimes that would be just a track, but mainly it was Australian bush – the dry, bushy landscape. In Cape York, there was another small settlement called Laura, where about sixty islanders and Aboriginals lived. There also were some Christians who had asked us to come. Moreover, and maybe at that moment an even more decisive factor, was the fact that we did not have the money to pay for the trip for ourselves as well as the car, to go by boat all the way to Cairns. So we decided to travel overland from Bamaga to Cairns. We realised this would be rather adventurous; but if we had known how adventurous it really was going to be, we probably would have prayed more urgently, to enable us to go to Cairns by boat. Leaving from Cairns, we would visit some of our contacts and slowly travel south to Brisbane. Along the way, we would preach at different places, and that almost always meant we would receive a love offering so we could continue our travel.

The boat was scheduled to leave on Friday. The people became sad. The pearl fishers would arrive on Saturday, after spending a week at sea. They really wanted to organise a great farewell party on Sunday. Some believers were on the mainland for work, and they would come home that weekend. The next boat would leave fourteen days later, and that would be too late for us to get to Brisbane in time. The people begged us to stay a bit longer, but we just couldn't. Then Grandfather Pitt, one of the people of the original group, and the oldest in age of the congregation, stood up and said, 'If you cannot stay until after Sunday, then I will pray that something happens to the ship and that it will not leave on time!' Grandfather Pitt's statement spread immediately throughout the entire island, and we wondered what would happen.

The week before we left, a police officer came to visit. There were four police officers on the island, and he was the commander. He had tears in his eyes while he spoke. He thanked us for the time we had been on the island, because their work had become so much easier, and things were much more peaceful. A few of the worst drunks and troublemakers had been converted and were now fiery witnessing Christians. The whole atmosphere on the island had changed. What a testimony! The police had noticed it and came to thank us. That moved us too.

Wednesday arrived, the day on which the ship, the MV *Malukka*, normally arrived and would unload. Grandfather Pitt had prayed. That morning two or three believers came running to us, out of breath and totally excited. 'Brother John, Sister Coby, the *Malukka* got stuck on a reef just in front of the island!' We really thought it was a joke, but they were very serious. We walked to the shore, and there in the distance we saw the *Malukka*. It had become low tide, and truly it was stuck on a reef. We went there with a dinghy to have a look and take some photos, which I still have. The *Malukka* had sailed from Cairns to Thursday Island for years, every fourteen days, and this had never happened before. The news spread like wildfire over the entire island. Most people had heard of Grandfather Pitt's statement, and now it had happened. Nearly everyone came out to see it. Grandfather Pitt himself was upset and felt very guilty. 'But I did not pray that the *Malukka* would get stuck on a reef,' he told everyone. 'I just prayed that it would depart later and that John and Coby would be here for the weekend, to be at the farewell party we wanted to organise for them.' That evening the *Malukka* remained stuck; but on Friday night during high tide, and with the help of other boats, it was pulled off the reef. It was unloaded on Saturday and Monday, and on Tuesday morning, it left for Bamaga. On Sunday we had a grandiose, moving, and unforgettable farewell party, including a huge island meal of deer, turtle, fish, fruit, and much more. Delicious!

Saying goodbye was difficult, very difficult. In four months, these people had become such a part of our lives, we had become family. Coby still remembers our departure very well. She stood at the boat railing for a long time, with tears in her eyes, watching Thursday Island as it disappeared beyond the horizon. Thursday Island and Daru were the first places where we were able to serve God as missionaries without a leader, which was a new experience for us. We had seen God move in a mighty way. Never before had we seen the Lord do so many amazing miracles. To this day, the name Thursday Island stirs up something within us. If this was a foretaste of what our life would be like, we looked forward to it with anticipation. Years later, there would be another farewell that would be even more difficult: after fourteen years, we left Papua New Guinea permanently; it was a land that we had grown to love so deeply. But more about that later.

After several hours, the ship arrived in Bamaga, and the Land Rover was offloaded onto the jetty. We went to look for the person who had contacted us and found the family that had asked us to come. They knew that the *Malukka* was not on schedule but did not know when it would arrive; otherwise, they would have welcomed us, island style. That evening we held a meeting in a crowded little house. There were family members of believers from Thursday Island, who had heard the testimonies and stories about the miracles. We prayed for a few people but decided to start our journey overland along the telegraph line the next day, because we had to be in Cairns on Sunday. We had taken a number of jerrycans with petrol from Thursday Island, a gift from Johnny Fell's father (Johnny was the crippled boy who had been healed). We also had food and drink sufficient for about two or three days.

The next morning we informed the police that we would start our journey along the telegraph line. They looked at us and probably saw how inexperienced we were, and I detected doubt in their eyes. *We have the Lord*, I thought, *and that is what counts most.*

Cape York Peninsula's landscape is dry and arid Australian bush. The journey along the telegraph line is actually over quite flat land and not too overgrown. The trees are mainly eucalyptus trees. There were many bushes, big termite hills, and a few rivers, which at times were no more than dry riverbeds, which only held water during the rainy season.

From Bamaga to the first river was a gravel road, which was in a quite reasonable condition. After an hour, we arrived at the river. It was a steep slope of loose sand going down and on the other side a steep slope with loose sand going up. I had a four-wheel-drive vehicle, but this was too much for the Land Rover. We looked at it from all angles, but this was really too much for our car. Desperate, we went back to Bamaga with the thought of having to wait there for fourteen days for the *Malukka*. We also went to the police station to tell them of our return, and then they told us that we had missed a turn-off and that there was an accessible way through the river a few hundred metres from where we had been. We went back again, and sure enough, there was a turn-off. It was quite overgrown, so it was no wonder we had not seen it. We stopped at the riverside, and I walked through the river a few times. The river reached to the top of my leg, so it was not more than a metre deep and a little deeper in some places. There were some iron strips from the war, but they were spread here and there in the river – probably pushed there by the heavy rain. In the rainy season, this river would become a wild torrent. I found enough strips to make it possible for the tyres on one side of the car to have something firm to go over. Then we prepared the car. The river was quite wide. We put a canvas sheet over the front of the car to try to keep the engine as dry as possible. We prayed, Coby had the camera ready, and we went. We were both very tense. I had never driven through such a wide river. We made it safely to the other side, thanked the Lord, and breathed normally again.

When I later shared about our journey through that river, some people gave me an anxious look. 'Don't you know that that place is reasonably close to the sea and that the water is brackish and that there are crocodiles!' At times it may be better not to know some things! After crossing the river, we travelled hour after hour along the telegraph line. The maximum speed was fifteen to twenty kilometres per hour through the real Australian bush. We saw nobody, just bushland. Sometimes we saw kangaroos or emus, the Australian ostrich. Those stupid animals would run in front of the car. If we drove ten kilometres per hour, they would run ten kilometres per hour. If we drove fifteen or twenty kilometres per hour, then they would run fifteen or twenty kilometres per hour, and they apparently did not think about moving aside. Even the Bible calls these animals stupid, which we saw confirmed before our eyes. In a way, it was fun, having those emus running in front of the car. We knew there would be another river on our way. At that river, there was a telegraph station, where someone was present from time to time. Late in the afternoon, we arrived there. This river was easier to cross than the first one. A little further was indeed a cottage, the telegraph station, literally in the middle of nowhere. For hundreds of kilometres all around, there was not a man in sight. We saw no one, so I honked the horn. A little later, a wild-looking man came outside cursing and shouting. We were disrupting his peace, beat it. Okay, we only wanted to be friendly and moved on. Endless bush, captivating, impressive, and beautiful. The feeling that there was absolutely no one else there, and that we were there, just the two of us, was quite an experience. Sometimes the road became pretty rough, and I had to put it in four-wheel drive from time to time. There were tense moments, but we could not go back; we had to move on. Around sunset, we ate sandwiches and made coffee. We unloaded the car and just put everything outside. There was no one there anyway. When it became dark, we slept in the back of the car. We had often done that. It was a little cramped, but in a happy marriage, that is no problem at all! At sunrise, we woke up. More sandwiches and on we went. It was the 14th of September, my birthday. The most peaceful birthday I have ever had. Together in the bush of Cape York in North Queensland. That day too, there were kangaroos, emus, and many birds. We went easily through a river this time. At that river, we met two other cars that were going north. They were together, so if something went wrong, they could help each other. We were alone and quite inexperienced. The police had given us instructions: 'If something happens or you get into trouble, you must climb up the telegraph pole and cut the wire. Then there will be a technical failure, and we will have to come.' I can't climb poles very well, so the advice was to throw a roll of metal wire over the telegraph line and cause it to short-circuit. We had the roll of wire with us, but we did not have to use this emergency measure.

Suddenly there were two cars with adventurous foreigners. You guessed it: they were Dutch too. You run into them everywhere! We talked for a while and moved on along the telegraph line which seemed endless. Sometimes we saw car tracks from other vehicles. Most of the time there was only flat, sandy, dusty ground. That night we slept in the bush again. We were actually hoping to arrive in Laura that day, but we had lost quite a bit of time on the first day. Just before Laura, there was a river we had to cross. The river was dry, only loose sand, but no iron strips or anything like that. For a brief moment, this thought crossed my mind: the Land Rover will not make it. But we had to at least try. We prayed; and with a screeching engine, in four-wheel drive and first gear, shaking, jerking, and tossing up sand, we made it through. We again thanked the Lord and thanked Him for the angels that we realised were there. We enjoyed the journey, the landscape, and the Australian bush; but we did live with a certain amount of tension for those few days. If anything was to happen, we could lose our gear and our car. However, the thought *But we have the Lord* was very real!

Laura was a very small place. There was a tiny store, if you could call it a store at all. The people there were either all involved in cattle farming at a large cattle station or worked on maintaining the telegraph line. We easily found the family who had invited us. With a population of only sixty people, everybody knows each other. The family was from Thursday Island. That evening we held a meeting. It was only a small gathering, but the people were so happy and thankful. We prayed for the sick, and it was just good to be there. And there was a meal. These islanders sure know how to cook!

That evening, while sleeping in that very simple house, we were awakened by a soft shaking and stamping sound. In the light of the almost full moon, we saw where the sound was coming from. Near the house was a well for animals. Grey and red giant kangaroos, who can grow to a height of two metres, came leaping to the well to drink and then leapt away. We had seen such kangaroos before, but not so many. The kangaroos one normally sees are smaller and are actually called wallabies. It was fascinating and impressive to see these huge animals leaping and drinking in the light of the moon. We watched them for a long time.

The next day we went on our way again. The road from Laura was at least recognisable as a road; there were little white pickets indicating where the road was. It looked as if, perhaps once a year, the road was graded; but that certainly had not happened that year. We drove endlessly through the bush. What a lot of space and no people! Then we saw a little truck by the side of the road which had broken down. I stopped to see if help was needed. The driver was completely, and I mean completely, drunk. There were quite a lot of cartons of beer in the truck, and a few cartons were opened. Coby stayed in the Land Rover, and I walked to the driver. He suddenly saw Coby, a woman, and started to walk up to her with a very strange look in his eyes. Blind drunk he shouted out, 'A woman!' I ran back to the Land Rover, started the engine, and drove off. The man shouted and screamed. I don't know what he said, but I still think it was the right thing to do.

Later that day, we saw the first signs of civilisation, at least, junctions with signs of the name of a cattle station and how many kilometres it was to get there. We once saw a sign that said that the cattle station was only twenty-seven kilometres away, with the remark, 'Radio, telephone present, only use in case of emergency.' So if your car broke down, you could walk for twenty-seven kilometres and find a phone. It seemed to us that the words 'Only use in case of emergency' were unnecessary.

Towards the evening, we arrived in Cooktown. It was a very small town, but it looked like the civilised world. At a camping area, like they have near every town or village in Australia, we slept in the back of the car. The next day we went on to Cairns. That part of the journey, from Daintree to Mossman, and then to Port Douglas and eventually Cairns, is indescribably beautiful. You leave the dry and arid bush landscape behind and enter the tropical, heavily forested mountains, a rainforest environment. The road is along the coast with green mountains on one side and the great blue Pacific on the other side. It is incredibly beautiful.

In Cairns, we had to check in with the police. They had heard via telegraph that a clearly inexperienced young Dutch couple had undertaken the journey along the telegraph line. They seemed to be surprised. In four days we had reached Cairns. 'In Bamaga, they thought that you were not going to make it, and we took into account that we might have to go looking for you.' The Lord had sent His angels with us, we were sure about that. That year, seven cars undertook this journey, and we were one of the seven. We were able to witness to the police because someone in the police station had heard about the miracles on Thursday Island.

In Cairns, there were letters with money waiting for us. We were able to move on. In various places, we preached in services or visited people we had contacted the previous year. After two weeks, we arrived in the Brisbane area. We set up our tent, which we still had from our first year, and visited some Dutch people who had heard about us and wanted to meet us. They were kind, friendly people. At one of the homes, we met a couple who had recently come to the Lord and were filled with the Holy Spirit. Later they told us that from that moment, they had felt connected to us. That couple was Hank and Lenie van der Steen. We promised to return, stay awhile, have some meetings, and then be on our way to Papua New Guinea.

In Brisbane, we preached for four days in quite a well-known Pentecostal church. The pastor had heard about us, and the small revival on Thursday Island, and had invited us. We knew that in most Pentecostal churches, not much was happening at that time, but the hunger and the desire to see God move was great. A few people came to Jesus, quite a lot were filled with the Holy Spirit and spoke in tongues, and several people were healed. On the second day, the pastor came to visit us at our campsite. When he saw that we stayed, or rather lived, in a tent, he was surprised. He had actually assumed that we had a caravan and toured around with it, as many people in Australia do. 'We will have an offering for you, because you need a caravan. You will leave Brisbane with a caravan behind the Land Rover!' was his firm statement. The second, third, and fourth evening, he told the people that this dedicated young Dutch couple lived in a tent and that they, as a congregation, would have an offering for them to purchase a caravan. There were some 250 to 300 people each evening. Some Dutch people we had become acquainted with had come to the services in that Pentecostal church, and Hank and Lenie were amongst them. We had four fine, blessed days.

The day after the fourth meeting, the pastor came to say goodbye, just before we were to leave for Sydney. He had brought the love offering, but he apologised for it. It was not enough for a caravan, not even for a second-hand caravan, but maybe it was enough for a spare tyre. The offering had fallen short of his expectation. I remember the amount well: thirty-six Australian dollars and sixty-four cents. Maybe enough to fill our tank twice. We clearly felt that something was not right. A few months later, when we were having meetings with the group of Dutch people, they were surprised that we did not have a caravan behind our Land Rover, and asked us about it. Though they did not mention the amount, some had personally given more than the love offering we had received. It was very difficult to encourage these people to keep going to this church. Later we heard that the pastor had subtracted the rent for the building, electricity, printing costs for the pamphlets, his own salary for four days, and some other costs from the love offering and had given us what was left. It was not the first time that we experienced dishonesty concerning money. But it was another good exercise in forgiveness and not to put our trust in people, but in the Lord.

One evening while on our way to Sydney, we had a practically empty tank and could not find a petrol station that was open. We had to drive the entire night to honour an appointment we had made for several meetings. Nowadays, there are petrol stations that are open twenty-four hours a day, but not at that time. The fuel gauge started to signal red, but there was no open petrol station. What to do now? We prayed and drove to the next place, about 100 kilometres away. The gauge was way in the red, so the fuel tank was practically empty or was empty. The Land Rover kept driving. After an hour, the next town was in sight, where we saw a petrol station that was open in the middle of the night. I drove into the petrol station, and on the turn-off into the station, the engine stalled. The car rolled on until the pump, and then we stood still! When we had filled up the tank, the engine made a bit of noise before it started again. The tank had been completely empty. But it had been empty for more than 100 kilometres! Again it was a miracle that the Lord had done, like the water bottle that did not run out on Thursday Island.

Once we had to preach in a church on a Saturday evening and the next morning in another church about 200 kilometres away. The idea was to drive all evening and arrive around midnight, to sleep there and preach in the church on Sunday morning. The pastor's home was easy to find, we had been told. When you get into the city and see the sign with the name of the city, then it is the third house on the left. As simple as that. However, when we came into the city that night, there was no light on in the third house, but there was light in the fourth house. That was the house of the pastor. But in his letter he had said he lived in the third house. What had happened? The pastor had mailed the letter, and later that same day, a huge truck had come with a complete timber house on it, and it was placed between the second and third house. So the pastor's house became the fourth house! This was typical in Australia. We once saw such a house transportation ourselves, so it really does happen.

At a certain moment during our journey to the south, the Lord spoke to Coby and said, 'My child, I want you to forgive people!' 'But I have forgiven everyone,' Coby said to the Lord. 'I have forgiven everyone. I do not have any bitterness in my heart anymore.' Again the Lord said, 'My child, I want you to forgive people!' Again Coby responded in the same way, but the Lord persisted. Finally Coby said to the Lord, 'But I have forgiven, haven't I? What do You mean?' The Lord spoke lovingly and tenderly, 'You forgive like people forgive. I want you to forgive people the way I forgive!' Coby realised that this was true. In her youth and as a young adult, but also in Australia, she had really been hurt by people, sometimes quite badly. Coby would then think, *I forgive you, but you must stay in the south and we in the north, but we should not meet again. Or you will stay in the Netherlands, and I will stay in Australia, so we don't have to meet again. But I have forgiven you.* It became the beginning of a process in which the Lord taught Coby and me what forgiveness really is. A deep, beautiful lesson that eventually led to a reconciliation between ourselves and another couple who also served the Lord. We then could help the couple, and especially the man, to come back to Jesus and be set free from demons that had entered his life during a difficult period when, as a Christian in the service of the Lord, he made a big mistake.

After having preached in Sydney, we travelled on to Melbourne to spend time with the Dutch group of immigrants who prayed for us so faithfully and who supported us financially as best they could. We would spend the month of December there and have a Bible study week in January, during the summer holidays, just like we had Bible Study weeks in Holland. Actually, we were convinced that we were spiritually rich in the Netherlands in the Pentecostal movement. Everything we had learned there we taught everywhere. And . . . it worked. The Bible study week was very special and very blessed.

Not long after this, the Lord brought across our path people who would greatly add to what we had received back in Holland. They would challenge us enormously and lead us into a whole new river of God's Spirit. From 1967 onwards, a whole new movement of God's Spirit was released in New Zealand and afterwards also in Australia. It was to greatly influence the work we were to do in Papua New Guinea. The first signs of a new movement of God's Spirit were already visible here and there.

During this Bible study week, Henk and Tanny Smit, a Dutch immigrant couple (with an extraordinary and almost funny testimony), were present. They had heard about the group through contacts and had come. In the beginning, it was especially Tanny who was very hungry for the Lord. Henk was not too sure about the whole thing and waited and wondered where it all would lead. One night Henk woke up. He heard his wife talk. He listened; and he heard his wife quoting verses from the Bible about the Holy Spirit, one after the other, very clearly and for quite a while. Henk told me how astounded he was as he listened, while his wife, who was asleep next to him, was quoting Bible verses about the Holy Spirit. Then she stopped quoting Bible verses and began to speak in tongues, clearly and for quite some time, and then she woke up. In her sleep, she had been filled with the Holy Spirit. Henk was flabbergasted, to say the least. Not long afterwards, he was filled with the Holy Spirit; and during the Bible study week, they were baptised in the sea.

Henk and Tanny discovered a small Pentecostal church near their home. We were inclined to think that this congregation was on the point of death. The congregation consisted of about sixty to eighty people, and there did not seem to be much life anymore. The Lord spoke to Henk and Tanny that they had to go to this church and stay there until there were 160 members, and then the Lord would lead them on. A little later, Tanny led the lady next door to the Lord, who had a Roman Catholic background. The Lord gave that lady a healing ministry, and for a long time, there was a healing service every week in that church. The church grew way beyond 160 members. Henk and Tanny will be mentioned again in a later chapter.

In the time we were in and around Melbourne, we visited Len and Joan Day. Len was in the process of buying his new plane, a Cessna 210. At the same time, he also began preparations to acquire a boat to evangelise from Daru along the rivers of the Western District. A young couple belonging to the group of Dutch migrants in Melbourne was later gone to work on Daru. It was also around this time that we came to know Jaap and Zwaantje Kooy, who are much loved in Australia and who are known there as Jack and Swanny Kooy. Jack and Swanny have visited us several times in Papua New Guinea, and we visited them in Australia on a number of occasions. Together we conducted special meetings or conferences. Spiritually speaking, these were very profitable times. But we also used to have a lot of fun and enjoyment in each other's company.

During this time, we also met Pastor Hal Oxley. Hal Oxley was a widower and was pioneering a church in Melbourne. Later he married Jill. Between this sweet, wise, fatherly man and his wife, Jill, and us, developed a warm and close friendship over the years. While I am writing this book, Hal is eighty-nine years old, almost blind but healthy and still active in counselling. Last Christmas he preached for the last time! I know of no other pastor who, at eighty-nine years of age, still preached.

During the farewell service with the Dutch group, they prayed for us. A brother had a vision. He saw a small township on the shore of a large bay. Around that place were seven volcanoes, and the sand on the beach was black, or at least very dark. That was the place where the Lord was sending us. When we arrived in Rabaul several months later, we were standing in a high place and looked out over the township and the bay. Surrounding Rabaul were seven volcanoes – six extinguished, dead volcanoes but one active one. Years later, when we lived in Japan, that volcano erupted. Because of this, the largest part of the city of Rabaul no longer exists; it is buried under a deep layer of volcanic ash. Several years after the eruption, I was able to visit Rabaul. It was bizarre; the place where we had lived did not exist anymore. And when we came to the beach for the first time, we were speechless. The sand had a dark grey colour, almost black. It was volcanic sand. We had never seen that before. We were convinced that beaches always have yellowish or white sand. It certainly gave us the assurance that we were in the right place.

The Dutch group was actually not very big, but they did so much for us and meant a lot to us. We wondered if they realised that themselves. We also feel that we never clearly expressed our gratitude to them. Not long after our departure for Papua New Guinea, the group discontinued, and most people became part of several Pentecostal churches. But individually a few of them kept supporting us for a long time. We'd like to take this opportunity to greatly thank them! I have dedicated this book to them as well as to the people in Holland who supported us.

In Melbourne, we tried to get a visa for Papua New Guinea, but the embassy did not want to give us one. We were under the impression that the person who was responsible and refused to issue us a visa did not like missionaries. Out of necessity, we decided to go north to Brisbane to try there. Sure enough, we received a visa for Papua New Guinea without a problem.

We went to Sydney and preached in several congregations. We also met people who knew the situation in and around Rabaul well and greatly encouraged us to go there. They told us that decades before, mainly Methodist missionaries had come to the area and had led people to the Lord. The missionaries who were there now were for the most part very liberal. Furthermore, the idea of black theology and nationalism that resisted the European influence was apparently promoted at that time. When we arrived in Rabaul several months later, we experienced how correct these remarks were. In Sydney, we were given the address of a Spirit-filled couple. They both worked as teachers just outside Rabaul. We got in touch with them, and they were able to arrange accommodation for us in Rabaul.

We had promised the group of believers in Brisbane to stay for a few weeks and have meetings and Bible studies. In those four to five weeks, a small revival started; and soon we came together several nights a week, with sometimes fifty or more people. One after the other, mainly Dutch people came to the Lord and were filled with the Holy Spirit. Hank and Lenie van der Steen were at every service. A few years later, they would form a team with us, and for seven years we worked together. Amazing people! Unfortunately, they are still in Australia, and we are in the Netherlands, so we do not see each other very often.

I held Bible studies like we did with Streams of Power in Holland, about the gifts of the Holy Spirit. As on Thursday Island, I taught about prophecy, a biblical characteristic of the outpouring of the Holy Spirit. Hank longed to be used by God in prophecy. One evening I felt that the Lord wanted to speak to an older brother and that He wanted Hank to prophesy over him. When I told Hank to do that, he did not feel anything and, not knowing what to say, started to speak in tongues. Then the Holy Spirit came powerfully upon him; and Hank shook and trembled, stood up, and walked straight up to the somewhat older man, who was actually resisting everything that was happening. This man only came because of his wife, who was filled with the Holy Spirit. Hank laid his hands on this man and prophesied with an almost thundering voice. His voice was so loud that he shouted to himself, 'Not so loud, not so loud!' It was a word of the Lord straight into this brother's heart. He gave up all his resistance and came to the Lord. He was filled with the Holy Spirit and baptised in water; and until his death, a few years ago, he testified about Jesus.

A lady, of Dutch origin, came to the Lord. She was married to a 'real Australian bloke'. He could have come straight from the television series *Flying Doctors*, or he could have been a mate of Crocodile Dundee. His name was Colin Noble. At first he wanted to have nothing to do with all that Christianity. He was a prawn fisherman, but a beautiful rough diamond. Finally, while at sea, he cried out to the Lord. His conversion was powerful. And when I say powerful, I am not exaggerating. Col realised that he could no longer be away from home for weeks on end. They had children, amongst them an adopted boy. Col wanted to sell his boat and prayed. A few hours before he had to sail off again and the boat already provisioned, it was sold. Col had prayed!

Col bought a heavy, second-hand dump truck and transported sand. One day he needed a part that he could not get right away. Col prayed, and the Lord showed him a garage that did have that part. He went there, and they had exactly one part left. It had been there for years, so he could take it for free. One day he noticed that one of his tyres was repeatedly going flat. 'That can't happen, Lord. I need money for my family and for the missionaries, John and Coby,' he said. He went to the petrol station and had the tyre filled with air, and he did not have a flat tyre after that. Col thought I had to learn to drive that heavy dump truck as well. 'You never know when you might need it,' he said. But when I almost scraped a lamp post for the second time, Col thought it wise not to try to teach me any longer. I agreed.

His adopted boy of about four years old had asthma. Col prayed, and the boy was healed. The asthma was gone. In Col you saw a principle: a deep conversion brings great faith. When the Lord Jesus called people to repent, He immediately linked it with faith: 'Repent and believe the gospel' were His words. Col saw miracle after miracle with his simple, childlike faith. The meetings were usually held at his home, and his hunger and desire for the Lord were great.

Col was doing really well until a Dutch man, who was quite dogmatic, heard about the group and came as well. He got to know Col, and one day he said, 'Col, you must realise that the Lord does not always answer prayers!' Col was deeply shocked. Col in his simplicity actually looked up to this man and all the other Christians who had followed the Lord longer than he had. This man's words greatly impacted him. He started to doubt, and that spontaneous, childlike, enthusiastic faith was gone. Col kept believing in the Lord but followed Him in his own way. Years later, when I was pastoring a church near Brisbane, I heard that he was in the hospital on his deathbed, and visited him. Col had a place in my heart ever since his conversion, and that was still there. Col is with the Lord now and has his simple and childlike faith back. In this story, there is a great lesson to be learned, about the importance of the words that we speak to new believers.

We were so desirous to go to Papua New Guinea that we did not really understand the extraordinary work of the Spirit that was taking place in Brisbane. Looking back, we should and could have stayed longer. The potential for a far greater movement of the Holy Spirit, resulting into the building up of a strong congregation, was clearly there.

The group and individuals from the group supported and prayed for us for years. We are still in touch with some of them at times.

The car went on the ship from Brisbane to Rabaul, and a week later, we said goodbye. It was quite a difficult farewell. Most of the people found their place in several congregations and churches during the months that followed. When a great movement of the Holy Spirit began in a church in Brisbane two years later, a number of the Dutch group joined that congregation!

The group waved us goodbye, and we flew from Brisbane to Port Moresby and from there to Rabaul, the place that the Lord had so clearly spoken about that night in Port Moresby. Rabaul, the place surrounded by seven volcanoes and with black sand on its beaches.

It was May 1968. I was twenty-three years old when we arrived in Rabaul. We would live, work, and minister for fourteen years in the nation of Papua New Guinea, the nation we have come to love so deeply.

CHAPTER 9

Rabaul

WE WERE VERY surprised when we arrived in Rabaul. We had heard that the countryside surrounding Rabaul was beautiful, but that was an understatement. We had seen lovely green Daru and dry, arid Port Moresby. Both areas were beautiful, but they were no match for Rabaul, which was bigger than we thought. It was a neatly built township. It could well have been a small town on the north coast of Queensland in Australia.

There were more expatriates in Rabaul than we had expected. They were people who worked for the government, for church organisations, or who were involved with plantations or business. Besides them, there were also Chinese; one part of Rabaul was actually called Chinatown. Then there was a group of people who were mixed race, often part native and part Chinese.

Rabaul is located along a beautiful bay. According to geologists, it is on the edge of a crater of a large sunken volcano. Seven volcanoes surround the city: six dead ones and one active one, the Matupit volcano. The bay has is connected to the sea, which makes its excellent harbour subject to low and high tides. After leaving the harbour, the sea is almost immediately quite deep – 2000 metres I was once told. The sea is a beautiful deep blue with many coral reefs. The area itself is mountainus and overgrown with jungle because of the fertile volcanic soil.

After the large volcanic eruption of Matupit on 19 September 1994, another volcano came into being on the other side of the large bay, five kilometres away from Matupit. It just came up out of the sea near the coast.

Rabaul is the centre of government for the island provinces all around, like Manus Island, New Ireland, and Bougainville, even though these islands also have government offices. Just outside Rabaul was the main hospital for the islands, the Nonga Base Hospital, where our eldest son, Mark, was born. The hospital was built outside the town because it is located at the foot of an active volcano. If the volcano were to erupt like it did in the thirties, then if the hospital was in the town, there would no longer be a hospital. The wisdom of building it outside the city was rewarded in 1994, when there was another volcanic eruption.

In Rabaul were several schools and government offices, as well as head offices for various churches. Burns Philp had a small supermarket in the town. Years later, after the eruption of the volcano Matupit, I visited Rabaul again. Not far from the bay, I saw a concrete wall on which was written in faded letters 'Burns Philp' – that was all that was left. Except for a small part of the town and its surroundings, the volcanic eruptions of 1994 had turned everything into a moonlike landscape. Metres, sometimes a dozen metres, of grey volcanic ash covered everything. Here and there were the remains of a building or the trunk of a palm tree. It was bizarre for me to see this beautiful city so utterly destroyed. From one point, I could estimate approximately where our house had stood, but that was now beneath metres of grey volcanic dust. The house itself was probably destroyed anyway, because it was made of timber, and the boiling-hot volcanic ash would have burned it down completely. We were in the Netherlands and saw the eruption on television. Later we saw extensive video footage of this disastrous event. The government decided that Rabaul was not going to be rebuilt; but thirty kilometres to the west, on the coast, there was a small government station called Kokopo. That place was extended and became the centre of the district. The original airport at the foot of the volcano was also covered by volcanic ash, and an emergency airport near Kokopo was developed and became the official airport.

From the beginning of the nineteenth century, the northern part of Papua New Guinea used to be a German colony. The southern part called Papua was an Australian colony. The Germans saw the potential of developing the area and built roads along the coast where possible.

The roads were constructed from coral gravel that made them nice and white, giving them a clean appearance. When the sun shone on the white road, it glistened so brightly that you had to wear sunglasses.

The roads with coral gravel were as hard as a rock and were easy to maintain. However, because of the salt in the coral, these roads are really bad for your car, causing a lot of rust. The roads were mainly along the coast, and sometimes a road went inland. Roads could not be built any further than forty to fifty kilometres along the coast, because of rivers running into the sea. The people who lived inland and to the west were very hard to reach; therefore, there was little contact.

The Germans had encouraged people to build plantations for copra and cacao. Copra is the dried flesh of the coconut, which is used, for example, in making soap. The cacao bean is used to make chocolate. Also timber was brought from inland. Because there were roads, everything could be transported to the harbour, so there was quite some development. The Germans brought Chinese people to their colony to work in the plantations and to teach the local population how to grow and prepare these products.

Because the ground was so fertile, people could grow a lot of food in their gardens and sell part of it at the market. Rabaul itself had a large market where you could buy staple foods in abundance – sweet potatoes, called 'kaukau', several local vegetables, and many kinds of fruit. Food that is closely related to 'kaukau' is 'taro' and 'yam'; all three grow like potatoes, in the ground. You could also buy fish, also woven mats and baskets and a carry bag called 'billum', which is used all over the country. Coby used to buy a lot of what we ate at the market. We still miss the delicious watermelons, the common melons, pawpaws, pineapples, and especially my favourite fruit: mangoes.

At the market, there were plenty of betel nuts for sale. A betel nut is a small nut which is grown on a slender and high tree that looks like a palm tree. It really is a nice tree. The local people open the nut and take the inside and mix it with coral powder, which is white. Once mixed, it becomes red. The people chew it, as it is a drug that causes them to become addicted. Many people are addicted to this betel nut; and after years of chewing it, it affects their teeth, their gums, and sometimes their mouth and can cause cancer. Often, you see people who are red all around their mouth. When there is nothing more to chew, they spit it out; and in many places, on the ground or on the street, you will see the red marks. If it ended up on your car, the paint would corrode.

In some districts, when they welcome you, they would offer you betel nut, like we would offer a cup of tea or coffee. We have never really preached against it, but we know few Christians who would still chew it. Once people are converted, it does not take long before they quit this addictive habit. The Christians in the villages will now offer visitors fruit, especially pineapple, as a welcome.

When you have walked for some hours through the jungle and came to a village and were offered some nice slices of pineapple, you really felt welcome.

Despite all the development, the villages still remain very basic, but nice and well laid out. Much later, they planted large palm oil plantations in the western area of New Britain, while Rabaul is situated on the east. The area Rabaul is in is the Gazelle Peninsula, which is still regarded as one of the most developed parts of Papua New Guinea.

In the Second World War, Rabaul was occupied by the Japanese and was an important Japanese headquarters. There are many reminders of that period, like the wrecks of Japanese aeroplanes near the airport, tanks, and small landing craft that the Japanese used to unload large ships. Furthermore, you can still see here and there various concrete ruins with large cannons. You can also still see the bunker belonging to the Japanese army commander in Rabaul, or at least parts of it. During the time we lived on the islands of Papua New Guinea, we regularly heard native people talk about how they had found grenades or ammunition. Often, they tried to open those up so they could use the explosive content to bomb fish. Unfortunately, even while we lived in the islands, this sometimes went wrong, and people would blow themselves up.

When during the Second World War the Japanese army occupied the island of New Ireland, they called for all the chiefs and witch doctors. They were the most influential leaders in the district. Then the Japanese shot these people, so there was no more local leadership, and they could easily rule on the island. The elderly people on the island remembered this only too well.

After our time in Rabaul, we lived for three years in Kavieng, the main small township on New Ireland. At that time, they even found a Japanese man who was still alive after hiding in the jungle, for more than thirty years. He had kept himself alive with food from the jungle and by stealing from the villagers' gardens. The man was welcomed in Japan as a hero, because he had refused to surrender!

Later, while we were working as missionaries in Japan, we had regular contact with a Japanese pastor, who had been a fighter pilot in the war, and had been stationed in Rabaul. He could tell me much about Rabaul. In Japan, there was even a song about it, the pearl of the Pacific. When we told people in Japan that we had lived and worked in Rabaul, we saw people, especially the older ones, nodding in recognition. This pastor, then pilot, started believing in Jesus after the war and experienced a powerful conversion.

Another Japanese pastor had also fought in the war and afterwards came to Jesus. He too had started a congregation. This pastor had a deep longing to make restitution and seek reconciliation. To do this, he asked the men in his congregation to build churches in places where Japan had fought during the war. Later a group of Japanese Christian men built several permanent buildings on Bougainville, where we had started a Bible school. They gave those buildings as a gift to the Christians. The Bible school is near the place where the aeroplane wreck lies of the famous Japanese admiral Yamamoto, who was in it when he was shot down. I went to see this wreck twice in the dense jungle. While the Bible school was being built, some students found a Japanese bomb of 500 pounds. Several Australian soldiers exploded the bomb safely, a few weeks later.

The local people of Rabaul and the surrounding area, the Tolai, have their own language: Kuanua. But there also were quite a number of people, especially on and around the plantations, who came from other districts of Papua New Guinea. The main language among them was Pidgin English, a language that came into use through contact with Germans, Australians, Chinese, as well as other nationalities. Pidgin

English has, for example, German words, many English ones, and words from Tonga as well as Samoa and other sources. The grammar is clearly of Papua New Guinean origin. You can compare Pidgin English with Papiamento spoken in the Dutch Antilles or Swahili spoken in Africa. Both of these are not original languages, but they developed over a period. Pidgin English is not a difficult language to learn, but a language represents a culture, and not knowing the culture, you do not really know the language. Coby and I are now able to speak Pidgin English fluently.

These days Pidgin English is sometimes jokingly called 'Pinglish' because more and more English words are being used.

Because of government and missionary influence, there were quite a lot of primary schools on the island of New Britain. Many children, though certainly not all, went to primary school because there were not enough schools for all the children. It is interesting to know though how children from less developed areas came to go to school.

Government officials who were responsible for all the villages in the area, and visited these regularly, were called 'patrol officers'. In Pidgin English, they were usually called 'kiaps'. When the kiaps or the missionaries went to a village, they called for all the children to come and play games with them. The games were actually tests to see how intelligent the children were. The parents of the most intelligent children were asked permission to let their children attend school. The primary school was like a simple boarding school, where the children would stay during the week. At the weekend, they would go home. In the first year, the children learned English; and after that, all education was in English. There are about 800 languages in Papua New Guinea. Some languages are spoken by a relatively small number of people. That is why English is the language for education.

The ages of these first children who attended school were unknown. A simple test was that the child would put his or her hand over his or her head and would try to touch his or her ear on the other side. A child under the age of six usually cannot do that, but children around six or older can. We never knew that, but it is true.

The first children going to school received their education free. In areas where there was more development and thus more employment, the parents need to pay school fees. To be able to do that, they often grew fruits and vegetables which they sell at the local markets. Because of this, the economy started to grow slowly but surely. To progress in the school, the results that the pupils achieved determined whether or not they could continue their education. There was no such thing as redoing a year, because there were many other children who wanted to go to school, many more than the schools could handle.

In order to pass from primary school to secondary school, a child had to have good grades. At secondary school, it is still about performing well; again, redoing a class is not an option. After four years of secondary school, a child could pass on to two years of higher secondary school. By then only a small group is left – only the best of them. Many schools are boarding schools.

Just before we came to live in the capital, Port Moresby, a small university was built. Only the best students from secondary school could go on to university. One of my good friends from Papua New Guinea was part of the first group of students of his tribe that went to the university. He is now, forty years later, one of the highest government officials and after university even studied and served his country overseas. When Westerners look at Papua New Guinea, they sometimes call it primitive. But what they call primitive has nothing to do with intelligence.

The religion of the entire population of the country in nearly all 800 or more language groups was animism. That means that their religion consisted of faith in spirits, good and evil, and worshipping them. The spirits are usually, if not always, the spirits of deceased people, especially ancestors. To them all of life is spiritual, and life is lived in a world of spirits. In most, if not all, language groups, there are many rituals concerning the death of a family member. If these rituals are performed in the right way, then the spirit of the deceased becomes a good spirit that will help and guide. If these rituals are not performed in the right way or are not executed at all, the spirit of the deceased becomes an evil spirit that turns against you. Speaking with spirits is quite normal.

Usually people are very afraid of them. All events in life are attributed to spirits. Especially in the cultivation of food, which is usually a family affair, the worship of spirits can play an important part. Throughout the years, we have seen Christians who did not participate in the witchcraft practices related to the family garden and were therefore forced to have a garden of their own. The much smaller garden belonging to the Christians often yielded a better harvest than the much larger family garden. For this reason, some people came to believe in Jesus.

The concept of a 'spiritual world' is not new to the people at all. Often, people see or experience the presence of spirits. We often needed to pray with students from the university, who would see the spirit of a deceased person in their room at the university campus. Witch doctors have power to let spirits be good to a person or to turn against a person. In general, witch doctors have great power and influence in their culture, often greater than that of the chief. There are male and also female witch doctors. The wooden masks that you see a lot in Papua New Guinea are, as far as we know, always or nearly always depictions of spirits, particularly of the spirit connected with that family or their language group.

Before we went to Papua New Guinea, and during the first months that we were there, I read every book I could find about the country. Christian and non-Christian. There were not many Christian books about the country, so most books I read were non-Christian, and sometimes even very non-Christian. There was one book that I did not read all the way through. The writer only seemed to be interested in the sexual lifestyle of the various tribes. I did learn quite a lot though, about the cultures of various language groups, from the books I read. In these books, a certain phenomenon was mentioned often: the cargo cult.

The simple native people saw that the Chinese and people from various different nations that came to their country had all kinds of things, cars, planes, furniture, boats, etc. Where did all that come from, and who had given that to them? They did not understand that all these things had been developed over a very long period through economic and technical development. The only source they had was their land and the ocean. Their lives had not changed and had remained the same for ages.

When the Europeans came, the Papua New Guinean people saw all the things they brought. For many there was only one explanation. The white people worshipped stronger spirits than theirs, and those spirits gave these things to the white people. The Papua New Guineans wanted that too! From time to time, a cargo cult prophet would call the people together to perform certain rituals. He promised them that on a certain day, usually at night, the goods would come. While we were living in Kavieng, on New Ireland, there was a cargo cult. Once, at night, hundreds of people waited on the beach for the cargo. Sometimes things did not end well for the cargo cult prophet! One of these cargo cults made the government so desperate that they brought several leaders to Australia to show them the factories. That way the people would see for themselves how, for example, cars and other things are made and that they don't just fall from the sky. When these cult leaders came back, they continued to perform rituals, because they now believed that the spirits of the white people would bring entire factories. Even though the cargo cult mindset started to disappear, it sometimes still shows up here and there. We once experienced that people who had only recently been in touch with Europeans and their world asked us through an interpreter if we could pray for them because they wanted a radio. This was a clear case of a cargo cult mindset.

On Bougainville a 'Christian' launched a financial pyramid scheme. Many people, including Christians, fell for it – all the more because it had a Christian flavour to it. The leader announced that the banks were earning a lot of money from our money and were actually profiting a lot more than the people. He knew of ways to invest money outside the banking system and make much more profit. Sometimes he spoke about 200% profit per month. Who would not want that? The people were interested. This 'Christian' quoted verses from the Bible about prosperity and that God wanted to bless the believers with riches. He also quoted verses that said that the riches of the non-believers would be given to the believers, and people believed him, because it sounded so biblical. The first people who invested in this pyramid did receive money, but after that, no one did of course. Amongst his own people of Bougainville, this man had followers. I was able to speak about this with various government officials and political leaders, and they all called it a 'Christian' semi–cargo cult.

During a visit to Bougainville four years ago, by strange coincidence, I discovered what probably happened to a part of the millions that man had collected. The money most likely was used to finance a movement that wanted to separate from the province of Bougainville. They were going to build a private kingdom in the south of the island. According to centuries-old legends, this kingdom existed long ago, even though the local people say that this is not true. I passed this on to an important Christian politician whom I knew. Later it was proven that my finding was correct. A few months before writing this book, I was in Papua New Guinea, and I was asked by several leaders to intervene concerning this. When I was back in the Netherlands, the Papua New Guinea newspaper, which I sometimes browse through on the internet, wrote quite a lot of news about this movement. There was an appeal by several political leaders for all the people connected to this semi–cargo cult to be openly prosecuted. Leaders who would not disassociate from this semi–cargo cult would be removed from their position and responsibilities. Later I read in that newspaper that the leader of this movement was shot by the police. However, his injuries were not serious, and he escaped into the jungle. The problem of this 'Christian' semi–cargo cult has unfortunately not entirely ended as yet. This cargo cult mindset can at times be the reason for people to seek out missionaries. We have experienced this a few times. This semi 'Christian' cargo cult of recent times has caused us some serious headaches.

In various books, I also read about the 'wantok sistem'. 'Wantok' is a word in Pidgin English. 'Wan' means 'one'. 'Tok' means 'talk' and means 'language' in Pidgin English. So it means someone from one's own language, a member of the same tribe. The word 'sistem' obviously means 'system'. The term 'wantok sistem' describes the strong connection and loyalty that exists between members of the same language group. That loyalty and dedication can go far, even so far that it leads to something known as 'payback killing.' Meaning, you killed one of us, we kill one of you. If we do not do that, the spirits will turn against us. Payback killing is probably one of the main reasons for tribal wars.

We will write about that a little more in a later chapter. When someone comes to Jesus, repents, and shows as much brotherly or sisterly love to people of another language (i.e. another tribe), then that is evidence that he or she really is a Christian and has truly repented. The command of Jesus to love your enemies, and to forgive, is a challenge for all of us. In this society, whether in the government or in the business world, the 'wantok system' can also play a part in preferring members of one's own tribe over others.

'Wantok' can also be used in a friendly and playful way for someone you like and to whom you want to say something nice. You would hear someone say, 'Hey, wantok.' On rare occasions I would meet a Papua New Guinean man with red hair. I would call someone like that 'wantok' in a friendly, smiling way, because I used to have, with the emphasis on used to, red hair too. Almost always I got a friendly response to that.

Let's go back to Rabaul where we had just arrived. The Baptist couple had rented a small apartment for us, which consisted of one room. A private owner had built about twenty of these small apartments and rented them out to people who worked there temporarily. Rabaul also had a station that monitored volcanic activity, because it is situated right on top of an earthquake zone. We experienced quite a few minor as well as bigger earthquakes, some even measuring 6 on the Richter scale. And once we even experienced a small tsunami. The water of the bay came a long way into town and carried small boats quite a distance inland.

After several days of our acclimatising, our car and luggage arrived. We now had transportation. We drove around to get to know the area and looked for places where we could evangelise. The hot weather was something we really had to get used to. Rabaul seemed warmer than Thursday Island and Daru, because it is quite near the equator. The temperature is about 33 to 35 degrees centigrade every day with a high level of humidity, nearly always more than 90%. In some ways, we never got used to it.

One evening we had visited the Baptist couple. After dinner, we talked and prayed together. When we arrived home later that evening, in our tiny apartment, we had a drink. Our apartment was on the first and highest floor. The stairs and the balcony were at the front, and at the back was no balcony or anything like that. The windows consisted of louvres, covered with insect screen to keep the insects out, which was really not a luxury but an absolute necessity.

It was dark, and outside were the typical sounds of a night in the tropics, especially the many insects. I got a feeling as if someone was looking at me, and I looked outside unaware of what was there. I stiffened. In front of our window was a large horrific mask. I had seen those masks before on Daru and in Port Moresby, and also in Rabaul, in various buildings like the post office. I do not remember ever having seen a mask that looked cheerful and happy. But this mask was no mask made by human hands; this mask was moving. The eyes moved, the mouth, the facial features, everything moved and looked at me in a foul way. I had at times read about, and heard about, the visible manifestation of demons. I now realised that this was a visible manifestation of a prominent demon. I was shocked. I had never experienced this before, but especially that look – those eyes looking at me. Someone was not happy with our arrival, that was for sure! After several moments, I regained my composure and started to call on the name of the Lord Jesus. After I had called on the name of the Lord Jesus several times, it gave me one more foul look and then disappeared. I did not sleep much that night. It became obvious that we had taken ourselves into some serious spiritual warfare. Though I had seen the amazing power of the name of the Lord Jesus so clearly, I was still shocked by this experience, though it was not only a negative experience. I had heard about this in missionary stories, but it was always in a faraway land. Now it had happened to me. I had general biblical knowledge about spiritual warfare, but that knowledge was mainly theoretical. It was on my mind for several days. It was the first time something like this had happened to me, but it would not be the last.

Years later, I was in Rabaul with Charles Lapa and a Tongan leader for a big crusade. I was invited to speak to hundreds of pastors in the Uniting Church of that time. A powerful movement of the Holy Spirit had been released in that church, and many pastors were converted and filled with the Holy Spirit. The bishop of that time had baptised many of his people in the harbour. I told the story of the living mask. A few leaders came to speak with me afterwards. They knew exactly whom I was talking about. They also knew this living mask. Nobody doubted that this was the demonic head of the tribe of the Tolais. Earlier on, I had come to know a Methodist missionary, in the area of Rabaul; and he had been greatly impacted by the charismatic movement in the seventies, in Australia. He too had experienced an encounter with this living mask. He and his wife became the instruments God used to lead many Tolai people to Jesus and to see them receive the baptism in the Holy Spirit.

After that night in Port Moresby when the Lord had so clearly called us to go to Rabaul, Kavieng, Bougainville, and then the mainland, I had bought the biggest map I could find of Papua New Guinea. I would spread that map out on the floor and kneel down, to pray for the country. I would also often kneel on the map and put my hand on New Britain, the island where Rabaul is the most important city, and on New Ireland where Kavieng is the most important township, and on Kieta, Bougainville. The most important centre of government in Bougainville was Kieta, a small government station. The word 'township' is actually too big a word; it was more an outgrown government station. But every time I put my hands on Bougainville, something happened. Something inside me would move. I felt God's heart towards all three islands, and all the surrounding small islands, but there was something special about Bougainville. I felt it, I knew it. The Holy Spirit in me moved strongly when I prayed for that island. I did not understand it then and kept praying in faith. Later we would realise how real and true these impressions and feelings had been.

From the moment that the Lord had spoken to me about Rabaul, Kavieng, Bougainville, and the mainland, we prayed a lot for these places. In one of these times of prayer, the Lord spoke to our hearts that our arrival in Rabaul would influence the Methodist (later called Uniting) Church. In our enthusiasm, and maybe even naively, we thought that this would be so from the very beginning. But when we arrived in Rabaul and wanted to get in touch with the Methodist

Church, it was made very clear that they did not want any contact with us. It became obvious that the missionaries and the workers of the Methodist Church were really unhappy with our arrival. Things would stay this way for quite a long time. But around the time we were to leave the country, after fourteen years, a remarkably powerful movement of God started amongst the Tolai, the people of the Rabaul area. Several years later, I was with a leader from our own work, Charles Lapa, and a leader of the Methodist Church in Rabaul. We held services and a big crusade at the sports oval in the middle of the city. I was deeply impressed by the impact of the movement of God's Spirit amongst the Tolai. In a book about the Uniting Church that appeared around that time, there was a chapter about Rabaul. In that chapter, it was written that at the end of the sixties, a young Dutch couple from the Pentecostal movement had come to Rabaul. Though the Methodists had at first been very sceptical towards their coming, eventually it had been a great blessing for the district and the other provinces. That was what was written. Unfortunately, we would experience quite a lot of resistance before that breakthrough came.

We desired to evangelise and have several small crusades, like we had done in Daru. On Daru, a few people spoke English, and this was a hindrance to effectually communicate the gospel to the people. I realised that the inability for people to understand English was also quite a problem in Rabaul, even though the region had been developed for quite some time and a good number of schools had been established. Apart from the Tolais' own language, Pidgin English was the main language spoken, but we could not speak that as yet. The Baptist couple had been in Papua New Guinea longer and had been in touch with Australian and American missionaries from the Foursquare Mission in the highlands. The couple got in touch with the missionaries. They were willing to send one of their Papua New Guinean pastors to Rabaul for a few weeks so that he could interpret from English to Pidgin English. The couple offered to pay for his trip. How wonderful that the Lord placed such a couple there and help us in this way.

In preparation, we spent two weeks praying and fasting; and after that, we were to start the meetings. We had the strong impression that

Rabaul was not as receptive as Thursday Island and Daru. Though the encounter with the demonic force over the area of Rabaul had clearly revealed the omnipotence of the name of the Lord Jesus, we also realised that there was a deep darkness over these people, despite the influence of the churches working in the area. But first something was going to happen that was clearly organised by God, and that would reveal the 'why' of our coming to the islands.

It was the 12th of June 1968, the Queen's birthday. Australia and her colonies were part of the British Commonwealth, and so they celebrated the birthday of Queen Elizabeth. The celebration was to take place on the sports oval in downtown Rabaul, and I went to see it. Coby stayed at home for some reason. I parked my Land Rover near the park and went to see the children's parade and to listen to the music. Then a man with very dark skin, really black, walked up to my car and kept looking at me and my car. He seemed to focus on the name on the car, 'Full Gospel Movement Streams of Power,' and the emblem of the cross and the dove. He looked at me intently and then at the car and then at me again. He appeared warm and very friendly. I had not seen anyone with such a dark skin before. The people on Daru and in Rabaul had a brown skin colour, but this man's skin was really black. He kept looking, while I watched the children. Then it seemed that he wanted to speak to me, but suddenly he walked away. I watched him as he left. There was something about this man. He obviously wanted to talk to me. Who was he? He did not come from Rabaul, I could see that. But where then was he from? Why did he look so intently at the name 'Full Gospel Movement Streams of Power' and the emblem of the cross and the dove on my car? Why did I wait so long and not walk up to him myself? This event stuck with me. At home, I told Coby about it. We prayed that the Lord would bring this man to us again and that he would talk to us. There was something about him. But what? And who was he?

CHAPTER 10

Siwai

ON THE SATURDAY after the Queen's birthday I drove to the little supermarket. When I came back to my car, the man with the very dark-coloured skin stood there! We greeted each other. He asked, 'Is that your car?'

'Yes, that is my car,' I responded.

'Full Gospel Movement, is that the same as the Pentecostal movement?' he continued.

'Yes, that is the same,' I answered.

'How long have you been in Rabaul?'

'About five weeks,' I answered.

'Are you here only for a short time or for a longer time?' He was clearly curious.

'I moved here and will stay here,' I could happily say.

'Are you then a missionary of the Pentecostal church?' he continued.

'Yes, I am a missionary of the Pentecostal church,' I answered.

'May I then ask you a strange question?'

'Of course you may.' My curiosity grew by the minute.

'Do you know the American evangelist T. L. Osborn?'

I was so surprised, I nearly fell over. How did this man from Papua New Guinea know the name of T. L. Osborn?

'I have met him personally a few times, and two years ago I worked in a team for his organisation to prepare crusades for him in Australia,' I could answer him.

'You know T. L. Osborn!' he exclaimed.

'Yes indeed! I know him,' I repeated.

'I come from South Bougainville, and we are friends with T. L. Osborn,' he said. I was stunned. In the south of Bougainville, there were people who called themselves friends of T. L. Osborn. My curiosity kept growing and growing.

'Do you have time to come to my home?' I asked. Yes, he had time and got into the car. A little later, we were with Coby, and I could proudly tell her, 'This is the man I saw on the Queen's birthday and who I told you about.'

Coby gave him a 'milo', a kind of chocolate drink. It is a popular drink amongst the people of Papua New Guinea. The Bougainville name of the man was Pinoko, but he had taken on the first names John Wesley, so he became John Wesley Pinoko. The fact that he called himself John Wesley revealed that he had some knowledge of church history.

Pinoko started talking, and we listened intensely.

A few decades ago, when there was no government or missionaries, there was a war between the tribe of the Siwai in South Bougainville and a tribe in the north of the British Solomon Islands. Those islands are close together. A political boundary had been drawn between these islands so that Bougainville belonged to Papua New Guinea, but ethnically and geographically it belongs to the Solomon Islands. Especially in the northern Solomon Islands and Bougainville, the people are related. In that war between the tribes, the Siwai finally made peace by giving a baby, a little boy, to the chief of the tribe of the northern Solomon Islands. The book *Peace Child*, written by missionary Don Richardson, describes the ritual of the peace child ceremony between tribes in West Irian. After the ceremony of the peace child, there was peace between the tribes in South Bougainville and the northern Solomon Islands, until this very day. Methodist missionaries came to the northern Solomon Islands, and many people believed the gospel, amongst them the now-grown-up peace child.

This man felt called by God to reach his original tribe with the gospel and went to South Bougainville as a missionary, the first missionary ever to go there. That is how the Methodist Church came to

South Bougainville. Through his preaching, testimony, and evangelism, people believed in Jesus. Afterwards, other missionaries came to South Bougainville. Through the story of Pinoko, we got the impression that the first Christians really knew the Lord.

Village schools were built, and the first children went to school. Years later, a training school was built on the Southern Solomon Islands by the Methodist Church, to train pastors for the villages. The men who were trained would go to the school for one or two years. Some men from Siwai came to be trained as well. The level of teaching and training was not very high, but this was the first generation of people who had become Christians. A few years before we met Pinoko, a minister from New Zealand called Allen Hall was the head of this school. Years later, we met Allen Hall in the north of Australia, where he had become a Bible translator amongst the Aboriginals. We were able to verify this story with him.

While Allen Hall was the head of the school, he was diagnosed with cancer. He knew about books by evangelist T. L. Osborn, and also by another famous American evangelist, who was extraordinarily used by God in healing, Oral Roberts. The teaching about praying and fasting had especially appealed to him. Allen Hall told the students he would fast and pray for forty days for his healing, and he was healed by God! He then taught his students about faith and healing. One of the Siwai students was Monturo, who had taken on the name Joshua, so he became Joshua Monturo. All the students were deeply impressed by what they had learned and seen, especially Joshua Monturo. The head of the school gave every student a few books written by T. L. Osborn.

Having completed their training, the Siwai students went back to their own area. Monturo became a village pastor in the Methodist Church, in one of the Siwai villages. In the beginning, he did not pay much attention to the message of healing, faith, and prayer and fasting; but after a while, he found T. L. Osborn's books again. He read them and was gripped by its message. He started to preach about it and formed 'healing teams', as they were called. If someone was sick, a team member would go there to pray. Various villages formed healing teams, and the most amazing healings and miracles took place.

Witch doctors and people who practised witchcraft repented. There was much openness, but from the non-believers, and especially the people who continued to hold on to witchcraft, came much resistance. Then another generation of missionaries from the Methodist Church arrived. They were sincere people but very liberal. They tried to discourage the existence of the healing teams and sometimes actually resisted them. Eventually the healing teams were actually forbidden.

At times we have been surprised about the authority that missionaries tried to exercise over the people and how fearful of the missionaries people could be. Often, a great sense of loyalty towards the missionaries was playing a part, because they had brought schools, simple medical care, and a measure of development. But we also heard about a different missionary – an unmarried New Zealand woman, who was translating the New Testament into the Siwai language. She was the only person who ever learned that language. Pinoko spoke about her with respect and great warmth. 'She is different. She is positive towards the healing teams. She is on our side but can't be so openly, because of the other missionaries,' was his opinion – an opinion that later proved to be true.

Monturo was the leader of the healing teams but became very discouraged. The people who could write tried to write letters to T. L. Osborn to ask for help, but they had no idea whether those letters ever arrived. Probably not. In any case, they never heard anything from T. L. Osborn. But they did call themselves 'friends of T. L. Osborn'. When the Methodist missionaries finally succeeded in stopping the healing teams, the people who really longed for the healing ministry decided to send a few men to the Methodist theological college just outside Rabaul in Raronga. These men could go there with their families and be trained for four years. When they had completed their training and became ordained ministers, they would come back and take the place of the missionaries and do things differently. They would then change direction and restart the healing teams and the healing ministry. Four men were chosen to attend the theological school. Pinoko was one of the four. Unfortunately, they found it very difficult at the theological college. It was all very liberal. The Bible was not believed literally, and there was absolutely no room for the message of faith, healing, and prayer and fasting, as they had learned from T. L. Osborn's books. On the contrary, at the theological college, they were opposed to it all. Pinoko was very discouraged, and the four wondered how to continue. Then when he was in Rabaul on the Queen's birthday, he saw my car. I asked, 'So why did you suddenly walk away and not come up to talk to me as you did today?'

'The head of the theological college, the principal, was standing near me and was looking at me. He knew about your arrival, because it had been mentioned during classes. We had been warned about you, and we were not allowed to get in touch with you,' Pinoko answered.

Pinoko asked another remarkable question, 'Did T. L. Osborn send you as an answer to our letters, in which we asked for help?' What a question!

'No, T. L. Osborn did not send us. God has sent us,' we were able to answer.

Coby and I held our breath, as we listened to this. What a story! Friends of evangelist T. L. Osborn in South Bougainville. Suddenly it became clearer to me why I had so often felt drawn to Bougainville while I prayed, kneeling on the map of Papua New Guinea.

We asked Pinoko to come with the other men and possibly their wives so we could get to know them. We told him something about the baptism in the Holy Spirit. Pinoko drank it in. He knew about it but did not know how to receive it.

The following Saturday, the four men came. We did not meet their wives until much later. We now understand that this is typically the Papua New Guinean way. One by one they shared their stories. We talked with them that Saturday and held a study about the baptism in the Holy Spirit. All four received the Holy Spirit and spoke in new tongues and not just a little. They were just overpowered by the Holy Spirit and overflowed with the Spirit. I needed to take them back to their homes at the college, which is quite a drive from Rabaul.

More Siwai people had moved to Rabaul, and the Gazelle Peninsula. They either worked or studied there. The news that a Pentecostal missionary couple, who were friends with T. L. Osborn, had moved to Rabaul, to work there, spread like wildfire amongst the Siwai people.

Several of them came to visit us. Those whom we met were devoted Christians and obviously born again. They were so hungry for the baptism in the Holy Spirit. One after another received the Holy Spirit in our small apartment. Amongst them was Amos Rorima, who joined us later on our first trip to Siwai and would be our interpreter. But there were also several people from other areas of Bougainville who had been in touch with the healing teams. One of them was Simeon Mimima from the Kongera District, which is in the mountains behind the government station of Kieta.

Mimima also heard about the missionary couple from the Pentecostal church and came to visit us. Mimima worked as a teacher at the Uniting Church primary school in Rabaul. When he came to our home, it struck us again what a deep hunger and intense desire for God the people of Bougainville had. We explained the baptism in the Holy Spirit and prayed, and Mimima received. He really received! He was completely zapped! Something happened to him that we had not experienced before. He was slain in the Spirit and fell to the floor without injuring himself and lay on the floor of our single-room apartment for two hours, completely 'lost' in the Spirit. After a while, he started speaking and described what he had experienced and seen, while he was on the floor. He entered heaven and came to the throne of God. Of all the things he said, the things that stuck with us most were his many remarks about the holiness and greatness of God. Apparently an angel spoke with him, and we remember that he said, 'God is one, but He is also three, and He reveals Himself as Father, Son, and Holy Spirit. People have tried to understand and explain this, but they cannot. The human mind cannot comprehend this. God is too great and too powerful.' I was deeply, deeply impressed by what was happening, but Coby did not know what to think of it. This 'falling down' – was that a good thing? Was it from God or not? In the Pentecostal movement in the Netherlands, we had been taught to watch out for emotionalism and for people who could not control themselves. Because God was a God of order, wasn't He? Coby touched Mimima to see if he was really lost in the Spirit. When Coby touched him, he turned around without opening his eyes and spoke to Coby, 'Sister, I rebuke you for your unbelief!' He turned around again and continued sharing how it was in heaven and what he was witnessing. Coby experienced a deep repentance that evening. We surely had never seen anything like this before.

Mimima was an extraordinary man. God spoke to him in visions and dreams and gave him assignments. No human is perfect, which goes for Mimima as well, but we can only remember razor-sharp and pure things. God spoke to him to pray for someone or go somewhere, and the greatest miracles happened. He often reminded us of the Old Testament prophets who were also called 'seers'. After some time in Rabaul, Mimima went back to his island Bougainville. In his own area, he pioneered a few powerful congregations. We always heard that there was much blessing in his ministry. He passed away during the great crisis on Bougainville years later. This was when Bougainville was completely shut off from the outside world for about eight years, because a civil war was raging. I was not able to find out whether he died of natural causes or if he was one of many who were murdered by the Bougainville Republican Army, a guerrilla movement that rebelled against the government.

At the end of this book, we will come back to this, because all this happened after we had left Papua New Guinea.

All four men and their families who attended the theological college in Rabaul were appointed to various locations. It would take quite a while before one of them was appointed to Siwai. We stayed in touch with Pinoko throughout the years. After his studies, he was appointed to the Southern Highlands, where development started to take place. He had worked there for a while as a teacher at the first missionary primary school and spoke the local language. Pinoko and his wife would, for a long time, experience an amazingly deep and powerful work of the Holy Spirit, amongst the people near Tari in the Southern Highlands, before they eventually came back to Bougainville.

Through contact with the people from Siwai and other parts of Bougainville, it became clear that we should make a trip to Siwai as soon as possible. That happened six months later. Our first trip to Bougainville started on the 1st of January 1969.

A somewhat amusing event was Pinoko's baptism. He was the first of the Siwai people who desired to be baptised by immersion. But because there was tension at the theological college between the Siwai students and the leaders, Pinoko wanted to be baptised in private. One evening the three of us went to a quiet beach: Pinoko, Coby, and me. We prayed, and I went into the sea to find a good spot. There were some waves breaking, but I found a good spot where Pinoko and I could stand. He walked into the sea and stood next to me. We prayed, and Pinoko delivered a short, beautiful testimony of his faith. I held his hands and put my other hand on his back, the way I hold people when I baptise them, and spoke the words of baptism: 'Pinoko, I baptise you in the name of the Father, the Son, and the Holy Spirit, in the name of our Lord Jesus Christ.' But a wave came and took Pinoko out of my hands, and I could hardly keep my balance. I saw Pinoko go under. Three times I saw legs, hands, and a head. The wave had a firm grip on Pinoko. When he got his feet firmly on the ground again, he threw his hands into the air and shouted, 'Praise God, I have been baptised!' We agreed. Three times overturned in the sea during baptism! It is one of the most humorous baptisms we ever experienced.

What we remember most of our first meetings with Christians from Siwai and other parts of Bougainville was their real hunger and desire for God. Their deep and simple faith and the depth of their experiences with God. The present pastor of one of the main Pentecostal congregations in Port Moresby, the capital city, is a Siwai man!

But now we need to go back to Rabaul; that is where we went to live and where we had work to do.

CHAPTER 11

Rabaul – We Start!

THE BAPTIST COUPLE had arranged for Pastor Metikau, from the Foursquare Mission in the Goroka area, to help us with our first evangelism crusade. Metikau was a man with a gentle character, straightforward, and humble, even though he was one of the first of his area who was well educated.

We would have loved to have a crusade in Rabaul. But no matter what we tried, we did not get permission to use the sports oval in the centre of Rabaul, or at another open area in the city. Clearly there was opposition and not only spiritually. More than twenty kilometres further up the coast, to the west, there was the second most important place in the district, called Kokopo. It was only a small town which had a few shops, businesses, a government office, a hospital run by the Catholic Church, and a school. In the middle of Kokopo, there was also a sports oval like in Daru. We did get permission to have meetings there, so we planned a crusade. Surrounding Kokopo were more villages than around Rabaul, so it was a good place to reach those villagers. The local small radio station promised to broadcast the news in the district. We also drove through the area announcing the crusade with a loudspeaker on top of the Land Rover. Metikau made the announcements of the meetings in Pidgin English.

We had prayed, fasted, and made all necessary preparations. We also asked both groups of Dutch migrants in Australia, as well as people in the Netherlands, to pray. And then we started. A few hundred people attended that first meeting. The weather was dry, which is quite unique in itself, because it rains quite regularly on the islands. In the meetings, we tried, like on Daru, to sing and teach the people simple songs. After that, a short message interpreted by Metikau from English to Pidgin English, followed by the call to choose for Jesus. Every evening a good number of people prayed the sinner's prayer.

Every evening we prayed for all those who were sick. We can clearly remember the case of an older man. Something was wrong with his legs, and apparently he was in a lot of pain which made it difficult for him to walk. But he also had damaged one of his ears so badly that he had become deaf in that ear. The man was healed! He walked up and down waving his stick in the air, and he could hear well again. The people saw the power of God and were deeply impressed. We noticed that the language was a problem as not everyone understood English or Pidgin. Many people only spoke their own language. The Kokopo crusade was not as powerful as the one in Daru and the breakthrough not as dramatic, but the Holy Spirit had moved.

We announced that in a few days, we would have a follow-up service and Bible study, on the same sports oval, thus in the open air. We invited people to come. A few days later, only a handful of people came, but these were people who apparently had really made a decision for Jesus. Among them was a man of mixed race who had repented. There was also a young man from the Tolai tribe, who spoke English very well and who had experienced a deep encounter with God. And there were more people like that. But where were all the other people who had prayed with us and had chosen to live for Jesus? Something began to gnaw away inside of me. We were new, and our Western culture and their Papua New Guinean culture were miles apart. Even with our 'Western Christian culture', we were still so different than these people. We had so much to learn.

When I now read the newsletters and articles that we wrote then, I read about the dozens of people who made decisions for Jesus, and then I also see our great enthusiasm, expressed in these letters and articles. Through what we learned later, I would now write differently about the crusade in Kokopo and put it in words like 'Dozens of people prayed the sinner's prayer with us and took the first step in following Jesus.'

In a later chapter, we will get back to this because the title of this book has everything to do with it.

The man of mixed-race background, who was truly converted, was named George. He made his house available for the Bible study, because it was not always dry outside. It was only a small house that could hold no more than ten people apart from George and his wife and children. George shared his testimony everywhere. He had been a drunk and had often been in all sorts of trouble and fights. Very soon George was filled with the Holy Spirit and spoke powerfully and beautifully in tongues. When I saw him again, he asked for the book so he could learn that special language better. After that first time, he had not been able to speak in tongues anymore. We had some explaining to do, but after that, he spoke in tongues often and much. When I now teach on the gift of speaking in new tongues, I often share George's story.

George was converted but had an anger problem. He could get strong fits of anger. When that happened, his wife and children were afraid of him. What was he to do? Was the Lord Jesus able and willing to help him? We did not know then what we know now, but with the knowledge we had, we gave him advice. George drove a 'grader', a big machine that is used in building roads. George drove the grader for about eight hours a day, building new roads through the jungle or maintaining existing coral gravel roads. Graders make quite a lot of noise with their diesel engines, so I advised him, 'Speak in tongues while you are driving the grader, speak loudly, and do it for hours. When you speak in tongues, your entire being is under the control of the Holy Spirit. James writes that when we control our tongue, we control our whole body and being.' George followed the advice. For hours, while he was driving the grader and his mind and eyes were focused on the job, he prayed from his new inner man, in new tongues. After six weeks, George was a completely transformed man, and his anger problem was no more! We often thought to ourselves, *If all Spirit-filled children of God were to speak and pray in tongues for hours, wouldn't the Holy Spirit then be able to do a powerful work in and through those believers?*

After Kokopo we received permission to have services on a little island near Rabaul that was connected to the mainland by a causeway.

You could reach this island, called Matupit, by car. The entire island was actually one big village, and all the inhabitants were Tolais, the local people of the area. The population of the village on the island was not very large, so the meetings were smaller than in Kokopo. We sang, preached, showed a film, and prayed for people. The people listened and prayed with us, but apart from a few people, there was not much receptivity. While we were praying for the sick, not much happened as far as we could see. In the newsletters, we mention that a native Methodist pastor was healed from some problem with his legs and that he was able to walk well again after prayer, but I was under the impression that he was not from the island itself.

On the third evening, when I was ready to preach, three men walked up to me and demanded that we stop immediately and leave the island. They had the Methodist Church on the island, and that was enough, they said. They were trying to intimidate us. I started to quote verses from the Bible. One man stayed and kept quiet while the other two slipped away. Later we found out, through some contacts, that one of the men was the local witch doctor. During the days of the meetings on Matupit, someone from the village passed away; and out of politeness and compassion, we attended the funeral. But a dark ritual took place at the funeral that included the famous, or rather infamous, Duk Duk dances. Spirits were called up, rituals took place, and there was a thick, dark atmosphere. Afterwards, the local native pastor of the Methodist Church came and prayed. The gospel was mixed with ancient practices. To us this was terrible. These people were still in darkness.

There were also people who were touched by the Lord, especially one man who was a teacher and who spoke English very well. He had an intense desire for God. I have forgotten his name; but this man had, during the meetings, really chosen to live for Jesus and had a deep experience with the Lord. He came to our house regularly, when we studied the Bible with him. He was so hungry. One evening I took him back to Matupit, and we were talking for a while beside the car. He asked me if I could pray for him to receive the baptism in the Holy Spirit. Beneath a beautiful starry sky, we prayed, and this dear man had a deep encounter with the Lord. The new language of the Holy Spirit flowed from his innermost being. We stood under that starry sky for quite some time. In the weeks that followed, we met with him often. He had been so touched by God. But then he started to tell us that resistance was growing on the island. His family rejected him. Several church leaders of the island started to turn against him, and he said that he would not visit us for a while to let things settle down. The pressure was too much. We were sad. He was a real Tolai man who had been deeply touched by God. We occasionally saw him, but he never sought contact with us again, and we lost sight of him. We sensed that the pressure and resistance from the Tolai population was growing.

One of the people who had prayed during the meetings in Kokopo was a young Tolai man who had taken on the name John. John had been in touch with the gospel before, but in Kokopo, he had accepted Jesus, and that had brought a powerful transformation into his life. He could not keep quiet about it. He came to our home, and when we told him about the baptism with the Holy Spirit, he was so desirous to receive that. In our small living room we prayed, and something happened that we will never forget. John slowly began to fall backwards and whirled slowly down to the floor, like a leaf falling from a tree. While on the floor, his arms and hands were raised, and he began to speak beautifully in new tongues. A river of new words flowed forth from his belly. For a minute, I did not know what to think about the falling-down bit. It was the second time we had experienced someone falling in the Holy Spirit in our little house. But when John was lying on the floor and beautifully spoke for a long time in new tongues, we could only conclude that this was genuinely the work of the Holy Spirit.

His life proved in the weeks following that it was real. We like the comment of the famous female evangelist Kathryn Kuhlman. She said, after years of seeing people fall in the Spirit, 'To this very day I cannot explain it, but I know that it is God's work.'

John testified everywhere. He prayed for people and saw God at work. I was convinced that a Papua New Guinean apostle was born. John was so hungry for the Lord. He was an educated man, spoke English very well, and even had a car from his work, which was very rare in those days. But he started to experience resistance, first from his family, later from the elders of his village. We prayed with him. He started to visit us less often, and eventually he told us, 'I cannot handle the pressure any longer. I need to stop visiting you for a while and let things settle down.' We never saw John again. It broke my heart. When John was doing well, I felt I was doing well; but when he was not doing well, I felt I was not doing well either. I went to the Lord, and He spoke to me through the words from Philippians 1:6 and 7: 'Being confident of this very thing, that he which hath begun a good work in you will perform it until the day of Jesus Christ.' But it were especially the following words that the Lord spoke to me: 'Even as it is right for me to think this of you all, because I have you in my heart.'

The Lord was challenging me! What were my thoughts about the believers? Did I have faith in the work of God in them? This experience changed my way of thinking about believers: God had started a work, and He would finish it! It was His work, not ours! Throughout the years, people asked me several times how I remained so positive towards some Christians. I believe in the work of the Holy Spirit in them. I have even been accused of being too positive about people, but I believe I am in good company; Jesus Christ Himself is very positive about you and me!

Shortly after the small crusade on Matupit Island, we held a crusade in one of the largest villages near Rabaul, named Pila Pila. People from the surrounding villages also came to the meetings. Again we noticed their curiosity and a certain measure of openness but also resistance. During the altar call, many people prayed the sinner's prayer, as far as we were able to tell. We prayed for the sick, but we don't know if anything happened. After the meeting, a group of young people stayed around. They had enjoyed the preaching, the singing, the film, and everything else. A few adults also stayed, but we sensed that they kept their distance.

It was the third evening. I started speaking, and while everyone was watching, a Tolai man walked up to me. He spoke to me loudly and in clear English and commanded us to stop and leave the village immediately. He sarcastically called me 'white man.' In our fourteen years in Papua New Guinea, I experienced this three times, and this was the first time. I understood that this was an important man. I later learned that he was a magistrate of the court and one of the first Papua New Guinean magistrates in the country. The atmosphere was thick, but I did not really want to stop. After a while, it became clear that it was wiser to do so. Many people left immediately, but again a group of young people stayed around. I was still able to announce that we would return for a follow-up meeting for all the people who had followed the prayer to receive Jesus. A few evenings later, we did go back. Eight teenage girls showed up; that was all. That evening a leader came to tell us bluntly that we were not welcome. The girls got scared, apologised, and then left quickly. The door to Pila Pila Village was tightly closed! I did not understand what was going on, and it remained a huge question for me. Despite the resistance, quite a few people had prayed the sinner's prayer, and they seemed genuine. When we arrived to hold the follow-up meeting and Bible study, there were only eight girls. Where were all those other people? Were they afraid to come because of that leader? I could hardly believe that, but it gnawed at me. In Kokopo, only a few people had come; in Matupit Island, hardly anyone had come. In Pila Pila Village, only eight teenage girls came. What was going on?

In the following weeks, it became clear that every opportunity to reach the Tolai people from the Rabaul area was exhausted. We asked ourselves how that was possible. What had happened? I had the confrontation with a demonic principality shortly after we had arrived, but there was more to it.

During that time, we prayed a lot and fasted often. How could we break through? Our contacts with the Siwai men from the theological college were very good, but they could not always come. There were other Siwai and Bougainville people who had been filled with the Spirit and came to our house, but there were only a few. We had a small meeting in Kokopo in George's house, but even that seemed to be tough going. What was going on? After another attempt to get permission for meetings in Rabaul, a government official sought contact with us and took us into his confidence. He told us that the leadership of the Methodist Church had warned all government offices and all Methodist leaders in the villages that we were a dangerous sect, which was against all medical help. It was said that we advised people not to seek medical help because we believed God heals. They also said we were a sect that was against the government. Now things became clearer to us. Once we knew this, we used every opportunity to make it obvious that we were not against medical services. When we had to take someone to the hospital or visit someone, we tried to do it as conspicuous as possible. On our Land Rover was clearly written, 'Full Gospel Movement Streams of Power', with the symbol of the cross and the dove. There was only one car like this in the area. I would make an elaborate turn in front of the hospital to get as much attention as I could. It did help somewhat.

Apart from the Methodist Church building in Rabaul, the church also had a Christian bookshop. The four gospels had just been published in Pidgin English and were sold there. But whenever I went to the store, it was nearly always closed. We did not understand it. Later, when our contact with the Methodists had become much better, two women who were in charge of that shop told us what had happened. They were given orders to close the shop as soon as they saw us and were not allowed to let us in. They hid in the adjacent room, and when our car left, they opened the shop again. We were able to laugh about it together then, but when it was happening, it was not so amusing.

The Lord was moving, but we just did not realise it! God was also working on the question that was gnawing at my heart, why so few people came back, even though hundreds of people prayed the sinner's prayer. Our search for the truth about this would indeed give us answers. Those answers would become a common thread in our ministry through the years, right until today, but we did not realise it then.

One positive thing was that after several months, we found a larger house with a room that could hold thirty to forty people. Our small apartment was in the small expatriate area of Rabaul, where some local people did not like to go. The house we found was the ground floor of a two-storey house and had a Chinese owner. The rent was high, and it was a great step of faith to do this. We were always able to pay the rent, and six months later, we were able to rent the whole house, so now we had a place for meetings. On top of that, the house was near the market, as it was in the centre of Rabaul, where the local people easily could get to and often came. This house was close to a 'compound' though, which is a sort of protected area where a certain number of people live together. In this compound lived several workers from different areas. The first Friday we lived there, we heard how they started a sing sing. A sing sing is the Pidgin English word for dances that are practised by every language group in the nation.

They sang for hours and hours. Well, singing is not quite the word. It was more like chanting. They were accompanied by drums. The drum is made from a piece of tree trunk which is hollowed out and given a particular shape. On one side the skin of a snake is tightened, and after they add some decoration, the drum is ready. A common name for such a drum is 'kundu'. For hours the chanting and muffled thumping of the drums sounded. Actually we thought it was quite interesting; we really had come to live in a third world country. Around four o'clock Saturday morning, they stopped. By that time, a whole lot of homemade alcohol had been drunk! The following Friday, it was again a sing sing night. The muffled thumping of the drums made it impossible to sleep. The third Friday night, it became annoying; and in the fourth week, I was getting really irritated. In my irritation, I said to the Lord, 'Why are they doing this? What has got into these people?' Immediately I sensed the Lord whispered to me, 'Satan just copies what I intended for my children!' That was clear! Sometime later we started sing sings for Jesus with the new Christians. The Christians would sing and dance for hours. They had hours of praise and worship. In those first years, I damaged my voice because we had no sound equipment, but those sing sings for Jesus were heavenly, and we cannot forget them. When we discovered the biblical truth about praise and worship several years later and started teaching it, the people understood it very well, perhaps even better than Westerners.

One morning we both had our personal, daily Bible reading time. Suddenly Coby said, 'John, listen to this! Cannibalism is explicitly mentioned in the Bible as the worst curse that people can get under!' Coby was reading Leviticus 26. I stopped my reading, and we read that part in Leviticus 26 together. I knew that horrible story in the Bible of the occupation of the city of Samaria, where a child was eaten because of hunger and hopelessness. I always saw it as a deed born out of sheer desperation.

Here it said that cannibalism is the worst curse that a nation can get under, and it became clear to us that when they do not repent, the next thing is that God removes such a nation from the face of the earth. In Leviticus 26, it says, after the part that speaks about cannibalism, that even the sound of a rushing leaf will frighten the people. What a sign of fear! To be frightened by a rushing leaf! Later on, during patrols through the jungle, I have seen men who came along as carriers, being frightened by some leaves that were moved by the wind. They would shout, pointing to the rustling leaves, 'A ghost, a ghost!' At the end of the chapter in Leviticus, we learned that if people will repent and confess their own sins and those of their ancestors, God will accept them and heal their land. I was totally absorbed by what I had just read. We had moved to a country in which some language groups had practised cannibalism. In the days when we came to Papua New Guinea, you would sometimes hear of cannibalism. In the following years, I spoke with men who had practised cannibalism. This land was not 'primitive' as Westerners often call it, but although it was a beautiful country, many people were in deep darkness.

I knew that what Coby shared with me contained a great truth. In Australia, we had become familiar with two English concordances, Strong's and Young's. In the weeks and months that followed, I spent hours and hours studying; and with the help of the concordances, I looked at every part of the Bible that spoke about curses. Slowly but surely I gained insight into a spiritual truth of which we had previously only theoretically known the word 'curse'. Several years later, I started preaching openly about this with astonishing results. This study or message was then called 'confessing the sins of your ancestors'. We would shortly afterwards hear about Derek Prince for the first time, but we did not know him then. When we met Derek Prince years later and he heard that I preached regularly on this subject, he told me of his discovery on the subject of 'blessing and cursing' and that he was writing a book about it. We talked together for several hours. His biblical insight was deeper than mine, but apart from a missionary in Africa who had pointed it out to him, we were the only missionaries and preachers who spoke about this.

Years after the discovery of this biblical truth, I preached at a big mission conference of the Assemblies of God in Auckland, New Zealand. One of the themes that I spoke about was 'confessing the sins of your ancestors.' It was received very well, but it was not new to them. Derek Prince had been there several years before me. In Australia, I was also asked by the Assemblies of God to speak about this; and I can remember those meetings as very powerful times in which God touched, healed, and set many people free. To avoid confusion, later when Derek Prince had written his book, we called the message also 'blessing or curse'.

When we later preached this in Papua New Guinea, it led to great breakthroughs in the lives of people, but more about that later when we write about our time in the capital, Port Moresby. In Rabaul, a foundation was laid for a truth that would later be a great blessing and bring breakthroughs for many people in Papua New Guinea, as well as in other nations where we would live and minister.

In the meantime, the Methodist Church had become part of a larger, new denomination called the Uniting Church of Papua New Guinea and the Solomon Islands. In the Uniting Church in and around Rabaul, quite a commotion had arisen about the fact that we had come into the district. Among the leaders of the Tolai there was resistance, but miracles had happened as well, even though the church had taught that miracles do not actually happen any longer. The head of the Uniting Church, an Australian missionary, who clearly had a hunger and desire for God, contacted us after a while and asked if we could come over one evening to tell the Tolai leaders who we were, why we had come, and if we could answer some questions. We accepted the invitation. About a hundred people came. Some native leaders told us bluntly that they did not appreciate our arrival in the district; but others had questions about healing, miracles, and the Holy Spirit. There were clear divisions that evening; some were possibly open, others opposed strongly. Also among the missionaries who attended, there was division.

At the end of a somewhat unruly evening, a small old woman stood up. She only spoke the Tolai language. A missionary interpreted for us. The old lady asked her question, and it grew quiet. We had no idea what she had said. I asked the missionary to translate it for us, but he hesitated. When I pressed on, he translated what she had said. Her question was 'We have had the gospel for a long time in our district. We are told that we are in the light, but we are not in the light. Many of us are still in darkness. Can we really come out of that darkness?' We were surprised and deeply moved by what we heard. The missionary was clearly embarrassed, and everyone saw it. Our answer was clear and spontaneous: 'Yes, through Jesus, you can get out of that darkness.' And with that, the evening ended. There was not much talk after that. Most people were obviously at a loss about what had just been said that evening. To us the statement of Jesus in Matthew 6:23 became clear: 'If therefore the light that is in you be darkness, how great is that darkness!' Years later, a pastor would tell us that until that moment, he had never known a Christian who did not also practise magic.

Our hearts were filled with even more compassion for the Tolai people, but the door seemed even more closed after that evening, and it would stay closed for quite some time longer.

Still things happened which now showed us that God was teaching and training us. One day two young men came to our door. They wanted to talk with us, so we let them in. They were university students who were on a holiday in Rabaul. They spoke English very well and started talking. Then the big question came out. 'In our country, Papua New Guinea, various churches have come like the Roman Catholic Church, the Anglican Church, the Lutheran Church, the Methodist, the Swiss Evangelical Church, Jehovah's Witnesses, the Mormons, and others. They all claim that they have the truth and that they are the one true church and that all other churches are wrong. Now you have come to our country. You call yourselves Pentecostal. Do you also believe that you are the one true church?' What a question! But a justified question. Coby gave an answer that became a revelation to me. She said, 'Jesus said, "I am the way, the truth and the life." Truth is a person, not a church or a teaching. And if you have this person, Jesus, then you have the truth.' The two students were quiet and thought deeply. I was very quiet too. The Holy Spirit had given Coby a 'word of wisdom', but to me it was a revelation that would play a big part in my way of thinking and working. Truth is a person! What an amazing truth! And when you have that person in your life, you have the truth! Years later, I shared this story, which was recorded on a DVD, called 'Furious Love'. Until today I have had reactions from all over the world, people and even pastors, for whom this was a revelation. Truth is a person, and that person is Jesus Christ.

There was another event that seemed very small and insignificant but which also greatly influenced my thinking and way of preaching. An Australian pastor visited us. In a conversation, he said, 'It must be very difficult to always preach at Sunday school level because these people understand so little!' What a remark, and certainly no 'compliment' to the Papua New Guinean people. For a moment I did not know what to say. But Coby said, 'You know, the truth that Jesus brought was so deep that it could only be explained in a simple way.' I thought much about that. The greatest preacher to have ever walked the earth is Jesus. When He spoke to the crowds, He very often used simple stories from everyday life, parables, to explain spiritual truths. I then decided to train myself to preach that way too. Later I was criticised in Australia and the Netherlands for telling too many stories. I find myself in good company. Jesus also told many stories. But I also regularly meet people who, after years, remember the stories. They learned from them.

We had a great desire to go to Siwai, but it did not seem possible as yet. The four theology students could not come with us because they were at college. Moreover, if they took us to Siwai, it would mean the end of their studies, which would not be wise. Someone had to join us, but that person was not there yet.

The dear Baptist couple had been in Papua New Guinea longer and were in contact with missionaries from the Foursquare Mission. Our interpreter came from there but had gone back in the meantime. He had helped us tremendously. We had thrown ourselves into learning Pidgin English and were beginning to master it.

The Foursquare Mission would have their annual workers' conference in Goroka, a small township and the government centre of the Eastern Highlands District. The Baptist couple offered for me to go there. What a gift! I went, and it was a week that made a deep impression on me.

There were signs in Australia that a movement of God's Spirit was beginning. One of the preachers from the USA, who went to Australia often, was A. S. Worley of the Pentecostal Holiness Movement. He was an amazing Bible teacher, and healings would take place in his meetings. We had met him and his wife once before but briefly. He would speak at the conference together with Norman Armstrong, the Australian representative of the famous American evangelist Oral Roberts. We had come to know Norman Armstrong well in our first two years on this side of the world. He had decided, we think, to watch over that 'young Dutch couple'. He was indeed a fatherly, friendly man.

A. S. Worley gave a series of studies about spiritual growth, inspired by the words of John in his first letter, where he writes to 'children, young men and fathers'. His studies made a real impression on me and greatly affected our lives. People who know me from training courses know that I like to speak about 'spiritual fatherhood'. The seeds of that truth were sown in my heart during that conference.

During that conference, I also came to know a few missionaries. Friendships that lasted through the years were born. The conference was held at a missionary post outside Goroka. We will write more about the Highlands later. After the conference, Norman Armstrong decided to come with me and spend two days with us in Rabaul. That was a gift from the Lord. His visit blessed us.

Another thing which I will never forget happened during the conference. In the little town of Goroka, a small supermarket had opened. This was mainly for the expatriates working and living there. The supermarket was very basic. In the Netherlands or Australia, one can choose between ten sorts of washing powder. Here, one could choose between one, maybe two kinds. There were no fresh vegetables available; you could only get those at the local native market. Still, it was a supermarket, the first in the Highlands.

I think I went there to get toothpaste. I regularly tend to forget to put that in my bag. I must have been looking for toothpaste; there were only two different varieties available. Then I saw something. A local Papua New Guinean woman wearing nothing but a grass skirt walked behind a shopping cart, while she shopped for groceries. Really, only a grass skirt as they are worn in the tropics. That was all she was wearing. I did not have my camera with me; otherwise, I would most certainly have taken a photo. I would have given the photo the following title: 'Stone Age Goes Shopping in Space Age'. This event showed how big the contrasts were at times and how rapidly new things were introduced into the country.

Back in Rabaul. For several months we asked ourselves, 'What now?' Almost every door seemed tightly closed. Looking back, we can so clearly see the hand of the Lord, but in those days clarity was missing. We had to fight discouragement. At last we decided to fast again. If we did not get an answer, we would give up on Rabaul. After three days of fasting, Coby asked me, 'Has the Lord spoken to you?' Yes, the Lord had spoken something in my heart. Coby was curious. The Lord only gave me one word: 'Stay!' The Lord had also spoken to Coby. He had spoken only one word to her as well: 'Stay!' We stayed, but it was not much clearer than just that.

CHAPTER 12

The Plantations

WE HAD PREPARED a room in our home for meetings. Several Siwai people were willing to come. Apart from them, there were various people we had come to know in the township. There were also some people in Rabaul who came from the mainland and had come to believe in Jesus, in Pentecostal churches there. They discovered that we were also Pentecostals. Apart from a few people, most of them were not strong or mature Christians. The fact that they had left their original area seemed to indicate a desire for adventure. Some of them had become Christians because a chief of the village, the head of the family, or some other important person in their language group, had come to believe in Jesus. Out of a sense of loyalty, they also became Christians, but it was not wholeheartedly. We discovered that they wanted to come to the meeting on Sunday, but that was pretty much the only sign of Christian living they showed. Some had discovered alcohol and prostitutes, and although they said they were Christians, they were a long way from being genuine Christians. Two rather funny events in relation to these people I can remember.

Smoking was a sensitive subject. The missionaries in their areas had been very clear about it: Christians do not smoke. Generally speaking, we totally agree with that. One Sunday a few believers came to the service, among them a few people from the Highlands. One of them had a cigarette butt behind his ear. I wanted to make a joke and said, 'I didn't know that you smoked.' The man was embarrassed. 'Uh, ah, uh, ah, uh, ah, you know, I met a wantok on the way, and he asked me to carry his cigarette for him.' Nobody believed it, and of course he knew it was a lie, as was clear from the look on his face. I did not know about the cultural phenomenon of 'loss of face' yet. I had let this boy 'lose face' in front of others, so he had to try to save his honour. I told this story many times, and the people of Papua New Guinea always laugh about it. They know their own people.

Another man from the Highlands had also asked for prayer, because he wanted to give up smoking. A few days later, I saw him in town, and he was obviously smoking a cigarette. I stopped the car and greeted him. He was taken by surprise; the cigarette left his mouth and was held in his hand behind his back. Behind and above his head smoke came up, and he pretended nothing was happening. I thought it was amusing and kept talking with him. The cigarette must have burned his fingers. We had much to learn about the mindset and culture of the various people groups, but loss of face was something that was present in all tribes. When a Christian was not two faced, but just, honest, and straightforward, then his conversion had done a deep work in his heart.

For several months we could not do much and spent a lot of time praying and fasting. Then George, the man who was converted during the crusade in Kokopo, had an idea. Beyond Kokopo were many plantations where a lot of people from the Highlands worked. He knew the manager of the Ulaveo plantation, and maybe we could have meetings there. At the plantation worked about 500 men, who all came from various areas of the Highlands, and they worked there on contract for a period of two years.

The coastal areas of Papua New Guinea did have contact with the outside world for a long time, some areas even for several hundred years or more. At that time, people thought that the high mountainous area in the middle of the mainland was uninhabited. Just before the Second World War, a pilot who flew over the area saw smoke and discovered a village. It was evident that the Highlands were not uninhabited. Because the Second World War broke out shortly thereafter, nothing could be done about this discovery. It was after the Second World War that the first well-organised patrols explored the area. After several years' exploration, they found the Highlands to be the most densely populated area of the entire country. Most, if not all, groups in the Highlands lived just like their ancestors had lived for centuries. There was much violence among the different groups. This violence is called 'tribal wars'. We experienced it twice at close range, but more about that later. Government stations were built, and missionaries entered the area. We heard many of their stories. It is amazing and sometimes almost unbelievable what they had to accomplish to establish those mission stations.

In an attempt to bring the men in touch with civilisation, they were asked if they wanted to come to the coast, to work on the plantations. They had to sign a contract with a fingerprint, because no one could read or write. In the fifties and sixties, the Highlands were brought under the control of the colonial government of Australia. The climate in the high mountains is ideal for growing coffee and tea, so that's what they started with, to develop the area economically.

For people from the Highlands to come to the coast meant flying in a 'balus', which is the Pidgin English word for aeroplane. That also meant that the people saw the sea. If you were born and raised in a mountain area, you never saw the sea. The men who came to the coast were picked up in an old DC-3 and flown to the coast. There they lived in barracks at the plantations where they were working. They made very little money, but after two years, they received a couple of hundred Australian dollars, the currency used in those days.

We and many others considered it almost slavery. The men lived under very primitive conditions and usually had no idea what a period of 'two years' meant when they signed up for it. Though most men were single, some of them were married and were actually torn away from their wives, children, and relations. Often, there were men of various and sometimes enemy tribes at one plantation, which could lead to very bloody scenes. One advantage was that most learned Pidgin English quite quickly and reasonably well. A certain local woman saw a source of income and prostituted herself. That went below any decent human standard and was humiliating. In several tribes from the Highlands, they adhered to high moral standards. But here the men let go of all these standards, and that often led to trouble after they went back after two years. The men could not read or write. Communication with 'home' did not exist or maybe some wantoks could sometimes deliver messages. There are stories about women who were convinced that their husbands were no longer alive, and remarried, as is normal in their culture. This had serious consequences when the original husband returned. Also young unmarried men, who were committed to the high moral standards of their tribe regarding marriage, became totally unhinged.

And yes, we received permission to have meetings on the biggest plantation called Ulaveo. Deep in my heart, I was not too excited, because we had actually come for the local people of the district surrounding Rabaul, the Tolai people. In those days, I sometimes felt as if I had 'failed'. We did not understand that God was doing something very unique, by reaching these men in the plantations with the gospel.

The Ulaveo plantation was about forty kilometres outside of Rabaul. The first part of the road was bitumen, but then it became coral gravel. A few believers from Kokopo came with us. There was a sense of excitement, this first time. When we arrived at the plantation, they were having a sing sing. The men had dressed themselves as they usually do for a sing sing. We told them that we came for a meeting and that we would show a film and wanted to pray to Jesus for their needs. We were surprised, but the sing sing was stopped, and they came, dressed up and all, to the open place between the barracks where we held the meeting. We drew a lot of attention. That evening a few of the men prayed with us, but we did not know how true or deep their commitments went. We promised to come back the following Sunday evening. One of the managers of the plantation was from Holland. He was quite happy for us to come, as it gave the men something to do.

That Dutchman told us that there were more Dutch people working at the plantations spread throughout the district. Most had come to Papua New Guinea from Indonesia. He also told us that for these Dutch people, every Monday evening at eleven o'clock, fifteen minutes of Dutch music was played on a certain radio station in Papua New Guinea. The following Monday evening, we turned on our radio; and sure enough, there was Dutch music. The first song was 'Oh, that

Elisabeth, who makes such great coffee.' The next was a street organ song. It felt weird. We were at the other side of the world, far away from the Netherlands, and then we heard this typically Dutch song, 'Oh Elisabeth', who makes such great coffee.

Every Sunday evening, we would go to the Ulaveo plantation. In the Rabaul District, it usually rains a lot; but for an entire year, it did not rain on Sunday evening in Ulaveo. Sometimes it rained in Rabaul or Kokopo but not in Ulaveo. Many people noticed this unusual fact. Starting from the first Sunday evening, there was a special presence of the Lord in the meeting, which was held in the open air in a space between two barracks. The believers from Kokopo who had joined also noticed how tangibly the Lord was present. Even when we went to other smaller plantations later and held meetings there, Ulaveo was the place where God worked in a unique way; it was as if the presence of the Lord there was stronger and more powerful. There were men from various areas of the Highlands, but particularly from Western and the Southern Highland Districts, a big area. Among the men working at the Ulaveo plantation were several language groups, such as the Chimbus from the Western Highlands District and the Pangias from the Southern Highlands District. Both areas had only recently come under government control and were now 'opened areas'. Some men had probably never heard the gospel or had barely been in touch with missionaries. We asked ourselves if they knew the gospel or understood it. At that time, we could not have imagined that twenty to thirty years later, some of the most prominent spiritual leaders in the entire national work would come from those language groups. God did know, and we realised years later that the major breakthrough in the home areas of these plantation workers was related to the services at the Ulaveo plantation, where many came to know the Lord Jesus.

Most plantation workers had already learned quite a bit of Pidgin English, so communicating went reasonably well. We were starting to get a grip on the language, but we still needed some help with interpretation from the Kokopo believers. From the very first evening, many men prayed the sinner's prayer, but we asked ourselves how much do they understand? Did they only pray out of some sort of politeness? But Sunday after Sunday the men earnestly prayed with us.

One of the first Sunday evenings, a young man, a worker at the plantation, came to us after the service and asked if we could pray that God would give him a radio. Immediately I had the impression that we were dealing with a cargo cult mindset. George, the faithful Kokopo believer, was also convinced of this. We spoke with the young man, but he did not really understand the gospel. We prayed that Father God in heaven would reveal His love to him, because God knew him through and through. His thinking really resembled a cargo cult mindset. So especially in the beginning, every time the men prayed, we wondered how much they understood. But we should not have worried. The fruit of the work on the plantations was phenomenal. But we had yet to learn a lot more about Papua New Guinean culture and their way of thinking.

After several weeks, we went to the plantation again on a Sunday evening; but near the plantation, we came across some workers who were covered in blood, and really upset. There had been a tribal fight at the plantation, and people were injured. Near Kokopo was a medical post, and they were walking there to get help. We quickly entered the plantation, and what we saw was horrific. The 'war' had ended, but there were various severely wounded people and much destruction. The manager and some of the staff were there. The men stood opposite each other in quite a hostile manner, but at a reasonable distance. A number of men had not participated, because they had become Christians. We spoke with them, prayed, and then helped to get some injured people to the medical post. During the first trip, we had a boy lying in the back of our Land Rover; he had a spear in the side of his head. The spear had not gone very deep, but it was not a pleasant sight. On our second trip, we took a boy who was missing a piece of his skin and flesh from his back. Someone had struck him in the back with a cane knife.

When we arrived back at the plantation, the police had arrived, and there were also more people to help. We went to the young Christians who were scared, and comforted and encouraged them and prayed again. Both injured boys whom we took to the medical post survived, which is a miracle. Afterwards, it became peaceful again at the plantation, and we did not experience big fights between the various groups again – only some fights between individuals. Later on we will tell you a little more about one of such fights.

After a while, we started speaking about the Holy Spirit; and in the following weeks and months, dozens and dozens of men were filled with the Holy Spirit and spoke in tongues. Many had extraordinary, powerful encounters with the Lord. While we initially had doubted when they prayed the sinner's prayer faithfully every week, that doubt was now gone. Many things happened among the men, because God was at work in very special ways. At the first baptism service at Kokopo, a few plantation workers were also baptised. Later, when we received more help, dozens of plantation workers were baptised by immersion, in the sea.

One of the young men who came to Jesus was Kawai, from the Pangia area. He had taken on the Christian name of Philip. Philip was married and had a daughter. He had not behaved well in his village, so he thought it wise to disappear for a while. He signed up for two years of work at the plantation. His wife, Bekki, and his daughter stayed behind. Philip worked in another plantation; but through wantoks, who worked in Ulaveo, he had heard about us and came to the meetings. Apparently he had heard the gospel before and now came to repentance in a very powerful way. Soon he was filled with the Holy Spirit. Several years later, Philip would become one of the full-time workers in Rabaul. By then he had brought his wife, Bekki, and daughter with him; so they were together as a family. When a Pentecostal missionary couple from Finland, with whom we worked together very closely later on, started working in Pangia, Philip became the first pastor. Several years later, this beautiful man died suddenly, which was a great loss to the work in Pangia at that time.

Not long after Philip had come to Jesus, he came to our house one morning very upset and knocked very hard on our door. It was about seven o'clock. Trembling, he told us that in a fight, someone from Pangia had been killed; and worse still, it was someone from his extended family, his clan. He was now obliged to kill someone from the Chimbus. He said, 'I have to kill someone. I have to repay the death of my wantok, but I don't want to do this. I am a Christian now. But the urge in me to kill is so great. Will you lock me up in the room where you have meetings? I will pray until the urge to kill is gone, even if it takes days. I will call you when the urge to kill has left me.' We were stunned; we had not experienced this before. A recently converted believer fighting against the urge to kill! Throughout the years, we learned how incredibly strong this urge can be. We locked Philip up in the room and gave him a bottle of water. There was also a toilet that he could get to. Every so often we would literally hear him scream and shout to God. We stayed at home the entire day because we had no idea how this would end. Around seven or eight in the evening, he called us. 'The urge to kill is gone. You can release me now.' That night he slept at our home, and the next morning I took him to the plantation and told the manager what had happened. Philip was a changed man after that day. We have asked ourselves more than once how many pastors would have ever experienced something like this. A recently converted believer asking to be locked up in the church because the urge to kill was so strong. It certainly does reveal something of the depth of conversion among the men at the plantation.

Someone else from the Highlands heard about us. His name was Yans; the name he had taken on was Joseph. He came from Laiagam where very recently Pentecostal missionaries from the Apostolic Church had started a work. Joseph had experienced some sort of conversion, but apparently not deep enough. He too had misbehaved in his clan, and it seemed wise to him to disappear for a while, and therefore, he went to work at the plantations on the coast. Joseph came powerfully to repentance shortly after we met him; he was filled with the Holy Spirit and became unstoppable. He too became a full-time worker in Rabaul, after his time at the plantation. Joseph was an intriguing, colourful person. He could testify and preach powerfully, and the examples he used were ones you would not forget. He often came to us on Saturday, spent the night, and went back to Ulaveo on Sunday; and from there he went to the plantation where he worked. His testimony and preaching were very colourful and full of cultural examples.

Coby often made lemon juice from lemons she bought at the market. She put sugar in it and cooled it in the fridge; it was delicious especially when the heat made you thirsty. Joseph did not know about the sugar, but he thought it was delicious. Once he testified that Jesus was just as sweet to your inner being as lemon juice.

Another time while he was preaching, he said in the middle of his passionate sermon, 'When you slaughter a pig, you want it to have much fat under the skin. But you don't know that until you cut the pig open. If there is a lot of fat, you are happy; and if there is not that much fat, then you are disappointed. That's the same for God. He looks at your heart and wants to know if you have much fat for Him.' How many Western preachers will use this sort of example?

The pig is very valuable in their culture. The dowry and many other things are paid with pigs. The event where the Lord Jesus delivered a possessed man from demons, and where the demons asked permission to go into the pigs, resulting in 2,000 pigs plunging into the sea and drowning, this made a deep impression on these people. Two thousand pigs are a lot of pigs. A bride in those days was paid for with about fifty pigs, so 2,000 pigs is the bride price for forty wives. Wow! That's how much a possessed person is worth to Jesus. Someone they would pay no attention to, and would just leave to starve in the jungle, was saved by Jesus at the cost of forty wives!

Another time we heard Joseph say, 'The love of God is so great. As you cannot empty the sea with a bucket, neither can you ever empty the love of God!' Joseph planted churches throughout the country until this very moment I am writing this. A few months ago, while I was in Papua New Guinea, I spent a morning talking with him. One of his children, his son Robert, was able to study in Australia. There he went to Hillsong in Sydney and met a girl from a Jewish background. They are now on staff at Hillsong. When we were there two years ago, a young man walked up to us. He was in charge of the team that kept order in the service. 'Do you remember me?' he asked. We had known him as a little boy. Here he was, in a suit, on the staff of Hillsong. From time to time, Joseph visits his son and daughter-in-law and attends Hillsong at those times. But it all started at the plantation. Joseph is a true Papua New

Guinean apostle. That the work at the plantations would bring forth these fruits, we never, never could have dreamed.

After two years, the men went back to their area, and especially those from Pangia testified and shared about what had happened at the plantations in Rabaul. After we had worked in Rabaul for two years, two prominent leaders from the Pangia area came to Rabaul, especially to visit us, and to ask if we could leave Rabaul and come to Pangia. We could not promise that, but we did promise to send missionaries, which we could eventually do because of our contact with the Finnish missionaries. Nowadays, there are many congregations in and around Pangia. Probably the most prominent leader who came out of this entire work, Charles Lapa, comes from Pangia; but we will share more about him later.

In those days, we wrote enthusiastic letters to the Netherlands about our work on the plantations, including letters to Karel Hoekendijk, the leader and founder of our Pentecostal mission movement Streams of Power. Karel Hoekendijk wrote us an enthusiastic letter back, and we felt quite honoured to receive a personal letter from him, because we looked up to this pioneer of Pentecost in the Netherlands. Streams of Power had designed a badge that men could wear on their jackets. The badge had the emblem of Streams of Power on it: a blue background with a white dove and a red cross. The image of the blood and cross of the Lord Jesus and the Holy Spirit. Karel Hoekendijk wrote that they had a lot of those badges to spare and asked if I perhaps wanted them for the believers at the plantations. We smiled when we read this, because the men wear shorts or a waistcloth called a 'laplap' and usually have a bare upper body. I wrote to Karel Hoekendijk that it was probably inappropriate to receive the badges, because pinning them on a bare upper body would hurt. We received a letter back from him telling us that he did not appreciate my playful remark, because I was actually mocking the emblem of Streams of Power. To us it remained an amusing incident, and we still smile about the response from Karel Hoekendijk. The newsletters that we sent in those days had a nice letterhead, 'Full Gospel Movement Streams of Power'. We had come from them and had been sent by them. But we would no longer use that name. A few years later, the work would be much more closely connected with, and become part of, what the Holy Spirit was doing in Australia and New Zealand. However, a good number of personal relationships and connections with various congregations in the Netherlands have always remained.

We had started a small meeting on Sunday mornings in Rabaul. It went all right, but it was laborious. The blessing was on the work at the plantations. A small number of believers came to the meeting. One Sunday morning, after the service, there was a knock on the door. We opened it. There were two men, an older and a younger man. They were dressed in white shirts, white shorts, long white socks, and white shoes. In those days, that was the normal way for expatriates to dress in the tropics. *These must be Jehovah's Witnesses*, I thought. They asked us if we were the young Dutch Pentecostal couple of whom they had heard. Yes, we were. 'We are Pentecostal missionaries from Finland,' they said. For a minute I wondered, *Am I crazy or what? We've been working here for more than eight months, and there are more Pentecostal missionaries in the area?* But that was not the case. They were visiting to explore the area, because they felt called by God to work in Rabaul and its surroundings. We invited them in, and for several days we talked a lot and prayed together. The older man, about forty years old, was Lauri Pesu, who had already been a missionary in Kenya and Sri Lanka. The younger man was Kari Harri, who had worked for about one year in the Sepik District, where the Australian Assemblies of God were already established. They both spoke English fluently, and we enjoyed our contact with them. After several days of conversation and prayer, it was decided that they would not start a separate mission but would work together with us. In the back of our minds, we remembered that God had said, 'Rabaul, then Kavieng, then Bougainville, and then the mainland.' Kari and his wife, Raakel, and two young sons could come from Sepik within a few months; Lauri and his wife, Martha, and their six children could come sometime in the following year. That is how it happened. Just before the end of the year, Kari and Raakel and their sons, Joel and Rauli, arrived; the next year the Pesu family arrived. Kari and Raakel rented the other floor of the house so that the entire house was now for missionaries and the work.

Shortly afterwards, Norman Armstrong, Oral Roberts's representative in Australia, contacted us. Norman was one of the speakers at the conference which I had attended in the Highlands. He had also spent several days with us. He had come into contact with a new powerful movement of young people, who were passionate and full of fire for missions and evangelism. The movement was called Youth with a Mission. A young couple from Tonga, which is a small island group in the Pacific, had come with a group from New Zealand to Australia, and felt called to go to Papua New Guinea. They were looking for contacts. Norman was very enthusiastic and told them about us. And that's how we got in touch with Kalafi Moala and his wife, Tapu. They intended to arrive around December. We were looking forward to their arrival. What we heard about them sounded very good.

In the meantime, there were several Siwai believers who contacted us and visited us. They had experienced the baptism with the Holy Spirit. Among them was a young man named Amos Rorima. He was prepared to join me during the Christmas holidays, for my first trip to Siwai. Rorima was a teacher at the primary school close to Rabaul and spoke English very well. The plan was to go to Siwai in the beginning of January, together with Kalafi Moala and Rorima.

When I reread the newsletters from that period, we wrote various times about young men who received visions while praying and to whom the Lord Jesus appeared. Several of them were slain in the Holy Spirit and had deep encounters with the Lord. A young man from Siwai saw the Lord, and the Lord said that He would move again on Bougainville around December! We intended to go there in the beginning of January. Every time we prayed, I would kneel on the map of Papua New Guinea and put my hands on Bougainville and pray for that island. Our expectations were high. We had to inform people well in advance that we were going to come, because communication with these areas worked best through people who travelled there.

In the meantime, the work at the plantations continued. There was much blessing in the meetings. The men who worked at the plantation were all healthy, because sick or needy men could not get a contract. Still, we saw many things happen among them. Not so much spectacular healings, but deep encounters with the Lord. The first baptism service was impressive. After a few new believers had been baptised, we celebrated communion on the beach. For most of them, this was their first time ever to celebrate communion. One of the men who had been baptised was healed that morning. I do not remember the condition that was healed, but the others were really excited, I do remember that very well.

Years later, when my parents were in Papua New Guinea for several months, we were able to visit Mount Hagen. From there we made a rough journey to Pangia with a four-wheel-drive vehicle. Not far from Pangia was an intersection, but we saw no sign advising us which way to go. We saw two young men and stopped to ask for directions. They exclaimed, 'Brother John, Brother John!' They were two men whom we had led to Jesus at the Ulaveo plantation. My father said, 'You meet people everywhere that know you, don't you?' We talked for a while, and both men were still fiery and enthusiastic followers of the Lord Jesus.

The Lord opened the door to start meetings in two other plantations, and occasionally we held meetings there. One day I had gone to one of those plantations to arrange some things. When several workers saw my car, they came to chat with me. One of them walked back to the barracks and came back with a gift. They had a cat that had become a sort of mascot for the entire group. This cat had given birth to kittens that were now over six weeks old. One of the kittens had the same hair colour as I had, red. That was our present! It was a cute little kitten. It loved pawpaw, and until this day we have not heard of a cat that likes pawpaw. The kitten had another amusing habit: when it would hear our car stop in front of the door, it would run to the door and sit there, waiting for us. That Christmas our dear friends, the Baptist couple, went on leave to Australia. They too had a red cat, and it came to stay at our place. Around us lived Asian people, but also local people from various tribes. It is generally known of these cultures that they occasionally eat cats. It is very remarkable that both cats disappeared the day before Christmas and were never seen again. Our neighbours had a big celebration and dinner that Christmas. We had our suspicions, but we could not prove anything.

Never, and I mean never, did we realise that the Lord used the work at the plantations to get us connected with the Highlands – the provinces Western Highlands, Eastern Highlands, and Southern Highlands. It was our vision and desire to plant congregations, but at the plantations we could only evangelise. Finally that evangelism resulted in dozens and dozens of congregations in other regions on the mainland. The Lord knew what He was doing, but we were not aware of it till much later.

In December, as planned, Kalafi Moala and his wife, Tapu, arrived. They were a delightful, enthusiastic, and fiery couple. We really clicked with them. In the tropical sun, Kalafi's skin became darker and darker, and people thought he was someone with a mixed-race background. They looked typically Polynesian. They told us a lot about the Tonga Islands. Often, we made plans to go there together. Unfortunately, that never happened.

In the meantime, it became certain: on the 1st of January 1969, Rorima, Kalafi, and I would go to South Bougainville and stay there for a month. The four theology students had gone to Bougainville in the beginning of December, for the holidays, and they prepared everything for us. They warned me. In South Bougainville there were hardly any cars; they knew of only two: one Toyota Land Cruiser belonging to a *kiap* (patrol officer) of the Buin government station and one old Land Rover belonging to the Methodist Church. Whether they would help us was uncertain. We could not count on it. Then there was a tractor with a trailer from a cooperative, and that was all the transportation. Often, roads could not even be used when it rained because of the mud and the chance of getting bogged. Therefore, walking was the way to go, most of the time. I managed to buy a pair of jungle boots in Rabaul, and boy, did I need them. It would be our first real journey inland, a journey that to this day has given us a great love for Bougainville and its people.

CHAPTER 13

Siwai

I GREATLY ENJOYED THE pleasant rumbling sound of the two engines of the old DC-3. It was my first of many flights that would follow in old DC-3s, which were still faithfully providing much-needed air services in Papua New Guinea. When several years later this reliable big old bird was taken out of service, because it was too old, I and many others thought it was a great pity. There is something very special about flying in an old DC-3. There was even a stewardess on board, and after we had taken off, we were served a few sandwiches and coffee or tea.

We flew from Rabaul to Bougainville. After flying for about an hour, I saw it. Right there beneath me was the island Buka that was separated from the main island of Bougainville by a narrow stretch of water. On Buka is a government post and an airstrip, and that is where we were to land. This island belongs to the province of Bougainville. My heart was pounding faster. So often we had put our hands on the map of Bougainville and prayed for it. After Buka, we would land in Kieta, the most important government post on Bougainville. Then all the way to the south, to the airstrip of Buin, which is close to Siwai, the destination for our trip. From there we had to walk or take one of the few vehicles in the district. Which form of transport it was going to be, we did not know as yet. There were not many passengers on board since it was the 1ˢᵗ of January 1969.

Coby and Kalafi's wife, Tapu, stayed behind in Rabaul and would take the meetings in Rabaul and at the plantations, with the help of the new believers like George. On the 31st of January, we were intending to fly back, that is, if a plane was leaving that day. Even though there was a schedule, it did not necessarily mean that there would be a flight. I once read a funny comment as to why a bus schedule was needed: the delay had to be based on something. That was certainly true for the flight services in Papua New Guinea in those days.

From Buka, we flew along the east coast of Bougainville to Kieta. Bougainville is very mountainous, covered with jungle; and in the middle of the island, there is a large volcano. The sea is a beautiful blue, and we could clearly discern the reefs in the water along the coast. Here and there we could see small white beaches. We flew over a place that had several buildings and houses, but it did not look much. A passenger told me it was Kieta, the main government station on the island. Just north of Kieta was a huge plantation, the Arawa plantation. Years later, when they found copper and gold on the island, the Arawa plantation became a beautiful little town that bore the name Arawa. Later we would live there for a couple of months.

After Kieta, it was about fifteen minutes' flying to the southern point of the island, to Buin. In the area between Kieta and Buin, the language of the Siwai people is spoken. Down there in the green jungle, some villages could be seen. Somewhere there was Siwai. So much had happened there, and even more was going to happen soon. There were the young men trained as village pastors, inspired by the head teacher of the theological school who taught them about healing, prayer, and fasting and faith. They had prayed for the sick, and so many miracles had happened. What would we find, and what would it be like?

The old DC-3 circled around Buin. On the south coast of the island, there were many islands, big and small. That was the neighbouring country, the then British Solomon Islands. Government authorities had drawn a political border on the map, right through the middle of the group of islands. Bougainville became part of Papua New Guinea, the rest came under British control. Years later, when a lot of political turmoil had broken out on Bougainville, the name of the province was changed to North Solomons Island Province, which indicates how much the people on Bougainville feel ethnically connected with the Solomon Islanders.

Buin's landing strip was built of gravel. Buin itself consisted of even fewer houses than Buka and Kieta. There was a Chinese shop and a government station. Its building was partly built with material from the jungle, with walls of woven bamboo and a roof of sago leaves. Somewhere, out of sight, a secondary school had just been built; and there was a hospital or, more accurately, a large medical post. In that area, the Methodist Mission had built a school for girls to teach domestic skills. Around Buin were a few plantations. Buin had a population of about forty-five people, not counting the students at the school and the patients in the small hospital. Compared with Buin, Rabaul was a metropolitan city (and Rabaul was not that large!). In Buin, there were a few cars. In Siwai, there were only two cars and a tractor with a trailer. If you had a car there, that would mean you could drive during good, dry weather; but if it rained, you would usually need a four-wheel drive. When it was bad weather, you would have to walk in the mud barefoot or with boots. I still have a happening that was recorded on a 16mm film. I was driving in a Toyota Land Cruiser and had several people in the back. I had to go through a large puddle, and at a certain moment, it looked as if the car was indecisive: am I going to fall over or not? That's what the roads were like in Siwai. Afterwards, they built slightly better roads, but many roads could only be used in reasonable weather.

We learned that Bougainville only has two seasons: a wet season and a very wet season. The month that we were in Siwai, it rained nearly every afternoon, usually late afternoon; and most times, the word 'poured' would be more appropriate to use.

I did not know about the pope's custom of kissing the ground whenever he disembarks from a plane in the country he is visiting. If I had known, I might have done so myself in Buin. Pinoko and several others were waiting for us. It was very special to see them. The kiap (patrol officer) had to go in the direction of Siwai, and we could get a ride with him. There really was no other option, unless we were prepared to walk for a few hours. So standing in the back of the Toyota Land Cruiser, we headed towards Siwai. We had to hold on tightly. It was just not practical to sit on the steel seats at the sides – it would not be pleasant for your bottom because of all the bumping and swaying of the car on the rough road. But you don't complain in such situations, and certainly not when you don't feel like walking for hours and carrying all your luggage. The road from Buin to Siwai crosses several rivers, and you always have to plan your journey making sure the rivers are reasonably low and one can cross them by car. You never undertake such a trip soon after substantial rainfall. We have made many trips to Siwai over the years and crossed these rivers often. Sometimes we had to spend several hours at the riverside, just waiting for the water to go down enough to be able to cross. I always took a good book with me on those trips and used the opportunity to read several books at those times.

The kiap was going to an area near the border of Siwai, and from there on we had to walk. At the border of the Buin-language area and the Siwai-language area, at the side of the road, there was the frame of a Japanese tank from the Second World War. There were heavy battles on South Bougainville between the Japanese and the Australians, English, and Americans. The Buin airstrip is not very far from Guadalcanal on the Solomon Islands, where the fighting was very intense. Buin was also heavily fought for, and there were quite a lot of air raids by the Japanese. The highest-ranked Japanese admiral Yamamoto and an accompanying plane were shot down above South Bougainville and killed, a severe blow to the Japanese. I have been to that plane wreck, deep in the jungle, several times. Near the location of this wreck, we would later build a Bible school, but more is yet to happen before we come to that.

Pinoko and others had arranged for us to visit Siwai villages where pastors of the Uniting Church lived and ministered – those who had been part of the prayer teams. They were willing for us to visit. The news that a team would visit them and that at least one person was a friend of evangelist T. L. Osborn had spread like wildfire throughout Siwai and its surroundings. They also had heard that we would pray for the sick. The Bougainville prayer teams and we ourselves strongly believed that the healing power of Jesus Christ is still the same today.

We started out in a village near Tonu and slept in a home of one of the leaders. The villages on Bougainville are well built and clean. The houses are built on poles to allow the wind to flow underneath the floor and enable the cool air to flow through the house. The floor is made of thin palm trees cut in half. The walls are made of woven bamboo attached to a timber frame made from small trees. The roof is a thick layer of sago palm leaves, watertight and able to keep the interior dry when it rains. Cooking takes place outside the house under a covered area, because a fire in the house would be too dangerous. The house has a number of rooms, but soundproof it is certainly not. The toilet is usually located a short distance from the house at the edge of the jungle. The bathroom is the river, because a village is always built near a river. Activities involving the river happen in a certain order. High up the stream, drinking water is collected, a little further down is a bathing area for men, and even further downstream there is a bathing area for women. Finally there is the area to wash clothes. Men and women strictly use their own designated areas for bathing. They have never heard about emancipation. I have really come to enjoy bathing in the river. Very refreshing after a scorching hot day!

The population of the village was not large. Most of the villages had a population of about 200 people. If a village had, say, 500 people, that would be regarded as a real big village. Nearly every village had a church. These churches were built on the ground, so the floor was even and hard. The walls only reached up to my waist and were made of woven bamboo like the houses. Above them it was open for airflow to keep the building as cool as possible. On a wooden frame of slender tree trunks was a roof of sago leaves. There would usually be a small platform of tree trunks cut longwise in half. The benches were boards that had been cut by hand from tree trunks, or they were tree trunks cut in half longwise, on supporting poles. They were not very comfortable.

From the first meeting, the churches were packed. People's hunger and desire for the Lord was impressive. Amos Rorima was a great interpreter. Some men spoke Pidgin English, but few women did. In Rabaul, many more people spoke it. We preached in English, and it was interpreted into Siwai, a beautiful-sounding but apparently very difficult language, especially grammar wise. The people of Bougainville had faith and great expectation. In the gospels, we read how the Lord Jesus could do nothing in some places because of their unbelief. In Siwai, it was the absolute opposite. There was great faith and expectation, and the Lord did wonderful miracles.

In every meeting, we would challenge the people to choose radically for Jesus and to repent. Dozens and dozens of people answered this call. I think that many of these people had already earlier on chosen for the Lord and converted; but they longed intensely for the Lord Jesus and did practically anything you asked of them, to get to know Him better, and to experience Him. Still, there were people who had set themselves against the gospel and who were living in darkness. We soon discovered that there was still a lot of witchcraft among these people – active witchcraft against others and protective witchcraft for themselves.

From the moment we entered the first village, the sick were brought to us so we could pray for them. We prayed for hundreds of sick people that month. When I read again the account that I wrote after I returned, it mentioned that many miracles of healing had taken place. In the ten villages we visited, more than twenty deaf or partly deaf people were healed. A deaf and dumb person was healed, also a totally blind woman was able to see and a crippled boy walked again.

After that first visit, we have never seen again so many great miracles of God happen under our hands in one month time. God had seen the faith, courage, prayer, and fasting of these people. The stories of the healings spread from village to village like wildfire. Sometimes people would come early in the morning, around six o'clock, asking for prayer. God was at work. Kalafi wrote afterwards that he had never experienced this before. Just about every day we had two meetings, one quite early in the morning and one in the evening, because during the day people would go to the jungle to cultivate their gardens. But many people stayed at home during the days that we were in their village and came to talk with us, attend Bible studies, or just be with us. We did not have much time for ourselves that month. Here we saw the gospel in a totally different culture, which did not resemble Western Christianity at all. People were so radical and devoted and had such a desire to follow the Lord Jesus as we had not seen in the Western world. We saw real Christianity on Bougainville.

The people's welcome was very special for us. The local people accompanied us and introduced us, as it is not acceptable for an outsider just to walk into a village. Often, you are not welcome at all, and it could lead to trouble and even violence. To show us how welcome we were, chickens were slaughtered, sometimes a pig, and fruit was provided in abundance. They have so much fruit! Sometimes someone was able to get coffee or milo for us. A month without coffee is quite hard on someone from Holland! After the evening meeting, the people often made a fire. They would sit around the fire and start talking or tell stories. I grew to love these moments very much. The people asked questions about everything. Did I know Osborn well? How many times had I met him? Had I been in one of his meetings? In his books, they had seen pictures of massive meetings; had I experienced one of those? And many more questions. We also had to promise that we would tell or write Osborn about our visit to the Siwai people and about the believers in Siwai who were his friends.

But there were very different questions as well. Had I ever seen an elephant or a giraffe or a lion? Was an elephant really that big? How dangerous was a lion? Those questions really amused me. The biggest animal that they knew was a pig. The children who attended school had brought along books with pictures of wild animals; that is how they knew about these animals. I had to tell them about my own country and my family. To my disgrace, I knew very little about my family, which they did not understand. One's origins and family are very important to them. In the years that followed, I started to look into my family origins, and I know now a lot more about it. When the fire finally went out, and there was not a single glimmer left, then the nights became indescribably beautiful. I often put my airbed outside and lay there watching the starry sky, seeing the greatness and majesty of God, our Creator. I had never seen the nights as beautiful as that. We had seen the night sky in Australia as well, but there had always been some source of man-made light somewhere close, but not here. I still miss those moments.

With those who were leaders or pastors, we spoke about the baptism in the Holy Spirit and had Bible studies with them. This was unknown to them. We read the story of Pentecost and the account in Acts where the believers received the baptism in the Holy Spirit and spoke in new tongues. We explained what speaking in tongues is, why the Lord gives it to us, and so on. Rorima interpreted for hours, but Pinoko and the others who were with us interpreted as well. We began to pray for the baptism in the Holy Spirit, and one after the other received the Holy Spirit, most often very powerfully. It was a feast, a real feast.

In my conversations with the people, I took every opportunity to ask them about the prayer teams and about the days when it all started. I held my breath at times as I listened to the stories, testimonies, and miracles that they had seen. Several times I even heard about the dead being raised. In these conversations and stories, I heard the name of David Pookaro many times, but I had difficulty believing the stories I was hearing. I thought that this could not be true, but later, I would meet Pookaro himself. In one of the following chapters, I will tell his story.

I also saw their great disappointment because Methodist missionaries had tried to stop their search for 'how to continue'. But time and time again I did hear people mention the name of that lady missionary, Pamela Beaumont. Time and time again they said, 'She is different. She believes like we do. She wants this too but is stopped by the other missionaries.' Facts that turned out to be very true. When we were in Siwai for the first time, Pamela Beaumont was on leave in New Zealand. Little less than a year later, we would meet this special woman and came to know her.

The people were very encouraged by our visit. 'You have to come and live here with us' was a remark we often heard.

After several days, we moved on to the next village. There was actually only one road through Siwai, and it was only accessible every once in a while. The road from village to village was often a jungle track, a narrow path where you walk behind each other, because the track is only wide enough for one person. These tracks went uphill, downhill, through the mud, through creeks, sometimes through rivers, and sometimes you had to cross a river over slippery tree trunks. The Siwai walked across such tree trunks without any difficulty. I sat down on some tree trunks and slowly shoved myself to the other side. My clothes got very dirty, but at least I did not fall into the water. I quickly learned something about their way of communicating. If they really wanted to go somewhere and it was still a long way away, then it was close! But if we wanted to go somewhere and they did not want to, then it was always far away, even if it was around the next bend of the jungle track. You quickly learned to ask some more questions. 'It is near' could mean two more hours of walking and tramping through the jungle. 'It is far away' could be ten minutes. We learned that they did not want to lose face nor disappoint you.

There was one village named Panake. We were asked to go there and pray for a man who had been sent home from the little hospital at Buin, to die. He had tuberculosis. We went to that village, and sure enough, in one of the houses lay a man who looked extremely sick. He was very skinny and lay there, waiting for his death. This man knew the Lord Jesus and had been active in a prayer team. We prayed for him, and he was healed. In the following years, he became the main leader of the work in Siwai. His name was Jacob Neewai. Not so long ago, while I was writing this, Jacob passed away and is now with his Lord. Jacob will always be one of my great heroes. Very rarely have I known a man who walked so closely with God.

Years later, I was in a monthly meeting, and the people sang an indescribably beautiful song in their own language. I had brought one of our missionaries, Hank van der Steen. He was crying. The Holy Spirit was present in such a special way. The way this song was sung was so moving. After the service, which lasted for five hours, I asked Jacob about this song. Very casually he told me that he and his wife, had been in prayer and that an angel had come to them and taken them to heaven. There they heard angels singing in their language. An angel came to them and taught them the words and said they had to teach this song to their own people. That's what they did! In Australia and in the Netherlands, I have heard that one could follow courses on 'writing new songs'. Of course that is a good thing, but I also sometimes think about Neewai and his wife, Raakel. What I heard that day was really a new song.

Neewai also had a great sense of humour. Though I did not always understand their humour, it was a fact that when Neewai was in the meeting, there was a lot of fun and joy. Neewai suffered immensely when the political turmoil broke out. Several times they tried to kill him. I still have in my possession a copy of a handwritten murder threat against him. The month flew by. It was a dream. Now I understood why I had always had that strong inner assurance of the Holy Spirit whenever we prayed for Bougainville.

When we had been in Siwai for about three weeks, Joshua Monturo came to visit us. I did not understand why he had not come straightaway, because he was the man who had actually started it all and had been the leader of the prayer teams from the beginning. It was so good to meet him. He stayed with us, and after several days, he also wanted prayer for the baptism in the Holy Spirit. This was entirely new for him. 'Does Osborn believe this too, and does he preach it as well?' he wanted to know. Finally we prayed for him, but nothing happened.

Then Kalafi had a word of knowledge about bitterness in his heart. That proved to be right. Because of all the resistance, slander, and criticism from the Methodist missionaries, he was deeply hurt. Kalafi spoke with him for a long time and was able to lead Monturo in a prayer, to forgive those who had treated him so badly. During the days that he was with us, Monturo was filled with the Holy Spirit and spoke in tongues. We had very good and enjoyable times with him, but he had been scarred by the sometimes-violent opposition he had experienced during his time as a pioneer. These wounds have more or less troubled him for the rest of his life, and from time to time I needed to speak to him about it. Despite that, I had great admiration and respect for Monturo. He had been a pioneer and had done something that was unheard of and had not been done before. Inspired by the teacher at the theological school, he taught people about prayer, fasting, and faith and also started prayer teams to pray for the sick. He had to pay a price for this. He was the one who had broken the area open, and without him, we could not have been there. They had sown; we were now able to reap.

Even though Monturo was the first leader, later on it was Neewai who became the recognised leader. And if there was a man who knew what it meant to forgive, then it was most certainly Neewai!

Just before we returned home, we had a meeting with the Methodist missionary who lived in Siwai at the Tonu mission station. We wanted to meet him. But it was a difficult meeting. It was clear that he would have preferred to see us go rather than come. 'This will divide the church,' he kept saying. In a way, he was right, but it was also his own attitude. The people were reaching out for more of the Lord, and he could not stop this. And if he were to stop it, then people would make their own choice.

Returning home, we first had to walk some distance. After that, the kiap took us in his car back to Buin. The kiap was a very agreeable man, a single Australian with whom we had a very good conversation. He knew about the prayer teams and was actually quite interested in what was happening and what our involvement was.

The old DC-3 was surprisingly on time, and we flew back, via Kieta and Buka to Rabaul. I was going home to Coby and Kalafi to his wife, Tapu. I was looking forward to seeing Coby again, to be with her after not having seen her for a month, during which we had not been able to communicate. *However*, I also left Siwai with homesickness. Part of me wanted to stay. I had to promise that I would come back soon and bring Coby with me. They promised that in various villages, they would build a special house for us so that we could have times by ourselves. They would also organise a special bathing area in the river. Four months later, we went together to Siwai and fulfilled our promise. They also kept their promise. In several villages was a small house especially built for us, and yes, there was a special area at the river, which was our bathing area.

That last part of the flight, from Buka to Rabaul, was indescribably beautiful. It was late in the afternoon, and the sky was already changing colour as the sun was setting. The sea beneath us was like a mirror, and at the horizon you could hardly see where the sea ended and the sky began. There were beautiful cloud formations. It was one of the most beautiful flights in Papua New Guinea that I can remember. I let everything from the past month pass my mind. The first time in a real jungle, life in the village, and especially the privilege of seeing God move in such a magnificent way. I felt so very small. What did God see in this little naughty boy from Holland with his red hair? It is a feeling that I still have sometimes. What a privilege to be used by God. I can think of nothing better or more beautiful.

At the Rabaul airport, a real blessing was waiting for me: Coby. I had so much to tell her, and the decision was made: she would join me on the next trip to Siwai.

CHAPTER 14

Coby's First Trip into Siwai, and Her Very Special Experience

BACK IN RABAUL, it took me more than a week to get both feet back on the ground. Never before had I seen God work in these ways in such a short period. One month! Dozens, maybe even hundreds, of people had repented and chosen for Jesus, to make Him Lord of their lives. Many miracles had taken place. Several believers, especially leaders, had received the baptism in the Holy Spirit. Several had very powerful experiences in the Holy Spirit. It was all so impressive, so overwhelming. This is what you dream of as a missionary, and suddenly it happens right before your eyes and under your hands. Not often have I seen people who were so hungry for God.

Kalafi and his wife were a lovely couple, and we got along well. Tapu was pregnant, and it looked as if their first baby would be born in Rabaul. They shared a lot about their native country, Tonga, a group of islands in the Pacific Ocean, but also about their time in New Zealand with Youth with a Mission. They told us about a new move and wind of the Holy Spirit that had begun to blow in New Zealand. This movement would become known as the charismatic movement. Traditional churches opened themselves up to the Holy Spirit and reached out for the gifts of the Spirit. They told us a lot about it, and they also had brought with them recordings of praise and worship, audio tapes of Scripture in Song that were recorded in Auckland. We enjoyed these and tasted the new, fresh movement of the Holy Spirit.

Kalafi and Tapu had become fans of a Bible teacher named Derek Prince, whom they had heard in New Zealand. They had brought some recordings to which we listened. They had also brought several books and articles by him. We devoured them. Derek Prince and several other preachers formed a team and published a magazine called *New Wine*. They also sent every month a 'tape of the month' free to missionaries. We applied for this, and after a while, we too received the magazine *New Wine* and the 'tape of the month' in our far corner of Papua New Guinea. I still remember the first 'tape of the month'. Derek Prince spoke about 'Christ's legacy to His disciples'. It was about the Holy Spirit and the Word of God. We were richly fed and wanted more of what we tasted.

The small services in Rabaul and Kokopo had continued, and also the services at the plantations. Coby and Tapu, Kalafi's wife, and several believers had taken our place while we were in Siwai. We took Kalafi and Tapu with us to the plantations where I or one of the English-speaking believers like George would interpret them. Kalafi was a fiery preacher and an amazing evangelist.

There was blessing, but my heart still went out to Siwai. I thought about it a lot and prayed for our next planned visit, which would be together with Coby.

Joshua Monturo had played a special part in the rise of the prayer teams, but he had become discouraged. But now he had also received the baptism in the Holy Spirit, so we asked him to come to Rabaul for three weeks. It was good to get to know him better. Every day Kalafi and I could train and further equip him more. Monturo spoke Pidgin English very well and also spoke English reasonably well because of his training as a village pastor and the fact that he completed primary school. We brought him along to the plantations, and we also tried to get Siwai people together in Rabaul so we could lead them into the baptism in the Holy Spirit. It was a good time. Monturo shared more about his life, how everything had begun and about the prayer teams. We heard stories of miracles, real miracles. He too mentioned Pamela Beaumont, the Methodist missionary who was now on leave in New Zealand. She clearly cared about the prayer teams and supported them, although it was not easy for her because the other Methodist missionaries were against it. Monturo also told us the almost unbelievable story of David Pookaro. Coby and I were really looking forward to meeting this man when we went to Siwai, and planned to visit his village.

In March, the Finnish missionary couple Kari and Raakel Harri arrived in Rabaul with their two little boys, Joel and Rauli. They rented another part of the house where we lived. Kalafi and Tapu, who did not have children yet, lived with us. In the house, we had a small room for meetings. Kari and Raakel had already served for over a year with the Assemblies of God in the Sepik District which is near the border of West Irian. They had learned Pidgin English there and spoke it well. A deep bond grew between Kari and Raakel and us. Several years ago when they were working as missionaries in India, Raakel unexpectedly died of a heart attack. We were devastated when we heard about it. Kari recently remarried a Finnish missionary from China, and together they now work in India. In Papua New Guinea, a third son was born. Their three boys are all grown up, and all three of them serve the Lord, two as missionaries! Very special!

Kari and Kalafi got along really well together. They formed a team and ventured out together. Kalafi, who looked as if he was from a mixed-race background, spoke in English; and Kari, a white man, interpreted him into Pidgin English. That was something the people did not understand at all – someone who was mixed race who could not speak Pidgin English? Around Rabaul, there were several settlements, villages built by people of other language groups. They lived there together as a group like the Sepiks and the Chimbus. Doors were opened to us in those settlements, and Kari and Kalafi held many meetings. They also visited the plantations, so we actually had two teams now. With the local people of the area around Rabaul, the Tolai, we did not get any contact, apart from maybe one or two people. It would be several years before the doors among them would open.

A mixed-race couple who lived in Rabaul had come to Jesus. Peter was originally from Kavieng on New Ireland. Because they were good in English and also in Pidgin English and even some of the local languages, they were a great help to us. Several expatriates living and working in or near Rabaul had also come to Jesus. We met one of those couples because the Chinese owner of our house wanted a water pump so that we no longer needed to depend on rain water that was collected in big tanks behind the house. We knew that this would happen but were very surprised when one day an Australian man with a dowser walked around our home to find the right spot for the water pump. Sure enough, he built the pump at the place that the dowser had pointed out, but we were not convinced that the dowser had anything to do with his finding water. The man was a real, somewhat rough Australian. Not long after that, he and his wife very radically came to Jesus. The interesting thing was that he did not want to work with the dowser any longer after his conversion. He decided to pray to find the right spot for water pumps. When I think about this couple now, I wish I had known about deliverance from evil spirits as we know now. The man did have an absolutely terrible time as a youth, and from time to time, he was literally tortured by demons. But insight into those matters would come later.

Because several expatriates also attended the small meetings, we were now sometimes asked to come to more official events. For example, we had been able to lead an Australian man, who suffered from cancer, to Jesus just before he died. Shortly afterwards, he passed away. The funeral was quite formal and was held in the Catholic Church. The expatriates who were there were quite officially dressed, but I only had sandals and no shoes. Most were wearing leather dress shoes, but I did not own those kinds of shoes, and you could not buy them in Rabaul. Besides, I need size 11!

Sometime later, an Australian pastor and his wife, whom we knew reasonably well, made a trip through Papua New Guinea. They visited Rabaul for several days and stayed at our place. When they left, the pastor said, 'Just before I left, I bought new shoes, but they are actually a little too big for me. What size are you?' The shoes were my size and fitted exactly, so he gave them to me. I have always had the feeling that the Lord sent someone all the way from Australia to bring me a pair of black leather shoes!

May was rapidly approaching – the month in which Coby and I would go to Bougainville. We would not fly to Buin this time but to Buka, because a month ago the Missionary Aviation Fellowship (MAF) stationed a plane there. The MAF pilot Harold Morton, who was known to be an outstanding pilot, and his wife, Hope, lived there as well. Tonu, the most important missionary post of the Methodist Church in the south of Bougainville, had recently made a little airstrip, a strip of grass, which was maintained by the staff of the missionary post. We would fly from Buka to Tonu and walk from there. Tonu would become quite well-known years later. After we left Papua New Guinea permanently, great political turmoil broke out in Bougainville which led to a sort of civil war that lasted for eight years. In that time, there was a camp in Tonu where people could live and where there was reasonable protection against the Bougainville Revolutionary Army. Though it was not easy in the Tonu camp, many people's lives were spared. In that camp, the difference between the Uniting Church, the former Methodist Church, and the Pentecostal church faded away. It was just Christians who came together. It was quite charismatic though! I have often thought that what happened in the Tonu camp was a more real picture of the body of Christ than the churches with their organisation and structure. Nowadays, these congregations or groups of Christians have taken on the name New Life Churches.

May arrived, and that meant going to Siwai for Coby and me! Kalafi and Tapu had a baby girl born to them, and they stayed in Rabaul with Kari and Raakel. By now we had been in Rabaul for a year. Though it was not always easy, here and there things started happening. Only to the local people, the Tolai, the door was still closed.

In an old DC-3 Coby and I flew to Buka. There Harold Morton, the MAF pilot, was waiting for us; and we continued in the MAF Cessna from Buka to Tonu. Harold knew the beautiful spots of the island and flew over them as much as possible. He flew past the volcano and circled around it. It was fascinating to see the hot, smoking lava coming out of the crater. He also flew over a deep, almost-round crevice between the mountains. At the bottom of the crevice, we could see a river coming out of a mountain on one side and entering the mountain on the other side. Nobody had been able to discover yet where this underground river originated and where it flowed to. The only place where you could see the river was at the bottom of that crevice which was about a hundred metres wide. Along the east coast of Bougainville, there are gorgeous white beaches. From the sky, we also saw the beautiful deep blue sea with the reefs. The southern west side of Bougainville, in the direction of Siwai, ended in a sort of swamp with mangrove trees that grow in salt water like on Daru. We also flew over the Arawa plantation, where several years later the small city of Arawa would be built. A little while later, Harold pointed out the airport of Tonu. In the jungle, there was an open place with grass, and at the end were a couple of houses and the school for the missionary post. According to regulations, the pilot had to circle the airport once before he landed, to make sure everything was safe. Of course there could be playing children or cattle on the airstrip. We saw a small group of people standing there. They were waiting for us. Landing on a strip like the one in Tonu is always a bit bumpy. But I like that. We were in Siwai, near Tonu, and we were most warmly welcomed. Especially Coby was warmly welcomed. European women do not often come there. During the flight, we spoke with Harold Morton. He knew Pamela Beaumont and also spoke with deep respect about her. However, she was still on leave in New Zealand.

From Tonu, we walked to our first village. The luggage was immediately taken from our hands as they carried it for us. For Coby, this was the first time she came into the villages in the jungle, the real Papua New Guinea! Again it became clear how important it was not to walk into an area or village as a stranger but to have contacts. The Siwai men who studied theology near Rabaul and the other Siwai believers had paved the way with their testimonies.

Also the visit with Kalafi and Rorima in January, the many miracles, and the people who had received the baptism in the Holy Spirit had caused us to be very well accepted. We often had the impression that because we, as European missionaries, believed like they did, this was an enormous encouragement to them. They had received quite a lot of resistance from other Australian and New Zealand Methodist missionaries. Questions that we were often asked during this visit, when we spoke about the baptism in the Holy Spirit, were as follows: Does Osborn believe this too? Does Osborn also preach about the baptism in the Holy Spirit? Is Osborn also filled with the Holy Spirit, and does he speak in tongues? It was very helpful that we knew the answers to these questions. It was special to hear how great the influence of Osborn's books were in Siwai and, as we heard later, in other areas on Bougainville.

I do not remember which village we visited first. I cannot retrieve this from the accounts or newsletters. It was probably Panake, the village where Jacob Neewai was healed of tuberculosis. Anyway, in that village, they had built a small house especially for us. It must really have been quite a lot of work. They had also built a toilet for us near to the house at the edge of the jungle. It consisted of three walls of woven bamboo and leaves. One wall could move; this was the door. There was a deep hole with boards that had an opening. Very often they built such toilets for us in the years to come. We gave such toilets the nickname 'post office', and this stuck. 'I am going to the post office,' we would say. Everyone knew what that meant. Toilet paper was something we had to bring ourselves. Using a certain type of big leaf was not our choice. Besides, toilet paper is not heavy to carry.

Because we spoke Pidgin English quite well, we could alternate between English and Pidgin English depending on who was available to interpret for us. Very soon we learned some Siwai words. The word I still remember is 'mirahu', which means 'good'. When I meet someone from Siwai nowadays, I often say, 'That is someone from Mirahu land.'

For me it was the second time I slept in the villages, but it was Coby's first time. There were so many new impressions: washing our clothes in the river, the food, sleeping in a truly Papua New Guinean home, sleeping on a mat on the floor, experiencing life in the village from so close, and the hospitality and love of the people. Life in a village is totally, and I mean totally, different from the life we were used to. What we noticed quickly was that in their culture, the community is very tight. Within the community of the village, you are safe and accepted. The way people treat the children is heart-warming. We have not seen children who suffered from rejection. You belong to your own family, but you also belong to the extended family, and that bond is really tight too. A cousin is therefore not called 'cousin' but 'brother' and is treated as such. What stands out in village life is the respect for the elderly and the place they have within the community. When elderly people become somewhat forgetful or senile, the people understand it and handle it well. In this tight community life, everyone has specific responsibilities and is aware of them and keeps them.

The people were clearly honoured by the fact that I had brought Coby. When expatriates came, they were mainly men. They had fruit in abundance for us: delicious ripe pineapple, banana, mango, papaya, coconut, and so on. So much tastier and healthier than all the sweet stuff in our Western society.

What especially impressed Coby had touched me too: the openness of the people, their deep, intense hunger for God and how easily they received from God. We just watched it all happen. There was a deep work of God in these people. Often, the people asked us to come to Siwai and live there. We considered it many times, but the Lord had so clearly called us to various parts of the land. We also saw that this was a work of God within their own culture and community. If we were to move there, the people would maybe consciously or subconsciously look up to us and make us their leaders. Then something unique that God was doing in their midst would be hindered by an outsider. Our task was to encourage, give directions, coach, and train. It was a work of God within their culture, and they had to lead it themselves.

During these three weeks, again many people came to Jesus, and many things relating to witchcraft were disposed of. Again many people were healed, and especially many Siwai believers were filled with the Holy Spirit. Often, it happened together with very powerful experiences with God. Praying for the people was not difficult as they received so easily. This time Monturo and Neewai were with us most of the time, and they were a great help.

We visited various villages. Usually we slept in their houses, but some villages had built a house for us. Coby still remembers the hours of walking single file over the narrow trails through the jungle, the beauty of the jungle, its sounds, and the peace of the jungle. On Bougainville, there are no dangerous snakes, so we did not have to worry about that. This was in contrast to the mainland where various dangerous species of snakes are found.

We were asked to pray for several sick people in a village near Panake, Neewai's village. We walked through the jungle for a while, following each other, and suddenly I heard the sound of an engine. That was not possible; there was only a path through the jungle, and there were no engines or motorcycles in the villages. But as we came closer, the sound grew louder and louder. When we arrived at the village, we saw that under a house, there was a red Honda generator running. An electrical wire went up through the floor of split trees. We were allowed to enter the house, and there stood a little fridge containing Fanta. There was supposed to be Coca-Cola in it as well, but unfortunately, it had run out. Coby felt like having a Coke.

How was this possible? We came to bring the gospel but Coca-Cola and Fanta were already there. We learned that a Siwai man had worked at the coast and earned money. The generator, the diesel oil, and the fridge had been carried to the village by the people. The people grew copra and cacao, so they had some money when they sold copra and cacao to the cooperation and were able to buy Fanta or Coca-Cola. The experience was amusing but also a little confronting. Coca-Cola had made it to the village when Christian influence was still very small.

The believers had arranged that we would visit the village Pike in the north of the Siwai District. I had been there before. From Tonu through the jungle, it had been a two-day walk for me. The local people did it in one day; but they walked for eight to ten hours, uphill, downhill, through rivers, and so on. That was too much for me, so we did it in two days with an overnight stay in a village. But now the MAF had begun a missionary flight service. Tonu had an airstrip, and near Pike, they also built a small airstrip near the small government post of Boku. From there, it was only a short walk to Pike Village. You could see it from the airstrip. It had been arranged that the MAF would take us from Tonu to Boku. Harold Morton, the pilot, came to pick us up at the arranged time. I recorded the time the flight took from the moment our wheels left the ground in Tonu until the wheels touched the ground in Boku. You will be surprised . . . six minutes! During my first visit, it took me two days, and I had to hire four carriers to carry my luggage. We now arrived fresh and cheerful and clean. Together with the loading and unloading, it had taken barely twenty minutes. After a short walk, we arrived in Pike; and because we were well rested, we could start our meetings that afternoon and evening. You possibly guessed it, but whenever it was possible, we made use of the special services of the MAF in the years that followed. We deeply respect the workers and pilots of the MAF. In those following years, I once flew to Siwai with another MAF pilot. A week later, he was dead. He had overloaded his plane and therefore could not get out of a valley and crashed into a mountain. During our time in the country, a few MAF planes crashed.

The meetings in Pike were unforgettable. God moved so powerfully. We met the man we had heard so much about, David Pookaro. I had brought a small tape recorder with me; and I had Pookaro, his wife, children, family members, and others who had seen the miracle of his life from close by share his story while I recorded it. None of them had ever seen a tape recorder, and they had to conquer some fear before they allowed me to 'catch their voice'. When we rewound the tape, they heard their own voices which caused great commotion and excitement. We had lots of fun with that tape recorder among the people. Years later, when the large copper mine had been established on Bougainville, nearly everyone carried a tape recorder. But back then with our little recorder, it was the first time they saw such a device. The remarkable story of David Pookaro will be told in the next chapter.

Many villages still had a 'house for men', a place where men would get together and endlessly talk. It was usually quite an open building with a high roof so that a fire could be made and the men could sit under the roof around the fire. Because of the great amount of smoke, the roof, poles, and all the wood were covered with a layer of smoke residue, and there was always the pungent smell of smoke. Especially during the first trips to Siwai, I often spent time in these houses for men. Just underneath the roof, I saw many skulls that were kept there. Those skulls were not of family members as is custom in other tribes or language groups! After several visits to Siwai, I did not see the skulls anymore, and often the houses for men were not rebuilt when they became too old. Part of the culture was disappearing. I never said anything about the skulls; but they were, as far as I know, removed on their own initiative.

In Pike, many believers were filled with the Holy Spirit; and during this trip, several people requested to be baptised by immersion. We had not actually spoken about that yet, but a few of the Siwai believers who lived in Rabaul had been baptised and had spoken about it. We knew that this could cause further conflict with the Methodist Church, but a few believers really desired to be baptised and were specifically asking for it.

Pike was the last village we visited, so we flew back from Boku to Buka after three weeks. During our time in Siwai, something happened which Coby will never forget. We had only been in Siwai for a couple of days, and it was arranged that we would go to a village. We walked for several hours and arrived in the village named Kuting. The pastor of the Methodist Church who was also a leader of the prayer teams was not there. He was visiting his family and would be away for a couple of days. Though we had understood that everything had been arranged, nobody knew we were coming. There was practically no one in the village; the people had gone to their gardens. We were resting for a while, and it looked like we had to go back. We were offered something to drink and some fruit to eat when suddenly Pastor Simon Oko came walking towards us. The night before, he had a dream; and in the dream, he saw that we were in the village. The Lord told him to go back quickly. That morning he got up early and walked for hours. What an encounter. We stayed in his house, and that evening we started the meetings. By using a large drum, the message was spread that we were in the village and that there would be a meeting that evening. That kind of drum, called a 'garamut' in Pidgin, has a sound that carries a long way. In the jungle, you would hear the sound of a garamut every once in a while. And with it they could convey all sorts of messages, and the people knew exactly what the garamut communicated.

God moved in an amazing way that evening. The next morning we held another meeting. We prayed for Simon Oko. He was very powerfully filled with the Holy Spirit and began speaking in new tongues. We also baptised Simon Oko in the river and announced that in the evening, we would have a healing service to pray for the sick.

Late in the afternoon, we were sitting on the small porch of Oko's house. The sun had nearly set. The people had returned early from their gardens. They had prepared food and washed themselves in the river and put on clean clothes to go to the service. They were standing in a long line in front of the porch so we could pray for them.

The people were standing close to us, and suddenly Coby exclaimed, 'Sjoerd, Sjoerd [my native Dutch name], come and see!' I watched and saw the people coming. Coby called out, 'This is what I saw in the dream which I had when I was eight years old.' I knew that dream, but I had not thought about it anymore. Coby was almost beside herself. 'This is what I saw, this village, these homes, these people with their almost-black skin colour.' Coby was stunned. She was now twenty-four years old. As I have mentioned earlier, sixteen years ago in Landsmeer, a small village near Amsterdam, she had a dream and told everyone that she was going to be a missionary. She had always thought that it was Surinam, South America. In the dream, she had also seen that someone was with her, but it was blurry. She had automatically assumed that it was a woman because women who become missionaries do not marry but form a team. What the rest of the meeting was like, I hardly remember because we were so overwhelmed by what had happened. What a confirmation from God! Coby sometimes shares that this gave her such an awareness of the fact that our lives are in God's hands and that He, without us realising it, directs our life. It revealed to her that she was doing God's will and that she was where God wanted her to be. It was now clear: the person who was with her in the dream was a man! If Coby had ever doubted whether or not I was 'the one' for her, something she really does not doubt, then the event in Simon Oko's village would definitely have taken that doubt away. I tease Coby sometimes by asking her if I am still 'blurry' because there is absolutely no doubt about it that I am that person.

That evening Coby told the people of Kuting Village about her dream. The people were deeply touched and moved. God knew the little village of Kuting and the people in Siwai long before. We saw many miracles happen in Simon Oko's village, and Simon continued in the power of the Holy Spirit. I have heard that Oko has passed away and is now with his Lord, but we will never forget him and his village Kuting. The dream Coby had as an eight-year-old girl literally came true!

CHAPTER 15

The Story of David Pookaro

WHEN WE MET the four theology students from Siwai, they told us about the prayer teams and the miracles that God had done through them. In those stories, we repeatedly heard what happened to Pookaro, a man who had taken on the biblical name of David. Altogether I have heard this story more than forty times. Honesty requires me to say that I had real difficulty believing it. But when about forty people tell you the same story about what they have seen with their own eyes, then you realise this is true. I came to believe the story without any doubt when I came to know Pookaro personally. Some years ago, I heard that he passed away. He is now really 'home' with the Lord Jesus. But neither we nor the people of Siwai will ever forget him.

During the second visit to Siwai, I let Pookaro, his wife, and several leaders of the prayer teams, who were there when it happened, tell their story; and I recorded it on a cassette tape. Later in 1969, when we had visited Siwai again, we wrote the story down and sent it to all our prayer partners and other believers who supported us. I will now give you the literal translation of the story, which was in Pidgin English, and which was then recorded on a cassette tape. Here and there I adjusted it a little linguistically so that it is easier to read. This is the story as we sent it to our prayer partners.

In the Siwai District, in South Bougainville, lives a Christian who became one of my best friends. His name is David Pookaro. This is the account of his conversion and how he accepted Jesus Christ into his heart. Before that time, he was an evil person, in the eyes of his own family, his language group, but also in the eyes of God.

Pookaro lived in the village Sikurai where his sinful way of life caused several people to go to prison. He regularly lost control of himself and would get extremely angry and start fighting. He committed adultery many times, and I have reason to believe he raped women more than once.

Preachers of the Methodist Church came to his village, but Pookaro hardly ever went to church. He was too proud and thought he was a strong man who could take care of his own business and did not need God. The few times he did go to church usually resulted in him becoming very angry, because he thought the preachers were focussing especially on him. He did not know the Lord Jesus and did not want to know Him either. The church told the people not to go fishing on Sunday, but Pookaro was disobedient and went fishing or hunting on Sunday but would, on purpose, give nothing to his wife and children.

His wife frequently became really angry with him. Pookaro listened to nobody and lived his own sinful life. One day the men of the village gathered to talk about a small pig breeding farm they wanted to start. After the conversation, Pookaro went to sleep close to the fire. Then something extraordinary happened to him. He woke up because he was feeling very cold, almost as cold as a dead body; and though his wife stirred up the fire, it did not make any difference. Finally he stood up, and while he was looking into the fire, he saw a demon in the form of a woman who had been murdered several weeks before. The devil had sent this demon to mislead Pookaro. Pookaro's mind became severely deranged by this appearance. The demon pointed its finger at him and said, 'You say that I am not here because they buried me, but I say to you now I am here. You know how they killed her with a big stick. Now I say this to you so that you will know.' Pookaro looked in total panic at this demon that he saw and heard speaking. Nobody else in the room saw the demon, but they did hear the voice. A child who was asleep near the fire woke up in fear and panic and started screaming. The mother said that there was nothing going on and told the child to go back to sleep. Pookaro said, 'The demon woke it, and therefore, the child is afraid.'

From the moment Pookaro had seen this appearance, he became crazy and possessed. The next morning he made a huge hole in the roof of his house. Near the house was a 44-gallon (160 litres) drum filled with water. Pookaro jumped off the roof into the drum. 'Where did he go?' everyone asked. They called his name and looked around in search of him. When he jumped into the drum, the water did not splash out; no water came out of the drum! After a while, Pookaro came out of the drum, and he was not injured (he was a small man). Many people saw this happen. Pookaro went back into his house to the place where the food is cooked and broke down the roof. Again he jumped down through some wires without breaking them. The people who were watching were surprised but were also getting scared. A few shouted, 'There is a demon in that man!' His actions really frightened the people. Sometimes he would sit in the fire but would not burn himself. Sometimes he climbed trees and walked on branches that would not normally have been able to support his weight. He did many what we would call 'supernatural things', and the people became more and more scared of him. One day he became very angry and was going to kill one of his (then) four children with a piece of wood. The people ran to the child to save it but also took Pookaro and tied his hands and feet with some rope. Pookaro called out, 'Okay, you have now taken me captive as they did with Jesus. Now I have to stay the way I am now: I will stand on one leg the entire day.' Pookaro was true to his word. From early morning till mid-afternoon, he stood on one leg.

A man in the village said, 'There is a powerful witch doctor in the village Tuurungung. We have to take him to Pookaro to heal him.' In order to cast the demon out of Pookaro, the witch doctor prepared himself by eating certain food and performing all sorts of rituals. As soon as the witch doctor came near the house, Pookaro knew what was going to happen. He said to the witch doctor, 'You think that you are ready to cast this demon out of me. You prepared yourself with witchcraft and by eating certain food. But I do not like this. I think we need to ask a pastor/preacher from a certain village to pray for me.' The preacher of the village came and prayed for him. Pookaro seemed healed and normal and went back home.

Things went well with Pookaro for a few weeks, but then the demon came back, and he became worse than before. The people of the village then threw him out of the village because he was too evil and caused too much harm. From that moment, Pookaro lived on his own in the jungle at a great distance from the village. Sometimes they took him food. One day they went to take food, and they saw that he was sick and dying. They brought him back to the village and hoped that he would die soon so that they would be rid of him. He died shortly afterwards in his village. The people called his family and friends together, dug a grave, and wanted to bury him.

Then something extraordinary happened. Pookaro saw a vision. In this vision, he was walking and came to a fork in the road. There were roads that turned right and roads that turned left, but there was a narrow road that went straight ahead and upwards. There was a large Bible at this narrow road. A man stood nearby and said, 'If you want, you can take this road because it leads to heaven. There are many ways in the world, but there is one way that leads to heaven, and that is the way of the Bible. When you walk this road, you must walk carefully and attentively because the road is narrow. You cannot look right or left or back because then you will fall. You can only look ahead, and you must pay attention to every step you take.'

Pookaro saw how he started to walk on this road. The road went up higher and higher until he came to an open place where a Person was sitting. That Person was whiter and lighter than a European and shone more brightly than the sun. The light beamed and shone in all directions from this Person. The light blinded Pookaro's eyes, and he realised this Person was Jesus.

He fell down at His feet like someone who has no more strength. Then the Lord Jesus spoke to him and said, 'Stand on your feet!' When Pookaro stood up, he could not see clearly, but the Lord Jesus touched his eyes, and then he saw clearly. The Lord said, 'Pookaro, look to your left and to your right, look in front of Me, look behind Me, and look up. Do you see anyone?' Pookaro said, 'No, Lord.' Then the Lord said, 'That is true because I am the Only One, the Almighty!' The Lord continued, 'Come and see My hand.' In the hand he could see the wound of a large nail. The Lord continued, 'This hand was nailed to the cross so that you could be saved and be forgiven. First you did not believe in Me, and you committed many sins. But now you will believe in Me and accept Me in your life. After that, you must preach the gospel. If you do this, I will especially bless you, and soon you will reign for a thousand years with Me [Pookaro still does not know what the Lord meant with those thousand years]. If you do not obey My Word and do not preach the gospel, you will become dust.' Pookaro solemnly promised the Lord that he would preach the gospel.

In the meantime, the people were standing around his body and wanted to put his body in the grave. Some cried but more out of superstition than out of grief. Suddenly Pookaro opened his eyes and sat up. The people were terrified and were so shocked that a few nearly fainted. I have actually spoken, during my first and second visit to Siwai and during the many visits that followed, to people who were there and who ran for hours to get away from the grave that had been dug for Pookaro and away from the dead man who suddenly sat up straight. Some did not dare to go back to the village that same evening. They were in total panic about what they had seen happening. It took some people a long time before they dared to meet Pookaro.

Pookaro stood up in the grave, took a knife, and walked to a tree. He chopped off a few branches and walked to an open place in the village. He marked a spot and said, 'Here we are going to build a church, and here we will preach the gospel.' Then he told the people of what had happened to him, how he had met the Lord Jesus, and what the Lord Jesus had said to him. The people were absolutely stunned about what was happening. As soon as they could, they started building a church. They chopped wood, bought cement, and brought it to the village and started building. After a few weeks, the building was complete, one of the very few buildings with a concrete floor. According to native custom, they had to have a great celebration to dedicate the building. Pookaro, who started calling himself David more often, gave his wife the task of killing their only pig and preparing it for the celebration. His wife protested because it was their only and last pig. David told her that if she was disobedient, the pig would die because the pig was for the work of God. When he went to see how things were going a while later, his wife told him the pig had died. Pookaro answered, 'I told you that it would die if you were disobedient.' David went to the pig and prayed for the pig, and it came back to life. Then they killed and prepared it for the celebration and dedicated the church.

Shortly afterwards, Monturo and a group in a neighbouring village held a meeting where they prayed for the sick. David heard about it and was excited. He wondered why he had not heard about this before. He said to himself, *I have to go there and learn more of the Bible.* In that meeting, he went forward to repent and was saved and powerfully touched by the Holy Spirit, when Monturo laid hands on him. From that moment on, David Pookaro was filled with compassion for lost people and the sick. He went from village to village and delivered a fiery testimony of what had happened. After a while, he ordered someone to go to a place where he could buy a Bible. That person came back with a big black King James Bible. Though Pookaro could not read or write, he always carried that Bible with him because he strongly believed that a soldier could never be without his weapons.

He prayed for many people, and great miracles happened. Near his village lived an older man who was dying. His family sent someone to call the Catholic priest. He said that he would come when they paid six dollars. The priest prayed for the man and said the man would go to heaven. David heard about this and became very angry because he knew that this man did not really believe and was not saved. David Pookaro went to the house of the dying man and prayed for him, and the Lord healed that man in one moment. The people were happy and excited. David told them more about Jesus. Several days later, the priest came and asked when the man had died and where they had buried him. When the people told the priest that David Pookaro had prayed for the man and that he was healed, the priest became very angry. 'This is witchcraft,' he said, and the priest went to the assistant district commissioner (ADC), the second highest Australian government official in Bougainville. He wanted to take David Pookaro to court to stop him from praying for the sick. But the Lord was at work. During the small trial, the ADC said, 'This is not witchcraft. I know this man. This is the work of the Holy Spirit!' The ADC then gave David Pookaro a letter which said that he had permission to pray for the sick and that no one was allowed to stop his work as an evangelist! We personally saw and read this letter signed by the ADC.

David Pookaro has won many people for Jesus. We met many people, also outside of Siwai, whom he led to Jesus. Various times David was asked to come to the hospital in Buin to pray for people, and miracles happened. We know that he had raised twice someone from the dead. One day he was asked to pray for a dying woman. When he came there, the people told him that the woman had just died. Many people had come to the house to cry and lament; this was just like the customs in the time of Jesus. Pookaro remembered what Jesus did when Jairus's daughter died. He went into the house and sent everyone outside. Then he knelt down and prayed for a long time. God answered his fiery prayer, and the woman came back to life. Then David returned to this village to preach. During our last (third) visit to Siwai, David had just been to the hospital to pray for a man with tuberculosis. He told the man about Jesus and prayed for him. Instead of staying in the hospital for a year, as he had been told, the man could now go home, totally healed. He has since accepted Jesus and was baptised. One evening, after we had preached, David prayed for a woman who was nearly blind. She was healed.

David Pookaro is now baptised in water himself and filled with the Holy Spirit. David had never heard about the biblical baptism by immersion. During his baptism, he saw a light coming from heaven to the place where he had been baptised. Praise the Lord! God's Spirit rests on this small, unlearned, but extraordinary man. We have grown to love him very much. He now preaches in many places. In the village where he now lives, Pike Village, he is busy building a church. His wife is now baptised in water as well. Their lives are an example to so many people. We thank the Lord for this small man in whom He has done such a mighty work. When David Pookaro shares his testimony (we heard and saw him do that many times), he often starts to cry. Jesus means everything to him. God has used him in a great and amazing way among his own people of the island Bougainville.

This is the story as we wrote it down in 1969 and sent it to our contacts. There are several interesting facts I would like to mention. Pookaro had four children before he died, met Jesus, and came back to life. After that, he and his wife had four more children. As far as we know, all the children follow the Lord; but between the first four children and the second four children, you can see a clear difference.

David Pookaro met Monturo shortly after his experience, and Monturo told him what had happened on the Solomon Islands during his training as village pastor. Monturo told him about Osborn and gave David Pookaro a book that contained many pictures of the great Osborn Crusades and the miracles. When David Pookaro prayed for someone, he first put the old, almost worn-out book by Osborn on the head of the person; then he put his hands on the book and prayed. When we met David Pookaro, I asked him not to do that because Brother Osborn has nothing to do with the healing: Jesus is the Healer. From that moment on, David Pookaro first put the big black Bible on the head of the person he prayed for and then put his hands on the Word of God. I tried to explain to David that that was not necessary, but I had no success. He always put the Bible on the head first and then his hands on the Word of God. Maybe there is something to be said for that . . .

David Pookaro always carried his Bible with him. This led sometimes to humorous moments. When, for example, I said that I would read from Matthew 18, then David would watch how many pages I had turned left and how many I turned right, and he would copy that so it seemed that he was reading along too, but he could not read. More than once I saw David with apparently the right amount of pages turned over left and right in his Bible but with the Bible upside down! We were often amused by Pookaro and had a lot of fun with him.

In Buin, a secondary school was built; and an Australian teacher named John, who was a Spirit-filled Anglican, came to work there and wanted to get in touch with us. He had heard the story of Pookaro but could not believe it. In his class were some Siwai students. At the end of the school year, they had an evening in which the students performed dramas they had created themselves. The evening arrived; and John, the teacher, was stunned when the Siwai students performed the story of Pookaro in a play. How he became crazy, died, came back to life, and started preaching. John later told me, 'I just have to believe the story of Pookaro. These students were not just doing something crazy.' If I still doubted, and I have not done that for quite some time, then also with me, just like with the teacher John, the remainder of any doubt would have been removed.

CHAPTER 16

Kavieng and . . . Back to Siwai

AFTER THREE WEEKS, Coby and I were back in Rabaul, but it took us a while to really 'land'. Our bodies were in Rabaul, but our hearts were still in Siwai. For a period of three weeks, we had seen God move in such special ways. It was my second time in Siwai, but it was the first time for Coby. We saw miracles happen before our very eyes, and it all was so easy. For Coby, this was the first time that she saw it happen like this. We had seen miracles before, but in Bougainville, so many miracles and healings happened, and more and more people were filled with the Holy Spirit. It was all so normal among the Siwai believers. It was a deep work of the Holy Spirit. There were many Siwai people who had met God personally and had experienced a deep work of God in their life. They were free from the darkness and wrong aspects of their culture. They paid the price to seek God, and touched Him. Such people are a key to see a deep work of God in a people group. Missionaries can come, but when the people themselves break through, then that is a deep work of God.

The trip to Siwai was not only special to Coby because she had seen God work in such ways but was also special because the dream that she had had as an eight-year-old girl was literally fulfilled before her eyes. That was a major event. Though Coby had no doubt that she was serving God at the right place, the experience in Kuting Village made her more certain that she was at the right place and doing with her life what God had intended for her.

We experienced blessing in Rabaul, especially on the plantations; but we longed intensely for a breakthrough among the original people from Rabaul, the Tolai, as it happened among the Siwai people on Bougainville. Coby and I had had the desire for a while to spend a good amount of time in prayer and fasting for the work in and around Rabaul. We were now able to do so because we had help.

In the meantime, we had been able to buy a little second-hand offset printing machine of a Chinese trader. He taught me to how to make simple offset prints, and we started making and printing our own gospel tracts. I had spent many hours beside that little machine. We printed thousands of tracts and lessons. When I enter a printing office and hear the machines, I feel the excitement again. Reading matter is so powerful. My knowledge was of course limited, and multiple times we had to pray for insight about how this little offset machine worked. The Holy Spirit apparently knows all about offset printing machines...

Peter, a man of mixed race who came to the Lord in Rabaul, came originally from Kavieng on the island of New Ireland. When the Lord spoke to me two years earlier that night in Port Moresby, the Lord mentioned Rabaul, then Kavieng and Bougainville, and finally the mainland. We lived in Rabaul and had been to Bougainville twice, but it was clear that sooner or later we would go to Kavieng as well. That's how the plan emerged to go to Kavieng with Peter. Kalafi and Tapu would stay in Rabaul with their daughter. Kari Harri, Peter, and I would go to Kavieng for about ten days. We prepared everything and prayed much before we left. We flew from Rabaul to Kavieng, a forty-five-minute flight.

Peter had many friends, family, and acquaintances in Kavieng and took us along to everyone he knew. Soon we had many friendly contacts, and we could testify and even pray for people here and there. Kavieng reminded me of Daru. But to me Kavieng is much more beautiful. It is a government post, and in the middle of this outgrown government post was a large field. We decided to have an open-air crusade there. We sent a telegram to Rabaul, and two days later, we had our sound installation, projector and films, and some lights. We had received permission for meetings from government officials who had heard about us. We had contact with the radio station in Rabaul. For several days, they broadcast a message that there would be an evangelistic crusade on the open field in the middle of Kavieng.

And so we started. The first evening already many people came, we estimated around one thousand or more people. That is quite something when you realise that Kavieng only had 2,500 inhabitants at that time. Many people had come from the villages around Kavieng and even from the islands around Kavieng. Many people knew Peter, the man of mixed race who had come with us to Kavieng. They quietly listened when Peter shared his testimony. Alcohol had played a large part in his life, but Peter had met Jesus. Many people prayed with us when we prayed the sinner's prayer that evening. There was an evident presence of the Holy Spirit. Only later we would hear that that evening, one of the most infamous drunks of Kavieng and his wife asked the Lord Jesus to come into their life. Later we got to know this man, his dear wife, and his children well.

The second evening we again estimated a crowd of more than one thousand people. The Holy Spirit was very present. Kari Harri, who spoke Pidgin English fluently, preached. We showed a film, and again many people prayed when Kari prayed the sinner's prayer. A boy with a very painful leg was healed, and faith began to arise in the hearts of the people.

Right before the third evening, it started to rain. But when the service began, the rain stopped. Again about one thousand people had come. Again many people prayed the sinner's prayer. An old man with a thick, swollen foot was healed in an instant and walked without pain. There was much joy among the people. They saw God working. It promised to be a powerful crusade.

The fourth evening arrived. About 1,500 people had come. Kavieng is a place where nearly everyone speaks Pidgin English well. They sang with us and clapped their hands. There was a joyous atmosphere in the meeting. Suddenly a white man entered the service, grabbed the microphone, and began ridiculing the gospel and shouting in rude language. I was able to turn off the sound installation just in time. Only a few people heard his words, but they saw what was happening.

Nearby a few police officers were standing. They watched but did not do anything.

Then a white man drove his car onto the field and started driving around the people that had gathered. The windows of the car were open. A man who was clearly drunk started to shout loudly. We were liars, imposters, God could not do miracles, and the miracles that happened were lies. Again the police did nothing. In the years at Papua New Guinea, we were often ashamed about the behaviour of white people, and I've been ashamed more than once about being white. But after driving several circles around the people, the man left. The peace and rest returned, and the meeting continued. Karri began preaching, and then it happened. Suddenly a police car came with their flashing lights and drove into the meeting till just before the microphone where Karri was preaching. The white police officer stepped out of the car and loudly shouted, 'Stop immediately or you will be arrested!' I asked why. We had to stop, and the police officer mumbled something from which we concluded that the sound was too loud. Later we heard that several Catholic leaders had protested against the service. 'But we have permission from the district commissioner, the government official in the district.' I tried to talk with the police officer, but it did not work. We had to stop immediately. 'Okay, we will pray and then stop,' I answered.

'If you pray, you will be arrested,' the police responded.

Kari prayed for the people, the police, and the government officials. We were not arrested. We did have to report ourselves at the police station the next morning. The crusade had ended. The people were angry with the police. Some almost fought the police, and we had to calm some people here and there. Other people cried. The police left. We stayed behind for a long time and prayed with the people. There were even some evident healings. We promised to return to Kavieng as soon as possible. The people promised to pray for us. Hundreds of people were hungry and longing for the gospel, but a few white people could stop everything. Sadly this is quite typical of what happened sometimes before independence came in 1975.

The next morning we went to the police station as we had been told. We also spoke to some government officials. It was evident that the police had exceeded their power. Several government officials were afraid that we would file an official complaint about the behaviour of the police. However, we did not get permission to continue with the services. We were allowed to go to the villages outside of Kavieng. In Kavieng, we had been able to get electricity on the large field; but in the villages, there was no electricity. We would need a generator, and we did not have one with us. We therefore decided to go back to Rabaul. The people in Rabaul heard what had happened as well. Because of the event, the nationalistic feelings were strengthened. We had to watch out because we could become a puppet between the people of Papua New Guinea and a white colonial government. A white solicitor in Rabaul whom we knew advised us to file a complaint against the police. We did not do that because we know that when the Lord is not fighting for you, it is all useless.

We had to wait for two days before there were seats available on a flight to Rabaul. Friends of Peter allowed us to stay in a vacant house near the airport. I had brought a book of the Bible teacher E. W. Kenyon. Kalafi had told us about his books and teaching. We had never heard of him. I had read a book of him and greatly enjoyed it. The book I had with me was called *The Two Kinds of Righteousness*. The afternoon before we would go back to Rabaul, I was reading about the righteousness that we receive by faith. God, the Father, had made His Son Jesus to be sinful with our sin so that we would receive His righteousness. God does not only see us as forgiven people but as believers who are righteous with the righteousness of His own Son. That is how God sees us! I read the chapter, I read the parts of the Bible, and I saw it. I saw what I knew in theory and also believed, but I saw it in my innermost being. I sat for a long time in that house with the book on my lap. I was stunned, excited, deeply touched, incredibly happy, but also filled with a deep awe and incredible thankfulness to God. I had a revelation. A revelation about the righteousness of God that we receive by His grace in Christ. I cannot remember the rest of the day. I was in another world, almost taken up in the Spirit, one could say. I saw it, I saw it, I saw it. I had never seen it this way before. I knew that I was forgiven, I knew with my head that God loved me, but I sometimes felt quite inferior and would then have the tendency deep inside to try even harder because I really wanted God to be happy with me. I wanted to do my best. But that afternoon I understood how God sees me. After several hours of prayer, I said trembling, 'Thank You, God, that You see me as righteous, not with my own righteousness but with the righteousness of Your Son Jesus Christ.' Somewhere I expected a flash of lightning from heaven to hit me for praying this prayer. But no lightning came from heaven. Instead, a deep and great joy rose up inside of me. I prayed it again and again and again. God has made me righteous with the righteousness of Jesus, and nobody can improve that righteousness or add to it. A better and greater righteousness does not exist, and God has put my sin on Jesus and gave me that righteousness. I can appear before God with absolute boldness and without inferiority or feelings like guilt and shame. For days I lived in another dimension. Righteousness is not just a biblical truth to me but a precious, very precious revelation from God. I saw it, and I got it. I knew it. I could shout for joy. David prays in the Psalms, 'Open to me the gates of righteousness: I will go into them, and I will praise the Lord' (Psalms 118:19).

I sometimes preach about seven or eight events that were a turning point and milestone in my life as a Christian, and this is one of them. The first was the deliverance of fear and panic when Coby prayed for me, the second was the lesson about forgiveness that God gave to Coby and which we made our own, and the third was this revelation about righteousness. Later another turning point and milestone would be added when I made a trip to Daru, and during the time we lived in Kavieng.

I could shout it from the rooftops: God has made me righteous in Christ. When years later I heard Derek Prince speak about the great exchange on the cross, my sins for His righteousness, I learned that sermon just about by heart, made it my own, and preached it very often.

In Rabaul, we received letters from people of Kavieng. They asked us to return quickly. We even received a letter from a boy that had accepted the Lord Jesus after reading one of our tracts. We also received a letter in typical Pidgin English. The man wrote about his physical condition and said that he had no more blood in his body, an expression that means that you are very weak. Only we did not know that expression yet, and we had to ask around for a bit before someone knew what it meant. Two weeks later, Peter and I went back to Kavieng. This time we went to several villages surrounding Kavieng. The people were happy that we had returned. In the meantime, an Australian couple that belonged to a Pentecostal church had moved to Kavieng where the husband did technical work. We could stay at their place. This happened a lot throughout the years. White, often Australian or New Zealand people, with a desire to do something for Papua New Guinea would take up a job in the country. In that way we were able to build very good friendships. We enjoyed their hospitality, and often they helped financially in the work. These people were a real blessing to us but also for the country.

In a village near Kavieng we held services. People came to Jesus, and the sick were healed. A deaf woman could hear again after prayer. A man with much pain in his body was healed. We met the infamous, now ex-drunk and his wife who had accepted Jesus in the first campaign, Percy and Margaret, names that became very precious to us throughout the years. At the time of translating this book into English, we heard that Margaret and Percy are with the Lord Jesus, home in heaven.

One Sunday we were allowed to preach in a small village church of the Methodists. Fourteen people came forward to choose for Jesus. An elder of the village came forward and testified that though he acted as if he were Christian, he was still living in sin but that he had now really chosen for Jesus. Not much later, the Lord healed him of painful legs.

We looked in and around Kavieng for a rental house or a piece of land to build on but could not find anything. But deep in our hearts, we knew it. Kavieng would be our next mission post.

We ourselves but also Kari Harri, Peter, and others went to Kavieng regularly to encourage the believers. More and more it became clear that someone had to go and live there.

At the end of June, Kalafi and Tapu Moala and their little girl Lisa left Rabaul. They went to Goroka where for two months a large evangelism outreach would be held by Youth with a Mission. A team of young people from Australia and New Zealand was coming. It was a pity that they left. We loved them and got along really well. Later, when they moved to the capital, Port Moresby, we again had much contact with them.

Peter and Norma were given a job as plantation manager on one of the islands of the Duke of York Islands, a group of islands between Rabaul, which is on New Britain, and the south of New Ireland. There was sufficient plain accommodation on their plantation named Makada. Coby and I went there to have a time of prayer and fasting for the future but especially for the original inhabitants of the district surrounding Rabaul, the Tolai people. That breakthrough eventually came, but then we no longer lived in Rabaul. During the visits after our stay of fourteen years in Papua New Guinea, we visited Rabaul several times. Especially within the existing Uniting Church, the former Methodist Church, a great work of God was happening. John Wesley, the man of God who started the Methodist Church, would, we think, be very happy about the movement of God's Spirit that came among the Tolai people.

After a time of prayer and fasting, we came back to Rabaul. We started to prepare ourselves for the third visit to Siwai, a visit of four weeks. After Bougainville, we wanted to visit Kavieng again. In the meantime, the second Finnish couple, Lauri and Martha Pesu, had moved to Rabaul. We got to know Lauri and Martha as very sweet, warm, hospitable people, genuine Finnish couple. In the period that we knew them, we drank many cups of coffee and tea at their place and ate 'pulla', a kind of cake that the Finns bake at every occasion, and which we liked!

In October, Coby and I went to Siwai again for four weeks. Letters had been written far in advance, and messages had been sent that we would come. We had been in touch with pilot Harold Morton of the MAF to bring us from Buka to Tonu. This trip would be special because from the Oral Roberts organisation in Sydney, which was led by Norman Armstrong, we had received a second lightweight projector and a small generator especially so we could take them inland to the villages. The small generator was just able to make the projector work. We had two colour films of T. L. Osborn that had been recorded during large campaigns. The films were in English, but we would turn the sound almost off, and I would translate into Pidgin English, which went well. On the films, there was a short sermon but mainly testimonies of people who were healed, often great unmistakable miracles.

One of the films was *Holland Wonder*, recorded in 1958 during the great and massive Osborn campaign in the Hague. That's how we repeatedly saw a bit of the Netherlands in the jungle. It remained amusing to us Holland people to hear the typical Dutch sound of a Dutch street organ in the jungle. I was never able to figure out how the people of Papua New Guinea felt about street organ music. I was always under the impression that they thought it was a bit strange, but from their perspective, we white people have and did more strange things. The other Osborn film we brought was about Ghana and actually came closer to their culture.

Coby and I flew to Buka, where Harold Morton with the MAF Cessna was waiting for us and loaded all our luggage in the plane, our projector, generator, films, and small sound installation. We had permission to bring a can of petrol for the generator in the small plane. We circled over Siwai and landed in Tonu, but there were no Siwai believers waiting for us. The staff of the mission post in Tonu did come to the plane because the pilot had brought some letters for them. I had already met the missionary couple during my first visit. They were not happy with the prayer teams and the attention given to the Holy Spirit in all of Siwai. With them was a woman, about fifteen years older than us, who greeted us and introduced herself. Her name was Pamela Beaumont. So this was the woman about whom the prayer teams had spoken and of whom they said that this missionary was happy with everything that was happening. Pamela was clearly reserved in greeting us, but the look in her eyes was warm and friendly.

Several months later, Pamela would receive the baptism in the Holy Spirit; and within several years, she would be used in a special way by God in Siwai but also in other parts of Bougainville. Pamela would also become a very personal friend of ours. I desired to speak with this woman, but it was clear that this would have to happen some other time. Pamela still remembers the moment we met well, but she could do no more than restrain herself and wait for a moment that we would be able to talk. The missionary post in Tonu was not a place where we were particularly welcome. But several years later, the then four foreign staff members led by Pamela Beaumont were filled with the Holy Spirit; and we have had many times of prayer, worship, and study in Tonu. The missionary post became a place where the Holy Spirit moved and was present in a very special way as, we think, God intended it.

From a distance, a man of the village had seen our arrival and had seen how Pamela Beaumont had shaken our hands and greeted us. This man, who was very intimidating but confessed to be a Christian, was still deeply involved in witchcraft. Shortly afterwards, he spoke to Pamela Beaumont and put a curse on her in her presence. When we got to know Pamela a few months later, we had to set her free from this intimidating curse that this man had put on her. The man really set himself against the work of the Holy Spirit and has made quite a scene more than once when we arrived on the little airstrip of Tonu. Once he almost beat me on the airstrip of Tonu. A few years later, I baptised him after he had powerfully repented. I felt a little like Ananias who baptised Paul.

Though there were no people waiting for us, we unloaded because the pilot had to go somewhere else. More flights had been booked that day. We were allowed to wait at the missionary post of Tonu. Two hours later, Joshua Monturo came walking up to us happy and cheerful. The letters had not reached him nor the others, but that morning he had heard the MAF airplane and seen how it circled above Siwai. The Holy Spirit had told him that we were on the plane, so immediately he started walking to Tonu. It was so good to see Monturo again. The missionary was not happy at all with Monturo because he was the one who had started it all, but Monturo did not care about that. We left most of our luggage behind at the missionary post of the Methodist Church and walked for two and a half hours to the village where we would start. We arrived in the village, but there was no one, except for a few children and elderly people. The pastor with whom we would stay also was not there. We waited again, and an hour later, the pastor came walking up to us elated and happy. He was visiting his family for several days in another village, but that night he had a dream and saw us in his village. The next morning he immediately started walking back to his village. He too had not received the letter and the message that we would come. In areas like Siwai, we often wondered what works better: our Western way of communication like letters or prayer and the Holy Spirit that warns and leads people. The latter seemed more reliable among the Siwai people than the former.

We held services in various villages and showed the Osborn films. That was a great success, to say the least. Hardly anyone had ever seen a film, and it was the first time in all villages that a film was shown. The people had heard of films, but we had to explain multiple times what films are and that what they saw had really happened. But there was one film service in the village of David Pookaro, which was very humorous.

Pookaro always carried that old book from Osborn with him. In that book were quite a few black-and-white pictures of mass campaigns and of people who were healed but also pictures of Osborn himself. When the film was shown in Pookaro's village and he saw how T. L. Osborn began preaching on the film, Pookaro ran up and down, totally excited, and shouted things like 'That's him! There is Osborn! That is the man of God about whom we have been told!' I tried several times to calm Pookaro down because I had to translate through a small sound installation, but it did not work. Pookaro was totally excited. When on the film the testimonies came and he saw people who were healed by God, he became even more excited. He jumped up and down, loudly screaming and running through the service. It was very amusing. It was also the first time that Pookaro ever saw a film. He saw the film many times, but it was always a feast when Pookaro saw a film about Osborn. About a year later, we would have five more Osborn films translated into Pidgin English, and that made it even more humorous and effective.

During this visit to Siwai, more people were converted, filled with the Holy Spirit, and baptised in water. Siwai was really a people group that was as a ripe harvest. All we had to do was harvest. Several villages had now built a house for us. That was nice and gave us some rest now and then. Often, there were three, four, or even six services in one day.

From early in the morning until the evening, people came to hear God's Word and to receive from God.

Of course we had to promise to come back soon again. Our main contacts were Joshua Monturo and Jacob Neewai, who had been healed of tuberculosis during the first visit. He was full of fire and had established several new congregations. The Holy Spirit worked, and it was a fire that kept spreading. Also the language group just north of Siwai, the Nagovisi, invited us; and we could have film services in their villages. In Nagovisi was a small missionary post of the former Methodist Church, but at the moment there was no missionary. When we went to Siwai again, Pamela Beaumont had been sent to this small missionary post with her co-worker Stephen Iroro. He helped her with the translation of the New Testament in the Siwai language. Stephen was a son of the man who years before had been given as a peace child to an enemy tribe and had returned as a missionary to Siwai. Stephen too became someone whom God would use very specially in the work in Siwai.

After four weeks, we had to go back to Rabaul. Rabaul was spiritually, apart from the plantations, a cold shower after Siwai. We longed intensely to see in and around Rabaul like we experienced in Siwai.

The Pesus encouraged us to visit the Finnish migrant churches in Australia and to tell them about the work in Papua New Guinea. Coby and I never sought a travelling ministry; it simply just started, often out of dire necessity to raise more funds. We decided to make that journey to Australia in November and December. The work in Rabaul was now mainly done by the Finnish missionaries. Joseph Yans and Philip Kawai had finished their contract at the plantation but had stayed in Rabaul and helped the Finnish missionaries with the work. We had no idea that the Lord had something more in mind than a visit to the Finnish migrant churches in Australia. During that trip, the Lord would deeply touch our lives and turn our whole life upside down, but more about that later.

I was twenty-four years old when this al happened. Often, I thought about that first service in Amsterdam in which the preacher prophesied, 'At a young age I will call you in My service and at a young age you will be in My service.'

CHAPTER 17

Australia – The Lord Turns Our Lives Upside Down

THE JOURNEY TO the Pentecostal churches of the Finnish emigrants started in Mount Isa, quite a big mining city in the state Queensland. When the plane descended, the sun was just about to set. The inland of Australia is very dry and desert-like, and because of that, there is often much dust in the air. This causes magnificently coloured sunsets.

In Mount Isa, we held several services. The Finnish people were very hospitable and warmly welcomed us and did everything they could so that we would be comfortable. We went for a picnic some distance away from Mount Isa, and from a high point, we could look out over the desert landscape. We never would like to live in that desert, but it was impressive to see.

The Finnish believers had organised evangelism services and had advertised well for it. They had rented a Baptist church because their own building where they held services was not big enough. Quite a few people came, among them a couple that would later be uniquely used by God in Papua New Guinea: Hilding and Ingrid Ericksson, originally from Sweden, but who migrated to Australia.

Just outside of Mount Isa, Hilding and Ingrid had a large chicken farm, and they were doing very well socially and financially. However, because of disappointments and the pressure and demands of the company, their faith in God was at a low tide. They did sometimes go to church on Sunday, but that was about it. One day Ingrid read in the newspaper about a service in which a young Dutch missionary couple would give a presentation about their work in Papua New Guinea. It did not let Ingrid go. Papua New Guinea!

It took her a while to persuade Hilding to come with her, but that evening they were in the Baptist church. We told about our work and showed slides including slides from Siwai. I shared the story of David Pookaro. According to Hilding, I then said, 'There is someone here who needs a miracle from God in your body; and God wants to touch you now, here tonight, just as He touched those people.' At that moment, the Holy Spirit touched Hilding, and he was healed from a heart condition. Hilding felt the power of God 'slap' him, and the pain left him. He knew that God spoke to him. Hilding later told us how several days later, while he was working in his company, everything suddenly became quiet; and he heard a voice that said, 'I have blessed your company. I have seen your business. But if you will go to Papua New Guinea, I will especially bless you.' Hilding was stunned. He heard the voice very clearly. The next day it happened again. He was busy with the machine that had to arrange food for five thousand chickens. All became quiet, and again there was an audible voice that spoke to him and asked him to go to Papua New Guinea. He knew that he had to give up his company and everything and go to that country as a missionary. He told Ingrid about it, and they decided to go. Hilding was in his late forties when this happened. We had no idea what had happened that evening in the Baptist church in the lives of this Swedish couple, but we certainly would know it later.

Hilding had an elder brother, Ludwig, who lived in Cairns. As a young man, God had shown Ludwig a vision and called him to work as a missionary in Papua New Guinea. Ludwig and Hilding grew up in a Pentecostal family. Shortly after the year 1900, the Pentecostal movement came to Sweden, but the Pentecostal church had no missionary work in Papua New Guinea. Whatever Ludwig did, he could find no church or organisation that could send him to Papua New Guinea. Ludwig and his wife decided to migrate to Australia because that was near Papua New Guinea; and then they would, so they thought, find a way from

Australia to the country of their calling. They migrated to Australia, and eventually they arrived in Cairns, and his younger brother later moved to Mount Isa. Because of Hilding's experience of healing in the service and later, when he heard God's audible voice, Ludwig went to Papua New Guinea as well. Hilding and Ingrid's story is so special that it deserves a separate chapter.

Lauri Pesu, the Finnish missionary who had come to Rabaul, had left a car behind in Mount Isa. He had lived there for a short time and had been pastor of the Finnish church before he came to Papua New Guinea. We could use that car for the trip in Australia, and from Mount Isa, we went to Brisbane by car, a journey of about thirty hours. I still enjoy driving long distances, preferably at night. In Australia, especially on the inland roads, it is very quiet, you get the feeling that you have the road all to yourself. The nights are often incredibly beautiful, and you can see numerous stars. Furthermore, it's cool at night, so the car engine runs much better. Two other people joined us, and we took turns driving. I drove around midnight when I saw a wallaby (a small kangaroo) jumping, and I realised that it would cross the road. I slowed down, but the wallaby did so too, and it seemed that it would wait at the side of the road. So I accelerated again, but the wallaby did so too, and a big smash was the consequence. Luckily the car had a bull bar for protection on the front. Everyone woke up. You don't stop because a wounded wallaby can attack you, and a dead wallaby is food for the birds of prey. In total, it happened to us four times throughout the years that our car hit a wallaby.

In Brisbane, we held services with the Finns but also met several Dutch people from the group that we had been in touch with before. The group no longer existed; most had become part of a Pentecostal church which had been deeply touched by the new movement of the Holy Spirit, which had started in New Zealand, but was now also touching Australia. Hank and Lenie van der Steen had joined that church too.

From Brisbane, we went to Sydney, and there happened several special things. I preached in a Finish church. I preached in English and was translated into Finnish by a female member of the congregation. In one of the services, I had preached and had invited people who desired prayer to come forward. Three people came for prayer, among them a boy of about fifteen years old. I asked Coby to come and help me, and she started praying for this boy, while I prayed for a lady. Suddenly Coby became very moved and spoke somewhat loud in tongues. I knew how she normally speaks in tongues, but this sounded different. I could not pay attention to it because I had to pray for someone else. Though the Finnish congregation was a Pentecostal congregation, I was aware that it was not as open to the work of the Holy Spirit as most Pentecostal churches are. There were Finnish migrants in the church who had difficulty with the manifestations of the Holy Spirit. I kept praying for the lady, but the music that had been playing softly had stopped, and it was dead quiet in the church. Everyone was listening. Coby spoke in tongues for quite some time while she prayed for this boy and then stopped. The pastor immediately came to us. Coby had spoken in Finnish and even in classical Finnish that foreigners never learn, a kind of 'King James Finnish'. Her message in tongues was a prophecy in Finnish to the congregation. The essence of the message was that the Lord asked them to be open to His Spirit; they had to give His Spirit room and opportunity to work. We were all surprised. Coby doesn't speak a word of Finnish but had spoken in tongues in the Finnish language. Our visit to this Finish migrant church in Sydney made a great impression, and nobody could deny how supernatural it was what had happened. We had heard stories of these sorts of miracles, but now it happened in our own lives, and you never forget that.

Another thing happened in Sydney that greatly impacted us. We knew Pastor Norman Armstrong of the Australian office of the American evangelistic movement of Oral Roberts. Every month this Australian branch organisation held a healing service in Sydney, and Norman Armstrong had asked us to preach that month because we were in Sydney anyway. We accepted the invitation, and we felt very honoured to be able to do so.

The service was held on a Saturday afternoon. About 300 people had come. After a time of singing, I preached. I shared about the miracles on Bougainville. It made an impression, and there was real expectation and faith among the people. Then came the time to pray for the sick. There were several pastors and leaders in the service including Dean Sherman from Youth with a Mission. Later the people who did not know us well would often confuse the two of us; we were both slim, and we both had 'red' hair. I did not have a beard or moustache yet.

Norman Armstrong had arranged that the four of us would pray for the people. True to the method of the famous evangelist Oral Roberts, the people had to fill out a prayer card so that we could read the card and then pray. So no conversation, only short questions at the most. We were standing left on the stage, and I led the prayer. The people stood in line and came on stage one by one via small stairs. We prayed for that person, and the person would walk over the stage to the right side and via stairs would go back to his or her seat.

We had prayed for several people when a young woman walked onto the stage. Later we learned she was nineteen years old. She was very slim and a bit small for her age. On her card she had written that she suffered from asthma. She was a Christian and attended a Pentecostal church. However, there was something strange about this young woman. Anyway, we prayed, and she began to walk to the other side of the stage to the stairs to go back to her seat. I looked at her; something seemed wrong with this young woman. When she was near the stairs, all of a sudden it looked like an invisible hand lifted her up and threw her like a missile ten to fifteen metres through the air over the stage, where she smacked into the wall and collapsed to the ground. She began to scream and screech with a sound which resembled that of a pig that is slaughtered.

Dean Sherman walked up to her to help her, but she was already on her feet again and grabbed Dean with one hand and lifted him over her head and threw Dean against the back wall of the stage. Dean was lying dazed on the ground. He did have a few bruises. One of the other four pastors walked up to her, but she kicked him really hard in the stomach, and he fell to the floor gasping for breath. Then I walked up to her.

She had grabbed a small wooden children's stool and tried to smack me in the head with it, which would undoubtedly have made me unconscious. I learned at life-saving swimming how to get hold of a person who is drowning and panicking and how to stop this by partly or entirely stopping the air in the throat. The philosophy behind this is simple: better to have a drowning person unconscious on solid ground and reanimate him or her than for both to drown. It was not very spiritual, but it was the only thing I could think of at the moment, and it worked. I got hold of her and started to push her head forward so that she got little to no air and weakened. In the service, everybody was totally alert. Nobody was drowsy or sleepy. Everybody was absolutely awake. Some were afraid, and others were wondering what we was going to happen next.

We tried to get her into a room behind the stage, and we managed to get her there. The wife of one of the pastors present joined us. With great effort, we got the frail young woman on the floor. She was raging like crazy. The worship leader had come on stage in the meantime and tried to sing with the people while we were dealing with this woman behind the screens. Later we heard that her screaming was louder than the music and singing. The woman who had joined us was sitting on one of her arms; one of the pastors held another arm down. Dean and I were both holding a leg, and that way she could not go anywhere or do anything. I knew that we were dealing with demons here, and I spoke to them and commanded them to go out. I had done that a few times with people that were calm and where nothing outwardly happened, but this was my first time with someone who was manifesting. Suddenly out of the mouth of the young woman came a growling, masculine-sounding voice which said in English, 'We will not come out!' We continued and used the name of Jesus. The language that then came out of the mouth of the young woman is something I will not repeat here, but I remember it well; it was horrible.

An incident happened in September of that year. A terrible massacre had taken place in the United States, in which among others Sharon Tate, the wife of the famous film director Roman Polanski was murdered. Later a guru, Charles Manson, and several others were convicted for the murder. Shortly before this incident in Sydney, I had read the story in the *Time* magazine. The murderers had written the most terrible words on the wall with the blood of the people who were murdered; the same words came out of the mouth of the young woman we were holding to the ground.

We continued and kept using the name of Jesus. Again that deep, manly voice that said, 'You are hurting us. You are hurting us.' *Good*, I thought to myself. *You are aware that we use the name in which is all authority in heaven and on earth.* Suddenly a terrible, bellowing scream came from her mouth; and she threw all four of us off her, jumped up, and shouted, 'I am free! I am free! I am free!' She began dancing with joy, and so did we. One of the pastors talked to her for a while. She had asthma, but more than that, she had been plagued by a deep fear for years. I must admit that I have not experienced it this spectacular again, except for maybe on one or two other occasions. How the service ended, I can't remember. We spent quite some time dealing with this young woman. Norman Armstrong prayed for the rest of the people.

For several years we regularly heard from this young woman, and she was doing well. Her life had really changed after this experience. She was a faithful member of a good Pentecostal church and remained very active. I myself think that the demons could throw such a show because we were so inexperienced. This is not the norm. I also think that God wanted to teach us something through this. Several years later, prayer for deliverance would be a regular part of our ministry. I sometimes hear Christians claim that Christians cannot have demons. I wish it were true. And I would really like to know what this incident was about then. It is impossible to attribute this to emotions or mental disorder. The deliverance of this young woman was a great miracle.

On this trip, another special thing happened in Canberra, the capital of Australia. After Christmas 1969, I had preached during a Finnish emigrant conference. A middle-aged couple had invited us for lunch, and we accepted the invitation. When we came, the husband told us that he had heard me speak at the conference about the baptism in the Holy Spirit. He really wanted to receive the Holy Spirit, but he had not dared to go forward in the service, so he had invited us for lunch.

I asked if he knew Jesus, and he told us elaborately that he and his wife were very dedicated Mormons. They had even visited one of the Mormon temples as a pilgrimage. Proudly he showed us the Book of

Mormon and several other important books. I carefully tried to tell him that the Mormons are a cult, but that did not go down well. He believed in God; he believed in Jesus. He was a Mormon and really wanted to be filled with the Holy Spirit. The man was genuinely desiring; that was clear. I prayed in silence and had a thought. I said that I would pray, went to him, and laid my hands on him; and in silence, I rebuked the misleading spirit and commanded it to go out in the name of Jesus and prayed for the Holy Spirit to come. And the Holy Spirit did come and filled this man. He fell to the floor and began to speak very beautifully in new tongues. He was totally lost in the Spirit of God. He moved his arms and hands, and it was as if he was having a very lively and deep conversation with someone. The language of the Holy Spirit flowed forth from him for half an hour. We sat there and watched. We knew what was happening, but his dear wife did not understand any of it and kept looking at her husband. Suddenly, after speaking in tongues for about half an hour, he stopped, looked incredibly happy, stood up, and walked to a room and came back with a stack of books that had to do with the Mormon faith and said, 'These books are wrong. This is lie. What I have now received is real.' All books went into the fire that day. That same afternoon, we could lead his wife to Jesus; and we later heard that shortly afterwards, she was filled with the Holy Spirit too. Several weeks later, they were baptised and became members of the Finnish Pentecostal church in Canberra.

We left Canberra on the 1st of January 1970, right in the middle of summer in Australia; but on the way from Canberra, we ended up in a snow blizzard. A snow blizzard in the middle of summer! We were one of the first cars that got stuck. We had no warm clothes with us, but luckily we did have a few blankets. We spent hours wrapped in blankets in the car. A low spot in the road had completely snowed in, and no car could pass through. After hours, a large trailer with a bulldozer and an excavator came that cleared the road; and after about five hours, we could continue on our journey. The first restaurant after that place with snow had a very busy afternoon, as many people who had waited in the cold for some hours wanted to eat or drink something hot. We bought a large cup of hot tomato soup, and our bodies warmed up a little. That evening it was on the national news: on the 1ˢᵗ of January, there was a snow blizzard just outside Canberra in which a few hundred cars got stuck. We were one of them. A very unusual experience in the heart of summer!

Back to Sydney. The whole trip was nicely planned till Christmas and a few days after Christmas. After that, we had no appointments or services, which is understandable because Christmas is in the middle of summer; and in Australia, that is holiday time. We had been in prayer about what we should do after Christmas. We got the impression that we should go to the summer camp of the Foursquare Church in Sydney. We knew that church because it was the first-ever Pentecostal church we had visited in Australia when we arrived in 1966. Henk and Tanny Smit from the group from Melbourne had asked us what we would be doing around Christmas. We had written to them that we would go to the summer camp just outside of Sydney. They wanted to come too and had registered. We looked forward to seeing them again. Tanny was the Dutch woman who some years before had been filled with the Holy Spirit in her sleep.

The day after Christmas, the camp started. The main speakers were Norman Armstrong of the Oral Roberts organisation and a certain Frank Houston, president of the Assemblies of God in New Zealand. We were honestly not too impressed with the Assemblies of God in Australia. To us there was not much life in it anymore. We presumed that it would not be much better in New Zealand. We came from Streams of Power from the Netherlands where we had really experienced something from God.

We arrived at the camp and had a lovely reunion with Henk and Tanny. In the camp were about 300 participants. We had heard that a movement of the Holy Spirit was taking place in New Zealand but had paid little attention to it. First see it, then believe it was our mindset. The camp started. Norman Armstrong spoke in the first service; and we enjoyed this dear, compassionate man, with his passion to evangelise in Australia. Then came the second service, and Frank Houston was going to speak. He was a small and slim man. Within a few moments, I was on the edge of my seat. There was a special presence of the Holy Spirit.

Frank Houston spoke simply, but it was so full of power and life. Then he started to call people forward with words of knowledge and began to pray for them. We saw before our eyes how people changed, were healed, and were set free from demons. It was incredible! It was so simple, so normal, and so special. In the Netherlands, we had been to services of Oral Roberts and in Germany of T. L. Osborn; both men are famous Pentecostal evangelists. In Streams of Power, we had experienced Karel Hoekendijk and had really seen the Holy Spirit move. What stood out to us immediately was that this was not a service around a man of God. On the contrary, the Holy Spirit was at work. We saw how he delivered a young woman of an evil spirit, and after a scream from her mouth, the woman began to dance with joy. Frank Houston danced with her.

In one of the services, Frank Houston spoke to two young men. 'Both of you there in the back, I see that you are hungry for God but don't know Him yet. Come forward, and I will pray for you.' The young men were seated some rows behind us and stood up a little sheepishly and shy. Frank Houston encouraged them, 'Come, God will touch you.' When they walked past us, they both fell to the floor and began to call out loudly, 'God, forgive me. I have sinned.' It came from deep inside. *That sounds good*, I thought, and I was deeply impressed. They cried and begged God for forgiveness. A while later while they were still lying on the floor, they began speaking in tongues. It flowed out of them. They just could not stop. After maybe about 15 minutes, they finally stood up and walked forward. Frank Houston prayed for them, and they both fell in the Spirit of God again. I saw them later, completely changed. Before they had even reached the stage, they had repented and had been filled with the Holy Spirit. We had not seen anything like that before. We could not get enough of it. In that camp we heard for the first time how an entire congregation sang in new tongues. It was heavenly. We had heard it once before when at the Bible school the student began singing in new tongues, but here several hundreds of believers were lost in worship by singing in the Spirit. We joined them, our first experience and the first time we sang in tongues ourselves. We knew that Paul mentioned in 1 Corinthians 14 about singing in the Spirit, but that was all. Now we did it ourselves.

We were introduced to Frank Houston as a missionary couple from Papua New Guinea. I think he saw our hunger and intense desire for the working of the Holy Spirit. He asked us to stand next to him when he prayed for people so that we could learn. He did not have to say that twice; we stood next to him and were like his shadow. This man was so plain, so loving, so respectful, so real, so full of compassion and just himself. We will never forget Frank Houston.

Frank told us how he had been an officer in the Salvation Army in New Zealand but became sick and was not able to do much anymore. He had to be cared for. A young man that was looking after him was filled with the Holy Spirit and testified about it and told Frank that God could heal him and fill him with His Spirit. One Sunday evening when he was able to do it, he went to a Pentecostal church. At the altar call, he went forward, and someone prayed for him to receive the baptism in the Holy Spirit. He told us how he knelt down and felt how the Holy Spirit filled him, and he began speaking in tongues. That was about nine o'clock in the evening. When Frank Houston, still kneeling down on the floor, came to himself, he looked around. There was no one left, but near the door was a deacon waiting who was half asleep. It was almost one o'clock at night! That evening he was healed and filled with the Holy Spirit. New Zealand and Australia came to know about it.

We got to know Frank Houston and his dear wife, Hazel, well. Frank visited us several times in Papua New Guinea, in the congregation we led in Australia, and he also once was a speaker at a conference week in the Netherlands where we both ministered. Few people have had such an impact on our lives. Because of him, we received an intense hunger for more of God. Coby was inwardly so sure that she had already received much in Streams of Power that she did not even think about going forward in the camp and ask for prayer. In the Netherlands, a leader or missionary would not do such a thing in public. Now we think very, very differently about that.

Frank told us that there were two other pastors from New Zealand that God was using so specially, Trevor Chandler and Bob Midgley. In the following years, we got to know both of them very well. Pastor Bob

Midgley became very special to me and for some years was a true father in the Lord. I learned much from him.

Some years ago, Frank and Hazel Houston have been 'promoted to glory', shortly after each other, to say it in the terminology of the Salvation Army. Bob Midgley is also no longer with us. Because of these men, we entered into a deeper stream of the Holy Spirit. We thank God for what we received in the Netherlands, but God took us further. Our lives were turned completely upside down in that camp. In the weeks that followed, I spent every free hour and moment to be alone and seek God. I wanted what I had seen. I wanted God to change me deeply and work through me.

One thing I saw so clearly in Frank Houston: he was absolutely not afraid of people, the devil, or whatever else. He did not care at all what people thought of him. He was very normal, but also very bold. What a key that is for the work of the Holy Spirit! The apostles in Acts did not pray for more power, but for boldness.

One event happened in the camp. I was standing next to Frank Houston when a man came to him and asked for prayer. Frank Houston looked at him calmly and said, 'I don't pray for proud people.'

The man looked at him stunned. 'I asked for prayer,' he said, 'not to be insulted.'

'I heard that, but I don't pray for proud people,' Frank Houston answered calmly.

The man began to get very upset. 'You are insulting me. How dare you say that I am proud,' the man snapped.

'You know it, God knows it, and I know it,' was Frank's calm answer. The man was of quite a big posture, and I became afraid that he would beat Frank Houston up. The man turned red. Frank Houston remained very calm. I stood next to him, but I was getting worried. Suddenly the man fell to his knees and cried out, 'Lord, You know that I am proud. I repent. Forgive me.'

Frank Houston said, 'Now I can pray for you,' and so he did. The man was set free from several demons and fell in the Holy Spirit and was on the floor for quite a while under the power of God. Inwardly I sighed with relief. Later in the camp, I saw the man several times: a completely changed man. Never had I been around someone so bold, so plain, but also so normal and so humorous.

Henk and Tanny Smit were deeply touched by the Lord in this camp. When Frank Houston shared in a sermon that his congregation in Lower Hutt, New Zealand, had a two-year Bible school, they made their decision. They sold their house in Melbourne and went to New Zealand with their three children. Later they became pastors there, and when I visited them years later, they were leading a flourishing congregation. When years later Coby flew from Japan to the Netherlands to attend the wedding anniversary of her parents, she met Tanny in the plane on the way back. Tanny had also visited her family in the Netherlands. They were still pasturing a church, and one of their two sons was the assistant pastor.

Frank Houston moved to Australia later. He was already way in his fifties then, but he founded many new congregations. In his home church in Waterloo, Sydney, his own son Brian Houston was the youth leader. After several years, Brian started a church at the other side of Sydney, the now-famous Hillsong Church.

When Frank was in his seventies, he was still a very beloved youth preacher, and he preached regularly at large youth events for thousands of young people. Frank Houston had a great love for young people, and you could not keep them away from him. Age and generation were no chasm for him. The ones who experienced Frank Houston in the Netherlands during the conference week saw the same. When during the summer camp most of the people would already be sleeping, Frank would be talking with young people until far after midnight. Years later, just before we left Australia, we visited Frank in Sydney. We were also attending a pastor meeting that day. With our forty-eight years, we were one of the five eldest pastor couples. The average age of the approximate 150 pastors of the congregations that Frank led was mid-thirties.

A movement of the Holy Spirit had begun, a movement that would later be known as the charismatic movement. Among traditional church people, this movement would have great influence. Frank Houston was chairman of the Pentecostal denomination called the Assemblies of

God, but that did not matter to him. He belonged to the body of Christ and spoke a lot and often about the kingdom of God.

A movement of God's Spirit had begun, and it was like a river which burst forth after heavy rain, and it began to break through everywhere. We had the great privilege to be part of this movement from the early beginning. We longed to bring this to Papua New Guinea, and that is what happened. Frank prayed for us and laid on hands for the work in Papua New Guinea. To us Pastor Frank Houston later simply became 'Frank' and a special friend. God sometimes uses people to give your life a completely new course and direction. Frank Houston was one of the people God used to do that in our lives.

In Australia, another thing happened that would greatly influence our service for the Lord in the years after that. While we were in Melbourne to visit our dear Dutch friends that prayed so much for us and supported us financially as much as they were able to, we heard of special services that were held by a New Zealand missionary who worked in India. We could only go one evening. That evening I heard something that got me to study. The preacher had mentioned 'David's tabernacle', and this had awakened something inside of me. In the months that followed, I discovered the truth of David's tabernacle by myself: what it means to be a royal priesthood, how to enter into the presence of God and what to do in that presence, what worship is, but also how praise is a powerful weapon against demonic princes. Psalm 149 is still one of my favourite psalms. Later, during our first leave in the Netherlands in 1972, I spoke about this in a series of services; and my first little book about David's tabernacle was published which, we now know, influenced quite some musicians and worship leaders. Several years ago, an extended version of this book was published. As a result of this truth, we would experience unforgettable things and see a great spiritual breakthrough in the lives of the children of God, but it also would deeply affect the beautiful people and land of Papua New Guinea.

CHAPTER 18

Tari in The Highlands

JOHN PINOKO, ONE of the four Siwai students who studied theology, and whom we met in a special way shortly after we arrived in Rabaul, had finished his studies and was appointed a minister of the United Church in the Tari District in the Southern Highlands. Before Pinoko studied theology, he had been a primary school teacher there for several years. His wife, Ruth, had been a nurse at a medical post. John and Ruth spoke the local language well. A minister is responsible for all the village churches of a district. He also conducts further training for the village pastors. Sometimes that can involve quite a number of churches and pastors. They took over from a missionary who had left and who had responsibility over a large area. John and Ruth wrote letters to us in which they told us about much blessing and many miracles. They especially mentioned one great miracle.

The Hong Kong flu spread through the Tari District, and many people died. In the village near the missionary post, a young woman became sick with it and died. The people gathered to cry and mourn. Ruth Pinoko knew the woman and went to the village, to show her grief. While everybody was crying, Ruth said, 'You must not cry any longer. I will pray to the Lord Jesus.' Ruth knelt down next to the body of the young woman and began to pray. God did a great miracle. Suddenly the woman sat up, opened her eyes, and asked for water. The people shouted, and great joy came into the village because this woman was raised from the dead. Spontaneously this woman gave her life to Jesus, and many believed. John Pinoko himself had prayed for a demon-possessed young woman. The people called her 'crazy' or 'mad'. The woman was delivered from evil spirits and became a normal, sweet woman who also gave her life to Jesus and began to follow Him.

I met both of them, and you sensed the presence of God with both women. The whole district heard about and saw the power of Jesus Christ. This opened the door for Pinoko and his wife wherever they went. It is so true: simple faith in Jesus brings about great miracles.

After the trip to visit the Finnish churches, we returned to the capital of Papua New Guinea, Port Moresby. Visiting the Finnish churches had been enjoyable and blessed; but our heart, our mind, and our whole being were vibrating because of a touch of the Holy Spirit. We had a deep hunger for the Holy Spirit as a result of the summer camp. How intensely we longed to see such blessing in the nation where the Lord had placed us. In the camp, we had experienced how a large group of people inspired by the Holy Spirit were singing together in new tongues. It was so beautiful, so heavenly. Everyone sang his or her own melody, but it sounded as if it was one sound, like the apostle John in the book of Revelations, who heard a great multitude but it was one sound, the sound of a great waterfall. Coby and I had been singing together in new tongues during our long trips in Australia. It was so beautiful, so rich, and so filled with the presence of the Lord. We longed to teach it to the believers in Papua New Guinea. When we first arrived in Rabaul, we sometimes heard people make their own music and sing all night long. In frustration, I then said to the Lord, 'Why do these people do this?' And clearly the Lord answered me, 'The devil only copies what I have intended for my children.' At the camp in Sydney, we heard people sing in intense worship in new tongues for long periods. We realised that the believers in Papua New Guinea would be able to do this for hours.

Kalafi and Tapu and their daughter Lisa had gone to Goroko in the Western Highlands, in June of the previous year, and they had evangelised with a team there for weeks. Around October, Kalafi and Tapu went to Port Moresby because the Holy Spirit told them to do so. They knew no one and had no place to stay. Several hours after they arrived in Port Moresby, they met a young woman who was born again and talked with her. She felt compelled by the Holy Spirit to offer them a place to stay. Remarkable! Just like Jesus told His disciples in the gospel of Matthew chapter 10. Shortly afterwards, they were able to get a large place for themselves in the suburb of Gabutu. Through publications, they asked young Christians in Australia and New Zealand to spend their summer holidays in Port Moresby to evangelise. Several young people came, including a recently converted young Australian named Tom Hallas. Most of them returned to Australia or New Zealand after the outreach, which is called Summer of Service (SOS). However, several stayed, including Tom. Tom Hallas became a well-known leader in Youth with a Mission and has led YWAM in Australia for many years. Youth with a Mission Papua New Guinea needed legal protection, and because we already had that, they worked under our legal covering.

In Port Moresby, they had organised various meetings, and what I remember of our short period there is that many newly converted young people were filled with the Holy Spirit. In one meeting, nine young people were filled with the Holy Spirit and spoke in new tongues. A boy from a totally different area than the capital began to speak in tongues and spoke in the local language of the area around Port Moresby. Others recognised the language and understood exactly how he praised the Lord Jesus in their language. A little later, he began speaking in another language. During our time in Port Moresby, twenty-one new believers were baptised in the sea. People from the nearby village were curious and came to have a look.

There was also an opportunity to visit the small university that was recently opened. There were also students who had come to the Lord including Lenden Butuna and Bob Lutu, who would later be leaders in the work of the Lord in Papua New Guinea.

Coby and I went to Goroka to visit an Australian missionary couple named Barry and Rosaly Silverback, missionaries from the Australian fellowship of Pentecostal churches named Christian Revival Crusade. Years later, they also came to work in Port Moresby, and over the years a warm friendship developed. Coby stayed with them for a few days while I went to Tari on my own because there would be a lot of walking in the jungle involved. But there was no problem in Coby joining me during the next visit.

I flew in a small aeroplane to Tari in the Southern Highlands. Tari was a government post for that area, and it was not really that long ago that the area was opened up by the government and also missionaries. The area is very mountainous. I have been told that the mountains in the Highlands are the highest mountains in the Far East apart from the Himalayas. The highest is Mount Wilhelm with a height of over 4000 metres.

In these mountains, they found fossils of shells, sometimes even at great heights. I once read an article by a scientist who had found the fossil skeleton of a crocodile high up in the mountains. The scientific explanation is that millions of years ago, the layers of the earth's crust collided with each other, and plateaus at sea level were pushed up to form what are now high mountain ridges. Or . . . was there a worldwide flood after all?

In books with pictures of Papua New Guinea, you will probably come across pictures of Tari and the 'Huli Wigmen'. From their youth, the men collect their hair when it is cut; and when they have sufficient hair, they make beautiful wigs, which they decorate with little flowers and wear at certain occasions. Often, they decorate the wig with the skin of a snake or lizard and with dried yellow flowers. They are very colourful and quite beautiful. Often, the men have a thin bamboo stick through their nose. Although I have not seen this personally, a good friend took a photo of a man who got hold of a screwdriver and put that through his nose. Whenever I showed this in the Netherlands or Australia, it always brought much laughter. The men carry a braided bag around their shoulders. In it they carry just about everything, such as a knife, an axe, or a pipe and food like sweet potatoes. Many men also wear a large flat pearl shell around their neck, called 'kina'. The shells made their way from the coast to the Highlands through trade. They are a sign of wealth. When Papua New Guinea released its own currency after independence and stopped using Australian money, the dollar became a 'kina'. The cent became a 'toea', the name that the people from Rabaul give to a beautiful little shell that they weave together in strings and which is used for payment.

The women also carry a large woven bag but with a strap over their forehead and the bag on their back. In that bag, called a 'bilum', they often carry their little babies or the harvest of their gardens. The women wear nice thick grass skirts, that is all. When I show photos, the men often ask me what I think about that, women who only wear a grass skirt. The truth is that after a while you don't notice it anymore; it is so natural and common. The women also breastfeed their babies at any time. But I have also seen how they breastfeed piglets. Pigs are very valuable, and if a sow can't feed its piglet, a woman will do it. I actually have a photo of a woman who has a baby on one breast and a piglet on the other. Piglets get spoiled because of their value. The bride price is paid in a number of pigs; it could be forty or more. Also on special occasions and feasts, a pig will be slaughtered. Several times when we arrived in a village, a pig would be prepared. When they gave me a piece of pig meat, it would have fat and skin on it. The meat was sort of okay, but the rest... The pigs in Papua New Guinea have a dark colour and a rough, prickly skin. When other people brought their pigs to Papua New Guinea, they brought light pink-coloured pigs with a rather smooth skin. Dark people have dark pigs, and white people have white pigs. Interesting, but hard to explain.

Because Tari is quite high in the mountains, the people often cover themselves with the fat of pigs to stay warm. The way the men greet you is with a firm hug... The men nearly always carry their bow and arrow with them. If things go wrong, then they have their weapons ready, and they surely know how to handle them.

The men also often had a pipe to smoke. The pipes were pieces of bamboo. At the end, they would put a sort of dried tobacco, and they smoked it. We had a pipe like that for years, but we lost it. I do remember that after several years of being in our possession, the pipe still smelled strongly of the 'Tari tobacco scent'.

At the market in Tari, I once bought a nice axe. The axe was made of the claw of a cassowary, a bird of the ostrich family. It was beautifully made; the claw of the cassowary was artfully woven and attached to the wooden handle. It was new, and we liked it. To us it was a beautiful artifact from Papua New Guinea. At our home in Rabaul and later in

Kavieng, it hung on the wall. Once a man from Tari visited us and saw the axe displayed on the wall. He asked us why we had that thing in our home. I told him that I bought it new, so it had never been used, and we thought it was very beautiful and like a piece of art from Tari. He told us that his ancestors used such weapons to strike hard to kill an enemy. To us it was art; to the Tari people it was a deadly weapon. We immediately took it off the wall and destroyed it. Years later, I received a little axe, cast in pure silver and put behind glass in a frame from the leader of the opposition and ex-prime minister who had come to Jesus. It was his way of thanking me for something I had done for him. That little silver axe hangs on our wall in our home in Rotterdam, the city in the Netherlands where we live.

Tari itself is in a beautiful valley, and when we landed, I was impressed with the natural beauty of the landscape. The Tari people love gardening, and flowers and beautiful bushes are everywhere. At the airstrip, several Tari people were waiting for us, some of them wearing their wigs. The men also carried their bows and arrows. John Pinoko with his black skin stood out among these people, and it was not difficult to spot him from the plane.

It was great to see Pinoko again. The last time I met him was during my first trip to Siwai. We respect people like him and Ruth. To us they are true apostles who opened up entire areas for the gospel. John had not been able to hire a car, but he did have two bicycles, only . . . their missionary post was uphill for nearly the entire road. He had come by bike, downhill; now it was back uphill! I could tie my luggage to the bike, but for most of the two and a half hours, we had to push our bike uphill.

Though the building style is simple, the houses are very attractive. The large church was beautifully made of woven bamboo and with a roof consisting of a thick layer of kunai grass. Services were held during the day because there was no light in the church. They had only a few kerosene lamps.

The inhabitants of the large islands like New Britain, New Ireland, Manus, and Bougainville are good singers. But the people in some areas of the Highlands sing in a different way; it is more chanting then singing. In my home country, the only comparison that could be made is with Gregorian singing that is used in the Roman Catholic Church. Pinoko had taught the believers many Bible verses by making them chant them. It really was impressive. The people could not read or write but in this way had learned many parts of the Bible by heart.

Preaching was an unforgettable experience in Tari. I spoke one or more sentences in English, Pinoko then spoke in the local language, and after every sentence the people would comment and respond in their own language so that you knew they understood. These people could not read or write and had no Bible, and this was their way of gaining knowledge. When I invited people to choose for Jesus, everyone came forward, knelt down spontaneously, and prayed. Many found Jesus as their Saviour and Lord, although I think a good number of them had already accepted the Lord, but this showed their deep hunger and desire for Him.

After that, we prayed for the sick. It seemed like nearly everyone was sick. The Lord touched many people. There was great faith among them. They had seen the power of God up close when someone had been raised from the dead and a woman who was delivered from demons.

After a Bible study, several people were spontaneously filled with the Holy Spirit and spoke in new tongues. I have always hoped that in these areas I would hear someone speak in tongues in the Dutch language, but unfortunately, I have never (or not as yet) experienced it. Speaking in tongues, says Paul, is the language of humans or angels; so it should be possible.

Pinoko took me to another village. Near the village was a big, tumultuous river about thirty metres wide. The people had very artfully made a bridge of bamboo. This bridge was wide enough for one person, and actually you had to put one foot in front of the other because it was too narrow to put your feet next to each other. On each side was a rail of bamboo, and in between was plaiting so that you could not fall off and thus made it reasonably safe for children. The bridge moved quite a lot and swung from left to right as you walked on it. Beneath you flowed the wild river. I estimated that the bridge was about ten metres above the river. Quite an experience to walk over a bridge like that.

In this village, the same happened. A crowded church and nearly everyone came forward to give their lives to Jesus. I got the impression that here too many people had actually already accepted the Lord but just wanted to pray again. The hunger for God was great, and one got the impression it was like the first congregation in the book of Acts. The grace of God was on this area. We prayed for the sick. A deaf woman was healed and could hear perfectly. An old blind woman accepted Jesus, and we prayed for her. She immediately saw. Her eyes were clear. I asked her to touch my nose, and with great joy and amusement among the people, she did. I asked her to count my fingers, and she could. Three other people who were blind in one eye were healed. Often, this blindness was caused by accidents. A chip from a stone axe or an arrow that hit someone's face or a branch in the jungle. With another blind person, I commanded the blind spirit to leave, and the man saw clearly.

Back in the village at the missionary post, a man who was blind in one eye was healed. I asked him to get his wife and children so that I could take a photograph. A little later, he proudly came back with two wives and several children. The photo turned out well.

A lot happened in Tari, and the miracles I described are the miracles that we could see straightaway. Undoubtedly there were many more miracles that we could not see right away.

John and Ruth Pinoko experienced a specially blessed time for several years in Tari. Actually one could say they experienced a small revival. It all began because the principal of the training centre of the Methodist Church in the Solomon Islands discovered the truth about healing, prayer, and fasting.

I went back to Tari several times. Coby joined me once, and we were even able to take a well-known Dutch evangelist to Tari. I understood that he had never seen an area as primitive as Tari and its people. The Tari people were just starting to leave what Western people call the 'Stone Age'.

In one of the villages, a man spoke to me through a translator. He was a typical Tari man with his wig, bamboo through the nose, piece of cloth and leaves covering his behind, and carrying a bow and arrow. He told me that his son had gone to university in Port Moresby. His son must have been one of the first children from that area to go to school and had attended both primary and secondary school. Later, in Port Moresby, I was able to meet his son; he was studying economics. Speaking of a generation gap . . .

In a neighbouring area where the former Methodist Church also had a missionary post, the minister had committed adultery. The people were furious and wanted to kill him, so the minister in charge had to leave the area in a hurry. The people in the village churches were angry and deeply disappointed. Because John and Ruth Pinoko were doing so exceptionally well, they were transferred to this place, and another Papua New Guinean minister came to their missionary post.

It was difficult at their new post. The people felt betrayed and were angry. Adultery is shocking in many cultures, but within some tribes in Papua New Guinea, the one who commits adultery can be killed. All the anger and disappointment that the people felt was directed at John and Ruth because they were the new ministers. It was difficult, and they did not break through. The new minister at their former missionary post was not charismatic and unfortunately did not continue in the work of the Holy Spirit. The movement of the Holy Spirit gradually diminished.

Throughout the years, the contacts with Tari remained. We were able to arrange for several young men from Tari to attend a Bible school. Years later, we regained contact with Tari, which came about because the Lord had opened a door in the area for Hilding and Ingrid Ericksson, the Swedish couple from Mount Isa in Australia. They were able to pioneer and establish new congregations in several places. While they were working in Tari, I was able to visit that beautiful area again. The photo on the cover of this book (as it was published in Holland) was taken during one of these visits. I was again and again surprised and blessed with the openness to the gospel and the powerful movement of the Holy Spirit among this colourful-people group. I often wondered as to how much John and Ruth Pinoko were used by God to break open this area for a powerful move of God.

John and Ruth became disappointed and eventually returned to Siwai. I met them often, and they helped build the work there. But I always felt that their time in Tari had been their most fruitful time. Recently I heard that Pinoko has passed away and is with his Lord. I often felt that John never fully realised what an instrument he was in the hands of the Lord, to begin a great work of the Holy Spirit in Bougainville as well as Tari, in the Southern Highlands. We will meet this precious man again in heaven.

CHAPTER 19

The Solomon Islands

AFTER THREE MONTHS, we were back in Rabaul. It was good to be 'home' again. The Finnish missionaries Lauri and Martha Pesu and Kari and Raakel Harri had continued the work in and around Rabaul. Especially the work on the plantations was blessed. By now many plantation workers had been baptised. Most plantation workers went back to their own areas after two years, and only the Lord knows how much they testified about Him and what influence it had among their own people. The number of contacts in Rabaul was growing, and the relationship with the missionaries of the Uniting Church gradually became better, mainly because of the efforts of Lauri Pesu. So we joined the work in Rabaul again . . . until in May 1970 a letter arrived.

An English couple worked for the government at a marine base on a little island called Tulagi, in the then British Solomon Islands. Tulagi had been the government centre for some time, but for the last few years, that was now Honiara. Still, Tulagi was an important place in this small island nation.

Because of his work as a technician, the husband had met a few young men from the island Malaita. These young men knew the Lord. They belonged to the South Sea Evangelical Church, a missionary organisation with its origins going back to the end of the nineteenth and the beginning of the twentieth century. Men of the Solomon Islands were encouraged to work under contract for three years on the sugar cane plantations in the north of the Australian state of Queensland.

Years later, similar arrangements were made on the plantations of Papua New Guinea. The men came from a background which many would call paganism and only spoke their own language. The Pidgin English that is now spoken on the Solomon Islands came into existence because of contact with Australians while they worked on the plantations. Several born-again Australians began to evangelise among these men. When you read reports from that period, you will read unusual stories and testimonies of many men who came to Jesus. A missionary organisation was founded and called the Queensland Kanaka Mission. The word 'kanaka' means 'a native from the Pacific Islands'. This word especially means someone who comes from the jungle or lives in the jungle and who has not been influenced by the outside world. The word 'kanaka' is used in Pidgin English in Papua New Guinea as well for someone who continues living in the jungle or who follows a primitive lifestyle.

The men who had come to know Jesus would usually go back to their island after three years, and they were the first ones to share the gospel with their own people. We think that the Solomon Islands is one of the most beautiful places on earth, but many people lived in deep darkness. Headhunting, cannibalism, witchcraft, and worship of spirits were then the way of life. In some places, there was a custom that when a newborn baby cried too much the first day, it had to be buried alive or a curse would remain on the family. It was the only way to break and stop a curse, so they believed. What effect must this have had on the mothers of these newborn babies?

Many of the men who had found Jesus could no longer live in their own villages and had to build houses elsewhere. That's how 'Christian villages' and 'non-Christian villages' came into existence. Early in 1900, missionaries went from North Queensland to the Solomon Islands. The courage and perseverance of these first missionaries demands great respect. In the first decade that these missionaries were working in these islands, a powerful work of the Holy Spirit took place. Though the first missionaries came from the South Sea Evangelical Church in Australia, the ones we met in 1971 were from New Zealand, sent out by the Baptist and Brethren churches in New Zealand.

In 1971, the missionaries often met with third-generation Christians, people who no longer knew the demonic darkness that their ancestors had lived in, but for whom faith was no longer a living reality. The missionaries and leaders were very concerned about this, and there was much prayer for a spiritual awakening.

The young men, whom the New Zealand brother had met, had heard of revivals and were very interested in the work of the Holy Spirit and eager to be baptised in the Holy Spirit. Roy Latter (the New Zealand brother) had written a letter to T. L. Osborn and asked if he knew Pentecostal missionaries in the area of the Solomon Islands who could possibly help him. T. L. Osborn replied that John and Coby Pasterkamp were the nearest missionaries he knew of. That's how we received a letter from the Solomon Islands. Roy and Margaret Latter asked if we could come for several weeks to help these young men receive the baptism in the Holy Spirit, and they would pay our airfares.

Geographically and ethnically Bougainville belongs to the Solomon Islands. A political, man-made border had made Bougainville part of Papua New Guinea. In the days that we prayed for Bougainville, we had often prayed for the Solomon Islands as well, and now there was an invitation.

Two weeks later, I left. An old DC-3 was the plane that day, flying from Rabaul, via Kieta on Bougainville to Honiara in the Solomon Islands. There were only a few passengers. Just before we came to the Solomon Islands, the pilot announced that a few whales had been spotted, and we were going to circle lower so we could see them. Those were interesting and fun flights. From the air, the islands in the blue sea were stunningly beautiful. You could see the white beaches, the palm trees, the villages, and the mountains. Finally we landed in Honiara on the island Guadalcanal. The New Zealand couple had asked a Pentecostal Australian couple living in Honiara to pick me up, and the next day I went to Tulagi by boat. A well-known local preacher of the South Sea Evangelical Church came with me. A few days later, he was filled with the Holy Spirit. It was so good to meet the New Zealand couple and their two little girls. They were very hospitable. Some young men with whom they had spoken about the baptism in the Holy Spirit had already received the Holy Spirit and spoke in new tongues. One of them was Arnon Sau, who would later take me to his village on the island Malaita. Other young men were very desirous to receive the Holy Spirit. In these meetings, the leader of the South Sea Evangelical Church who was with us said, 'What you preach, we have heard before, but not with such power and penetration. It is familiar and yet so different. It is like it was with Jesus because He spoke with authority and power.' Indeed, the difference is the Holy Spirit.

Every evening we held a meeting. In the morning and in the afternoon, I held a Bible study about the nine gifts of the Holy Spirit. In the evening meetings, it did not take long before fifteen young men were filled with the Holy Spirit. Some of them danced for joy. It was a lovely time.

Arnon Sau wanted to take me to his village on the larger island of Malaita, east of Tulagi. I stayed on Tulagi for ten days and then travelled by boat via Honiara to Auki, the government centre on Malaita. Several men who also lived on Tulagi but also came from the same area as Arnon Sau joined me. In Auki, the young men could stay acquaintances, while I rented a room in a simple guest house. In my room, we had a Bible study every morning, afternoon, and evening; and we prayed together. I shared with them everything I knew about repentance and the person and work of the Holy Spirit. Then we went to the village of Karkara in an old Land Rover they were able to charter. What I experienced there during the following days I will never forget. The people had prayed for revival, and that is what we would experience. God had heard their prayer. We had experienced a special work of the Holy Spirit on Bougainville, but what we experienced here was probably even of greater depth and power.

We arrived in the late afternoon. After having eaten a locally prepared meal, I really needed to use the toilet, but I couldn't discover anything resembling a toilet. I told Arnon Sau of my need, and he asked me to follow him. We walked a long way into the jungle, and then Arnon said, 'Somewhere here.' I now understood that toilets did not exist in this village. I had learned, after the first trips to the inland of Papua New Guinea, to always take a roll of toilet paper with me, a habit I still practise when I travel to certain countries.

We began having meetings in the village. In one of the first ones, I was about to begin preaching when an old woman in the back of the church became very emotional and loudly called out things in her own language. I asked her, through my interpreter, to calm down so that I could preach. The interpreter communicated my request, but I sensed that he did not really want to. Because the interpreter was a young man, and I knew that younger people were not allowed to correct older people, I asked some older people who were sitting near the woman to calm her down and ask her to be quiet. A few of them looked at me strangely, and I did not understand why. I asked again, and then the woman calmed down, and I could preach. About seven people received the Holy Spirit and spoke in tongues, and I prayed for several sick people. It was a good meeting, I thought. When it had ended, I asked Arnon Sau and the others who had joined me what actually had been going on with the old woman. I did not understand their response, but when I persisted, they told me that this woman had seen Jesus standing next to me, and she tried to tell everybody what He looked like. I felt terrible! And that is a total understatement! The revival on the Solomon Islands was characterised by deep repentance, maybe first of all my own. I offered my sincere apologies and asked for forgiveness. From that moment onward, I became more cautious about stopping something that I did not understand.

We continued having meetings, and the blessing broke out among the people. About forty people came to Jesus. In that same meeting 'happened to be' a young man who heard me speak about the Holy Spirit and who asked me afterwards to tell him more. Especially the younger people spoke reasonable English, because they had attended primary school. Furthermore, a sort of Pidgin English was spoken on the Solomon Islands, similar to that of Papua New Guinea. Communicating with younger people went pretty well; with the older people, it happened through an interpreter. The young man had just recently come to Jesus and had read about the Holy Spirit in the Bible. In the next meeting, he was powerfully filled with the Holy Spirit and spoke in tongues.

In the gatherings that followed, there was great conviction of sin among the people. I marvelled about it. I had not experienced it like this before. People from the surrounding villages started coming. One evening around midnight, several young people came to Arnon Sau's house where I was staying. They did not want to wait until the next day to accept Jesus and be saved. In the middle of the night, Arnon Sau led them to Jesus. There were several people who had never come to church before and who had always rejected the gospel and the missionaries and preachers. With tears running down their faces, they came to Jesus. People came to confess hidden sins like witchcraft. They brought amulets and other witchcraft objects and destroyed them. Others were delivered from evil spirits. There was great joy.

Every morning I held a study in which the people learned how they could receive the Holy Spirit. In the evening meetings, there were first seven, then nine, then fifteen, and in the service after that, even thirty believers, who received the Holy Spirit. In a little over a week, about a hundred people were filled with the Holy Spirit. Some danced, others laughed, and others sang in new tongues. We prayed for a woman, and she was filled with the Holy Spirit. Her hands went up, and she began to sing in new tongues. The melody seemed to come straight from heaven. She was completely lost in the Spirit. It was moving to see and hear. Later we asked what had happened to her. She only remembered that when we started praying, she saw the Lord Jesus on His throne and the angels around Him. The angels sang a beautiful song to worship the Lord Jesus, and she had joined the angels in singing. We heard it! It was indeed music from heaven.

I know seven people who saw Jesus in visions when they were filled with the Holy Spirit. They also saw in those visions that the Lord Jesus would return soon. Some meetings lasted for three and a half hours or longer. Until late in the evening you would hear people in their houses singing, praying, reading the Bible, and exalting the Lord. One night, around twelve o'clock, Arnon Sau took me to every house in the village; and we listened outside. Nobody was sleeping! Everywhere we heard songs, prayer, and people reading the Bible out loud. Even at half past four in the morning, I heard people singing and praying. In Karkara, there were apparently only three people who were not converted after the ten days I had been there.

We walked to the next village for several hours in the burning sun, and there too many things happened. People repented, were filled with the Holy Spirit, were touched by the Lord, were delivered from evil spirits or healed. The day after, we made a trip along the coast in native canoes. It was a magnificent trip, for me too short. The crystal clear water of the sea, the coastline, the palm trees, the mountains in the background. Simply beautiful. I can imagine that when you read books or accounts by anthropologists about this area, you get the impression that this is some sort of last paradise on earth and should be absolutely left alone so that it can remain 'a paradise'. Concerning nature that is true, but concerning the hearts of the people, it is not a paradise, but often great darkness of need and fear. It might not be like it was a hundred years ago, but there still is much demonic darkness! We must bring the gospel. In this seaside village, we again had a specially blessed time in which many things happened. The wind of God's Spirit was blowing through this area!

In the newsletter we sent after this trip, I wrote about several tuberculosis patients who were healed, nearly blind or damaged eyes that were healed, and skin diseases that disappeared. We mainly prayed en masse. There were too many people asking for prayer. A special miracle was the healing of a young girl who had suffered from leprosy for five years. She was under medical supervision. God healed her in an instant. Several days later, she again visited the medical post, but the medical workers could not find any trace of leprosy anymore. The girl testified how Jesus had healed her. She also asked for prayer for her brother who was in the hospital with tuberculosis. Later we heard that the day after, there was no more sign of tuberculosis on his X-rays, and he was allowed to go home.

As mentioned, there was a deep conviction of sin. We heard of someone who had to walk for almost a day to return a stolen axe and other people who had walked for two days to ask people in other villages for forgiveness. There was much reconciliation between people.

Forgiveness was asked and given to each other, while in Western countries sometimes even a phone call seems too difficult.

Along the coast were plantations, also in the area of Karkara Village and the surrounding villages. There were no more contract workers on the Solomon Islands. The men of the villages worked at the plantations and were paid for it. A few men did not show up at work because they were too busy repenting and coming clean with God and others. I have wondered what it would be like in the Netherlands or Australia if the wife called the boss and said, 'My husband cannot come to work because he is still busy repenting.' Or the other way around, if the husband called his wife's boss with that announcement. Critics and the media which were criticising the revival also mentioned it: men were not showing up at work. I had to smile when I read that later and wished it was like that in more places.

I saw a depth of repentance here that I had not seen before, and the whole subject and meaning of 'repentance' began to gain significance and meaning that would become a red thread in our service for the Lord in the years that followed.

It was very difficult to say goodbye to these people after these special days of revival and blessing. Some 350 people came to the last meeting, many from surrounding villages, because Karkara Village itself was not that big. People came to Jesus, the sick were healed, and again people were filled with the Holy Spirit and others delivered from evil spirits. There were many testimonies from people who shared about what the Lord Jesus had done for them, and those testimonies touched many hearts.

From Malaita, I could fly back to Honiara in a small plane. Arnon Sau and the group of men stayed behind. Much later we heard from them how wonderfully God used this team of men. For me, these are real heroes of faith, and they belong to chapter 11 of Hebrews.

In Honiara, we also held meetings. The news of the outpouring of the Holy Spirit in Karkara and the surrounding area had already reached Honiara, and here too hungry believers came to receive the Holy Spirit. Satan was clearly not amused, and attacked. One afternoon around four o'clock, I was writing a letter to Coby. At six o'clock, I had a high fever. I became delirious and did not know where I was or what I had to do. The couple with whom I was staying told me about it later. I had malaria for the first time. I can remember that the next morning I had to go to the toilet and crawled out of my bedroom to the toilet because I could not walk anymore. I felt so awful. On the toilet door hung a calendar with Bible verses for every day. I forced myself to look at my watch to see what date it was, and then on the calendar. There were the words of Psalm 118:17, 'I shall not die, but live, and declare the works of the Lord.' I got hold of those words and made them my own. Later I saw that the calendar was years old. That day I still had malaria, but that evening I had to preach. However, I was too sick; but regardless of that, they still took me to the meeting. All I could do was sit down. Before I was to preach, a few big, strong, muscular men from the Solomon Islands prayed for me. They grabbed my hair (which they call 'laying on of hands') and began to pray passionately. I don't think they realised that they were shaking me quite strongly. Anyway, God touched me, and that evening I preached and was able to stand. Several days later, the malaria came back, but again I was touched by the Lord. On the Solomon Islands, I did not have malaria anymore after that; but unfortunately, I did have it again in Papua New Guinea.

In the meantime, Coby had come, and together we went back to Tulagi. There we held meetings, and in one of those, we saw a woman who began dancing when she was filled with the Holy Spirit. With her arms raised and eyes closed, she danced for about an hour in that crowded small building in between the people, without bumping into anyone. We were stunned and so enjoyed what we saw. It was so supernatural.

After Tulagi, we went back to Honiara and held more meetings. The hunger was great. I spoke one afternoon for quite a while with a converted secondary school teacher about the baptism in the Holy Spirit. It was a very pleasant conversation. Whether this teacher has ever received the Holy Spirit I don't know. I do know, however, that when independence came several years later, he became the first prime minister. His name is Stephen Kenilorea.

We heard of a group of girls who were at a boarding school and who were praying to receive the Holy Spirit. One evening the Holy Spirit fell on the girls. They spoke in tongues, fell in the Spirit, and had amazing experiences. The head teacher did not know what to do about it and forced them all to take sedatives. We wondered where all those sedatives came from; but that, I suppose, is not our business.

We wanted to stay longer in the Solomon Islands, so I asked for an extension of our visitors' permits at the immigration office. When they saw our names on the passports, the answer was a definite no. Our visitors' permits could not be extended under any circumstance. We had the impression that something was going on.

Someone told us about an American who had come to Honiara and wanted to meet me. I met him and heard a gripping story.

In the north of the Solomon Islands on the islands close to Bougainville, a cult had come into existence named after its leader Silas Etho, the Ethocult. I had heard about it. I had also heard that it started well and that in the beginning the leader had been a devout and deeply committed Christian. This fact made me curious, and I had once expressed the desire to go to that area. There was an anthropological report published about it, which I had read. Though the writer was not a Christian, I could see from the report that it had started out well but that it had gone off track.

The American man, an incognito missionary, had entered that area in a unique way; and he had met and spoken with several leaders of the Ethocult. It is in the area where John F. Kennedy nearly died during the Second World War but was saved by local people. When this American missionary was there, several men came to visit him and told him that they were the ones who had saved John F. Kennedy and other crew members when, on the 3rd of August 1943, the US Patrol Boat 109 was hit by a Japanese warship. John F. Kennedy was one of the crew who survived the disaster. Together with several other crew members, of whom several were wounded, they reached an uninhabited island after hours of swimming. Then, after more hours of swimming, they reached another island where they were helped by the local men to get to the Australian coastguard. These men later heard that John F. Kennedy had become the president of the United States but later on was murdered. As a symbol of the American victory over the Japanese, they had made a wooden carving of an American soldier holding a Japanese head. Their question was if it could be taken to America and given to the Kennedy family as a memory and token of appreciation. And that happened. The missionary was able to personally hand this wood carving to the Kennedy family. Now it is on display in a museum. He was on his way back to this area because the leaders of the cult had invited him. These men told him how the Ethocult had started, and the American shared it with me, and I was spellbound listening to this.

Through missionaries, Silas Etho had come radically to Jesus. One evening he was fishing in a lagoon. In his canoe, he began praying and had a deep encounter with the Lord. He saw the heavens opened and the Lord Jesus Himself. He saw the angels around the throne and experienced the glory of God. I understood from the story that Silas Etho also spoke in new tongues. Etho was overwhelmed. He told his story to a missionary who worked there. The missionary was an evangelical but was not open to manifestations of the Holy Spirit. He warned him that this was not of God but a deception of Satan. Etho could not believe that; he knew what he had experienced and seen. Etho told it to his own people, who did believe him. Eventually they broke away from the missionary's church and began their own church, but no one helped or guided them. From the side of the missionaries, there was only resistance. Slowly but surely things went wrong, and finally Etho claimed an experience in which God had told him that he was to be part of the Trinity. So that became now a Unity of Four: Father, Son, Holy Spirit, and Silas Etho. They opposed the government, development, and any influence from the outside and totally retreated from contact with other people. The American missionary, who was a wise Pentecostal man, did sense in the people of the Etho movement that he spoke to an openness and hunger for the truth. He had to promise to come back.

Normally speaking, nobody could enter the area because of the government, so he had to work under some sort of cover. It was a moving story of which I now had some understanding. Our meeting made a deep impression on me. We prayed together for the people in the Ethocult. After we had left the Solomon Islands, we heard that the missionary did not get there, because he was put out of the country. The government had a policy that only allowed five church organisations to work in the country. Coby and I, the American missionary, and later on someone from New Zealand did not belong to one of these five churches. So we all had to get out of the country and could not return. We heard about all this after we had left but had always noticed this resistance. However, the Holy Spirit did not leave and could not be put out of the country. He continued unabated!

In the days that we were on the Solomon Islands, a New Zealand Maori evangelist, Muri Thompson, had come to the Solomon Islands to hold campaigns at the invitation of the South Sea Evangelical Church. Although we did not meet him, we heard that he had been touched by the charismatic renewal that was deeply impacting church after church in New Zealand.

Muri Thompson started his campaigns on the southern islands, and God began blessing mightily. Especially a conference with missionaries and leaders was quite unique. There was deep humbling, much confession of guilt and repentance towards God and towards each other. God blessed and responded to these men and women with a deep work of the Holy Spirit. After that conference, Muri Thompson and a team went to other areas, and they also went to Malaita. Not only Muri Thompson but also his entire team were powerfully touched by the Holy Spirit. On Malaita, some of the men with whom I had just spent weeks joined Muri Thompson's team. It was now a bigger team of which each member was filled with the Holy Spirit. When, at meeting after meeting, the Holy Spirit fell on people, not only did Muri Thompson know what to do, but his entire team as well. I have read their letters, and we rejoiced with them about what was happening. Thousands of people were touched by a powerful revival that lasted for years.

When we could not extend our visas, the custom officers made it very clear that we had to leave. When the airport customs saw the names in our passports, we again saw that strange reaction. We now understand that our names were apparently known everywhere, and we had the honour of having our names put on the blacklist.

Several days after we were back in Rabaul, we received a certified letter from the Department of Immigration of the Solomon Islands. If Coby and I ever intended to visit the Solomon Islands again, they would not be able to give us a visa. The last sentence was 'Your willing servant', and the name of the immigration official. I smiled: 'Your willing servant'. Of course that is just formal language and the man was doing his duty, but we never asked him to do this.

In the islands of the Pacific, there was in those days, and maybe still today, a magazine called the *Pacific Island Monthly*. In the November edition of 1970 was the following article:

THEY'RE BEING REVIVED ON MALAITA

On a recent visit to Auki in the Solomons, we were chatting with one of the residents. In the course of conversation he said one of his sons had died a few years previously. We expressed the usual condolences.

Then his eyes lit up and he went on to say that just two days ago, three of his children had gone to heaven; but he said it with such an expression of joy and delight we didn't know whether to express sorrow or join him in his apparent rejoicing.

We played safe and gave a serious nod of the head and waited for him to continue. He then told us that the children had returned the same day and had told him all about it and of their meeting with their brother. He related to us a graphic description of heaven, and the nice room his dead son had there. Finally he explained, to our relief, that his other three children had not themselves died but merely gone up to heaven briefly during a revival meeting.

Revival meetings, as their participants call them, have been held recently in several areas on Malaita, following the visit of a Dutch Pentecostal missionary, and they apparently have had a considerable following among the adherents of the South Sea Evangelical Church.

This movement even has had some affect in Honiara, where it followed a recent crusade in the SSE Church there. Boys left school to hold prayer meetings in the bush, and healing sessions were held. But though claims of healing and even raising of the dead were made, no one actually knew of any particular instances. But the main effect has been on Malaita where children have in some cases have been withdrawn from school to follow the new faith, andmen have left their work.

At one time some thought that it would get a real hold on the people, but perhaps because the local leader was a former mental patient and some of his followers have ended up needing treatment, most Malaita people treat it as the latest joke especially after one adherent was stopped by the police from beating a woman to make her confess and thus relieve her of any devils that might have resided in her.

The following letter was a response to the article, and was published in the January edition 1971 the *Pacific Island Monthly*:

MALAITA'S REVIVAL

Sir, - On seeing the report in your paper under the heading "They're Being Revived on Malaita" I would be grateful if you will give me space to state some real facts concerning this revival. I feel, since the subject has been opened, a movement vitally affecting the lives of over 10,000 people in three months deserves more than a sketchy, misleading report such as was in your November issue.

I have been very closely connected with the revival since it broke out in August and only want to state what I have personally seen and shared in. One very pleasing feature of this revival has been that very many are being used and not any one particular leader.

As with most spiritual revivals, after the first upheaval there is steadying down to to consistent Christian living, but the movement continues unabated on Malaita and is extending to other islands also, and I believe this will eventually have far-reaching effects for the good on the whole country.

Personally I have seen hundreds of people delivered from immoral living having been slaves to alcohol and other vices of the white man as well as demon possession, something of which we Europeans know very little, no one having come into contact with such possession would ever think of it as something of a "joke".

These deliverances are real and only in very isolated instances have I heard of any turning back. Rather are they rejoicing in the joy of coming to know the living God as a mighty reality in their lives.

I have been present when longstanding feuds over land and other matters have, I believe, been permanently settled in a spirit of love and forgiveness. As one, I am told, a revived backslider for many years, said to a government officer, "If all Malaita were truly Christian you would have a lot less work to do.'

Yes there are excesses as with all revivals, these are our major problems; the enemy is most real and the spiritual warfare intense, at the same time these excesses are grossly exaggerated by some and give misleading impressions. This applies to your correspondent's reference to a former mental patient being a local leader.

I hesitate to say anything about miracles of healing; it is easy to exaggerate so it's best for those helped to speak for themselves. If your correspondent comes to our house the next time he visits Auki and happen to be home I will take him to a case where he can see and hear for himself and so get reliable information first hand.

Lastly let me say that attitudes to revivals vary greatly depending on the person to whom one is speaking. It is true what the OLD BOOK says, "The natural man receiveth not the things of the Spirit of God for they are foolishness unto him, neither can he know them because they are spiritually discerned." 1 Cor. 2:14.

GEORGE STRACHAN
SSEC Missionary.
South Sea Evangelical Church,
Auki, Malaita,
British Solomons.

I also felt the need to respond, and in the same edition of the *Pacific Island Monthly*, I wrote a letter to the editor of *Pacific Island Monthly*, which was published. This is the letter I wrote:

> Sir, the signer of this letter, Rev John Pasterkamp (from Holland) is the Dutch Pentacostal missionary referred to n the article on the Malaita revival. It is clear that your correspondant who visited Auki recently only heard some of the story but was not well informed at all. This whole article gives a wrong impression of what is happening.
>
> The signer visited the protectorate from June 16 until August 2. Places visited were Tulagi, Honiara, and two villages north of Dala station, North Malaita. At the same time many crusades were held all over the Solomon Islands. These crusades were conducted by Rev. Muri Thompson, from New Zealand, who was invited by the SSE Church. What is happening is part

of the charismatic movement which is touching man churches in many countries. Through this movement many people have found new realities in their christian life.

However we regret that your magazine associates his movement with a former mental patient and his followers near Auki, which is certainly *not* the case. This former mental patient was already known in this area long before these revival meetings were held. He is absolutely *not* the leader and has no connections whatsoever with this movement, as your magazine likes to state.

If there are any leaders, we like to refer to some pastors and elders of the SSE Church, North Malaita. Every normal thinking person wil abhor the very thought of beating up people.

We would appreciate it very much if you would make rectification of this statement in your magazine as it puts many people in the Solomon Islands and followers of SSEC in a bad light.

Rev. J. Pasterkamp

My letter was published in the January edition of the *Pacific Island Monthly*.

The editor responded to both letters with the following remark:

> We've had some other letters on the subject besides these. Some of the other letters indicate that the church really is faced with some "excesses" over the revival, and that it has got a lot of unwanted fellow travellers who are doing nobody's image any good. We hope the church can overcome the problem, but we're cynical about its chances.

In the weeks and months after our return to Rabaul, we received letters containing extraordinary accounts. A very powerful revival had begun. For example, Arnon Sau writes, 'In one month we baptised 569 people by immersion and about 800 people were filled with the Holy Spirit.' Arnon Sau and George Strachan also wrote about a meeting in which the people heard a very loud noise and thought that a plane was coming. The noise came closer and stopped above the roof of the church. At that moment, the people began to weep and cried out loud in repentance.

They had to take some people out of the meeting to administer deliverance of demons. There was deep repentance. After this the people shouted for joy and danced while others began speaking or singing in new tongues. For those who were present, it was unforgettable. In the book *Fire in the Islands*, the history of the South Sea Evangelical Church is described, and much is also written about these revival meetings.

In the months that followed, reports kept coming in about hundreds of people who were converted and hundreds of believers who were filled with the Holy Spirit. We tried to go back to the Solomon Islands, but we were not able to get a visa. Maybe it was better for us not to go, because the Solomon Island men and women continued among their own people and led this revival.

In response to our newsletters that we wrote in the days after our visit to the Solomon Islands, we received letters from people in Australia, New Zealand, and also the Netherlands, who were eager to visit the revival and asked us if we could give them contacts. We did not do that. We received letters from people who felt called to go to the Solomon Islands as missionaries. We even received a letter from a person who wrote that after he had read our newsletters, he knew he was called as an apostle and asked if we could give him contact details so that he could go to the Solomon Islands as an apostle and lead the revival. Of course we did not do that, but we also stopped writing about the revival. I have no doubt as to who the real apostles in this revival are. This revival was among the people of the Solomon Islands. God had chosen to use their own people in a powerful way. It would not be the first time that people from the West stopped or disrupted a work of God because of inexperience or insensitivity to the culture.

Though it is not as spectacular as it was during the revival which started in 1970, there is to this day a powerful and strong church on the Solomon Islands.

Years later, I met Arnon Sau again during a conference in Australia. After the country became independent, an Australian Pentecostal church had begun to work in the Solomon Islands, and Arnon Sau had become one of its leaders. It was very special and moving to meet this servant of God as well as several other leaders of the Solomon Islands again.

A year and a half later, Coby and I went on our first leave to the Netherlands and flew from Port Moresby via Hong Kong to the Netherlands. On the flight from Port Moresby to Hong Kong, there were not many passengers, in what was then a quite modern Boeing 707. In the plane I saw two men of Papua New Guinean appearance. I went to them and spoke with them. They introduced themselves and told me that they were members of the self-government of the Solomon Islands. When I introduced myself, they exclaimed, 'Are you John Pasterkamp?'

'Yes, I sure am,' was my answer.

'Are you the Pentecostal missionary who went to the Solomon Islands?' was their question.

'Yes, I am,' I answered.

'In government circles, your name was a highly debated subject; and even recently in the self-government, your application for a visa to visit the country again was debated. We pleaded for a visa because we are Christians, but with a small majority, your request was declined after all,' they told us. It became a long and moving conversation, and after praying together, we said goodbye in Hong Kong. Precisely the ones who had defended us in the government of the Solomon Islands were on the same plane as we were. Could it be that God had arranged that?

When we shared about the revival on the Solomon Islands, we often were asked questions like how does it come, and what did you do to get such a revival? Some ask such questions because they have a deep hunger and intense desire for the Lord and because they want nothing more than for God to move and for Him to be glorified. But with others, you sometimes sense the thought: what method or what principle were you practising, because when we know that, we can do the same, and then we will also get revival. We don't have an answer to this, and we don't want to seek an answer either. It was God's work!

On the Solomon Islands, we saw what can happen and what does happen when God moves by His Spirit. In the years that followed, I sometimes said with great respect, 'What we have seen and experienced on the Solomon Islands has spoiled us. We now know what God can and wants to do. Never will we be satisfied with less!'

Years later, something happened which deeply touched us. I was in Afghanistan to lead a retreat of Christian social workers. After being there for a few days, I spoke with a couple from New Zealand. They had heard me say something about my experiences in the Solomon Islands. They said, 'A couple, and very powerful prayer partners for us as workers in Afghanistan, worked in the Solomon Islands years ago as well.' I asked for their name. It was the same couple who invited us to come to the Solomon Islands. I could not believe what I heard. I got their address and wrote them a letter. Soon we received a long letter in reply. They had retired, but their hearts were still moved for missionaries, and they spent much time in prayer. Without children of God like this couple, the work of the Lord could be a whole lot different. Now they are again praying for us too!

A verse that really came alive for us and became very meaningful was Isaiah 42:12: 'Let them give glory unto the Lord, and declare his praise in the islands.'

Once we asked T. L. Osborn the secret of the great revivals he experienced. His answer was surprising: 'To be at the right place at the right time. All else is God.' That is the way we felt too about our visit to the Solomon Islands. We were in the right place at the right time. I was twenty-five years old when we experienced the beginning of this great and deep move of God.

In prophecy the Lord had said, 'At a young age I will call you, and at a young age you will serve Me.' These prophetic words were certainly fulfilled!

CHAPTER 20

A Few More Months in Rabaul and Then . . .

QUITE A LOT of preparations were needed for the visit of Mrs. Daisy Osborn, the wife of evangelist T. L. Osborn, and two team members. For quite a while we had been communicating with the Osborns about the possibility of translating several films and ten of the best messages by T. L. Osborn, into Pidgin English. They would be in Rabaul for eight days to record translations of the five films and ten tapes. These would then be processed further in the United States. Several missionaries and leading national workers of the Foursquare Mission in the Highlands had specially come over to help us.

Mrs. Osborn was loving, compassionate, and warm, yet unpretentious. She had, together with her husband, led some of the biggest mass crusades in the history of Christianity and had seen tens of thousands of people come to Jesus. In those days, we once heard the remark that Billy Graham and T. L. Osborn in their crusades led more people to Jesus than anyone else in history. And now this special woman and her team were with us for eight days. We spent six days on translating under the leadership of Mrs. Osborn. We worked from morning to lunch, after lunch until right before dinner, and again several hours in the evening. Two Papua New Guinean workers spoke the text of the films and sermons onto a recording tape in the studio of Radio Rabaul, under the supervision of a technician. It was hard work. What stood out to us was how disciplined Mrs. Osborn and the two team members were. Five films, among them *Holland Wonder*, and ten messages were translated and then recorded. *Holland Wonder* is the documentary that was produced when T. L. Osborn was in the Netherlands, when he held a large evangelism and healing crusade in our governmental city of the Hague in August 1958.

On Saturday afternoon around lunchtime we were finished, half a day earlier than planned. We thanked the Lord together! Then Mrs. Osborn said, 'What is the most exciting thing that you can do around here for the remaining part of the day?'

One of the missionaries said, 'Catching sharks in the bay tonight.'

'Then that is what we will do tonight,' she replied, and so we did. We hired a boat and tried to catch sharks until midnight, by the light of the moon. The only one who caught a shark was Coby. It was a shark of about 150 centimetres long. Very exciting and a little scary. Coby did not get the shark on board herself; she was glad to accept help to do that.

We had a long conversation with Mrs. Osborn about the use of literature. She encouraged us to increase our capacity for printing and to buy a bigger offset printing press. The Osborns were also willing to help us print their gospel tracts in Pidgin English. A little while later, we were able to buy a bigger offset printing press and to print many gospel tracts as well as other Christian literature.

We held a prayer meeting on the evening before the Osborns' team was to leave. Jack and Swanny Kooy, Dutch missionaries who worked in Australia, were spending some time with us and had also been able to see the work that the Osborn team had done. That evening everyone was in the small room where we held church services: the missionaries, the national workers, Mrs. Osborn, and the two team members. Both Jack and Swanny have strong voices as well as some of the workers who were present. It became therefore a powerful and rather loud prayer meeting. It reminded me of the comment in Acts where it is said that they raised their voices to God with one accord. The prayer meeting had barely ended when there was loud knocking on the door. The Finnish missionary Lauri Pesu opened the door. The police commander stood there and said, 'We received a complaint from the neighbours about excessive noise in this house. What is going on here?'

Lauri innocently said, 'Commander, we just finished a prayer meeting.'

The commander turned around abruptly and said, 'Then it could not have been here,' and walked away. When he drove off with several other policemen, we had a good laugh. If only he had come ten minutes earlier . . .

We told Mrs. Osborn about the seven weeks we spent on the Solomon Islands. She listened attentively. We also told her that we were planning to leave Rabaul in several months' time, to go to Kavieng. We would hand over the work in Rabaul to the Finnish missionaries. Mrs. Osborn said that she could give us a 'mobile evangelism unit' for the work in Kavieng. Such a unit consists of a vehicle, a generator, a film projector, films, a screen, small sound equipment, and everything needed to evangelise in the villages. We were surprised. In total we received four units, completely equipped for evangelism, from the Osborn organisation: a unit for Port Moresby, a unit for Rabaul, a unit for Kavieng, and a unit for Bougainville. The Foursquare Mission in the Highlands received one as well. In Australia, I sometimes heard people criticise the Osborns because they so often asked for money to support missions. The people in Australia and other countries were asked to give. We were on the receiving end and are very grateful to the Osborns for all they did for the work in Papua New Guinea.

I made another trip to Siwai, this time with Joseph Yans, who was now working with us in Rabaul full-time. It was the first time for Yans to go to Bougainville. He stood out with his red-brown skin among the people whose skin is pitch-black. Again it was a specially blessed visit. Jacob Neewai, who was healed of tuberculosis during our first visit, was wonderfully used by God. He travelled throughout the entire district and pioneered quite a number of churches. Many miracles happened through his ministry. It was so encouraging to meet him again and hear the testimonies of what God was doing. During this visit, we could again baptise new believers. But the real highlight of this visit was my meeting with that extraordinary missionary, Pamela Beaumont. Pamela had just been appointed to a small missionary post in the area north of Siwai called Nagovisi. I borrowed a bicycle and had to ride for quite a distance. Sometimes I had to walk instead of ride because of the poor condition of the road, but Yans stayed behind in the village.

In Nagovisi, Pamela was able to continue translating the New Testament into the Siwai language, which she had learned and was still learning. Pamela is, as far as I know, the only Westerner who ever learned that language properly. Her dedicated assistant in this big project was a Siwai man called Stephen Iroro. Stephen too was filled with the Holy Spirit around this time. We came to know him well. He was a very gentle and intensely dedicated man. Pamela spent three years in Nagovisi, a period which she received as a gift from the Lord.

When we met, we spent hours talking. I was deeply impressed by this loving and brave woman. Pamela was really longing for the baptism in the Holy Spirit. She had read books about the Holy Spirit, and during her leave in New Zealand, she had been in touch with charismatic believers. Harold Morton, the MAF pilot, had often given her the magazine *Voice* of the Full Gospel Businessmen that contained testimonies of people who had received the Holy Spirit. Before I left, we prayed together for the baptism in the Holy Spirit, but it took some weeks before she received the gift of speaking in tongues. That happened while she was praying alone. In the following days, Pamela realised that she had to be baptised by immersion as well. She asked her loyal worker Stephen Iroro and David Pookaro to baptise her in water, in private. Near the missionary post was a little creek, but because it had not rained much for the past few weeks, there was not much water in it. Pamela proposed that she would sit in the water, and then Iroro and Pookaro could baptise her. That is how it happened.

When they baptised her, her nose flooded with water because the current of the stream was flowing against her. Gasping for air, she came up from the water, but she was overjoyed and happy. She was baptised! Though she was baptised in private, the news eventually reached the bishop of her area, and tension began. After a few more years, Pamela realised that she would be dismissed because of her baptism in water. She took the honourable way out and resigned. But in those few years, she was an enormous blessing to Siwai and to us. After her return to New Zealand, she attended a Pentecostal Bible school for a year. Then she came back to Bougainville and joined our work and led a Bible school in Siwai where many young people were trained. That school would become known all over the island and beyond. Pamela's most fruitful time on the mission field was yet to come.

In Nagovisi, she finished the translation of the New Testament. Throughout the years, we developed a deep admiration for Bible translators. Because of Pamela, we came to know the challenge of an almost impossible task.

How do you translate 'grain' and 'bread' on an island like Bougainville? What is a grapevine, what are grapes, and what is wine? What are sheep and goats, and what is wool? In Paul's letters, he writes about leaven. What is that, and how do you explain it? How do you describe the rituals in the temple with the ark, the washbasin, the lampstand, and so on? And in the book of Revelation, it mentions horses and lions. What are they? And then there is the grammar. No one had ever put the Siwai language on paper or compiled a dictionary. Pronouns like 'I' and 'we' are unknown in the Siwai language, but they can be understood from the conjugation of the verb. So a verb like 'to walk' reveals in a certain conjugation that it concerns 'I' but in another conjugation that it concerns 'we'. But 'we' also shows how many people are involved, two, three, four, or five, for example. When Paul writes 'we went somewhere', then one wants to know how many people were involved. In this way, Pamela had to learn the past, present, and future tense of 'I' and 'we' (two, three, four, or five). An almost impossible task. Westerners sometimes call these people groups primitive, but their language and grammar is anything but primitive.

Another very difficult translation challenge: take for example the well-known verse John 3:16, 'For God so loved the world that he gave his only begotten Son.' The concept of 'giving' is not very difficult for Westerners to understand. I can give something to someone and that's it. It is a gift or present, and the one who receives it is not obliged to do anything. But in the culture of Papua New Guinea, 'giving' is a very different concept. When I give something to someone, the one who receives it is under an obligation. Someday the one who received it or a family member has to give back something of the same value to me or my family. This means that throughout my life I am in debt. In their culture and way of thinking, that is an established concept. Now God gives us His Son out of love for us. Is that a giving as the Western people know it, or is it a giving as these cultures know it, meaning that we have a debt towards God? I experienced some intense debate about this issue among missionaries and Bible translators. I personally believe we have a debt towards God. God gave His Son; and that Son, Jesus Christ, gave His life for me. My only right response is that out of love and thankfulness I give Him my life. That is how we handled this cultural problem. You don't have to agree with me, but we saw good fruits from this approach. When we mentioned in a sermon or testimony that people now had a debt towards God, their Creator, they understood; and the responsibility weighed heavily on them.

Though usually only the New Testament is translated, a beloved verse for many born-again Christians is Isaiah 1:18, 'Though your sins be as scarlet, they shall be as white as snow.' Papua New Guinea is located just south of the equator; it's a tropical country, so what is snow? Try explaining that to people who are not familiar with snow and ice. But Bible translators found an excellent solution: 'Though your sins be as scarlet, they shall be whiter than the inside of a coconut!'

Many times when we spoke about missions, we mentioned Bible translators. A question that we heard them ask is something we ask the people we are speaking to: 'What is the most difficult book of the New Testament to translate?' Usually Revelation is immediately mentioned, but that is not the case. In Revelation, you read for example, 'And I saw a white horse.' That is not difficult to translate, once you have figured out what you are going to call a 'horse'. The most difficult book to translate is the letter to the Hebrews. The prophetic symbolism of the tabernacle, temple, sacrifices and service of the priests, and Jesus being the fulfilment in the New Testament is most difficult to translate. The second most difficult book is said to be 2 Corinthians, a book that contains difficult grammar.

Pamela came to Bougainville in 1951 as a teacher, and after living near Buin for a year, she came to Tonu in 1952. She soon discovered that the people needed the Bible in their own language, and in 1958, she followed a training course at Wycliffe Bible Translators in Melbourne, Australia. In 1960, she began translating; and in 1977, she finished this enormous task: 17 long years. In 1962, she was consecrated as a deaconess, which gave her the authority to preach and do pastoral work.

In the translation of the New Testament, Pamela had found a Siwai name for God: Tantanu. 'Tantanu' was also the word for God in a neighbouring language group. But when Pamela received the baptism in the Holy Spirit, she felt less and less comfortable translating God with 'Tantanu'. She began to research the exact meaning of the name again and discovered that there were several other gods beside Tantanu and who were equal to him. Tantanu was the god who gave food and all good things. She discovered that the Siwai people from their ancient history knew another god. A god who had no equal and who was the creator of everything and who was 'good', the highest giver of all good things. His name was Kupuna. Pamela decided to use that name, and though there was some misunderstanding at first, it eventually had a great effect.

In many people and language groups, the concept of the real, true God exists. But sometimes one has to dig deep to find it. I have heard people speak about that real, true God whom they no longer knew because of disobedience. Therefore, they now served those other gods: evil spirits.

As a young girl, Pamela wanted to become a missionary. She listened to a missionary from the Methodist Church who was working on the Solomon Islands, well before the Second World War. He called for missionaries to come to this country, as only little about the gospel was known there. Pamela answered that call. Bougainville is in a political sense part of Papua New Guinea, but geographically and ethnically it is part of the Solomon Islands.

In our bookcase is a very precious little red book, titled *Ma'ma'ni Dirokisa*, the New Testament in Motuna, the language of the Siwai on Bougainville. In the front is a personal message from Pamela and Stephen Iroro. I cannot read it, but to us this book is very precious, and it will always have a place in our bookcase.

Back in Rabaul, something happened that did not seem to be so important at first. However, it would have positive and far-reaching consequences for the work in the years to come.

We received a letter from the founder and leader of the youth training centre called Young and Free in the Netherlands. It was a friendly letter, but in it the leader asked a question. The Great Commission of the Lord Jesus to His followers is to make disciples of the nations. 'But,' he asked us, 'what do you think is the best way for us to make people disciples of Jesus?' A very good question. We thought about it for a few days and came to a certain conclusion which I wrote him in a letter.

How do you make disciples? Very simple: how did the Lord Jesus do it? He spent time with a group of men, very informally, for three years. It seemed like He had no schedule or program. His teaching and training were spontaneous. But the distinguishing mark was His relaxed, friendly, and intimate relationship with those men. They did everything together whether it was eating, walking, or sleeping; in short, they were inseparable. I wrote that to this brother and took the letter to the post office, bought a stamp, and dropped the letter in the mailbox. When I posted the letter, I sensed that the Lord spoke to me, 'And what do you do with this yourself?' For a brief moment, I wanted to stick my arm through the slot in the mailbox and get the letter back, but of course I couldn't do that. 'What do I do with this?' I knew that in some amusing way I was caught by my own answer. We had never heard about people who had discipleship groups. We had never yet heard about the Argentinian preacher Juan Carlos Ortiz and his messages about discipleship groups. In the years that followed, I tried to apply this principle, but it was when we were living and working in Port Moresby that this principle of a discipleship group really got off the ground, with astonishing results. But more about that in a later chapter.

It was clear that the Lord led us to the next island to live and work. That night in Port Moresby, during our first visit, the Lord had spoken about Rabaul, Kavieng, Bougainville, and the mainland, in that order. There had been several short visits to Kavieng. A group of believers met together, but they needed help. Renting a house in Kavieng seemed impossible, so we tried to get some land to build a simple house. After several attempts, that succeeded. The owner of a plantation next to the township of Kavieng was willing to lease a part of the plantation to us for thirty-five years. Hank and Lenie van der Steen, whom we had met in the Brisbane group, had received the Lord's call to go to Papua New Guinea and help us. Together as a team of four, we would go to Kavieng. Even though we had found a piece of land that we were allowed to build on, we had not been able to find a house that we could rent while we built the house. God would provide! But something had to happen in my heart.

Something was going on in my heart that no one noticed except Coby – something I had to be freed from. The work was growing. There were two Finnish missionary couples working in Rabaul. Kari was our age, but Lauri was twenty years older and an experienced missionary. He had served several years in Sri Lanka and Kenya and had been a pastor in Australia for a number of years. In many ways he was our senior, although we had started the work in Rabaul.

Hank and Lenie van der Steen were on the point of moving to Papua New Guinea to work with us. Hank was an accountant by profession. Besides Hank and Lenie, there were three other indications of interest by people who wanted to become involved in our mission work. I read their resumes: quite competent people.

I did not have such higher education. After my conversion, I decided not to go to teachers college to become a teacher, which made my father very angry. I took up an office job. I did some more study in a night school, but I thought that all these people were more competent than I. Deep in my heart, that made me very insecure, and a fear began to grow that they would not accept me and that they definitely would not accept me as their leader. I wanted them to come so that we could carry a greater workload, but I was also afraid and even noticed that inwardly I sometimes resisted it. I struggled with this, but I took no responsibility for those inner feelings and actually blamed the others. I caught myself with the recurring thought, *If only I had followed a higher education, then I could have done so much more for God and would have been able to serve Him better, and I would surely have been totally accepted.*

One time I was praying about this again. Nobody, except Coby, knew my inner feelings and struggle. Then God spoke to my heart and said with unmistakeable clarity that I had a problem, and He challenged me to look deep into my own heart and deal with my own wrong thoughts and insecurities. Paul writes in the second letter to the Corinthians, 'Bringing every thought into captivity to the obedience of Christ.' I did that, and the Holy Spirit helped me. I faced my own insecurity and feelings, acknowledged them, and brought them into the light. Instead of saying, 'If only I had a higher education . . .,' I began to say something else to myself, namely 'It would have been nice if I had a higher education, but my service for God is not dependent on it. The first disciples were plain fishermen. My competence is God Himself.' When I remembered that several of the first disciples were fishermen, that struck a chord, because on my father's side of the family, there are quite a few fishermen and also outside of the family I know some fishermen. Even when they take a shower six times, you can still smell the fish. I think that for these first disciples, it would have been the same.

I would have loved to be able to say that my inner insecurity was gone in an instant, but that was not the case. What did happen was that my deepest inner feelings and thoughts began to change. In the years following, I worked together with twelve foreign missionary couples and with Pamela Beaumont who was single. As far as I know, my leadership was never a problem for them, and it was never challenged. And the fact that academically nearly all of them had a higher education and were in their sphere of expertise more competent than I was never was a problem for me. On the contrary, between those missionaries and us grew strong relationships which remain to this day.

Three builders from Melbourne had promised to come to Kavieng in the beginning of 1971 to help build our house. Only, we had not found a place to live as yet for the period during which we would be building our house. Leaving Rabaul and our decision to go to Kavieng was a big step of faith.

We handed the work in Rabaul over to the Finnish missionaries, and in December 1970, we went to Port Moresby for two months to help with a large summer outreach: A Summer of Service by Youth with a Mission. About twenty young people from Australia and New Zealand would come for six to eight weeks to evangelise; most came from churches that experienced the new movement of the Holy Spirit. Hank and Lenie would come from Australia and be in Port Moresby those two months, and then we would go together to Kavieng.

Kalafi was going to lead a team for several weeks in the Milne Bay Province, and another team would go to the Gulf Province. Most members of the team would evangelise in and around Port Moresby. I myself would lead a team to an island in the Fly River, not far from Daru in the Western Province. We did not realise then that I would nearly get killed during that trip and that afterwards, in Port Moresby, we would almost lose one of our team members, who became very sick. A Summer of Service with Youth with a Mission can be exciting and adventurous, but this time it would be very, very challenging as well as very adventurous.

CHAPTER 21

Kiwai Island

KALAFI AND TAPU Moala of Youth with a Mission had welcomed a few new team members in Port Moresby. Kalafi Moala, the young Australian Tom Hallas, and the American Dean Sherman were now in charge of the whole team. We had met Dean Sherman in Sydney where he was present in the meeting in which a young woman was delivered, in quite a spectacular way, from demons. Furthermore, there were several other young people who had stayed on in Papua New Guinea, after they had participated in evangelism outreaches of Youth with a Mission in the Highlands, several months earlier. About twenty young people from Australia and New Zealand would join the team during the summer holidays. In addition, some local Christians who had come to the Lord in Port Moresby, as well as Hank and Lenie van der Steen who had arrived from Brisbane, Australia.

In Port Moresby, the team had led several young people to Jesus, among them a young Australian woman named Diana. Tom Hallas and Diana fell in love and wanted to get married in Port Moresby. I had just received my official recognition as a marriage celebrant in Papua New Guinea and had the privilege of conducting the wedding ceremony and praying for their marriage union – my first wedding ceremony ever. I don't know who was more nervous, the bridal couple or me? Tom and Diana's first baby, a daughter, is named Coby, named after . . . you're right, my Coby.

Dean Sherman had heard God speak to him after a time of prayer and fasting. Though there were various churches in Port Moresby, and quite a lot of people called themselves Christians, they were still bound to sin. Many so-called Christians practised witchcraft. Even when people were warned about it in church, it did not make any difference. Dean heard God say, 'Praise is the key to break the powers of darkness that have held this city captive from the beginning. These powers have never yet been challenged.'

Dean was stunned. Never before had he thought about the possibility that spiritual powers could hold a city captive. In 1970, you would not have heard anyone speak about that. But Dean had heard of people who appeared to have a ministry of deliverance – setting people free from demonic powers – but he had never met any. The team began to spend time in praise and worship every morning, sometimes for hours. God began to confirm this truth in multiple ways, and when I began to teach the team about David's tabernacle, that was again a confirmation. After a while, the result became clearly visible. There was a much greater openness among the people who heard the gospel, and the conversions were deeper and more radical.

The young people from overseas could now begin their Summer of Service outreaches. In the team was a young, newly-wed Australian couple, Barry and Joan Winton: they were modest and a little quiet, but when practical work needed to be done, they were there and served wherever they could. This soon caught the eye of the leaders.

Just before Christmas, I left for Daru with four young men who originally came from the area of the Fly River but now lived in Port Moresby. From there we would try to get to Kiwai Island by boat, the largest island in the eighty-kilometre-wide estuary of the Fly River. We wanted to evangelise in the villages where the young men originally came from. The work on Daru was led by a Dutch couple who had also been part of the group in Melbourne. It was nice to see them, but also to be back on Daru, the place where it all started some years earlier. The congregation there steadily grew, and there were good contacts on the mainland where several other congregations were forming as well.

We looked for a way of getting to Kiwai Island from Daru, but there was no boat to be found. It was just before Christmas, and the four young men really wanted to be with their families for Christmas. Finally we found a few men who were going to Kiwai Island with a large canoe, called a 'lakatoi'. They estimated that it would take two days of sailing and that they would arrive on Kiwai Island the day before Christmas; if not, then we would spend Christmas travelling. There was, however, a big problem. The canoe was a sailing canoe and had no outboard engine, and the monsoon wind had turned unusually early. The monsoon wind comes from the north-west from December to April. From May to December, the wind comes from the south-east. We would have the wind against us instead of for us, and the current of the Fly River is also from the north, so it would be against us as well.

With the current of the river against us and the wind from the north-west, it was nearly impossible to reach Kiwai Island with such a heavy lakatoi. What do you do then? Pray! Together with the Christians on Daru, we prayed, and what is impossible happened: the monsoon wind turned, and we could go. Shortly after Christmas, the monsoon turned again and kept blowing as usual for three months. Everyone was talking about it. The monsoon had come very early but had turned around again after a few days. That had not happened before since time immemorial. It seems that God likes doing things that have not happened before.

The Fly River is an enormous river. Where the river flows into the sea, it is about eighty kilometres wide. In a report in 1976, I read that the amount of water that flows from the Fly River into the sea is enough to supply every inhabitant of the world with forty litres of water each day. The Fly River carries mud up to sixty kilometres out into the sea, and the mud colours the sea into various shades of brown. Much of that mud returns to the coast and causes the river delta and coastline to keep expanding. Kiwai Island is in the estuary, in the delta. The coast is mud. In other parts of Papua New Guinea, the sea is crystal clear, but here you cannot even see your own hand when you put it in the water.

The canoe was a very large hollowed-out tree with outriggers on both sides to make sure that the canoe cannot turn over. On the canoe was a little platform where six or eight people could sit. The canoe had a simple sail, and the rudder was a large board that went through a groove in the hollowed-out tree trunk into the water. Western people would call it 'primitive', I think. There is no cabin, so you are outside in the open, no matter what weather it is. Think about it: me with my red hair and my skin which is sensitive to the sun taking a trip of two or maybe three days, on a canoe in the sun and with the glare from the sun's reflection on the water. I had been able to get my hands on a sun helmet and wrapped up my face and bare areas of my body in linen-like cloth. I must have looked like a Muslim lady. Despite that, I was quite sunburnt, right through the linen cloths. We had brought several boxes with food: rice, cans of fish and meat, dry hard biscuits, sugar, coffee, and tea. We also had some bananas and coconuts with us. The boxes were on the platform because on the bottom of the canoe, they would certainly get wet.

On our first day, we sailed in the direction of the Fly River. We made less progress than we had hoped for, and in the evening, we decided to spend the night in a small village by the coast. The canoe was brought as close to the shore as possible, and we made our way through the mud to the village. The men with the canoe were familiar with the village. There was a canopy of sago leaves under which we could sleep. I longed to sleep, but I could not. There were millions of mosquitoes, and I was completely devoured by them. I had brought some insect repellent cream, but it did not seem to help much. Day 2 did not bring us far either simply because there was not enough wind. We were not going to be able to cross the river and get to Kiwai Island before Christmas. So we again spent the night in a village near the coast.

It was Christmas Eve, the 24th of December. In this village, there were also canopies that we could sleep under. It was very hot – I estimate around 30 degrees centigrade and a humidity of about 90%. On the water it is cooler, but on the shore the heat is just stifling. That evening there seemed to be no wind at all. We did not have much to do, and after we had talked for a while in the dark, we tried to go to sleep, but we could not. It looked like the mosquitoes had travelled with us from the other village to join the mosquitoes here. How sorry I was for not bringing a mosquito net. We were completely devoured by mosquitoes. In the village, people were drinking alcohol because it was Christmas Eve, and they were very noisy. In the past, I have spent Christmas Eve in ways very different from this. The next morning we travelled to Kiwai Island, quite a distance away. I estimate about thirty kilometres. There was not much wind, and we were going against the current, so the going was slow. Often, we had to tack the unwieldy canoe. During one of these moments of tacking, the canoe shook, and the biggest box of food slid off the platform and disappeared into the depths of the water. We should have tied the boxes to the canoe, but we had not done that because there had been so little wind. I looked for quite some time at the place where the box had disappeared. If the people on the island would not give us food, then after a few days, we would have to go hungry.

Finally we arrived late in the afternoon of Christmas Day 1970 in the northernmost village on Kiwai Island. The young men who were with me saw their families again. They were happy and excited. But it soon became clear that the people of the village were not so happy that I had come with them. They had heard that several young people from their village, who lived in Port Moresby, had joined another church; and I was from 'that church'. Formally the village belonged to the area of the former London Missionary Society, usually abbreviated to LMS. The LMS also became part of the Uniting Church.

There was a small empty house that we could use. Though the young men had planned to sleep at their families' homes, they came to sleep in the same house where I was, probably to stay close to me, because on our arrival it had become clear that we were welcomed with mixed feelings. We did decide to have a meeting that evening because there were several young people in the village who were spending their Christmas holidays at home. All through the year they were at school or were being trained but lived at boarding schools, and during the two months of summer holidays, they went 'home'.

We were told that it had not rained for quite some time, and there was not much water left in the village. Washing yourself was therefore not possible, and we had to be careful when using water. We also did not have much food left. That evening we received food from one of the parents: sago. Sago is powdery and comes from the inside of a sago palm. The sago was rolled into a sort of sausage and roasted over a fire. The outside then had a crust, but the inside was just warm sago powder. I had never eaten it this way before, and my first response was that blackboard chalk tastes better. But . . . the Lord said to eat whatever you are served and to be thankful. That was difficult! The water was scarce, but there were coconuts in abundance, so we did get coconuts to drink and eat, only . . . coconut is not my favourite fruit. The water of a young coconut is very good to quench your thirst, but I just do not like it.

That evening a few young people came, and we sat in a circle and tried to have a meeting. We had brought a guitar and taught the young people an English song. After that, the four young men shared their testimony, but it seemed as if all the mosquitoes of the mainland had come with us to reinforce the mosquitoes of Kiwai Island. I wore a shirt with short sleeves, and my arms were covered with mosquitoes. Everyone tried to kill as many mosquitoes as they could. I had never before experienced so many mosquitoes. Therefore, it became impossible to have a meeting.

We decided to stop, and with the four team members and some young people who stayed, we sat around a smoking fire. We tried to make as much smoke as possible so that we would be rid of the mosquitoes; we partly succeeded. We then prayed together and rebuked the mosquitoes and commanded them to disappear. I would like to tell you they all disappeared, but they did not. But there were far fewer mosquitoes after that, and we were much less troubled by them in the following days. The people in the village on the island noticed this! They also heard that we had prayed.

When we talk about Papua New Guinea, people often ask if there were many dangerous animals. There sure are, millions and millions. Through malaria, the mosquito has killed more people than any other animal.

The next morning, Boxing Day, we held a Bible study about how you can be saved and why Jesus had come. The young people had heard the gospel in the mission church but often in a traditional way, and without explanation of how you can get to know Jesus personally.

About twenty, nearly all young people, had come. There was nothing else to do anyway. That morning we were able to lead a few to Jesus. There was celebration in our hearts. That afternoon, I was reading in the little house when I heard screaming and shouting. I went to see what was happening and saw a man chasing a woman with an axe, wanting to beat her up. The woman ran in circles shouting and screaming for her life. She was the wife of the man with the axe. Finally several men got hold of him and calmed him down, but it was almost an all-out fight between various men and women of the village. The atmosphere was tense. The team members told me that the man was the chief of the village, clearly quite a hot-tempered and violent little man. These people might be familiar with Christian things, but they certainly did not know the Lord. That evening we were served sago again, this time with little sardines in it, including the heads and everything. It was hard for me to thank the Lord, but I did.

That evening we were able to have a meeting around a fire with several young people. There were few mosquitoes, which was surprising. Later that evening, there was again a fight in the village. Everything in the village seemed to be restless, and there was an atmosphere of tension.

I had not had a shower or a bath for several days. On Bougainville, there are wonderful rivers with crystal clear water where you could have a great bath. Bathing in the Fly River was a possibility, but the river was brown and muddy, and you would get out of the water dirtier than when you entered it. It was extremely hot, though it was a little cooler on the bank of the river. I had sweated quite a lot for several days, was covered with mosquito bites, and had not eaten much. I had already decided I would rather be on Bougainville than on Kiwai Island. I missed Coby and felt far away from the inhabited world. We had sailed three days from Daru, the nearest government post, and any means of communication with Coby and the outside world was at least three days away.

Despite the fact that several young people had clearly chosen to follow Jesus, I did not feel so happy. That afternoon, I was in the little house feeling sorry for myself. I was deep in thought when I suddenly said, 'Lord, why did You bring me to this hole of a place?' The answer came immediately and very clearly, 'To please Me, son.' Immediately the verse of 2 Timothy 2:4 came to mind, 'No man who goes to war entangles himself with the affairs of this life; so that he may please him who has chosen him to be a soldier.' I was ashamed and said that to the Lord. I was not on Kiwai Island to have a good time or see big results, but I was there to please the Lord! What a revelation!

I had brought a book with me by Watchman Nee. In my own times of study, I had begun to discover something about the inner feelings of our born-again spirit, the place where the Holy Spirit lives. When I bought a particular book by Watchman Nee, I realised that he wrote about that subject too, and I wanted to read it. I had not heard anyone speak about this subject. In the book *The Spiritual Man*, I had come to the chapters about the flesh and the motivations of the flesh and the command of the Lord not to please the flesh but to crucify it.

The words 'to please Me' that the Lord had spoken so clearly and the book that I was reading became an absolute milestone and turning point in my walk with the Lord. The Lord had been working deeply within me in the weeks before, and together with this experience on Kiwai Island, I went through a sort of inner crisis. Suddenly I saw my own inward self very clearly. When everything was good and nice or adventurous, I loved serving the Lord. When missionary magazines wrote about the blessing and results we had and about that 'courageous Pasterkamp, missionary couple', it flattered me. But now I was on a muddy island covered with mosquitoes, without my preferred food, no shower, no bath, and in an atmosphere where I knew I was not really welcome. I saw motivations in me that I did not know I had. In those days, but also in the weeks following, I felt as if two doors of my heart were wide open; and the whole world could see what was actually going on in there and that not all my motivations were as pure as I thought and wanted. Every time I read another page in the book by Watchmen Nee, I was confronted with my deepest feelings and motivations. I began to understand that the Word of God separates what is spirit from what is flesh. Sometimes the confrontation with my own heart hurt quite badly. I was ashamed towards the Lord. I was quite willing to serve Him when the conditions were fun, pleasant, or adventurous; but on a muddy island called Kiwai Island with still too many mosquitoes, and far from the inhabited world and away from comfort and ease, and above all far away from Coby, then it was a different story. I repented, deeply repented, and spent hours during the day but also during the night alone with the Lord.

Every morning we held a Bible study, and one morning I gave these only recently converted young people a study about the woman about whom Mark tells us that she had a little jar filled with precious oil which she broke and poured out over Jesus. The gospel of John describes a similar story which tells us that the scent of the precious oil spread throughout the entire house. I shared that the Bible compares our life to a clay jar in which the Lord places a treasure. That treasure should not stay in the jar. They got the idea of clay jars, because in the area where we were, the people made simple clay pots and jars. Looking back, I wonder if the young people understood the rest of it. It was actually not a study for them, but I shared with them what I was personally going through. I realised that this was personal, and in the days following, I gave studies about the baptism in the Holy Spirit.

Close to New Year's Eve, most of the twenty young people were filled with the Holy Spirit and spoke in new tongues. Some had very powerful experiences with the Lord. After that, I started the studies about the baptism in water.

One day we were served sago with small sweet fruit. That was a feast after the dry sago for breakfast and dinner. Unfortunately, we were served dry sago again the next day. Luckily we did have some tea and milo and could have a cup of tea or milo every day. After several days, I decided to take a bath in the river after all. Even though I would come out dirtier than before I went in, at least I would have had the feeling of having been wet. The young men also wanted to go into the river after all those days. However, when we arrived at the muddy beach and wanted to go into the water, we saw what looked like a tree trunk floating against the current not too far away from us. A crocodile. The bath was cancelled that day. The day afterwards, we were able to take a bath. My whole body had been wet; what a luxury!

New Year's Eve arrived. All day there was a restlessness in the village. There was quite a quarrel between several men which almost turned into a fight. The chief seemed to be the one who had started it. I began to notice how afraid the people were of him. When he saw me, he did not greet me, and the look in his eyes told me clearly that I was not welcome. On New Year's Eve, a lot of beer appeared from somewhere. That must have come from Daru or a camp a little further up the bank of the Fly River, where they were looking for oil. The beer was warm because there were no refrigerators in places like Kiwai Island. The people don't drink just for the pleasure of drinking; no, they drink to get drunk. It became quite noisy in the village. We decided to stay with the young people. Towards midnight, something happened that I had seen before. They had obtained quite a few cans of some sort of baby powder from somewhere, and for fun they started powdering each other. I could not escape it. They came to get me, and so I started the New Year being white. I was a white man, but now a very white man!

At the Bible study on New Year's Day, I started to share about baptism by immersion. The four team members shared about their experience when they were baptised. For two or three Bible studies, we considered what Jesus said about baptism, all occurrences of water baptism in the book of Acts, what the New Testament teaches us about baptism, and the metaphors about baptism in the Old Testament. After the studies, fourteen young people announced that they wanted to be baptised. We promised to go to the river the next day and baptise them.

After the study, I sat in the house chatting with the young people, when the chief and two other men came to the house and called for me. I remained standing in the doorway. The chief's face did not predict good news. He spoke in his own language but was interpreted into poor English, but what he had to say was very clear. 'White man,' he began, 'I have heard that you are going to baptise my young people. Is that right?'

'Yes, that's right, sir,' I responded. 'That is the order of the Lord Jesus for everyone who believes. Tomorrow in the afternoon fourteen young people want to be baptised.'

His answer left no room for doubt. 'If you baptise my young people, you will not come off this island alive. I warn you.' Abruptly he turned around and walked away. We were quiet and had to let his message sink in. What I had already seen of his behaviour made this certainly no harmless threat or warning. What should we do? I told the four team members that I did not want to take them into danger and asked them to pray, think about it, and let me know that evening what they wanted to do. If they said no to the baptism service, then we would not baptise. I could not endanger them because of my conviction. I needed to know what their own conviction about this was.

That evening we gathered as a team. We did not eat that evening, if I remember correctly. I did not want to make a decision, but deep in my heart I knew what my choice would be, but I could not ask the team to do anything that was not their own deep conviction and decision. The team of four young men had evidently thought about it and were unanimous. 'We cannot give in to fear. The baptism service must go on.' I admired the courage and faith of these young men. I too had the conviction that we had to go on and not be afraid. I took into account that the chief might be bluffing and intimidating. But I also took into account the possibility that the threat was real. A leader in a culture like this one, who openly says something like that, must live up to his word or he loses his leadership.

We gathered the young people who wanted to be baptised. It was clear that the whole village had heard about the threat from the chief. When the whole village knows, that indicates that it is serious and not bluff. Of the fourteen young people to be baptised, five said they wanted to postpone it. Some of them were relatives of the chief. I could understand their decision. But it meant that nine young people were willing to be baptised. We prayed for quite a while that evening. That night I did not sleep much. *Is this my last night on earth? Is the baptism service tomorrow the last service I will experience on earth? At this time tomorrow, will I be in heaven with the Lord? Will I ever see Coby again, or was our goodbye in Port Moresby the last time we saw each other on earth? If they are going to kill me, how are they going to kill me? With traditional weapons because there are no guns here, right?* Many things went through my mind. I longed intensely to see Jesus and be with Him forever, but I was only twenty-six years old. I was eager to win many more people for Jesus and tell them about the great work of the cross by which we can be saved for all eternity. How would my father and mother respond when they hear that I had been murdered? I realised that would be devastating for them. Didn't the Lord promise a long life? But one of the first missionaries who ever tried to reach the area around the Fly River, Reverend Chalmers, was also killed. Wasn't it an honour to die for the gospel? What would happen to the team? A night with many thoughts and yet . . . that deep peace and quietness.

Morning came, and we had breakfast. Was this my last breakfast? I didn't know. Would I be in heaven that afternoon? Many things raced through my mind. One thing I decided, if this baptism service this afternoon would be my last meeting on earth, then it had to be a good one. I prepared well and made a short, simple, but clear message.

The afternoon arrived. We went in a procession to the most northern point of the island, a short walk over a narrow path with jungle overgrowth on both sides. A number of people from the village joined us. The muddy beach was small; the rest was covered with vegetation to the water's edge. One could not go anywhere except over the narrow path back to the village or into the water.

We sang, prayed, and sang some more. Suddenly the chief and two of his accomplices showed up. They stood at the beginning of the path. They had brought their weapons, a bow and arrows and spears. Was it pure intimidation, or was it serious? A few people became scared, that was clear, but nobody could leave because the chief and his mates literally blocked the path. *Is this then truly my last meeting, and will I never see Coby again?* These were the thoughts that ran through my mind. The nine people who were to be baptised were steadfast, and the team of four young men were strong and very brave. I admired them and was proud of them!

I began preaching, and the nine young people one by one shared their testimony. Two team members then baptised them. It was a moving experience. I think I only looked behind me once to the three men blocking the path. But I felt their eyes burning in my back. Everyone felt the tension. The nine were baptised. We thanked the Lord and sang again. The three men remained standing at the beginning of the path.

We sang again and thanked again, but sooner or later this meeting had to end. We had obeyed the order of the Lord, but we had disobeyed the order of the chief, and I was a guest in his village. *What is going to happen now?* raced through my head. *Will I be in heaven in a few minutes? Am I going to meet my Lord and Master Jesus in a few minutes?* Thoughts continued to jostle in my mind. Everyone wanted to return to the village, but the chief and his accomplices were still standing there. Then I decided to do something. I started to speak out loud in the language of the Holy Spirit: that is speaking in new tongues. I walked straight up to him and kept looking at him. The team members later told me that I appeared to be very calm, but inwardly I was not really calm. Speaking in tongues loudly, I walked slowly up to him. If he was going to kill me, then I would leave the earth and enter heaven speaking in tongues.

Suddenly something happened. The chief's whole body began to shake like a leaf on a sago palm, which can shake and move even when there is no wind. His whole body was shaking, and he grabbed both my hands and said something. The team members translated it. 'I am an evil man. Pray for me,' he said. *You are indeed an evil man*, I thought, and I prayed for him, first in tongues and then in English. I only prayed briefly, and then he let go of me and ran back to the village. His two accomplices followed him and also disappeared. We were stunned. God had intervened, that was sure. In the days following, it slowly became more and more clear to me what had happened here. That he was planning to kill me was evident. He had not bluffed; he had meant it. Since that moment, I became convinced that speaking in tongues saved my life at least once. That was on Kiwai Island in the Fly River. We did not see the chief or his accomplices anymore during the days that I was there. He obviously stayed far away from us. In his culture, he had suffered an immense loss of face; I understood that much. Much later I heard that three weeks after the event, he suddenly dropped dead in the village, something that left a deep impression on the island.

In the area of the Fly River and in the Western Province are now quite a few churches. I often wondered whether these churches would have been there if we had cancelled the baptism service because of the chief. Personally I think they would not have been there. Through this happening, a spiritual breakthrough took place over that area.

A few years later in a village on the bank of the Fly River, we experienced something similar. Seventeen people were going to be baptised, but when the baptism service began, the husband of one of the women who was to be baptised came walking towards us with a big iron axe and shouted that he would kill his wife if she was baptised. It seemed wise to us to have the baptism service and not a funeral right after it. The woman was baptised later, but not on that day. During the whole service, her husband was standing there with his axe. He watched us intently with a fierce look in his eyes.

A small open boat with an outboard motor had arrived at the village on Kiwai Island, and the owner told us that within a few days, a boat would leave for Daru from the camp where they were drilling for oil. I had been away for over three weeks and had said that I would try to get back to Port Moresby within four weeks. So I decided to go on that boat. The owner had been living on Daru for years, and I had met him before. A sailing canoe took me to where the boat was, and that took half a day to get there. The team stayed behind on the island to encourage the young people and be with their families a little longer.

There still is a Pentecostal congregation on the island. Jack Laukepe led the work in the Western Province for years and worked as an apostle visiting the island many times.

When I arrived at the camp, I heard that the trip to Daru had been postponed for two days, but I was welcome to stay on board. And that is what I did. I needed to be alone, to pray, to read, and to think. God was really working on me. However, there was an Australian crew member who apparently thought that it was interesting to have me on board. He filled his time with reading and looking at various *Playboy* magazines. He constantly came to me to show another picture and get my approval. I made it clear to him that I was not interested, but he pretended not to hear, and he came up to me a few more times, to show me what he thought was beautiful. Pathetic, absolutely pathetic, when a man is so occupied and fills his thoughts and life with this. I tried to speak to him about Jesus, but that was not successful.

The idea of going to the cafeteria of the oil drilling camp did not appeal to me either, because in their free time there was a lot of drinking, and the language spoken there was not what I wanted to hear. But the meals were in the cafeteria. When the men heard that I was a missionary, they did not know what to do with me, and I was treated and looked upon as someone from another planet.

When the boat finally left, it took only a day to get to Daru, and I can say that I did not mind leaving the boat. People have accused us many times, saying that missionaries destroy the culture of the people. But I wonder what causes more destruction, the gospel of Jesus Christ which changes people's lives or the alcohol and impurity, the various sexually transmitted diseases, the broken marriages, the way Western women sometimes dress and behave, etc. It is beyond dispute that there were also many good and wonderful expatriates in the country to serve the people, but there were also those of whom we were ashamed.

Several days later, I was back in Port Moresby, with Coby and the team. But God, deep in my heart, was still dealing with me, even weeks after my visit to Kiwai Island.

Kiwai Island became a precious memory to me, a milestone, and a turning point. More than ever I realised that I only have to do one thing: please my Master who called me. Also on a muddy island full of mosquitoes where they wanted to kill me.

CHAPTER 22

David Wallis

DAVID WALLIS, A young man from New Zealand, aged about twenty-four, had come to Papua New Guinea during his summer holidays. He was joining with twenty others for two months, to be part of the Summer of Service, an initiative of Youth with a Mission. David was going with several young men to their 'home area' in the Gulf Province. David's father owned a company in New Zealand. David had graduated from university where he was converted, and instead of being 'heir' of the company, he had heard the call of God and had only one ambition: to become a missionary. This did not have his father's approval, and his departure to Papua New Guinea had not been without tension.

When I left to go to Kiwai Island, David and his team also left. They first made a flight of about an hour with a small one-engine aeroplane to an inland government post. Then they had to walk. There was no radio contact, and the plan was that this team would be away for six weeks.

I came back to Port Moresby after four weeks, but David Wallis and his team had not returned as yet. Neither had the newly married couple Tom and Diana Hallas who had gone to the Milne Bay Province. Together with the team in Port Moresby, under the leadership of Dean Sherman, we prayed much for them. But every time I prayed for David Wallis and his team, I had an uneasy feeling. Something was not right; there was something going on. I shared this with Dean, and he also sensed that anxiety. Every day it grew stronger, so strong in fact that I decided to visit David and his team. I could get a seat on a small plane to the government post the next day and decided to go. But that night it was as if the Lord said, 'Don't go, stay home, and keep praying,' so I cancelled the flight in the morning. Later that day, we received a phone call from David who was at the airport. David and his team had returned and wanted to be picked up, only David did not sound well, and he did say that he had been sick but that he was doing better now. He also mentioned that they did have a rough time.

We picked up David and his team, and at the airport, we immediately saw that David was not looking well. The boys of his team said that he did have a severe fever several times, probably malaria. The food had not been good, neither the drinking water. They had also not been very welcome. It often happened that those coming from overseas could not handle the food, but that was not unusual. But we were happy that they were back. We could take care of them, and they could rest and regain strength. David rested for several days. He particularly wanted to eat fresh fruit. Soon he indicated that he was feeling better. We had prayed for him and also broken every influence of satanic opposition in the name of the Lord Jesus. However, although David said he felt better, he did not look better. We especially did not like the colour of his skin. David had been back for several days, and one afternoon he went to rest again.

Dean Sherman had to get something from the room where David was resting. He very quietly walked in and looked at David, whom he thought was sleeping. At that moment, Dean knew things were very wrong. David was unconscious and had not been able to control his bowel movements and had also vomited. Dean called for help, and I came. We immediately prayed for him again, and those who were in the house started praying too. We cleaned David up as much as possible. Dean called an ambulance, something expatriates have to do in case of an emergency. The ambulance came and took David to the hospital. Dean and I followed the ambulance in the car. In the hospital, we had to wait an hour or two while David was being examined.

After a few hours, the doctor came to the waiting room and asked us to come with him. 'You are the ones who arranged to have this young man brought here?' was his question.

'Yes, we are,' Dean answered.

'I have bad news,' the doctor continued. 'Your friend has cerebral malaria in a very advanced stage.' We asked him what cerebral malaria was, and the doctor explained that it is a very severe kind of malaria in the brain. Cerebral malaria is a combination of at least two different types of malaria and is about the worst malaria one can get. The chances of survival are very, very slim.

'I don't think he will make it to midnight. Four-fifths of his red blood cells are gone, and his brain is severely damaged. He has lost most of his functions, and there is nothing we can do. Cerebral malaria can hide for a while, but when it strikes, it is usually all over in several hours. Where is he from?' When we told him that he was from New Zealand, the doctor asked, 'Does his family know that he has been brought to the hospital?'

'No, they don't know.'

'Then immediately contact his parents. I think their chances of seeing him alive are very small, but if they are coming, we might be able to help him to live a bit longer.' We were dumbfounded and totally shocked. David was dying; and there was, medically speaking, no hope.

Dean asked, 'Doctor, but what if he lives, what then?'

The answer of the doctor was more than clear. 'Don't hope that he will live because then he will go through life like a vegetable. He won't have any brain functions and won't be able to do anything. Do not even hope that he stays alive because that life will have no quality whatsoever. Again, do not even hope for it. Your friend is dying, and like I said, he will probably not even make it till midnight. He is too far gone.' We were quiet and did not know how to respond. Totally beaten, we went home to inform the other team members. We came in touch with David's father by phone, and he was to take the first possible flight. There was no dinner that evening. Nobody was hungry. We only wanted to do one thing: pray.

After the whole team had prayed for several hours, we came together. 'Has the Lord spoken to one of you?' was the question Dean asked. Yes, He had. Two team members had received John 11:4, 'This sickness is not unto death, but for the glory of God, that the Son of God might be glorified thereby.' Another team member received John 9, the second part of verse 3, 'the works of God should be made manifest in him'. Several other team members had received Acts 12:5, 'but constant prayer was offered to God for him by the church'. I had received from the Lord the story of the conquest of Jericho in Joshua 6. The people had to walk around the city for seven days, and then the city would fall. When we shared these words and put them together, we understood that the Lord had spoken and had given clear instructions. We had to pray for seven days and call on the Lord as a team and as a congregation. We also understood that God would be glorified and that the Son of God would receive the honour.

We immediately put this in action and made a schedule. Two team members would pray for David every hour. We would do this from six o'clock in the evening to six o'clock in the morning and when possible during the day. Activities had already been planned, announced, and prepared; so it was decided that those would continue as well. The devil was not going to stop our evangelism. It was about ten o'clock in the evening, and the schedule started immediately. Coby and I prayed for an hour also that first night.

Early the next morning, Dean and I went to the hospital. David was still alive and was in intensive care. He was a mess to look at. Blood transfusion, infusion, ECG, everything. He was now in a coma. An Australian lady doctor worked her shift in intensive care. She came to us and asked, 'Are you the leaders of that group of Christians of whom this young man is a part?'

'Yes, we are,' was our answer.

'Has this young man taken malaria tablets?' was her next question.

Dean answered, 'We advise every team member to take malaria tablets, but we cannot force them. This young man is older than twenty-one. We advised him to take them, but he decided not to.'

The doctor was angry. 'I know you Christians. You believe that God protects or heals. This young man is going to die, and I will hold you responsible. When he is dead, I will have you before court because of irresponsibility resulting in death.'

Dean looked the doctor in the eye and said, 'Doctor, this young man will not die but live. We have a house full of young people who are praying for him day and night, and God will answer.'

The doctor was furious and shouted, 'You are crazy, and I will take you to court!' Then she turned around and walked away. We both had to take a deep breath. We went to David and prayed for him. Dean said something, but there was no response at all. In the car, on the way back, neither of us spoke.

That afternoon David's father arrived at the airport. It was not a cordial meeting. We immediately took him to the hospital. David was still alive. His father was visibly upset when he saw his son like this. Understandable. The father spoke to the doctor. We were not allowed to be part of that conversation. A room had been booked for David's father in Mapang Missionary Home near the hospital, a house for missionaries who are passing through and in walking distance from the hospital. When we came there, David's father was told that he could not get a room by himself but that he had to share it. His roommate turned out to be one of the leaders of the Solomon Islands. I knew him, and he was very happy to see me. We spoke for a while, and I explained the situation. He understood and promised to pray, which he also told David's father. This leader witnessed and prayed with him. Had God organised it this way? David's father rented a car and did not need our services any longer. He made that quite clear.

That evening and night, at least two team members prayed every hour, fervently and passionately. The fellowship also gathered to pray. More Christians joined us and also prayed at night. In between shifts several slept on the floor; there were no more beds.

The next morning David was still alive but totally unresponsive. He looked terrible. We stayed with him for a while, prayed, and left. Were we avoiding the doctor, or was she avoiding us? That was unclear. Late in the afternoon, the situation remained unchanged, and also the next morning. Once or twice we met David's father. He stayed with his son for hours. In the evenings and nights, people prayed fervently. They cried out to God. In the morning, during breakfast we shared what God had shown or which verses he had given us, which was very special and very encouraging. God spoke and built up our faith and trust.

That morning Dean and I went to the hospital again. Against all expectations, David was still alive. The doctor was not there, and neither was David's father. Nobody but his father, Dean, and I were allowed to visit David; and we were only allowed for brief moments. David's father was allowed to stay longer. There was only a nurse present. We stood next to David's bed. Dean leaned forward and said near David's ear, 'David, praise the Lord.'

Very softly and very slowly, but very clearly he answered, 'Hallelujah.'

The nurse saw it and exclaimed, 'Did he speak?'

'Yes, he spoke,' was our answer.

'Oh, but he does not speak to me,' she said.

'That's right,' Dean said, 'because you don't speak the right language.' The nurse looked at us with big question marks in her eyes. To us it was clear. David's body was so close to death; but his inner man, his spirit, was alive. The nurse apparently told David's father about it. But when he said something, there was no response. Only David's spirit was accessible.

We kept praying, often also during the day. On the fourth or fifth day, a missionary who was passing through came by for several hours to the Youth with a Mission house. We told her nothing about David. The woman did not know him. Suddenly she said, 'You know, I am so thankful to God. I should have been dead, but God healed me of cerebral malaria.' We could not believe our ears. Then we told her about David.

Every hour during the night, at least two team members prayed. After praying for an hour, they woke up the next two. These were unique hours. There was an overwhelming presence of the Lord in our midst. It was exciting, and it was serious, because we fought a spiritual battle for the life of one of our team members, but God was so tangibly close.

I must mention here that throughout this time, the doctors and medical staff worked around the clock and did their utmost to keep David alive. We are very thankful to them.

On the seventh day, David woke up from his coma and ate a small meal while sitting up in bed. What a feast. He was very weak but quite clear-minded and had all his faculties. He could move everything. His was speaking well; everything was in order. He remained in the hospital for a few days to regain strength and be under supervision and then was allowed to go to the Youth with a Mission house to recover further. The entire team was so happy. God had answered. For seven days we had cried out to God, and David was well again.

Dean and I asked to speak with the doctor. She refused to meet with us. David's father went back to New Zealand. We took him to the airport, but he did not say much. Later we heard that he had visited several traditional church leaders in Port Moresby, and those conversations had clearly not been positive. Youth with a Mission in Port Moresby experienced difficulties because of that for years.

A month after his healing, David fasted for several days, skinny as he was. David's father had seen his son get healed before his eyes. We don't know how that affected him. As far as David knew, he did not become a believer. The tragic thing is that David had to fly to New Zealand a year later to attend his father's funeral. He died of a stroke.

For some time David stayed with Youth with a Mission in Port Moresby. We loved him. He was a very dedicated and sensitive team member. He married Marilyn in New Zealand, and together they were sent as missionaries to the Philippines by the Assemblies of God in Auckland. I visited David and his team in the Philippines several times, to speak at conferences and crusades. Later David and Marilyn and their two children went as missionaries to India where they especially supported existing churches with crusades, conferences, and teaching. I also visited them there a number of times.

In a large meeting in Madras, India, I shared the story of David's healing. David, Marilyn, and their children were present. The two children were spellbound as they listened. Afterwards, they were very excited. Their father had told them about his healing, but now they heard the story from someone who had been there. It touched them deeply, and also the congregation where we were was moved. They knew David very well.

It is now more than twenty-five years since David's healing. The last thing we heard about David and Marilyn was that they lived and ministered in the United States of America.

Throughout the years, I often preached on 'the law of faith' as Paul calls it in Romans 3:27, and I take the conquest of Jericho as an example. Then I mention four points: (1) God speaks, (2) we have to act, (3) the test or trial of our faith, and (4) the answer. I then usually tell the story of David Wallis. It was a fulfilment of God's words; God's work became visible through him, and God received all the honour!

CHAPTER 23

Kavieng

THE DAYS AFTER David's healing were fantastic. Everyone was happy and encouraged with a sense of victory reigning throughout the entire team. Nearly every evening we held meetings, and God's Spirit moved. The new believers had also seen the miracle of David's healing, their faith was built up, and they were encouraged. It was not difficult to testify during the evangelism outreaches. Regularly young people and sometimes older people came to the Lord Jesus.

There were also several expatriates, mainly Australians, Spirit-filled people who lived and worked in the town. It was not unusual for us to have meetings in one of their homes. One evening the home of one of the expatriates was packed. There was an archway between the living room and the kitchen, and I was sitting underneath the lower part of the arch.

We could not get enough of praise and worship, which brought us into the presence of the Lord. We wanted to stay there forever, but I still felt it was going too far to show one's exuberance and joy by dancing. This critical attitude masked the fact that I simply did not dare to do it! But that night there was such joy in the meeting I decided to release the brakes and dance, for the first time in my life. I closed my eyes and taking a leap started dancing. Well, skipping is probably a better word. However, I was sitting right underneath that arch, and as I leapt, my head hit the arch. It did not hurt too much, but it did leave me with a bump on the top of my head for some days. That was the first time I danced before the Lord. I could see the funny side of it: me with my critical Dutch attitude! I had a good laugh about myself. In my imagination, I saw the Lord smile. Moving about a metre away from the arch, I danced. That was a great victory.

While we were in Port Moresby, we received a message that the land in Kavieng had been approved, and we could lease a beautiful piece of land for thirty years. We also received the confirmation that three builders from Australia would give up their holidays and come to Kavieng to help build the house. We cheered. They paid their own way! Now all we needed was temporary accommodation for Hank and Lenie, the three builders, and ourselves. We had looked around in Kavieng, but we were told that renting a house there was impossible. We enquired if there was perhaps an expatriate who was going on leave and we could take care of the house, but all we heard was no. We realised that we might have to arrange to have a native house in a neighbouring village. And though that may sound easy, in reality it was not.

Hank and I decided to go to Kavieng before the others, to arrange something, while Lenie and Coby stayed behind in Port Moresby. As soon as we had arranged accommodation, they could come. It was over two months since we had left Rabaul and gone to Port Moresby, when Hank and I flew to Kavieng. We had only our luggage but no use of a car. But four hours after we had arrived, we managed to rent a very basic house for several months. It was a few minutes' walk from the piece of land we were going to build on. It had two bedrooms with a partial wall so that fresh air could flow through all the time. It did not have much privacy. If someone coughed, everyone could hear it. The builders had to sleep on inflatable beds or mattresses on the floor in the living room. A big bonus was that the house was near the beach. Between the house and the beach was only a small path and a strip of grass. The sunsets behind the island Mussau, which was close to the coast, were magnificent. Many times we just sat down and enjoyed the beauty of these tropical sunsets. Now, after years in the Netherlands, we still miss the beautiful blue sea and the tropical sunsets. The owner of the house was an expatriate who had lived in Kavieng for years but had become an alcoholic. Sometimes he came to the house while drunk and talked a lot, but the next day he could not remember any of it.

On the next flight, several days later, Lenie and Coby arrived; and the team of four was complete. We were able to spend much time in prayer in that early period. The group of believers that regularly gathered in Kavieng was very happy. We now lived in Kavieng, and they were no longer alone.

Hank and Lenie came to Kavieng, trusting the Lord to look after them and to provide what they needed. They had saved some money but gave that away, so they were totally dependent on the Lord. God particularly used friends of theirs to provide, for the first few years.

In the meantime, we received a large part of the estimated costs of the house through gifts. All the lights were on green.

There 'happened to be' a bulldozer in Kavieng just after we arrived. Normally there was no bulldozer on the entire island. The bulldozer came from Rabaul. We could hire it for several hours to flatten the piece of land before building on it. Quite a number of coconut trees had to be removed, and on the land were also four small bomb craters caused by Japanese bombs that been dropped during the war. These had to be filled. Also the left corner at the front of the land was swampy because of a small crater filled with water. There were quite a few big frogs in there and sometimes harmless snakes. According to the native people, it was a place where an evil spirit lived, and they avoided that spot. Now we were building and going to live there! The bulldozer arrived, and despite the fact that it got stuck for a while in one of the craters, the land was flattened in several hours, and we could set out the perimeters for the house. Now the heaviest task began: digging the trenches for the foundation. The ground was mainly coral, so we had to break it up with a pick and shovel it out.

We hired a couple of young men, and also the Christians helped wherever they could. We were digging for nearly three weeks. We started at half past five in the morning until about eleven o'clock. After that it was too hot. In the afternoon, we continued from three to about six o'clock. Then darkness fell. I could wring out my shirt at about ten in the morning, and there would be quite a bit of water in a bucket. The parable of the wise man who dug deep to lay the foundation on the rock became more real to us.

During the long lunch and afternoon break, we tried to pray. But sometimes that did not work out. Because we were tired, we sometimes did not really get to prayer, and one or more of us fell asleep. We also discovered that iced tea is very good to quench one's thirst. During the digging and building, we drank gallons and gallons of iced tea.

We needed to provide a simple drawing of the house we planned to build, and this was approved. We had no finance to build two houses, so it became one large team house. We planned an elongated house so the wind could blow through the house. On both ends, there were a large living room and a bedroom, one for Hank and Lenie and one for us. In between were two extra bedrooms, a simple shower, and a large living room with a kitchen so that we would also be able to have meetings in the house. On the farthest end was an extra room for the printing machine and our equipment like the generator, projector, sound equipment, etc. In Kavieng, building material was easy to get, and what was not available came from Rabaul. Just outside Kavieng, bricks were made but only on order. The bricks were made of cement, sand, and coral that had been washed really well and contained no more salt. The bricks were very brittle and soft, but they were all we could get and were allowed to use. With a wood saw, we could saw the bricks to size when necessary. It sounds strange, but I have cut this kind of bricks to size many times with a wood saw. The front and back walls of the house mainly consisted of louvres. The house would get a slanting roof providing shade so that the sun would never shine directly into the house.

We still had no car, but there was going to be a sale of used government vehicles including several utilities, ideal for us. We made an offer and could buy one of these cars for a few hundred dollars. It drove quite well. Now building could begin.

The three builders arrived. Two of them, Ray van Netten and his son George, we knew from the Dutch group in Melbourne. Bill Bines, an Englishman whose son had married Ray's daughter, was new to us. They were professionals, and they knew how to build properly. While they were building, Hank and I were often busy buying or searching for materials so the men could continue to work.

We have to share one amusing event that happened in the early stage of building. Julius, a young man who lived near Kavieng and was originally from the Sepik Province, close to the border with West Irian, offered to work for us. He said he was a bricklayer and even had his own tools. He was looking for work. We agreed that he would work for a few days, on a trial basis, and then work on a daily basis until his help was no longer needed. He began to lay bricks for the farthest outside wall. Ray had set the corners, and Julius needed only to lay row upon row of bricks in between. After several hours, Ray went to see how things were going and then called us. Julius had almost finished another layer of bricks, but the cement between the bricks at the end of the row was almost as thick as the bricks themselves, and Julius did not understand it. Ray then showed him that his string was one brick high on one side and two bricks high on the other side. He had put more and more cement between the bricks until the cement was as thick as the brick itself. Julius stayed, but not as a bricklayer but as a labourer. Shortly afterwards, he came to the Lord, was filled with the Holy Spirit, and was baptised in water. After a while, he went back to his own province where the Assemblies of God worked. He followed a basic training course and became a village pastor in his own area, one of the fruits of Kavieng.

After four weeks of very hard work, the house was almost finished. We could move in. We were able to get a table and chairs in Kavieng and made the beds and cupboards ourselves.

Hank and Lenie had become members of a congregation in Brisbane that was perhaps the first congregation in Australia to embrace the new movement of the Holy Spirit, as we had experienced it during the conference with Pastor Frank Houston. The pastor of this church was Pastor Trevor Chandler, who had been Frank Houston's associate pastor in New Zealand for many years. The congregation changed its name to Christian Life Centre, adopting the name from the New Zealand congregation. It grew rapidly. In a short period, the congregation had grown from 200 to 800 or 900 visitors and members. Sometimes there were more than a 1,000 people in a meeting, which was still very uncommon in those days in Australia. Christian Life Centre was in the limelight and soon became known as a place where God's Spirit moved. People from all over the country came to Brisbane. Many came to the Lord, and many were deeply touched by the Holy Spirit.

After some time, the congregation began to support Hank and Lenie financially as their missionaries, and the work in Papua New Guinea began to build a relationship with Christian Life Centre in Brisbane. Shortly after the house was finished, several young people from that congregation indicated their desire to come and join us. Within a short period, we had a small team just like Youth with a Mission in Port Moresby. We did the same as they did. Five mornings a week we gathered to worship God, have times of intercession, study the Word, and build relationships. It was very special, and we experienced the Lord's presence and reality in our midst. Often, the new believers from Kavieng joined us and experienced the wonderful presence of God.

It was around that time that the Jesus revolution began in America, and soon it began in Australia as well. We noticed its influence. The charismatic movement in the traditional churches grew stronger and stronger. We began to receive teaching tapes from Derek Prince on a regular basis. Everything was new, sparkling, adventurous, and refreshing. A wind of the Holy Spirit was blowing.

Throughout the world, the sign of the Jesus movement was the hand with the index finger pointing upwards: Jesus, One Way. We also adopted that sign, and on the door of our utility truck was the One Way sign. Together with Youth with a Mission in Port Moresby, we were able to print T-shirts with the One Way sign and the words 'Jesus One Way'. Before long, we were known in Kavieng and the surrounding areas as the One Way Mission, a name that stuck for a very long time and which identified us with the worldwide movement of God's Spirit. Something we were happy to be identified with.

I began to experience something new, something that I never experienced before. There were times when for weeks at a time I woke up around five o'clock in the morning, and in those early hours, the Lord began teaching me. Entire passages of the Bible opened up to me. It started with the Sermon on the Mount. I spent hours and hours studying the Bible, and then I shared with the team what I had learned.

For example, I started to see how God worked in the lives of well-known people in the Bible, especially David. The Psalms became more precious than ever. David experienced the Lord's working deep in his heart, which made him stronger on the inside, until he could exclaim, 'My heart is fixed, O Lord'(Psalm 57).

Walking back home one day, after an outreach meeting, Arlene, one of the team members, asked me, 'John, do you really know God as Father?'

'Yes, of course,' I snapped back. 'What makes you think I don't know God as Father?'

Arlene gently answered, 'Because I hardly ever hear you pray to God as Father, but you usually pray to the Lord Jesus or to God.' I was upset. She was one of the youngest and newest team members. Where did she get the courage to say this to me, the leader? I felt offended. Wasn't I the team leader and an experienced missionary? What was she thinking? I was quite irritated and told Coby about it but could not shake it off. Slowly but surely I realised that Arlene might be right. Arlene had lost her father in a tragic way at a young age, and she really knew God as her Father. So I started to reach out to know God as Father. This process is not finished yet, but I began to get to know God more and more as Father, a loving Father, a Father with whom one is always safe, a Father who encourages and is genuinely interested in you, a Father who does not criticise you but who understands you completely, One who embraces you as a father does a son. I am glad and thankful that Arlene talked to me and had the courage to challenge me.

A nice seventeen-year-old boy had come to the Lord. At birth, a Roman Catholic priest had given him the name Darius. His own name was Kiumat. Although he was usually very cheerful, I sometimes noticed a sad look in his eyes. One day Darius wanted to talk with me. He came from New Hanover, an island that was part of the province. He told me that his mother was not married, and she did have one relationship after the other. Darius was born out of one of those relationships. He had no idea who his father was. When he grew up in his mother's village, he got a nickname. He was called 'pamuk pikinini' in Pidgin English, which is translated as 'bastard'. As a young boy, he thought it was funny, but when he became a teenager, he began to understand it, and after a while, he decided to leave the island and live with an uncle in Kavieng. He had attended primary school and was able to attend a school to learn a basic trade in Kavieng. Nobody knew his history, so his name was simply Darius Kiumat. That's how we knew him. But that week he had met an uncle who had called out to him, 'Hey, pamuk pikinini, how are you doing?' It had hurt him so deeply to hear that nickname again, as well as the fact that a grown-up family member called him that. The pain from his youth had surfaced once again.

What was I to say? I came from a good family. I am the fourth child of married parents, and although I was born in the 'hunger winter' of the Second World War, I was more than welcome.

In my heart I prayed, saying, 'Lord, what can I say to Darius? I don't know.' Very clearly I heard the Lord speak into my heart, 'Tell Darius that I had the same nickname as a child. I was also called pamuk pikinini.' I was dumbfounded. I suddenly realised how true that was. In the culture that Jesus was born in, a pregnancy before marriage was unacceptable. You can actually read how the Pharisees try to point that out to Jesus, saying that therefore Jesus had no right to preach. Doesn't it say in the law of Moses that a bastard may not enter God's house to the tenth generation?

After a time of silence, I said to Darius, 'Did you know that the Lord Jesus had the same nickname when He was a child? He knows exactly how you feel and what it is like to be addressed in that way.' Darius was quiet for a long time, and tears welled up in his eyes. He understood. We prayed together. The part in Hebrews 4 that teaches how Jesus can sympathise with our weaknesses because He was in all ways tested as we are became a lot more meaningful through this event. I have shared Darius's story many times throughout the years. But this story also characterises our time in Kavieng: a time of much learning.

At the trade school Darius had attended was a Dutch teacher whom we later met. He had taught Darius a Dutch word, and Darius was proud he still knew it and was able to say it, but he did not understand its meaning. The word was 'dom oor', which means 'stupid' in English.

Just outside Kavieng was the village Kopkop, where Julius, the bricklayer, lived. We held outreach meetings there. One evening we had a meeting, and there was a call to give one's life to Jesus. A man on crutches, called Wanga, came forward. Leaning on his crutches, he prayed the sinner's prayer. Suddenly Wanga gave a shout. He threw away his crutches and walked. During the sinner's prayer, he had been healed. The whole village was turned upside down. Wanga walked without crutches. Kavieng is only a small place, and everyone had seen Wanga walking on crutches. He had become crippled because of a severe accident in a game of rugby, which is very popular in Papua New Guinea. The testimony spread like wildfire throughout the area. Wanga was walking again. Nobody had specifically prayed for him. While he prayed and accepted Jesus into his life, he was healed. In Kopkop, a small fellowship soon started; and the majority of the village, which was quite small, became Christian.

A boy came to Jesus. Originally he came from another area. His father and mother, and afterwards a brother and a sister, had all passed away. Everyone in his village was convinced that they had died as a result of witchcraft. One child was left, and that was this boy. Acquaintances and friends collected money and put him on a plane to Kavieng, fearing that otherwise he might also die because of witchcraft. In Kavieng, he found Jesus. He radiated with joy and testified everywhere.

Regularly we could lead people to Jesus. Several girls from our team held children's meetings in the villages around Kavieng. About sixty kilometres from Kavieng, people invited us to come. There too a small congregation was planted. A young couple from our team lived there for quite a while and continued to build the small congregation.

The Osborns had promised that we would get a completely equipped utility truck for evangelism. The Osborns called such a vehicle a 'mobile evangelism unit'. Everything was arranged; and the unit was bought, with generator, projector, five Osborn films in Pidgin English, ten tape recorders each with ten tapes, sound equipment, a large screen, and much reading matter. The Osborns themselves would come to Kavieng to dedicate the unit to the Lord and present it to us. When I was visiting Siwai on Bougainville, I shared that Osborn himself would come to

Kavieng. It caused a commotion. Several Siwai believers scraped money together and flew to Kavieng to meet T. L. Osborn. David Pookaro was one of them. We had told the Osborns the story of Siwai, and they were looking forward to meeting the Siwai believers. The meeting between the Osborns and David Pookaro was moving to watch. David Pookaro had never, never thought that he would personally shake Osborn's hand. He just kept shaking Osborn's hand and looking at him.

There is only one hotel in Kavieng, and we booked the Osborns in for three days. They would have a small crusade in the evening during those days. The Osborns came, and the unit was dedicated to the Lord. The Christians had already seen the Osborn films, and now here was the real, living Osborn. It was a great honour to them. On an afternoon, the Osborns came to our house to spend time with the team. If a thermometer of faith had existed, then it would have shown a considerable increase above normal. Osborn told about the work they did, the great crusades they had held, and the miracles of God they had seen. One of the gifts of the Holy Spirit is the gift of faith. That gift was clearly present in the Osborns, and they definitely left something of that with us. That was an afternoon we would never forget.

The crusade was held on a large open field not far from our house. Osborn always prefers a local, national interpreter, but none of the local Christians spoke sufficient English to be able to do that. That's why I became the interpreter. What a privilege to stand next to this man of God and to interpret his message.

One evening it was raining heavily, and practically no one showed up. When it rains in tropical Kavieng, it really rains. This meant the crusade would only last two days. The crusade evenings were unique, especially the second one. About 1,500 people had come. Halfway through the sermon, we heard a growling noise above the people. Everybody noticed, and people were looking to see where the noise came from. It grew stronger. The growling noise was clearly in the air just above the people. When it grew quite strong and began disrupting the service, Osborn stopped preaching and turned to me. 'Does this bother you?' he asked.

'No,' I said, 'because I know what it is.'

Osborn continued, 'I experience this often. When I proclaim God's Word, the demons cannot take it any longer and start to manifest. If you feel comfortable with that, we will go on.'

Osborn continued preaching, and the noise grew very loud. Suddenly about half of the people ran away into the dark. The noise stopped, and Osborn invited the people who stayed to accept Jesus. Everyone who had stayed came forward and prayed the sinner's prayer. A great peace and rest came over the meeting. It was very impactful, to say the least. The entire team was present and will never forget this. This was not the last time that we would meet the Osborns. They passed through Port Moresby once, while we lived there, on their way to the Highlands. And years later we saw them again in Australia.

On behalf of the team of Youth with a Mission, we invited the Osborns to have a crusade in Port Moresby; but unfortunately, that wasn't possible. Their schedule was full. They suggested that we invite the well-known Dutch evangelist Johan Maasbach to have a crusade. The Christians knew Johan Maasbach from the Osborn film *Holland Wonder* in which he interpreted Osborn. Several months later, Johan Maasbach came and held a crusade. About 5,000 people came over five evenings. Again souls were saved, and the sick were healed. What touched us deeply were the great needs evident among so many people. It was a blessed crusade, but years later, after we had permanently left Papua New Guinea, we would experience very special and bigger crusades led by Charles Lapa from Pangia in the Highlands. He was one of the young men we trained in Port Moresby, who became a well-known spiritual leader in the country.

Johan Maasbach was eager to visit an area which had minimal development. Papua New Guinea still rates as one of the third world countries that is only beginning to develop. We took Johan to Pangia in the Southern Highlands, an area that had not been open for very long. It was clear that Johan was deeply impressed. He tried to film it with a 16mm camera, but something went wrong. My little 8mm camera was working, and during our leave in Holland, I was asked to show that short film in the large former cinema in the Hague, where Johan's congregation met.

We used the Osborn films often, and they did their job well. But during our time in Kavieng, we were also once able to rent the old black-and-white film *King of Kings* produced by Cecil B. DeMille, which is the first film ever about the Lord Jesus. It was more or less a silent film with background music but no speech. Sometimes the spoken words were written on the screen, and I translated these parts into Pidgin English. The film had a great impact. During the crucifixion, people cried and wailed or sometimes ran back and forth shouting, 'No, no!' At the resurrection when the stone was rolled away from the grave, and the Lord Jesus came out of the grave, some people cheered, and others clapped their hands or cried for joy. We even saw people running around and cheering. Many people saw the film, and only the Lord knows how many came to believe in their hearts. During our time in Kavieng, we actually did not see great results, but years later thousands of people in the province would choose to live for Jesus, but more about that soon.

During our time in Kavieng, I regularly went to Siwai. Going to Siwai was always a very positive event. A deep, great work of the Lord happened there. On the way, I always passed through Rabaul, and then it was good to see the Finnish missionaries. I also went to Tari once and also again to Daru. At those times, Hank and Lenie and the team remained in Kavieng. Most team members had mastered Pidgin English quite well. A young man from the Netherlands, Hans van der Wal, also joined the team. A year later his fiancée, Dorothy, arrived; and I consecrated their marriage in the congregation of Kopkop. After Hank and Lenie joined us for several years in Port Moresby, Hans and Dorothy led the work in Kavieng for some time.

Around Kavieng are many inhabited islands. There is only one way to reach those islands: by boat. Kari Harri had been able to buy a small boat which could sail along the coast, but he was not using it. We offered to buy the boat, and Kari Harri accepted. The congregation of Christian Life Centre in Brisbane gave us the money. All these things strengthened our bond with that church.

Hilding and Ingrid Ericksson were already in Rabaul at that time and helped wherever they could. They mainly did practical work. Kari Harri and Hilding Ericksson brought the boat from Rabaul to Kavieng.

It was nice to see Kari again. But it was also special to meet Hilding, who regarded me as the leader. He told me he had met a young man from the Western Highlands whose home area had until now rejected the gospel as well as any missionaries. From the moment that Hilding and Ingrid heard this, it stayed with them. But they wanted to have my permission and blessing before they went there. I gladly gave it. None of us realised what a great work of God they were going to see in the following years in the Western and Southern Highlands.

The boat was named *Gut Nius*, which is Pidgin English for 'good news'. On the bow we put the Jesus One Way sign. The Dutch teacher at the school where Darius had been educated came to us one day and asked if the boat with the hand and index finger upwards belonged to us. Yes, it did. The Dutch teacher made a One Way sign and moved his hand and index finger downwards and said, 'I have seen many boats do this, sink I mean.' The boat needed quite a lot of work, and the whole team spent many hours working on it. When the boat was finally in use, it only served for a short time because it ran onto a reef and sank, just like the Dutch teacher had said. We realised we had too little knowledge of boats and the dangerous reef-filled waters around Kavieng. From that moment, we hired a boat when a team wanted to go somewhere.

Coby and I had been married for six years now, and it had also been six years since we left the Netherlands. We longed to have children, but Coby had not become pregnant yet. We began to pray and ask God to give us a child. Coby had been examined once by a doctor in Australia, but that examination had not revealed much. Coby just had not become pregnant yet.

The fact that we did not have children was sometimes a problem for the national people. In the mindset of the people of Papua New Guinea, a man is only a man when he is married and has children. But we had no children. I was the leader in Kavieng, which gave me respectability in their culture, but I was not a father.

During one of the many visits to Siwai, I spent several days in David Pookaro's village. Two meetings a day was not unusual. One time, while I was preaching, an influential man from the village stood up and asked a question. His question was 'Coby and you have been married for several years now but have no children. In Kavieng, there is now a new couple [he meant Hank and Lenie] who have also been married for a long time, and they don't have children either. Just before you left Rabaul, there was a missionary couple who visited, and they too were married for a long time but did not have children either. You all come from the same country called Holland. I have heard that some white people do not want children and do something to prevent having them, though I have no idea what they do and how it is possible. Don't you want children, or can't you have them?' What a question and in the middle of a sermon!

Luckily I was able to answer, 'Until now Coby has not been able to have children, but we do long to have children and are praying that we will have them.'

The man was still standing and answered, 'That is good. Then I will pray too, and God will give you children,' and he sat down.

Difficult questions were often asked in a meeting. During a visit to a place near Tari in the Southern Highlands, someone asked me, 'People who can read well told me that before the Lord Jesus came there were laws. One of those laws said that a man could not have physical contact with his wife during her monthly period. We know that law too in our tribe. Women in their monthly period stay in a big house outside the village until their monthly period is over. We are doing that right then, aren't we? But why is that exactly that a man cannot have physical contact with his wife then?'

I knew the laws in the Old Testament but had never thought about it or paid attention to it. After thinking awhile, I responded, 'When the Old Testament speaks about blood, whether it is from humans or animals, then it's prophetically speaking about the blood of the Lord Jesus that He would give. Blood is therefore always holy. That's the thought behind that law.' The answer was clear to the one who asked the question, and with a pleased look, he sat down. Through the years, I was asked that question many times, and I would then give that same answer. Maybe missionary training courses should pay more attention to such difficult cultural questions.

On the island of New Ireland were four secondary schools, which were also boarding schools. A Roman Catholic teacher at one of these schools had been in touch with the charismatic movement and the Jesus movement while on leave. He had seen the One Way Jesus symbol often. When he was going to buy his weekly supplies in Kavieng, he saw a vehicle with a One Way Jesus symbol on it. He recognised it and was surprised. This kind of people were also in Kavieng? He found out that we really were genuine charismatic people, and he regularly visited us. He had wanted to become a priest but had been disappointed and had chosen to go into education. His name was Peter Clyburn. He came to Jesus, was filled with the Holy Spirit, was baptised in water, and experienced a deep healing in his life. Later he attended the Bible school at Christian Life Centre in Brisbane and came back to Papua New Guinea as a missionary. He married, and together with Pamela Beaumont, he led the Bible school that was established in Siwai, Bougainville. Once I heard Peter share a testimony that made a deep impression on me: 'I am not what I want to be. I am not what I should be. But thank God, I am not what I used to be.'

With Hank and Lenie and the other team members in Kavieng, it was now possible for us to go on leave to the Netherlands. In 1972, we went to the Netherlands for six months.

It was a long flight: Port Moresby, Manila, Hong Kong, New Delhi, Bahrain, Rome, and finally Amsterdam. But seeing our family and friends again was wonderful. When we arrived in the Netherlands, we had been away for six years and had much to tell. We enjoyed the many contacts. We loved seeing our native country, the Netherlands, again, though we also noticed that we had become very attached to Australia and Papua New Guinea. We had experienced a lot, mainly because of the new movement of the Holy Spirit that we had wholeheartedly embraced. Spiritually so much had happened in us. We spoke in many meetings and enjoyed the love and the warmth. We actually found that the spiritual climate in the Netherlands had deteriorated. When we left, there had been quite a lot of life in the congregations that we knew, but that was much less now. Worse than that, we noticed there was sin in some congregations. After we were back in Papua New Guinea, we heard that in several churches many problems had arisen, and some congregations that we knew well had ceased to exist. Although we still received support from the Netherlands, mainly from the Pentecostal congregation in the village where Coby was born, we also felt closely connected to Australia, especially spiritually. We had an intense longing to see that the Netherlands would also experience such a renewal.

While we were in the Netherlands, something very special happened. Coby discovered that she was pregnant. It was almost too good to be true. Because she did not want to be disappointed by a doctor, she did a test herself. It was positive. Coby was indeed pregnant, and the baby would be born in January 1973. We were thrilled.

Through contact with Open Doors, we spent two weeks in Manila on our way back. We felt drawn towards the work of Open Doors in Asia, but the Lord showed us clearly that Papua New Guinea was our place. In the Netherlands, we had been spoiled for six months, but we were also treated very well for those two weeks in Manila. Back in Kavieng, we of course had no longer cake every day or those Dutch delicacies or delicious Chinese meals, but plain everyday food from Papua New Guinea. I started with about ten days of fasting so that I would be able to handle plain food again. After ten days of fasting, I was back to liking Papua New Guinean food again.

It took a while to get completely back into the work environment of Kavieng. During our leave, the work had grown, and the Christians had grown in their faith and walk with the Lord.

While we were away, Hans and Dorothy had met the head teacher and his wife of the secondary school in Manggai. David and Beryl Odd were already Christians, but through the contact with Hans and Dorothy, they were both filled with the Holy Spirit and spoke in new tongues. They began to share this at their school, and for seven years, that school was a place of revival. They had more than 300 students per year, and for seven years, two-thirds or even three-quarters of them came to Jesus and were filled with the Holy Spirit, and many were baptised in water.

During one of the many visits to the school in Manggai, I saw on the wall of David and Beryl's simple home a poster which impressed me. On the poster was written the following:

> We, the unwilling,
> led by the unqualified,
> have been doing so long,
> so much, with so little,
> that we now will attempt
> to do the impossible,
> with nothing.

This saying was typical for David and Beryl who with practically nothing, because the boarding school possessed only the most necessary items and no luxury, saw a great work of God. When the revival began at the school, there were meetings evening after evening in which God's Spirit literally fell on the students. After seven years, David and Beryl went to Pastor Hal Oxley's Bible school in Melbourne, Australia, for two years. After those two years, they became one of the pastoral couples in Pastor Oxley's congregation. Several years ago, they went back to New Ireland Province, and they led a Bible school for the Uniting Church. The Uniting Church in the province had, during their absence, become quite charismatic. When we met David and Beryl during a visit to Australia, they told us about an incredible move of God's Spirit and meetings in which God's Spirit fell and where people lay on the floor for hours and hours under the power of the Holy Spirit. After their time in New Ireland Province, David and Beryl led a Pidgin English–speaking Bible School in Port Moresby and worked closely with Pastor Charles Lapa.

Before we had gone to Papua New Guinea in 1968, a brother from the group in Melbourne saw in a vision a field with people praising God with hands raised. It was a ripe harvest field, the brother said. We always felt that this vision was fulfilled when, on a piece of land belonging to the school in Manggai, about 4,000 believers praised God with hands lifted up. When we went to Papua New Guinea, God spoke to us that our arrival would have a great effect on the Uniting Church, which was then the Methodist Church. Though we received much resistance from them in the beginning, later this word became true.

Coby's due date was around the 12th of January 1973. It was exciting. She was very visibly pregnant, and the people were happy for us. But on the 12th of January, there was no baby. Neither on the 13th, the 14th, and following days. In Kavieng, there was a doctor who came from one of the former Eastern Bloc countries. Two weeks later, there was still no baby. It was the 26th of January. That evening Coby was taking a shower, and suddenly a big centipede came into the shower with its tail up ready to strike. The poison of a centipede can be deadly for people who are weak or sick. Coby managed to hit and kill it. She experienced it as something demonic.

Every day we went to the nearby hospital. The doctor was no longer comfortable with Coby's situation. The baby was fourteen days late, and it was big. The doctor said, 'If I am called to an emergency situation at the time that the baby decides to come, then I, being the only doctor, will not be able to help you. This afternoon there is a flight to Rabaul, where there is a gynaecologist. I will arrange that she will help you.'

There were enough spare seats on the plane, and that afternoon we flew to Rabaul, a forty-five-minute flight. The Finnish missionaries were waiting for us and had arranged a car. Coby and I could go straight to the hospital. The female gynaecologist from New Zealand was waiting, and immediately she began to induce the birth. I asked her if I could be present at the birth. In the English-speaking world, it was not the custom at that time for the father to be present at the birth. She looked at me and said, 'You are Dutch, aren't you? No more Dutch people in my delivery room. The last one who stayed during the birth fainted when I had to make an incision. A while later he woke up, saw blood, and fainted again. The baby came, and we just shoved him under the delivery table and woke him up later. So no more Dutch men at a birth.' It was clear. I was eventually allowed to stay with Coby but had to solemnly promise that when the gynaecologist told me to leave the delivery room, I had to leave and not object. I promised. Around midnight, it was clear that the baby was on its way. The gynaecologist looked at me and said, 'I think you are different. You may stay, but when I say leave now, then you are to go immediately.' That I promised to do. The contractions were coming faster, and just before the birth, Coby spoke briefly but very loudly in tongues. The doctor looked at me surprised and said, 'You are from the Netherlands, right?'

'Yes, we are from the Netherlands,' I answered. The doctor did not ask any further. However, Coby's speaking in tongues was definitely not in Dutch.

The gynaecologist had to use forceps to get the baby out, but she was not able to do so. She looked at me and asked me to help, which I did. I thought for a moment we were about to pull the baby's head off, when we were both pulling so hard. Several moments later, the baby was there, a big boy of nine pounds. No wonder it was a difficult birth. We had already decided that if it was a boy, his name was to be Mark John. The doctor cut the umbilical cord and laid the baby on a table and helped Coby. But Mark John was screaming and moved in all directions. The gynaecologist said, 'Mr Pasterkamp, hold that baby or he will be on the floor.' Mark was not even two minutes old, and already I had to watch him so he would not fall. A lively baby, for sure. We were ecstatically happy. Mark, our first child, was born a little after two o'clock in the morning, on the 27th of January. He was not only lively and adventurous after two minutes. He still is.

I stayed with Coby for a while. We could not get enough of looking at the baby. But around four o'clock, Coby had to rest, and I got into the car to go to the home of one of the Finnish missionary couples. The Rabaul hospital was just outside the township. There was no one on the road around that time, and my mind was not really focused on driving. I am the father of a son. I was so happy within myself. In deserted Rabaul, near the Finnish missionaries' house, a car suddenly came racing out of a side street. The driver clearly did not expect another car. I still don't know how we missed each other. I experienced this near crash as something demonic. Our first baby and now Satan was trying to get rid of the father.

After several days, Coby was allowed to leave the hospital; and together with our son Mark, we flew back to Kavieng. Mark was only about four days old when he flew for the first time. He still flies often, usually for work. The Christians in Kavieng were thrilled, and the baby was handed from one person to the next, something that is typically done in Papua New Guinea. I noticed an immediate change in the way I was accepted. I was now a father and even the father of a son; I was therefore a full-fledged leader. When, much later, I grew a beard, I was totally complete as far as the believers in Papua New Guinea were concerned. Among some people groups in the Papua New Guinean culture, you are not a man or a leader when you do not have a beard.

With Easter, we had a small conference for four days. At that conference, Mark was dedicated to the Lord by Ben, the first full-time worker from the Kavieng area.

Percy Mattias, who had been a drunk but came to the Lord with his dear wife, Margaret, in the first crusade, lived in the village Omo, near Kavieng. Every year a big pagan feast was held there. Powerful rainmakers from Rabaul had always been asked to come, to make sure that through witchcraft rituals, it would not rain that day. Since time immemorial, it had not rained on that day. Percy and Margaret were invited by the villagers to join them, but they refused because they were now Christians. Margaret felt an anger well up inside her and said, 'I will pray that it will rain that day, then you will know who has all the power.' Percy and Margaret were laughed at. It had never rained during the feast. Margaret prayed, and though the rainmakers had come and performed their rituals, rain poured down that day. After that, the feast went into decline because the rainmakers had not been able to stop the rain. I understand that the village did not want to pay and reward the rainmakers, because they had not done their job – a great victory for the gospel. This event illustrates the atmosphere of faith that was among the believers as they confronted the surrounding darkness.

The work in Kavieng grew slowly but steadily. There was a good team. I could go to Siwai every now and then and know that the work was in good hands. It became especially clear that Bougainville needed help, and the idea that we had to leave Kavieng and go to Bougainville grew stronger.

We had a very good relationship with Christian Life Centre in Brisbane but also with Youth with a Mission. Although YWAM initially did not want to establish churches, preferring to work together with existing churches and organisations in evangelism, some congregations were planted. Our home front of Streams of Power in Holland had completely fallen apart due to serious internal problems. Various congregations of Streams of Power continued but were going through a tough time.

Youth with a Mission planned a leaders' conference in Japan, and we were invited, as were Hank and Lenie. Hank had not been in the Netherlands for years and really wanted to visit his family. God made it possible in a supernatural way for us to go. When we were checking for the best price, it appeared that a world ticket, Papua New Guinea – Japan – the Netherlands, was cheaper than a two-way ticket, Papua New Guinea – Japan. So we went away for six weeks. The other team members were to look after the work in Kavieng during those weeks. A week in Japan and five weeks in the Netherlands. The family had not seen Mark yet, and we were looking forward to showing him to our family and friends.

Mark was ten months old when we arrived in the Netherlands, and he could already walk. With Mark walking between us and the two of us holding his hands, we arrived at the entrance to Schiphol Airport in the Netherlands. Everybody was surprised. Mark was already walking. The family was so happy and excited to see Mark, and the five weeks went by quickly. But in the Netherlands, something else happened. When we were back in Kavieng, we discovered Coby was pregnant again.

Shortly after arriving in Kavieng, we left as a small family and moved to Bougainville. Hank and Lenie stayed in Kavieng to lead the work there. It was difficult for us as a team to part. Hank and Lenie had become such very close and good friends. Together we prayed a lot, had times of intercession, evangelised, and built the work; but we also laughed a lot and had fun together. Hank has a great sense of humour. We did not know then that we would be together again for several years in Port Moresby.

We remember the three years in Kavieng foremost because of what the Lord did in our lives: renewal and an increased depth in our relationship with Him. And in one spiritual truth the Lord gave us in those three years a very special insight. It was of such nature that I have written the entire next chapter about it, and later a complete book. It is the truth of repentance.

CHAPTER 24

'Yu Mas Tanim Bel!'

WHEN WE BEGAN in Rabaul and conducted several crusades, we wondered about the fact that hundreds of people earnestly prayed the sinner's prayer with us; but when we organised follow-up meetings to help the new believers, practically no one came. What was happening here? Why did they not come? Where were those hundreds of people who had prayed? Were they not genuine? Was it a show? At the time, we understood little of the culture and wondered if that had something to do with it. Although several great miracles happened on Daru, also there, only a few people came to the follow-up meetings. Around Rabaul, that percentage was even lower, and it was the same in Kavieng. During the first crusade and all the other visits since, the number of people who prayed with us had been considerable, but here too only few people came to the follow-up meetings. In Siwai and the Solomon Islands, things were different, because in both of those places was a much more powerful working of the Holy Spirit.

I had started to read the book of Acts again, and I read it over and over again. How did the apostles preach? What did they preach? Which message did they bring? How did they win people for Jesus? After reading the book of Acts several times and crying out to the Lord from the depth of our hearts for insight and breakthrough, it slowly but surely became clearer. We started to see something.

We often preached along the lines of 'Jesus came to save you, to heal you, and to change your life. He loves you. He wants to forgive your sins and wash you clean with His blood. He wants to give you peace in your heart. He wants to take all darkness out of your life. He wants to take the fear of evil spirits out of your life and give you strength to conquer that fear. He wants to remove the fear of death and give you eternal life so that when you die you will not be lost but go to heaven.' Then we would ask, 'Who wants to accept Jesus and invite Him into their heart?' The people were willing to receive, more than willing. So many things that you can get for free by simply praying; that was very easy and what everyone wanted, wasn't it?

What we preached was true, absolutely true! Jesus does want to give you all these things. But when I read the book of Acts again and again, I saw what the apostles preached. I will put it in my own words. 'God has created everything, including you. When man turned his back on Him, He did everything possible to open the way for man to get back to Him. He sent His only begotten Son Jesus Christ, the dearest and most precious gift that He had and could give. This Jesus died for you, but He was raised from the dead, and He is alive. Now He is Lord, because God has given His Son all power in heaven and on earth. Therefore, He has complete right to your life and calls you to repent and make Him Lord of your life. His message to you today is 'I love you, and I ask you to come to me, to repent, and to make me Lord of your life and let me be Lord in your life.'

I saw in the book of Acts the continual call for repentance and the challenge to make Jesus Lord of one's life. Isaiah 53 teaches us that the essence of sin is that man goes his own way and not God's way. Repentance is not only repenting of all sin but also repenting of being self-centred and going one's own way. Repentance means turning around and going all the way with the Lord, asking Him to be Lord in every part of one's life. Repentance is taking absolute responsibility for your life, your actions, your sin and (where it applies) for the situation you are in. In Australia, we heard a pastor say in a message, 'If Jesus is not Lord of all, He is not Lord at all.' I had preached the gospel, but I had not spoken much, or hardly at all, about repentance.

Besides the truth of repentance, I saw something else in the book of Acts that hit me. The first Christians saw many miracles but also endured much persecution. Those two things seemed to go hand in hand. But now back to 'repentance'.

A parable that came very much to life for us was the parable of the two men who were building a house. One dug deep to lay the foundations of his house on the rock. The other did not dig deep and laid no foundations but built his house on the sand. The memory of digging the foundations for our own house in Kavieng was still fresh.

Papua New Guinea is a very mountainous country with the exception of the swamp areas on the south-west coast. The mountains are well covered with lots of vegetation. The mountains are rocks covered with a thick layer of soil, leaves, branches, and whatever. On that layer grow the trees, bushes, and everything else that is green. In some parts of the country, it rains and rains. With long and persistent rain, that thick layer on the rocky surface of the mountain can get very soft. This makes it possible for a big or minor earthquake to cause a landslide. We have seen that several times. Once we also saw the remains of a house at the foot of the mountain, a tragic sight because there was not much left of it.

Jesus told this parable to his disciples as part of the Sermon on the Mount. He did not tell this parable to non-believers. This parable therefore means that there are two types of Christians. There are Christians who take time and make lots of effort to lay a good spiritual foundation in their lives. They are the ones who dig deep and get rid of all the clutter so that they can lay the foundations on bare rock and build their house on it. There are also Christians who don't bother about all that and do not take the time and trouble to dig deep and who don't build on bare rock, but on what is still on the rock, the soil, the sand, etc. From the outside, both houses look the same; but in reality, there is a difference, a big difference. One house has a foundation; the other does not. By appearance, they look exactly the same, until the storms, rain, earthquakes, and winds come. Then it will be revealed which house has a foundation and which house does not.

Generally speaking, both look fine, until the storms come, and then you see the difference. Throughout the years, practice has taught us the truth of this parable. When believers experience difficult times or storms in their lives, then the one will remain strong and stand unmoved. Maybe the storms will shake the house and the doors and windows will rattle, but the house will remain standing.

But the other believer goes through a storm, and everything falls apart. It is as if the house ended up at the foot of the mountain and everything is destroyed. Though it is not up to us to judge, we often asked within ourselves, how strong was the foundation?

Hebrews 6 teaches us that the first aspect of the foundation of a Christian life is repentance. Verse 3 of that chapter tells us that a believer can only grow to maturity when God Himself gives permission. Does that mean that God does not allow some believers to grow further and go on to spiritual maturity? Yes, that is absolutely what it means! God is like a building inspector. When the foundation is not rightly built and therefore not strong, He does not give permission to continue building, because without a good foundation, there will be disasters once the storms come.

Though we have read this often we now saw more:

The first thing that John the Baptist preached was repentance.

The first thing that Jesus Himself preached was repentance.

When the Lord Jesus sent His disciples out on a short mission, He gave them the command to preach repentance. Repentance is therefore the first thing they preached.

In the Great Commission as written in Luke 24, the Lord Jesus gave His disciples the task of preaching repentance for the forgiveness of sin to all nations.

On the day of Pentecost, when about 120 disciples of Jesus were filled with the Holy Spirit, the first thing Peter preached was repentance.

In Acts, this truth continues. In Athens, Paul preached that 'the times of this ignorance God winked at; but now commands all men everywhere to repent'. Peter writes that God does not want even one person to be lost but that all people everywhere should come to repentance.

Repentance was always the first thing that was preached!

We also began to see that the Bible speaks about two types of repentance. Second Corinthians 7:10 teaches us that there can be godly sorrow or grief about sin, and that sorrow (the word is sometimes also translated as 'repentance') leads to a turning around and a salvation that one will never feel sorry about.

That same verse also teaches us that there is a worldly sorrow about sin, and that kind of worldly sorrow or regret about sin leads to death. This feeling of being sorry or having regret is towards people and towards oneself, but not towards God.

The parable of the two houses teaches this also. There are two ways to build your house: dig deep or only superficially.

Peter, the disciple who was so close to the Lord Jesus, denied Him at a most critical moment. His disciple Judas betrayed Him and handed Him over to his enemies. Both had sorrow, but Peter came clean with God. Judas also had sorrow, but it was more that he felt sorry. I can imagine that people pointed at Judas, saying, 'That's him. He did it. He betrayed Jesus and handed Him over.' People were talking about him. Judas had lost face and his reputation. So he tried to fix that by returning the thirty pieces of silver. But that did not remove the guilt, and in desperation he hung himself.

When the rooster crowed and Peter remembered the words of Jesus and realised that he had denied Jesus three times, something happened. Luke 22:61 tells us that at that moment, Jesus turned around and looked at Peter for a brief moment. What did Peter see in those eyes? Love, nothing but love! Peter went outside and cried bitterly. But Peter had only one motivation: I have to come clean with God. Peter went back to the disciples, though they probably all knew what he had done. Peter did not care about the shame. When, after three days, the women came to say that Jesus was alive, Peter ran to the grave. When, several days later, the disciples were fishing and realised that the person on the beach was Jesus, it was Peter who was the first to jump into the water without thinking, to be with Jesus. The reconciliation between Jesus and Peter is for me one of the most moving events in the Bible.

If Judas had experienced godly sorrow and had come to Jesus like Peter did, would Jesus have forgiven him? In my mind, there is no doubt about it! But Judas thought only of his honour, reputation, and loss of face.

One day in Kavieng, I was intensely thinking and meditating about this, and I had an experience. I can never feel what Peter must have felt, yet it was as if I felt something of it. His cry to Jesus. His intense sorrow and deep desire to come clean with God and his master Jesus. It was as if I felt just some of the emotions that Peter experienced. Those emotions were indescribable for me. Peter experienced real repentance. Jesus also said to Peter that there was a time in his life when he went wherever he wanted but that there was now a time coming in his life when someone else would have control over him, and he would be taken to where he would not have chosen to go.

In the Old Testament, we also see the example of two men and two different conversions. In 1 Samuel 15 is the account where God tells King Saul to destroy the people of Amalek. But Saul does not do what he is told. When the prophet Samuel confronts him with this, King Saul has excuse after excuse. When the prophet walks away from King Saul, the king says something that characterises him. King Saul then exclaims, 'I have sinned: yet honour me now, I pray thee, before the elders of my people, and before Israel.' That was typically King Saul! His position, the respect of the people, his reputation, his honour—all those things were important to him. He did in fact not care much about God. The fact that Saul in his days had not cared for the Ark of the Covenant says enough, he had not sought the presence of God at all!

King David had also sinned. He committed adultery and arranged for the husband of the woman to be killed. When the husband died, King David took the woman to be his wife and created the false and untruthful image of a sweet and caring king who had compassion on a widow.

It is clear from the Psalms that David cried out to God and felt deep sorrow. Because of the inner storm and pain he was going through, he even had major physical problems. David was king, but he was also subject to the law of Moses. That law was unmistakeably clear. Adulterers must be killed. But not only had King David committed adultery, he had also arranged the murder of a man. That too carried the death penalty. If David openly confessed his sins, he would have to be stoned to death. King David was wrecked by inner misery and struggle.

Then the prophet came and openly confronted him. Most likely this happened in the throne room with all the important people from his government present. David had no excuse. He confessed his guilt. In Psalm 51 King David cried out, 'Against thee, thee only, have I sinned, and done this evil in thy sight.' The prophet assured King David that he would not die. That is something very interesting. Why does the prophet say this, and what does it mean?

King David had godly sorrow over his sin, while King Saul had worldly sorrow (felt sorry) over his sin. King David came clean with God and recovered. King Saul lost everything and died a tragic death.

Again we saw two types of repentance: the outward repentance of Saul and the heart repentance of David.

There is another example in the Old Testament: Esau. Esau was indifferent and despised things that were holy. On the spur of the moment, he sold his birthright to his brother Jacob. When Esau came to his senses, he cried and regretted it. He was sort of willing to repent because he wanted his birthright back. He wanted back what he had despised. But he did not feel sorrow towards God. He did not get his birthright back. His brother Jacob was really not a nice guy, yet he had a deep desire for God. God persevered with him despite his faults. God let go of Esau.

In Kavieng, a young man came to the meeting. He had just been released from prison. He had sexually assaulted a young girl. Everyone knew about it. He came forward and cried. I prayed with him, and he prayed the sinner's prayer. In the weeks afterwards, he came forward multiple times, apparently to repent. But something was wrong. After a while, we did not see him anymore and enquired about him. We heard that he had done it again and was back in prison. Long after that when he was released again, I saw him in Kavieng. Again he came forward crying, but shortly after that, he went the wrong way again and had to go back to prison. Why did he come forward so often? Why did he pray again and again? Did he not mean it? I think that somewhere he did mean it. However, his desire to get rid of the shame and recover from his loss of face was greater than his repentance towards God.

That became very clear later. Through all this, God was teaching us something very precious.

A man of mixed race, whom we knew, came to us totally upset. His wife had left him. We were not too surprised, because we knew how he treated his wife. He came and cried and cried. We had to pray that his wife would return. I asked him if he had ever repented and asked Jesus into his life. The answer was no, but he was willing to do anything as long as his wife would return. I challenged him. 'Even if your wife never comes back, are you prepared to accept Jesus and follow Him?' Through his tears, he nodded affirmatively. I prayed with him, and he prayed the sinner's prayer. Inwardly I was still unsure how real this man was. Again I challenged him. 'Even if your wife does not return, will you follow Jesus?' He promised. We spoke for a while and prayed, and then he left.

I later heard that he got drunk that same night. His wife did not return. Three months later, he had a new girlfriend who moved in with him. We never saw him after that. Was this man sincere? He did regret his actions and wanted his wife back, but that was more important to him than repenting towards God and following Jesus.

We discovered more about repentance. The Western mindset is individualistic. Repentance in the Western mindset is therefore an individual and personal matter. But people in a culture like that of Papua New Guinea have a different mindset. On the one hand, they are of course also individuals. But in many ways they are also part of a bigger entity: their direct family, their extended family (a part of their tribe: the clan), and the entire tribe. Apart from that, they are part of a culture that has existed for many generations. Repentance is not only an individual matter to them but is also a repenting from the wrong and ungodly aspects of their culture, traditions, or family. Several years later while we worked in the capital, Port Moresby, we saw a real example of this.

A student at university wanted to repent and choose for Jesus. I led him in the sinner's prayer. This sinner's prayer is the one we always used, with little variations from time to time. This student earnestly and sincerely repeated the words after me, sentence after sentence. But suddenly he prayed a sentence that was not a normal part of the sinner's prayer. He prayed, 'Lord, will You forgive me because my father is a witch doctor.' That sentence was absolutely not part of our normal sinner's prayer, but I did understand what he was doing. He was also repenting from what he came out of, the wrong aspects of his culture and family background. Several years later, his father, the witch doctor, became a Christian. Did the prayer of repentance of his son anything to do with that? I am sure it did!

On the day of Pentecost when the Holy Spirit was poured out, the people asked what they had to do. Peter challenged them to repent, to be baptised in water and you shall receive the Holy Spirit. But he said something else: 'Be saved from this perverse generation.' That generation were the Jewish people of their day! The Jewish people are God's chosen people, but things had infiltrated the Jewish faith that were introduced by men and which were not of God. People had to repent and be saved from this. The people who repented were Jews and remained Jews; but they had to come out of a family, out of a generation, out of a culture, and out of a mindset.

This is something we hardly ever see in the West. In the Western mindset, repentance is an individual matter, but true repentance is deeper than that. I never heard someone pray in the West, 'Lord, forgive me because my parents are alcoholics,' or 'Lord, forgive me because my parents are divorced,' and there are many more possibilities like this. 'But I can't help the fact that my parents are alcoholics or divorced,' they could say. No, you cannot help it, nor are you responsible for it, but you do have to disassociate yourself of those aspects of your family.

The people in Papua New Guinea who repented remained real Papua New Guineans; but they had to be saved from the wrong aspects of generations, culture, and family.

In Port Moresby, years later, I experienced a very beautiful example of true repentance. Though Robert is not his real name, I often shared the story of Robert.

Robert was about twenty years old and attended a technical college which was a boarding school. He was a cheerful fellow, maybe a bit shy and modest, but he came across as being friendly. He seemed to be happy with who he was. He had chosen to follow Jesus when he attended the fellowship at Port Moresby and faithfully came to the meetings. He also was not hiding the fact that he followed Jesus. Everything appeared to be going well.

One Sunday evening he came forward for prayer. I asked him what he wanted prayer for, and he whispered that he was bothered by unclean thoughts about girls and sex. He did not want that. He wanted to live a pure life for Jesus. I prayed for him, and there was an evident touch and presence of the Lord. Robert went home that evening after the meeting, cheerful and happy.

About three weeks later, he came forward again during the Sunday evening meeting. He had felt that the problem was gone for about two weeks, but then it came back. He was plagued by thoughts about girls and sex. Robert was very honest and sincere and really wanted to live for Jesus. We prayed again, and the Lord clearly touched him. Robert went home happy and cheerful. But a week or more later, he again came forward for prayer. For two weeks again he had not been bothered by it, but it had returned. We prayed again, and we prayed earnestly. But several weeks later, Robert came for prayer again. I admired him for his honesty and that he was not ashamed to come for prayer again. We talked briefly, and I asked him if we could talk a little more sometime. I was wondering what was going on, and I also wanted to get to know Robert better. That evening we prayed, and again it was clear that the Lord touched him. But we also made an appointment. I would come to his school at a pre-arranged time, and then we could talk. And that's how it happened. One afternoon, after school, we met and talked in my car.

I asked Robert about his tribe, the people group he came from. What were the moral values like in his tribe? Those could differ quite a lot from tribe to tribe. But Robert's tribe had high moral standards and principles. As a man, you would not even think about touching a woman before you had married her. I asked him, since he now was in the capital city of Port Moresby, and no longer in his tribe, whether he did have sexual contact with girls. 'Absolutely not,' was his answer. 'I never slept with a girl or even touched a girl.' I asked him about specific reading matter. Magazines like *Playboy* and *Penthouse* were coming into the country and were available in shops. But there was not anything in that area that could be connected to his problem. Out of curiosity, he had looked at a *Playboy* magazine once, but then he stopped. 'I did not want this,' he clearly stated. With the knowledge and insight we then had, I could not find a cause for his problem.

We spent some more time talking when he suddenly said, 'I think there is something I need to tell you.' I pricked up my ears. What was he going to tell me?

At the college, there was a young female Australian teacher who taught English. Though the students spoke English well, she continued teaching them to improve their language skills. She was still young, but she was married. Her husband also worked for the government. One day this teacher gave Robert a note in which she wrote that she thought he was nice and attractive. She asked him to respond, and Robert wrote a note back which read, 'I think you are also very nice and attractive.' This exchange of notes and flattering compliments lasted several weeks until Robert received a note with the invitation to meet the teacher one afternoon around four o'clock at a desolate place. Robert knew that place. The afternoon came, and Robert wanted to go. He was quite sure about what was going to happen.

It was about a forty-five-minute walk, and Robert was ready to leave when an important uncle from the tribe who 'happened to be' in town came by. He stayed for a while to talk, and time was ticking away. 'When the uncle left, I ran to the place we had agreed to meet, but she was not there anymore,' Robert said. He was forty-five minutes late. When he shared this, I think I saw a look of disappointment on his face. Very shortly after that, the teacher was fired because she had done this not only with Robert. She was sent back to Australia.

I asked Robert a question, 'Deep in your heart, do you regret that you missed her?'

Robert was honest in his answer. 'Yes, deep in my heart I do regret that I missed it. I would have liked to know what it would be like to be with a white woman. I often think about it.'

I admired Robert for his honesty. 'There is the root of your problem,' I said. Robert saw it clearly. Suddenly, in the car, he cried out, 'Lord Jesus, forgive me that I kept this feeling and this thought deep in my heart and that I am actually quite sorry about having missed her.' Robert cried out to the Lord.

Suddenly there was a very unique and strong presence of the Lord in the car, and Robert was quite powerfully touched by the Lord. The root of his problem was gone. We prayed for a while and said our goodbyes. Robert was so happy, and I was deeply impressed and knew that I had learned a very important lesson. Robert had never committed adultery, but deep in his heart he had cherished a thought and a desire. In the car, Robert dealt with the root of his problem and firmly closed the door to the devil.

I kept in touch with him for quite a while, and his problem never returned. He did tell me once that he longed to be married, but the earlier thoughts were not there anymore. And the desire to be married is a healthy and normal desire.

After we began to see what repentance is, we often preached about it. In evangelistic meetings, we challenged people to repent and make Jesus the absolute Lord of their lives. In comparison to the years before, fewer people prayed the sinner's prayer. But as far as we could check, many continued and became followers of the Lord Jesus. Repentance brings joy in heaven and touches the heart of God. It is the first foundation stone of our Christian faith.

When you say in Pidgin English, the language we mostly spoke for about fourteen years, 'You have to repent,' then you say, 'Yu mas tanim bel.' Literally translated, 'You have to turn your stomach around.' Your 'stomach' is in Pidgin English the most inward part of man. And that is what repentance is: a deep, inner, radical turning to God. The deepest things in your heart must come into the light and be turned around. So repentance is to turn your stomach around!

CHAPTER 25

Two Very Precious People

THERE ARE PEOPLE one will never forget. To us Hilding and Ingrid Ericksson are such people. They were originally from Sweden. We told about them before in chapter 17, when we were visiting the Australian city Mount Isa at the beginning of our time as missionaries. In a meeting where we shared about Papua New Guinea, Hilding was touched and healed by the Lord and a few days later called to go to Papua New Guinea.

The following chapter is therefore not about our own ministry, but about Hilding and Ingrid's. It is an amazing story. Their story must be told, and may it not be lost.

In the years after we left Papua New Guinea, we had lost contact with Hilding and Ingrid. In order to write this chapter, it was necessary to get in touch with them to complete various details of the story. We knew that their cousin and her husband were missionaries in Kazakhstan and also that friends in Australia probably knew how and where we could reach them. We called Australia, and indeed our friends had a telephone number in Kazakhstan. We called Kazakhstan, and as if by a miracle, the cousin answered phone. The cousin and her husband knew us and were very surprised that we called. They told us that Hilding and Ingrid lived again in Mount Isa and gave us the phone number. We knew that Hilding and Ingrid would be in their eighties by now. We telephoned them in Mount Isa, and Hilding answered the phone. I immediately recognised his voice. Hilding had a strong accent, and probably because of his age, his accent had gotten stronger. I said my name, 'This is John Pasterkamp from Holland.'

Hilding did not hear me correctly and said, 'No, I am not from Holland. I am from Sweden.'

I said, 'I know you are from Sweden, but this is John Pasterkamp from Holland.'

Then he recognised my voice and shouted, 'John Pasterkamp from Holland, how are you?' It was very moving to hear his voice after more than twenty years.

I told him that I was writing a book about our time in Papua New Guinea and that we also wanted to tell their story. So we spoke for a while. Ingrid was not doing so well physically, but she also came on the phone. I made notes of the things Hilding told me in answer to my questions. Several days later, I called him again, and Hilding told me other facts and events that I had asked about. I then asked him to record his story on a tape or video or DVD, and a week later we received a cassette on which Hilding shared his story.

Here is the story of Hilding, with a little editing by me to make it readable. His English was somewhat broken, which is exactly how he spoke, but I have tried to leave that as much as possible. In two more phone calls, I received some more information, which I have used in this chapter. I have also included some facts which he did not mention but were known to us. Hilding was forty-six years old when the story of his calling began. Here is his story as told on the cassette:

> I also started to write a book for my family and friends in Sweden about all we did in Papua New Guinea, but that book is in the Swedish language. I will tell you in a shorter version what I have written.
>
> I grew up with my eight years older brother Ludwig in a Christian family on a farm in Sweden. When Ludwig was seventeen years old, he had a dream. In that dream, he saw himself working as a missionary in a faraway land. He saw rolling hills and mountains with high grass, different than that in Sweden, and

villages of grass huts. Ludwig understood that he would become a missionary. He also understood that the country was Papua New Guinea. He made enquiries but discovered that the Swedish Pentecostal churches had no missionary involvement or connections with Papua New Guinea.

Shortly after that dream, our father died. He was still young, only forty-eight years old. My mother was forty-four years old. She cried and said to Ludwig, 'We lost our father. You must take over the farm.' The calling that Ludwig had felt disappeared as snow before the sun, and he had to let go of the desire to go to a Bible school or get missionary training.

Years later, we migrated to Australia because it was close to Papua New Guinea. In Australia, Ludwig heard that the Pentecostal churches of the Assemblies of God did missionary work in the Sepik District of Papua New Guinea. The Sepik District is named after the great Sepik river which flows in the north-west, not far from the border with West Irian.

He went up to the Sepik Province where the Assemblies of God were working, met missionaries, and shared his calling to be a missionary. They asked him to become a missionary there. Well, my brother Ludwig was not satisfied, because the Sepik District is flat land along a big river. In the dream, Ludwig had seen mountains and hills covered with grass. Ludwig even chartered a MAF airplane for half a day to have a look around in the Sepik, but he did not recognise the landscape he had seen in his dream. Ludwig went back to Australia, discouraged, because this is not what he had seen in the dream. However, he carried it deep in his heart; it would not leave him.

I was very happy that my brother also settled in Australia just like me, and I wondered many times when he would go there again to find what he had seen in the dream, but he was busy. He had a big family. His children were in school in Cairns, and he was working hard. Ludwig and I had first settled in the mining town of Mount Isa, but he had great difficulty handling the heat and the perspiration of working underground in the mines. So he moved to the town of Cairns, a city on the north-east coast of Australia.

Then came the meeting at the Baptist church. I think it was 1969. On the notice board it was advertised that a young missionary couple from Papua New Guinea would share about their work. When I saw that, I knew that I should go there. I was ill, and already for some time I had real pain in my chest, but I had told nobody. I knew I was working too hard. Because it was a bit of a hard time for me in Mount Isa, when I started the chicken farm, I had a lot of things to do. I first worked hard in the mine. Then I bought the land at the end of the airstrip. It took a lot of energy for me to build a modern shed and modern machinery. Five thousand laying chickens in cages. It was around that time that I felt I had started a good business, because all the stores in Mount Isa wanted to have fresh eggs, because in that time it was not easy to get fresh eggs. They had to come by train or by truck from places on the coast, but when the road turned to mud because of rain, or the train could not go, you could not get eggs.

I was sitting and was so touched, tears running down my cheeks. You talked about Bougainville. You were talking about how good God was to you and the miracles you had experienced there. Your love for the people of Bougainville touched me. You told about a great miracle which had happened there (the story of David Pookaro). And then you were saying that if somebody is sick here, you would like to pray, so I did.

I was healed immediately. I felt like a big 'bang' in my chest. It was as if a fire went through my chest. The Holy Spirit met me with the healing power, and from that time, change began in my life. Revelation came into my heart, and I felt that I should pray more, and I started to think about all you were talking about in this meeting. I realised that great peace of Jesus had come into my heart, and the calling of God to go to the mission field had started. I knew something had happened to me; such a wonderful peace came into my heart, because God was working in me. Thank you, Pastor John, for coming to that meeting. I believe that was the real turning point in my life, and I can tell about what followed from there on.

I was really, really happy. I loved to go to the meetings. I had started to become very slack. I think I would not have been ready if Jesus would have come back. Now I knew that I have got something in my heart. Yes, I felt the call that took place, and that was wonderful. I got into my heart that something had started to happen. I just waited for what would happen now. I worked on the farm, but I realised that was not my life. I looked at all the eggs of the poultry farm, but that was not what I wanted to do with the rest of my life. I prayed to Jesus and asked, 'Show me something. Let me know something. Reveal to me that something will happen. Jesus, let me know where I must go.' And the answer came!

One day I was just feeding my 5,000 chooks. I filled my feeding machine. The whole process takes about 15 minutes from start to finish. But then something happened. All of a sudden all the noise from my machines and chooks disappeared, but now I heard a man's voice starting to speak to me, coming from above, saying, 'Hilding, I have given in the past blessings to you, but I have a request. I want you to go to Papua New Guinea for Me to bring the people the good news, that I, Jesus, have suffered for them. But now I am alive. Just preach the good news to them. This is not a command from Me which you must do. You have a free will, Hilding, and you can choose to be My servant.'

I was very surprised about what happened to me. What happened was so great to me. I went to see Ingrid and asked her, 'How do I look?' Then I told her what had happened. My son heard it too but did not like it.

My son's feeling was not the best after some trouble we experienced. He came to see me. I was on the cement path leading up to my shed. We had a cup of coffee. I had to leave him to go up to the shed to finish the feeding. What happened? I was just going past my son's car towards the shed, when I saw a very big snake, nearly two metres long and thick like my arm. It jumped over the bonnet and rolled over it. It only took a few seconds, then it was gone. No sign of it. No snake. I walked up to the shed.

The next day, about the same time, I experienced the same thing. This time the voice was full of love. My tears were running. The voice was just the same as I experienced the day before. The very first thing the voice said was 'What was that you saw yesterday? Did you understand what it was? That voice wants to mislead you and bring you on the wrong path. It almost destroyed your life. (Hilding understood that the Lord spoke about the snake – the devil – who had tried to ruin his life.) Once again, I will tell you, Hilding. Only if you want, I will help you in finishing the business and to get your farm sold. I will look after you because I have heard you calling Me. When you start to work in Papua New Guinea, I will help you through all the difficulties that will happen to you. If you will go as my servant, this is My promise to you.'

Yes, I talked to my darling Ingrid, and she was willing. We both prayed, and we both said yes to Jesus, because we both wanted to obey Jesus. After we decided, everything went so fast. I of course wanted to talk to my brother and his wife, but he was in Cairns, hundreds of kilometres away. At first I thought, *I will write a letter to him*. But it felt like it was important to talk to my brother personally, so I went down to the airline office here in Mount Isa. I was almost there but turned around and thought, *No, I want to write*. But I could not really concentrate. It was a fear on the one hand and a surprise and joy on the other hand. I went to the airline office again and asked, 'Do you have a ticket for the flight to Cairns this afternoon?' There were seats available, so that afternoon I flew to Cairns. I came to the house of Ludwig who was still working in the rose garden. He looked very surprised when he saw me. He said, 'Where is Ingrid?' Their son had just arrived the day before with his wife from Sweden; they had gone through the Bible school there. I thought they would be full of fire for the Lord, but that was not the case. That was disappointing.

My brother had to go somewhere, but later in the evening, I told him and his wife the wonderful experience, that I heard the voice of Jesus. That made such an impact upon Ludwig and his wife. They too decided to go to Papua New Guinea. Yes, that is how I got my calling.

From there on, everything went very quickly. We went to Papua New Guinea, and we visited you there in Rabaul. Pastor George, my nephew, who just finished pastoring in a small township in Australia, also came with us to Papua New Guinea.

And I remember how you were working there one day, and you were printing gospel tracts. Not having a shirt on, you were sweating. It was very hard, and I said, 'You should not work so very hard, Pastor John.' But you commented, 'No work, no souls. It is as easy as that.'

Anyway, now we had to go back again to the farm, but there was a strike, so we had to stay a week longer in Rabaul. You asked George, my nephew, to preach on the plantations. Eleven times he preached on the plantations. So he made a comment to you, 'You let me work too much.'

'No, that is how we like to do it when we get visitors from Australia,' you answered.

We came back to the chicken farm and sold everything. We moved to Papua New Guinea on May 13, 1971, to live and work there.

I knew that you had moved away from Rabaul and had taken up position in New Ireland. Together with Kari Harri, we brought the boat that you had bought to Kavieng, and we talked about the possibility to go to Mount Hagen in the Highlands. You said, 'Hilding, take Philip Kawai with you and keep him close to you. He left his district because of some difficulties. Help him to return without problems.'

We stayed in Rabaul for nine months, and we experienced a strong earthquake there. Very strong, 8.2 on the scale of Richter. The water from the bay was rising up a couple of metres and ran into the street and came into the shops. Nobody died, but the experience showed how vulnerable we were in Rabaul.

Someone came up from Queensland who wanted to find out if he was called to do missionary work there, but he was not quite sure of the call of God to come to

Rabaul. Then came the earthquake, and he knew he was not called for this place.

Before Christmas, my brother came. The schools of his children were finished. After my experience, he stayed for two more years in Cairns with the children. We had a wonderful time together. We went to the plantations and experienced much blessing on what we were doing. Philip Kawai was always with us and translated. Philip and I were inseparable. The people on the plantations had often begged us to come to their home district, Mount Hagen, to live and work there. After we had talked with you in Kavieng, we decided to go to Mount Hagen.

First we stopped over in Goroka in the Eastern Highlands. An Australian couple who first had lived in Rabaul, and with whom we, but you too, had become friends, was living there. They had just bought a caravan that he wanted to use to do outreach in the highlands. He had plans to go to the government station at Kundiawa. However, he had been transferred to Lae. Anyway, we had a good time talking together. Ingrid and I told how we felt about our calling to the Western Highlands. Our friend decided to sell the caravan to us.

Ludwig was not totally sure about his calling to Papua New Guinea. He was still looking for the place which he had seen in the dream. Ludwig had to go home to Cairns to sell his house. I had sold my farm in Mount Isa, so we had cash at hand. He said, 'No problem.' We remained in Goroka to wait for Ludwig and his wife. I remember the wonderful atmosphere in the air when we talked about winning lost souls for Jesus. Ludwig went back to Australia and sold his house in ten days and came back. We stayed in Goroka where we met Brother Mason Hughes, the superintendent of the American Foursquare Mission, who lived in Lae.

We talked to him and told him about our calling to come to Papua New Guinea to preach the gospel – the good news. We just wanted to put it before him, because they worked also in the Highlands. He gave us his blessing. He told us about the years that he himself worked on a mission station in the area of Kundiawa. We said goodbye to him and left in a good spirit and atmosphere.

We could buy a new four-wheel-drive Toyota to continue our journey to Mount Hagen. Everywhere they were working on new road construction, so it was very difficult to come through, but we had a good car and came through safely. In Mount Hagen, we found a hotel which was run by German man. We went to the hotel. I think you saw us there once, John. He arranged a good price for us to stay. Later we lived in the caravan on the grounds of his hotel.

Ludwig was very keen to go onto the streets to evangelise. He took his violin and began to play. The people had never seen or heard a violin. He had not learned Pidgin English yet, so after playing the violin, he played tapes from T. L. Osborn in Pidgin English, and it went well. Then he would put his violin under his cheek and play again.

At the hotel in Mount Hagen, we met a lovely brother from Denmark who had been to Papua New Guinea, and he asked us what we were going to do in Mount Hagen. And there was a Swedish brother too. So we said, 'We are going to preach the good news here in Mount Hagen.'

'Oh,' he said, 'not here in Mount Hagen. If you stay, don't tell anybody that you are Pentecostal. I am also a Pentecostal missionary, but the churches here have more or less chased me out of town.' Then I went to Wabag and Mendi and then came back to Yalibu.

We visited him in Yalibu, a very long drive. He had already established a mission station there. There were sisters from Denmark who did medical work. The mission station was in a beautiful surrounding. We visited him there later on more, and we had a good time together. We just experienced living and working there, and we discovered there were also other Pentecostal missionaries.

A young man from Wilpul Village had accepted the Lord, and through him we got contact with the village. Wilpul and the surrounding villages were not open to the gospel and to missionaries. They opposed anything which was Christian. But they did allow us to show a film. With the help of a generator, we showed a T. L. Osborn film, translated into Pidgin English. The attention was good, but we did not get any further than that. They allowed us to show a film a few more times. The people in the village thought it was interesting, but they did not understand what a film was. I had an idea: with my 8mm camera, I would take some movies around the village and the people in the village and show these to them. So that is what I did, only I had to send these little films by mail to Australia to be developed, and that took several weeks. When we came to the village again and could not show the film we made, some people in the village became angry. They thought we had lied, because we had no film. We prayed that the developed films would soon arrive. When they arrived, I spent that evening and part of the night to mount the films and prepare them for showing. The next day we went to the village with our generator and 8mm film projector and showed them to the people. Great consternation was the result. On the screen they saw their own village, the people of the village, and themselves. Then we tried to explain again what a film was. They had seen it: a small film of their own village and themselves. We explained that it was the same with the miracles in the T. L. Osborn films. Those miracles had really happened. Through this all more openness began to come, and I asked if they would allow me to build a small church in the village. That was all right. We poured a simple concrete floor; and from their own material, trees and bamboo, we built the church with a roof of kunai grass, like all homes have. The church was ready, but when we were away, it was burnt down. They did not want a church, but out of politeness, they had given permission. They explained that something had gone wrong, but of course they had done it themselves. They demanded that the concrete floor would be removed also, and they went to the government officers. Within a week, everything had to be away. The highest government official in the province, the district commissioner, who had come shortly before this, agreed with the villagers and gave an order that everything had to be removed. No pole or whatever could stay in the ground. I told the district commissioner that his predecessor had given permission. I kept pushing him, and finally he phoned Australia, where his predecessor now worked. Indeed, he had given permission. We did not have to remove everything. What was left over of the church was allowed to remain standing, and we even got permission to build the church again. Then it happened.

Early one morning I went up to the post office, and a man stopped me. I thought he wanted a lift. 'What do you want?' I asked.

'You must come into my village, because my sister's baby died,' he said. Some women were sitting in the village on a kind of blanket, one with a little baby. It looked dead to me. I looked at it. The girl had died, no doubt possible. God wanted us to do something and step out in faith. When the Lord called me to go to Papua New Guinea to bring the good news, He promised to do miracles. There we were. So I said, 'Come on and we will pray for the baby.' The baby came to life again. We were all stunned. I ran into the neighbour's house and said, 'We have prayed, and a miracle has happened.' We prayed again and thanked the Lord Jesus. I had difficulty believing it myself, but I had seen an amazing miracle.

A local brother had come with me. This brother Kissap jumped, clapped his hands, and raised his hand and praised God. Luckily the house was high enough for him. There was a great commotion in the village. The mother and the family of the baby went to the hospital, which was not far from the village. The doctor examined the baby and said, 'There is nothing wrong with the baby.' That was his conclusion. But he said to the mother, 'You must feed the baby, because it is hungry.'

Brother John, that was the first real miracle, and you know the story. We started from there, and we got more and more courage to preach the good news. We baptised the first people of the village who had become a Christian, in the stream near the village. There we had an amazing experience. A crippled man was carried into the water to be baptised. He walked out of the water. It is amazing what God can do when you have a touch of God upon your life. I had no experience, never had a missionary training, but God was there. God did great wonders. But, John, you must keep this story in your book short. God must get all honour. You asked for my testimony, but you must not talk about it too much. You have much to share yourself, because the door is wide open to the gospel. There was nothing to hold us back anymore. We experienced so much joy in that time.

You know there is a big market in Mount Hagen, but we were not allowed to do anything. I went to the policeman in charge there. He was in his office, but he did not even listen to me. The following day I went again, and the day after I went again and asked permission to evangelise in the market. I persevered like the widow in the parable Jesus told in Matthew 18. Eventually he said, 'Mr. Ericsson, you are just wasting my time. You can use your energy better than to try to talk to me.'

Well, I said, 'This country really needs the gospel. I received a call from the Lord Jesus to come to Papua New Guinea to bring the good news. What more can I do?' He listened, and we received permission to hold a few meetings on the market. Later we got permission to hold more meetings.

We felt so at home in Mount Hagen and to bring the good news there to the people. A couple from Finland who had worked for a while in Rabaul visited us in Mount Hagen. After prayer, we felt that they should come and help us, and they did. So Marti and Lisa Kumpulainen came. The wife was a wonderful singer. After that, Marti and his wife continued to bring the good news in the market. She was singing, and that was exactly what we needed. So Marti and Lisa Kumpulainen continued the good news at the market. And it was at the market that Kundipok came to give his heart to the Lord. He heard Marti Kumpulainen playing his trumpet on the market. He heard the noise, which was an unusual noise, so he drew closer to see them, and there we were. He was sitting at the market, selling a few things. But there Kundipok believed in Jesus and gave his heart to the Lord. Kundipok came to believe and became an important Christian leader among his people of Mount Hagen.

Yes, praise the Lord, yes, we were able to buy the house up in the mountain at the edge of Mount Hagen and started meetings there. I could buy some land on the mountain – named Kondep. There we started a little Bible school. In the beginning, there were sixteen people, but later we extended and could take twenty-four students. There is still a Bible school up there now. The work expanded and expanded, and we were really happy. And I saw that the Lord opened up doors, exactly as He had promised. We continue there in Mount Hagen, and many souls came to Jesus.

On September 16, Papua New Guinea became independent from Australia. A visitor from Sweden came. He had heard that Swedish Pentecostal missionaries had started a work in the Western Highlands, of which Mount Hagen was the important town. He also heard that the missionaries had not gone out from Sweden. So he had written a letter to me and said that he would love to come and meet us. At that time, an Australian missionary, Murray Tomlinson, was with us and helped us in the work. So we continued. God really let us see revival in this area. We had many odds against us, and there were difficulties to overcome. The work became very big. We were able to buy a joinery at Warakum, and later on we were able to buy a Chinese hall right over the road from the joinery. Many people came to the meetings.

Ludwig's daughter Marion and her husband, Sven, came to join us. They were sent by the Swedish Free Mission to come to establish a small vocational school. Before the independence, there was no good road from the coast to Mount Hagen. The government used Hercules planes to transport everything. But now there was a road, and you could go by car. It all became a little easier.

So we continued and reached out more. We went up to Tari, 300 kilometres from Mount Hagen. A good work developed up there too, and some brothers went up there to lead the work.

One thing I have not told you about yet. It happened when we came for the first time by plane to Mount Hagen. Some of our friends were with us. When we got out of the plane, my brother said, 'Now I can see the grass hills and mountains with grass and villages of grass huts and a high mountain in the background, exactly like I saw in the dream when I was a seventeen-year-old young man.'

So far is what Hilding shared on the tape. What a story! What a testimony! A man, fifty-six years old, without a missionary education or Bible school, was touched by God in a meeting in Mount Isa and several days later was called to the mission field by God Himself. Hilding and Ingrid spent a total of fourteen years in Papua New Guinea. Over the phone he said, 'They were the best and most beautiful years of my life. We were so happy in Papua New Guinea.'

The Swedish government wanted to do something for Papua New Guinea through the Pentecostal churches, only it had to be through a recognised organisation or church. Our organisation had the official name Christian Life Centre, which was of course totally unknown in Sweden. The only Pentecostal movement they knew was the Assemblies of God, and they wanted to work through them. That is how it was agreed that the work in Mount Hagen and the surrounding area became part of the Assemblies of God in Papua New Guinea. Tens of churches were established, among them a few big ones. Just before we left the country, the congregation just outside of Mount Hagen had about a thousand members.

Hilding was a businessman, and you could tell that by the way he handled things. When a congregation was founded in a village, he asked the people to make land available and to grow coffee or tea, involving all the church members. A kind of cooperative. The proceeds were for the church and the pastor. In that way they were not financially dependent upon help from outside. It was a system that worked very well and took away much pressure and tension. Several villages built permanent church buildings, which they paid for with the proceeds of the collective coffee or tea plantation.

After Hilding and Ingrid left Papua New Guinea, they worked in Australia for several years in a shelter for Aboriginals who were addicted to alcohol. They were already in their seventies then. Now they are in their eighties, and especially Ingrid is not strong physically.

We have deep respect for these dear, plain, but brave pioneers. Hilding and Ingrid will always be very special to us.

When my parents visited us in Papua New Guinea, we took them to the Highlands as well. There we stayed with Hilding and Ingrid. My parents said about them, 'Hilding and Ingrid might just be the sweetest people we ever met.' During that visit, we also visited the Bayer River Bird Sanctuary, a government post where you can see various exotic birds in huge cages: birds like the beautifully coloured birds of paradise and also eagles.

We could use the Toyota Land Cruiser, a four-wheel-drive car belonging to Hilding. Bayer River is about an hour or so driving over an unpaved road from Mount Hagen, where Hilding and Ingrid lived. Coby and the three boys were also with us. The winding road through the mountains and hills was narrow. Suddenly in front of us there was a complete tribal war going on. The hills on both sides were filled with armed men, many decorated for war. Screaming and shouting, they ran into each other. Here and there were houses on fire. The atmosphere was full of danger, hate, and tension. I knew enough about tribal wars to know what to do. 'Everybody down!' I shouted, and everybody ducked. I accelerated because when you stop in the middle of a tribal war, it is possible that the warriors will suddenly turn on you and that you would not survive. Unfortunately, there are examples of that. When you hit someone, you don't stop but keep driving fast to the nearest police post because if you stop, it will surely mean death by arrows and spears.

I drove as fast as I could and swayed between the warriors. Some jumped aside. Thank God, I hit no one. We were out of the danger zone pretty quickly. Everybody had been scared, but we had survived and could get up again. On the way back, the police was present throughout the entire area. A part of the village had burned down, and several wounded men were picked up. Later we heard that three men had been killed, which is few for a tribal war. The birds in Bayer River were very beautiful and absolutely worth seeing, but my parents remember the tribal war better than the exotic birds.

I also was able to bring my parents to Pangia, the place of birth of Philip Kawai and of the later well-known leader Charles Lapa.

Pangia was then a less developed area. When we visited a village, my parents were offered a piece of sugar cane as a sign of welcome just as we offer our visitors coffee or tea. My mother began to eat the sugar cane, and a tooth broke off. That was her first experience in Pangia. And there are no dentists in Pangia . . . My parents were invited into a house of Christians, built on the ground. Sitting around a fire, they were offered roasted sweet potatoes. There was also an older man present. He was only wearing a piece of cloth on the front and some leaves on the back. He wanted to be in a picture with my parents, and we still have that picture. My parents could not even have thought about this in their wildest dreams.

Just before he died, my father said that the visit to the Highlands and Pangia had been the most beautiful moment of his life.

CHAPTER 26

We Are Moving to Bougainville!

WE HAD COME to love Bougainville very much. Bougainville gave us a feeling of being home. We had been there quite a few times and had seen God move so uniquely and had seen so many miracles. We tasted an atmosphere of revival. What we experienced in Bougainville was something we had not experienced before except for the Solomon Islands. Now we were going to live there. We were excited. However, there was a problem: we could not find a place to live. There was a possibility to live in Siwai. That meant that we had to build a house of bush material. To us that would be fine, but we thought it wouldn't be wise. What was happening in Siwai was so true Siwai, so much something of the people themselves, so unique. Apart from that, we also started to get open doors into other places on Bougainville.

In the small government post Kieta was no house for rent. Kieta actually only existed of a handful of houses and buildings. The mine was building a small town named Arawa, named after the former big plantation that had been there. It was being built only for the workers of the mine, mainly expatriates and a number of public servants. All houses belonged to the mine. Renting a house there by people who did not work for the mine was impossible. Arawa was a kilometre or eight away from Kieta. Near the mine itself, a place named Panguna, houses were also built, all for the workers of the mine, not for rent.

We prayed and asked the Lord for help. Next to this airport, the Missionary Aviation Fellowship (MAF) had built a few houses, surrounded by a fence. Three pilots and two employees lived there. The MAF had two airplanes on Bougainville. We knew the pilots because we had flown regularly with the MAF. One of the houses would be empty for a few months until a new employee would arrive. We could rent that house, and we lived there for three months. The airport was ten kilometres from Kieta, but the road was an unpaved road. Especially after rainfall, and on Bougainville it rained often and much, the road was very bad. From Kieta to Arawa, it was about eight kilometres, but that road was of asphalt. From Arawa to the Panguna mine, it was over 20 kilometres, also an asphalt road which swayed over a mountain pass. It was not unusual to drive there in thick fog, when you could only see the white line beside the road which you had to follow. The road from Arawa to Panguna is dangerous, and many accidents took place.

The house that we moved into was very basic, but safe, because of the fence surrounding the houses. That was good, because when I was not there, then Coby and little Mark, now one and a half years old, were safe. Coby became pregnant again and therefore often stayed at home.

The island of Bougainville is in an earthquake zone. Often, there were earthquakes, usually light ones, but one afternoon the ground began to shake again, and it grew stronger. We took little Mark and ran outside. Through the open front door, we saw how the big upright refrigerator was unsure whether to fall down or remain standing. It is quite frightening to experience an earthquake of that strength.

A promise made by the Panguna copper mine was that the whole island would get more roads and better facilities. That happened only partly and would eventually become one of the reasons why the great conflict arose that ended up becoming a kind of civil war between various tribes who were mainly fighting for the rights to the land on which the mine was located. This conflict would cost between 15,000 and 20,000 lives and for more than eight years would completely close Bougainville off from the outside world. When we moved to Bougainville, we had never thought that such problems would arise on the island and neither the unique way in which the Christians would stand strong and be a great witness of the gospel.

Several years later, an unpaved road was built from the Panguna mine to the southern point of Bougainville, named Buin. That road, which would cross more than ten big and small rivers, went straight through Siwai and past Tonu. From that time, we would not fly with the MAF to Siwai anymore but go with a four-wheel-drive vehicle. The MAF left Bougainville not long after that, because more roads had been built, and there were more cars in the province. In the meantime, we had made many flights from Kieta to Tonu, about twenty minutes flying in the small single-engine Cessna airplane. We have much respect and admiration for the MAF pilots. Once they flew to Tonu for a medical emergency. The birth of a child was in danger of going wrong. When they landed, it was very bad weather. But in order not to lose lives, they immediately took off again in the stormy weather. The birds were not even flying anymore. The woman and her baby made it alive and well.

In the mountainous area behind Kieta, a man had read a tract and came to the Lord. His name was John Tako. This led to the beginning of a new congregation and the opening up of a new area where John and his wife became the leaders. The name Tako is also a Dutch boy's name. We seriously thought about naming our second child Tako, if it was going to be a boy. Tako was to us a Papua New Guinean but also a Dutch name. But we did not get inner peace about this name and decided to give our second child a biblical name as well. His name became Stephen. When we moved to Japan, we discovered that Tako is also a Japanese word: it's a term of abuse with which you can offend someone quite badly. We think Stephen was very grateful that his name was not Tako when we lived in Japan.

I often went to the area of Tako. You had to drive over an unpaved road for more than an hour, past the airport and along the coast to the south. Near his village was a river. Usually you had to leave the car at the side of the river, wade through the river, and then walk for half an hour over a narrow path up the mountain. You would then arrive at a level area where the beautiful village of John and Anita Tako was located.

During one of my trips to Bougainville, I was asked to consecrate two marriages in one service in their village. Barry Winton had done all the preparations, and we went there. Only, it had rained a lot, so we brought dry clothes just in case. The car was unable to cross the river, and we had to leave it, but we were able to wade across the river a little further upstream. After walking up the mountain and changing our clothes, the feast could begin. Both grooms, who were brothers, had their work shoes on and work pants and work shirt that read 'Panguna Mine'. That was their special wedding suit. Both brides had been able to get totally wrinkled white wedding dresses from somewhere. They had no shoes but walked barefoot. A bunch of flowers from the bushes in the village had to be the bridal bouquet. It was firmly held in their hands, and while they stared straight ahead, the wedding ceremony began. With their nearly black skin, it was very colourful and very non–Papua New Guinean. But that's how they wanted it.

When both couples stood before me and were about to say their marriage vows in Pidgin English, I looked at the feet of the brides. Wide, flat, rough feet appeared from underneath a wrinkled white wedding dress because in the village everyone walks barefoot. Because of the rain, water had run into the church building, and the ground was wet. It was therefore a little slippery and muddy. One bride was nervous, and her feet and toes moved slightly up and down. Between her toes, the mud came up and down, and the sole of her feet was covered with mud. What a combination: a white European wedding dress and bare feet partially covered in mud. I wish I could have filmed it. I heard that both couples are happily married.

In the Panguna mine also Papua New Guinean Christians from the mainland worked, who had started a congregation. They contacted us. In Arawa, we came to know several Spirit-filled expatriates who worked for the mine, with whom we started meetings. This led to the conversion of a sizeable number of expatriates. Sometimes there were about eighty people present in those meetings.

But there was another very special thing going on: the charismatic movement was more and more accepted in one traditional church after the other in Australia and New Zealand. Many people who attended church and especially church leaders were filled with the Holy Spirit. That movement also began to influence Bougainville. Shortly after we had moved there, Bible studies started with leaders of various churches.

Especially leaders and workers of the former Methodist Church came to these Bible studies and prayer meetings. Leaders were baptised in the Holy Spirit and began bringing this message to their churches. We also got in touch with Roman Catholic priests and nuns who during leave in their own country either had received the Holy Spirit or received it during the charismatic meetings on Bougainville.

During a visit to Port Moresby, we met Maria von Trapp, daughter of the famous Baroness von Trapp, known because of the famous film *The Sound of Music*. She had come as a missionary from the Roman Catholic Church and worked as a teacher in a Catholic school. She was Spirit-filled, and wherever she could, she was involved in the charismatic movement. She introduced us to several nuns and priests. These contacts later led to a meeting with the Roman Catholic bishop who was very open to the Holy Spirit. The contact with the nuns and several priests continued for a very long time. When we left Bougainville six months later and went to Port Moresby, it was not unusual on a Sunday evening to see nuns in the meetings, in their white habits with hands lifted up praising the Lord, or sometimes dancing before the Lord. When we now go to Papua New Guinea, part of the visit is to see the nuns of the Carmelite Monastery in Port Moresby. That God's Spirit was moving, even far beyond the boundaries of the Pentecostal churches, was clear to everyone. We sometimes think back to those days with a feeling of longing and homesickness.

In America and many other Western countries, the powerful Jesus movement had begun, and that influence was also noticeable in Papua New Guinea. The Christians in Papua New Guinea had a strong and appropriate feeling that they were part of something which was global. A phrase like 'this is the outpouring of the Holy Spirit about which the prophet Joel spoke' was often heard.

Pamela Beaumont, who was now in charge of the missionary post at Tonu in Siwai, her closest medical worker, and the young couple that took care of the practical things, like the church plantations, were Spirit-filled Christians. During my first visit to Siwai, I encountered hostility from Tonu. Now, when we came to Siwai, we held prayer meetings and Bible studies there and experienced unusually blessed times.

From the moment that Pamela was baptised in the Holy Spirit, God began to use her powerfully. Her life and service had already been a blessing to many; but now she received, as she said herself, 'a dimension that she had not known before'. What had cost much struggle and effort before that time in the service of the Lord was now very easy for her. Soon Pamela was used several times to set people free from evil spirits, a fact that caused a powerful witch doctor to be mad at her. She had a confrontation with him, and the witch doctor had to give up and acknowledge that Pamela now had a greater power than he did. Pamela experienced special things, but her position within the church became more and more difficult. It would not be long before she chose to take the honourable way out and resign; otherwise, they would fire her.

Several team members from Youth with a Mission in Port Moresby wanted to join us, but also this time accommodation was a problem. However, several expatriates, who were Christians and lived in Arawa, had spacious houses and offered them a place to stay. Two young women could stay there, and a young male team member who came from South Africa could stay with another family. Also the young dedicated Australian couple that had come to Port Moresby during the Summer of Service came to Bougainville. They had stayed behind and now joined us. They were Barry and Joan Winton. Their accommodation was a 'leave house'. That is a house of people who go on holidays and don't want to leave their house without someone looking after it. Regularly things were stolen from houses of which the owners were away on holidays. They spend a year on Bougainville. Their first child was born in Arawa. Around Kieta and Arawa, opportunities arose for us to have house meetings and also children's meetings. The team members of Youth with a Mission had enough to do.

One time I was in Siwai again and stayed in the missionary house in Tonu. It was always a feast to be in Tonu and to be with the believers. Time was too short to visit the churches in the various villages. The believers began a monthly service to which as many believers as possible could come. The service began when there were enough people, usually between ten and eleven in the morning. Many people had to walk for hours to be at the meeting, but that was a price they were gladly willing to pay. The meeting lasted for hours; five hours was not unusual. The singing, the worship, and the strong presence of the Lord are unforgettable for us. There was always time to pray for people and to share testimonies. Miracles were commonplace among the Siwai believers. And we did not only hear testimonies of healings but also regularly heard about appearances of angels. Like the time when I was there, when a couple thanked Monturo for the fact that he, during a journey to the villages on the north side of Siwai, had come to them and had spent the night in their house. That visit of Monturo had especially blessed them. Monturo was surprised. He had not visited them; he had not even come near their village. Slowly we realised that it must have been an angel. When we shared this possibility with the hospitable couple, something became clear. The conversation from dinner until they went to bed and the next morning at breakfast had only been about the Lord and the miracles of the Lord.

Jacob Neewai increasingly became the acknowledged leader in the work in Siwai. I sensed that Joshua Monturo was struggling with this development. Joshua had experienced much persecution, opposition, slander, and even physical attacks from the time he started the prayer teams. At times he had become bitter. But he forgave, but sometimes the bitterness surfaced again. I prayed with Monturo several times for this. I think that we never could fathom the opposition and persecution he had experienced from the time he began the prayer teams. Yet he was the man God used to open Bougainville for a mighty work of the Holy Spirit. We honour and deeply respect this courageous man of God.

In the monthly meeting, there was always a little old lady. We called her 'Grandma'. She had experienced the arrival of the first Europeans. I often saw Grandma dance with her eyes closed in the crowded meeting without touching anyone. Grandma was lost in the Spirit. The Christians of Bougainville had their own style of singing. They could sing well, often spontaneously singing in harmony. Just to experience a time of singing and worship was an event. And those times of singing and worshipping did not last ten or fifteen minutes! When the people of Bougainville sing, they really sing!

The monthly service was always on a Friday. Just outside of Jacob Neewai's village, the Christians had built quite a big church building from bush material. I would usually be there early for the meeting on Friday, and it seemed that everyone was late every time. Only, nobody made a fuss about it. They simply began when everyone was there.

While I was waiting, I was sitting on a tree trunk, which served as a bench, and was reading Philippians 2:9, 'God also has highly exalted him, and given him a name which is above every name.' I had noticed again in my studies the week before that God Himself reveals His name several times in the Old Testament: Lord. In Hebrew that is JHWH, which is Jehovah or Yahweh. I understand that most theologians believe it is Yahweh. Soon after God gave the Ten Commandments to Moses, the people did not speak the name of God anymore, out of fear they would use His name 'in vain'. When the Jews saw JHWH, they would say 'Adonai', which means 'Lord'. When the Old Testament was translated from the Hebrew to the Greek language, wherever the name of God is mentioned, they used the Greek word 'Kurios', which also is 'Lord', for the name of God.

On the day of Pentecost, Peter proclaims that God had made Jesus 'Lord'. Paul writes to the Philippian Christians that God had given His Son 'the Name above all Names', the name 'Lord'.

The name 'Jesus' was given by the angel before the Son of God was born. Suddenly I saw something: God had given His own name 'Lord' to His Son.

God could not give His Son greater honour than giving Him His own name, 'that at the Name of Jesus every knee should bow, and that every tongue should confess that Jesus Christ is Lord, to the glory of God the Father'. I saw that the name combination 'Lord God' appears often in the Old Testament but barely in the New Testament. The New Testament does say 'God' and 'Father of our Lord Jesus Christ'. I sat on that tree trunk lost in something majestic. God had given His own name 'Lord' to His Son. That truth made a deep impression on me. The name of the Son of God was Jesus at His birth, but after His transfiguration, His name was Lord Jesus, and to be even more precise, Lord Jesus Christ. Out of deep respect for His willingness to suffer and save mankind from their sin, God had given His Son the name above every other name. From that moment on, I called the Son of God 'Lord Jesus' as much as possible. A feeling of overwhelming awe filled my heart.

When I spoke about this years later at a large conference, the pastor who was in charge came up to me afterwards and said, 'This truth will have made a great difference in your ministry of deliverance.' It sure did. He got it.

I wanted to visit Monturo's village and could borrow the old Land Rover from Tonu. I had to cross two rivers. The first one was no problem. Drive in a low gear, use the four-wheel drive, and the river was crossed. When crossing the next river, the narrow road immediately climbed for quite a distance and was on a ridge along the mountain leading to the villages. I crossed the second river, and immediately the car had to go on the steep incline. I was almost at the highest point when I heard a loud noise. The Land Rover slowly began rolling backwards. Nothing was working anymore. I accelerated, but the car rolled backwards. I tried to hit the breaks, but the soaking-wet breaks were not working. I realised in a split second that if nothing changed, I would fall off the ridge, fifteen to twenty metres below. I turned the wheel and smacked the car into the mountain and ended up diagonally on the ridge with one wheel over the edge. I looked out the window and saw no road. Below me I saw a river. I turned the engine off and began to shake like a leaf on a tree. Then I realised what had happened. The transmission box of the old Land Rover had jumped out of gear to neutral because of a shock caused by a hole in the road or a stone, and I was left without a clutch, and the engine ran free.

I walked back to Tonu, about a two-hour walk. Later that day I went with a worker from Tonu with a tractor to the Land Rover, and we were able to free it. These sorts of things are not uncommon on the mission field. The people of the village heard about it, and the next day, those I wanted to meet with came walking to Tonu.

The house next to the airport was fun for Mark. He had a big field of grass to play on, and he was nearly always outside. Children in warm countries don't play inside: they play outside, and when it rains, it is often even more fun to play in the rain! We could only rent the house for three months, and the three months were almost over. Contact with the Uniting Church had become much better because of the influence of the charismatic movement. They offered us a small house on the hill behind Kieta. We had no other choice and accepted it. But the house was old and ramshackle; I once fell through the floor. But the view was indescribably beautiful. I think that some people would offer millions of dollars for such a view. We looked out over this little place Kieta and the beautiful bay where it is located. A little off the coast, there was a beautiful island named Pukpuk Island. In the vernacular, 'pukpuk' is the Pidgin English word for crocodile, because this island had the shape of a large crocodile. The sea was blue, and you could see the reefs. Every once in a while, a cargo ship came to Kieta, mainly to bring supplies to the shops and take back copra (dried coconut). Many times we stood or sat and enjoyed the fantastic view.

Unfortunately, it was not very safe. Because the house was just outside of Kieta, it was unprotected. Therefore, two team members came to live with us so that Coby or they would never be alone. Even with that precaution, we sometimes had stalkers around the house in the evening or at night. These were nearly always people from other areas who had moved to Bougainville or worked there. We never experienced this from people of Bougainville. They are people with high moral standards.

There were a few smaller meetings taking place around Kieta and Arawa, but the congregations in Arawa and Panguna began to take shape. Sometimes we actually were busy and . . . we only had one car, which was difficult sometimes. After two months, we could no longer stay in the little house on the hill, because the Uniting Church was going to take it down and build something new. We could not find anything else except a 'leave house' for one month, so the four of us and little Mark moved to this house. Around this time, Coby was well and truly pregnant with our second son.

In that month, a team of eight people from Youth with a Mission came to help for about two weeks, in and around Arawa. It was a good time. They could do much among the local people but also among the expatriates in Arawa and Panguna.

When they arrived, they were taken from the airport to Arawa in a little bus, but when they left, we had to bring them back ourselves. The road from Arawa to Kieta was bitumen, but from Kieta to the airport, it was an unpaved road. I had to make the trip twice to take all eight people to the airport. Every trip took one and a half hours. When they were all at the airport, they went to check in at the counter. Then it turned out that their names were unknown and that the old DC-3 was already full. But they had reaffirmed their flight! I became so angry that I nearly climbed across the small counter to hit the man in the face. Luckily I did not do that, but I was furious. The next airplane would leave three days later, and according to the man behind the counter, that was fully booked too. I was boiling and made sure that the man behind the counter knew about it. When I walked back to the car to bring the first four back, the Holy Spirit clearly spoke to my heart. 'Go back and ask the man behind the counter for forgiveness for the way you behaved.' I calmed down and walked back. The passengers were already in the plane, and the engines of the DC-3 had started. When the man saw me returning, his face turned white because I really had not been friendly. I asked him to forgive me for my behaviour and anger. He was kind of surprised and accepted it and shook my hand. Then he said, 'All eight of them can leave in three days.' First he had told me that that plane was also fully booked, but that was probably his reaction to my anger. Three days later, the team left for Port Moresby and from there to Australia.

Two more weeks and then we had to leave our house. We prayed and prayed, but nothing happened. Slowly we began to realise that our time to live on Bougainville would only be short. Tom Hallas had asked us to come to Port Moresby to close the base of Youth with a Mission and care for the small congregation that had come into being. Port Moresby needed help urgently. Kalafi and his wife had left some time ago, and now Tom and Diana Hallas had been asked to come to Hawaii for more training. The leaders saw the calling on their lives and their abilities and wanted to train them further, which is what happened. Tom is to this day a well-known leader in Youth with a Mission in Australia. The base of Youth with a Mission in Port Moresby needed to be finalised. The small fellowship had been able to lease some land from the government and been able to erect a small building. A great achievement in itself. Several Australian couples had helped the group of believers financially. One of the expatriates had designed the building and supervised the building of it.

Two more weeks and we would not have a home anymore but . . . we did not want to leave beautiful Bougainville and trade it for hot, dry, and dusty Port Moresby. But it seemed that there was no other possibility. Port Moresby was the only open door! With grief in our heart, we said goodbye to Bougainville. We went to Port Moresby, not knowing that we were about to begin our best years in Papua New Guinea.

The two female team members and Barry and Joan Winton stayed for a while and lived in 'leave houses'. But then the doors were also closed for them, and they left Bougainville. The work was now entirely in the hands of the local Christians.

Three years after we had left Bougainville, the work in and around Arawa had grown to such extent that they urgently needed help. Barry and Joan Winton then returned and led the congregation in Arawa for seven years. The congregation grew a lot in that period. We had applied with various authorities for a piece of land to build on so that the congregations in and around Arawa would be taken good care of. Barry and Joan moved thirty-nine times from 'leave house' to 'leave house'. Barry told me that more than once, when he had been somewhere and was going home, he had to really think about where he lived at that time. Everyone, local people and expatriates, saw the sacrifices they brought to be able to do the work; and they were respected for their dedication. Finally they were given a piece of land in Arawa, and they experienced living in 'their own house'. Unfortunately, this house was destroyed during the crisis.

Pamela Beaumont resigned and left Bougainville and went to Christchurch in New Zealand where she attended a Bible school for a year at the well-known congregation New Life Centre of Pastor Peter

Morrow. In that year, she was also healed from a severe physical illness. After a year 'home' in her original home town, it became clear that the Lord was calling her back to the island and people she loved so much: Bougainville.

In the meantime, Peter Clyburn, the teacher at the secondary school near Kavieng, had attended a Bible school in Brisbane. He also felt called to go to Bougainville to train and equip young people.

The work in Siwai grew and grew, and we realised that we had to do something about training for the people in the villages. After much prayer and advice, Pamela Beaumont and Peter Clyburn started a Bible school in Siwai. First in a village in the middle of Siwai, but when the school continued to grow, it was moved to a beautiful piece of land along the river on the border of Siwai and the district of Buin. For years, this school trained many young people and experienced great blessing. I understand that all through the later crisis the school kept functioning, and still functions today.

When Peter Clyburn was on his way to Bougainville, he spent several weeks with us in Port Moresby. Peter needed a car, a four-wheel drive. Peter set his heart on a small Suzuki. That type of Suzuki could be lifted up by four people, which was very practical when you would get stuck in the mud. And that happened quite often.

As usual we had no money and prayed. I advised Peter to go to the dealer in Port Moresby and get himself a poster of that model Suzuki. The Suzuki came in three colours: green, white, and orange. Typical of Peter Clyburn: he wanted an orange Suzuki. The poster he received was of a green one. Every day Peter looked at that poster and prayed for a Suzuki and believed the Lord. After a while, we received a phone call from Australian Christians who were returning to their own country and had a small Suzuki. They had heard that we urgently needed one. They wanted to give us their Suzuki. We cheered! The first question Peter asked was 'What colour is it?' It was a green one! Peter had looked at the poster of a green Suzuki for weeks and had believed God. We and Peter made jokes about it. 'You should have hung up a poster of an orange Suzuki. You receive what you look at!' Maybe there is a great truth in that, despite the joking. Begin to see in the Spirit what it is that you're believing for. The Suzuki was shipped to Bougainville and served faithfully for years. When later the school grew, they received a Toyota Land Cruiser which by then they really needed.

When the piece of land on which the Bible school was going to be built was cleared with a bulldozer and many trees had been taken down, they found a 500-pound bomb from the Second World War. The bomb had not exploded. They contacted the army that sent several soldiers a few weeks later to detonate the bomb. The bang could be heard throughout Siwai.

The Haari Bible school became a piece of paradise in the middle of the jungle. The atmosphere in and around the school was filled with the presence of the Lord. Even non-believers spoke about it. There were several buildings from bush material: a house for Peter and a house for Pamela, and also a house for the girls and for the boys. The classrooms, a building where the cooking took place and a room for meetings, were all made from material out of the jungle. Apart from that, there were gardens where the students grew their own food. Flowers and beautiful bushes were everywhere, and here and there were bunches of orchids that grow everywhere on Bougainville. And then the beautiful river that was also the bathing area. The boys bathed upstream and the girls further down the stream, strictly and clearly separated as the culture demanded.

Dozens of young people were trained for one year, sometimes for two. The results were impressive. The work began to grow everywhere and even extended to the surrounding areas like Buin and Nagovisi and beyond.

We often went to the Haari Bible school. The Bible school became very well-known in Bougainville but also outside of Bougainville. Even students from other areas than Bougainville came to it.

Once while I was visiting Bougainville again, I went together with the American missionary Sam Sasser. Sam Sasser had worked for several years on the Marshall Islands in the Pacific and had experienced a powerful move of the Holy Spirit there. We had been to Siwai together; and on the way back, not far from Panguna, it started to rain. It was raining cats and dogs. Close to Panguna you did not need to cross any more rivers, but the rain had caused a landslide. The road was totally blocked. It would need a bulldozer or many men with a shovel to open the road up again. We drove back because we wanted to try to spend the night in a village, but behind us there was also a landslide across the road. We were captives. We drove back to the first landslide and realised that we could climb, scramble, and slip across but would get very dirty. After that, we could walk uphill on the road to Panguna: an hour or two walking. That's what we did. We locked the car and left it behind, took as little luggage as possible with us, and went on our way. Totally filthy we arrived in Panguna and were able to clean up and change clothes there. We were even able to have the meeting that had been planned for that evening. We stayed in Panguna for two days. Then we heard that they were clearing the road. We were taken back, and after several hours, it was possible to get across the road in our four-wheel drive and continue our journey to Arawa. Working and living in Papua New Guinea was always somewhat adventurous. I still miss that!

Pamela and Peter came regularly to Arawa to buy supplies for the school. From Arawa to the Haari Bible school it was, in dry weather and good conditions, about a two-and-a-half-hour drive. It often took many more hours. I never made the journey without bringing a good book. On the bank of one of the rivers, which often had a too-high water level, because of the rain, I spent hours reading while we were waiting for the water to subside.

After several years, Peter married Marion whom he knew from the church in Brisbane. The team of the Haari Bible school then consisted of Peter, Marion, and Pamela.

The road from Arawa to Buin went past the Haari Bible school. You did have to cross several rivers though. One river, near Boku on the border of Siwai and Nagovisi, was often too high; and then you had to wait again, sometimes for hours, sometimes for days. Then it was decided to build a bridge over the river Boku. Well, bridge is too big a word. It became a long one-way lane of concrete, about two metres above the river. What a relief, no more problems at Boku. There were still few cars in Siwai, but because of the mine, more were coming.

Once it rained for weeks. And when it rains on Bougainville, it rains. After those weeks of rain, the bridge over the river was gone, simply gone. They found the bridge: half a kilometre away in the sea. The few cars that belonged to Siwai were back to where it was as at the beginning: at high water they had to wait by the river until the water had gone down.

T. L. Osborn had given a fully equipped car for evangelism to Bougainville. It was used in many places on Bougainville, but one time when it was further inland, it was damaged severely. To take the car back to Arawa, where there was a garage, was nearly impossible and definitely too expensive. So this was the end of the car which is still rusting away somewhere in the jungle. The generator, projector, and films, however, were used often for a long time after that.

Years later, we were able from Japan to help several Japanese Christians to go to the Haari Bible school. They built a building of durable material. The school itself was near the place where during the Second World War a plane had been shot down that carried the famous Japanese admiral Yamamoto. For the Japanese Christians, it was an act of reconciliation to build permanent buildings for the Bible school near that place.

We had not seen Monturo anymore until I visited Bougainville again after the crisis. There were only flights to Buka, the island north of Bougainville. From Buka, you had to go to the main island Bougainville by crossing a narrow passage of water between the two islands. There we would be picked up with a four-wheel-drive car.

The airplane had landed on Buka, and several people who were waiting on the airport recognised me. It spread like wildfire: John Pasterkamp is here. After having met a few people, we went to the boat to go to the main island. While I was waiting there, suddenly Monturo came running towards me, fell into my arms, and cried and cried. He hugged me and did not let me go. His whole body was shaking. It was moving.

He told me that his first wife had passed away and that he had remarried. His new wife became very sick, and with a lot of effort, they had gone all the way north to Buka, where she had been in the hospital for a while. He was at the government post and heard that I was on the plane that had arrived. He realised that the best chance to meet me was where the boats were, and he had come as soon as possible. His wife was still recovering, but she was with him. It was very moving to meet again after so many years. We could not be together long because the boat was leaving, and on the other side a car would be waiting. The car came three hours later, which is not uncommon. We called it PNG time.

When the crisis broke out, Bougainville was closed off from all contact: no mail, no telephone, no radio, no airplanes, no ships, no medical care, no education, nothing. Very sporadically someone had found a way to the northern island. Then you heard some news, but that news was usually not good.

The rebels did not tolerate any opposition and took Neewai. Neewai refused to be loyal to the rebels. They beat him up and hung him by his legs and left him behind. Neewai realised that in this position he would soon die. He prayed, and there came a wind that moved him back and forth until he could get hold of a high fence and was able to pull himself up and untie the ropes on his feet. When the rebels beat him, they broke his jaw. Wounded and with a broken jaw, he was able to reach Buka after three weeks. He was skinny and in a very poor condition. The government flew him to Rabaul where he spent weeks in the hospital. When he was well again, he came to Port Moresby to meet the leaders there and then went back to Siwai to be with his people. What a man of God he was! However, from that moment on, things became worse for him; and he experienced much persecution.

In the crisis, many Christians were killed. But as always in times of persecution, the believers brought many people to Jesus, and many new congregations were founded. Believers of the Uniting Church and Christian Life Centre gathered together. In times of persecution and pressure, differences fall away. Maybe it is then that we see true Christianity as the Lord intended it.

After eight years, some kind of peace was established. A small unit of peacekeepers from Australia and New Zealand established themselves on Bougainville. Shortly afterwards, I was able to visit Bougainville, which started with meeting Monturo on the beach near the boats. My travel companion was a good friend from Holland.

Arawa was a shock to me. Nearly all houses had been burned down or destroyed. The roads were in very poor condition and often entirely overgrown by the jungle. There were only a few houses still standing. In one of these houses lived Uzziah and Darucilla Movo, former students of the Bible school in Port Moresby and the pastor couple who cared for the church after Barry and Joan left. My Dutch friend and I were welcomed as kings. Peter was a stranger to the people. To me it was moving to meet them again. About sixty Christians and leaders had gathered, also from Siwai. Among them was Neewai. Only he was no longer the vital and powerful Neewai. The eight years of crisis and what he had been through had left its marks. In some sense he was a broken man. But it was deeply moving to see him again. About a year after this meeting, this special man of God passed away. He is with the Lord now.

We drove to Kieta, but with the exception of one or two houses, it no longer existed. Everything was broken down, destroyed, or burned. It was sad, very sad to see it all. There was no electricity, so everything was done with kerosine lamps. When I would ask someone how things were going, I received answers like 'My parents were killed. My sister was beaten to death. One of my children was murdered. My wife was kidnapped and was in the hands of the rebels for two years.' What do you say to Christians that suffered so much? I had the feeling I could not say anything to these people but that they had much to say to me. From the stories, I concluded that the Haari Bible school continued to function as best as possible during the crisis.

When I left after three days, they gave me a love offering. I left this money behind in Port Moresby for the work among the criminal youth. I could not take this money and use it for myself.

While I was in Arawa, I came into contact with several interesting men. I then discovered what probably happened with the money of the financial pyramid scheme that had been started several years before by a Christian on Bougainville. Bougainville wanted to separate itself from Papua New Guinea, and this was also the intention of the rebels. They say that according to legends, there had existed a kingdom called Papala in the south of Bougainville in and around Siwai. In my questions and research about this later, I got no further than that this was a legend. The tribal structure of Siwai was arranged in such a way that there could never have been a king or royal family. However, the one who began the financial pyramid scheme was busy building this kingdom, with himself as king. Later, from a report published on the internet, I learned that the man who started this financial pyramid had become the successor of Francis Ona the leader of the Bougainville Republican Army.

Back in Port Moresby, I was able to talk for hours about what I discovered with the leader of the opposition of that time, who was a former prime minister. I knew him reasonably well. He was a born-again Christian and came to one of our churches. Later, all the things that I discovered and shared with him proved to be true and correct.

It was hard to say goodbye to the dear, dedicated Christians who had gathered in Arawa. Some had come in the midst of very difficult circumstances and with great effort. I understood that some of them had walked for many, many hours . . .

I was warned that the driver of the car who would take us back to the north of the island was second in charge of the rebels. His name was Ismael. I was told to watch what I said and did. The journey went well. But when we arrived in the north and had to go to Buka in a small boat, to go to the airport, the driver wanted to speak with me. We walked to a quiet place near the water, and he began to ask questions. He spoke English well.

'Are you John Pasterkamp?'

'Yes, I am.'

'You lived on Bougainville, didn't you? And you are the founder of Christian Life Centre, aren't you?'

'Well, not entirely, it actually started with Siwai people, but I understand what you mean. Yes indeed, I lived on Bougainville, and I visited there regularly.'

'Do you know who I am?'

'Yes, they told me who you are.'

Then came the question I will never forget.

'Can and will God forgive me for what I have done?'

'Yes, God wants to and is able to forgive you. But why do you ask this?'

'I killed many people. It is so-called peace now, but we still have many weapons everywhere, and we could continue fighting anytime. Twice I should have been dead, but something happened. One time soldiers were lying in an ambush, and we did not know. Suddenly a big snake fell from the tree right before my feet, and I knew it was a warning. We went back and later heard that an ambush had been waiting. We would have certainly been killed. Another time someone warned us. Otherwise, we would have been dead. I think that God saved my life those two times.'

'I think so too,' I responded.

He continued, 'When we began as BRA (Bougainville Republican Army), Catholic leaders fled but also the leaders of the Seventh-day Adventist Church. Many leaders of the Uniting Church joined us. But there was another group, Christian Life Centre, of which you are the founder. They did not flee and remained neutral. They refused to choose. If we needed help when there were wounded people, they helped us. But when the enemy was wounded and needed help, they helped them too. Those were real Christians.'

The Christians of Christian Life Centre had obviously made a deep impression on him. Honesty bids me to say that I was quite moved when he said this. Again he asked, 'Does God want to forgive me for what I have done?'

'Do you know what it means to be reborn?' I asked him.

'I think so,' was his answer.

'Do you want to accept Jesus, repent, and be reborn?' I asked nervously.

'No, I am not ready for that yet. But you must promise me that when you visit Bougainville again, you come and visit me.' I promised.

The little boat left for Buka, and I had to say goodbye. I wished I could have stayed. This man was looking for help.

When I returned to the Netherlands several weeks later, I came home early one afternoon; and while I drank something, I turned on the television to the National Geographic channel. To my great surprise, it was a documentary about the crisis on Bougainville. This had been made by several New Zealand journalists who had managed to get into Bougainville during the crisis and filmed it. Suddenly, in my living room in Rotterdam, the face of Ismael appeared on our television screen. I cried and prayed for him. Ismael has been often on my mind and in my prayers.

When I was back in Port Moresby five years ago, I went out for dinner in a restaurant and recognised a man from Bougainville. He was a government leader, and he was a Christian. We greeted each other, and then he said, 'Do you remember Ismael?' How could I forget Ismael? 'He has repented and testifies everywhere about Jesus. I had to say hello to you from him. He really wants to meet you.' My visit to Port Moresby could not get any better. I promised that when I was able, the next time I would be in Papua New Guinea I would also visit Bougainville and especially Ismael.

The crisis on Bougainville has ended. The leader of the Bougainville Republican Army, Francis Ona passed away. The second man, Ismael, is now a Christian and testifies everywhere. But there still seems to be a political disquiet. What we do hear is that many people have become Christians and that many new congregations have been formed on Bougainville. The Christians of Christian Life Centre have played a special part in that.

CHAPTER 27

The Capital – Port Moresby

IT WAS NOT easy to exchange the beautiful, green, humid, and jungle-overgrown Bougainville for a dusty, dry, and hot Port Moresby. But it was clear that the Lord had closed all doors and had opened a new one. Port Moresby was our next assignment. That assignment would fill the coming six years, and the last years of that period would be the best years in Papua New Guinea – a time in which we would see a very powerful work of God. I was twenty-nine when we moved to Port Moresby, and many times I have recalled the prophecy I had received. It was spoken when I was for the first time in a Pentecostal meeting in Amsterdam: 'At a young age I will call you, and at a young age you will serve Me.'

The first weeks we lived at the Youth with a Mission base in Port Moresby. Tom and Diana Hallas were preparing to move to Hawaii. There were several team members who would stay, but there was no real leader among them. Unless the Lord was going to lead differently, it was obvious that this base in Port Moresby had to be closed.

Port Moresby was a fast-developing and growing city. It is the city where the government is located and also the city where the higher educational institutions were being established. A few years before we arrived there, the first university was built, with capacity for about 1,000 students. These were students from all over the country, who were the first ones to complete primary school and six years of secondary school and who had finished with high scores in their subjects. There was also a higher technical college and a higher administrative college.

The small fellowship consisted of sixty to eighty Papua New Guineans and a handful of expatriates. It was a friendly, enthusiastic group, but it had not much structure as yet. The fellowship had taken on the name Faith Fellowship. The Sunday before Tom and Diana left, Tom consecrated two men as elders. With hindsight, that might have been a little too soon, but it was on Tom's heart to convey a clear message: this fellowship is and will be your fellowship. One of the elders was Stephen Stephens, a man in his fifties from the area around Port Moresby. He was a real father figure among the people and was much respected. His wife, Rose, was truly a treasure. Later she worked at our office for several years. They had six children. The name Stephen Stephens was unusual. Stephen was his chosen first name. Stephens was a composition of his father's name. The government later introduced a law making that no longer possible. A child received a personal first name, and the surname was the birth name of the father. In that way the government tried to bring order into the naming of children and to establish proper registers. At the beginning of the colonial time, when Port Moresby was being built, Stephen's father was someone who was suspected of having committed a crime, though it was never proven. Together with several other men, he was hanged as a warning to others. Stephen hated white people, but when he was converted, he was able to forgive the perpetrators, and his hatred for white people disappeared. He became a dear and sweet friend. Two years later, he was diagnosed with cancer; and despite much prayer, he passed away.

Stephen worked at one of the few petrol stations in town. When, after the medical diagnosis of cancer, I had to tell his boss about this, he, an Australian, took me to his office, sat down, and cried. He said, 'I have never met such an honest and sincere man as Stephen. He never tried to put money in his own pocket although he had many opportunities to do so.' Stephen's life was a powerful testimony.

After several weeks at the Youth with a Mission base, we were able to live for a month in a 'leave house'. The birth of our second child was approaching. A man who came from Europe, a somewhat introverted man, had come to the Lord. He was the owner of three home units and was willing to sell them to us. Christian Life Centre, Pastor Trevor

Chandler's church in Brisbane, gave us the money for a down payment to buy those units; and the bank gave us a loan for the rest.

Christian Life Centre in Brisbane did much for us in the years we were in Port Moresby and invested quite a bit of money for the work in Papua New Guinea. But we also received gifts from the Netherlands, and that's how we were able to function.

Just before our son Stephen was born, we could move into one of the three units and decorate it, though very basic. Shortly afterwards, the fellowship in Brisbane sent a few builders and carpenters who renovated, restored, and painted the three units. It was the first time, after Rabaul, that we had our own home, our own spot. To both of us, but especially to Coby, this was a great gift; and she felt very much at home in this cosy small dwelling. Our second son, Stephen, was born at the maternity ward of the hospital in Port Moresby. There were now four of us. Mark was very pleased with his brother but also a little jealous of the baby that suddenly got so much attention.

In the fellowship, something was starting to happen that would clearly give direction for the years to come. When we arrived, there were two university students in the congregation: Francis and Margaret. But very soon many more students came to the Lord. Within a short period, many students had come to the Lord and were filled with the Holy Spirit. In the years to come, some of them would hold very responsible positions in the country.

Unexpectedly, someone came to visit us; it was the former owner of the Youth with a Mission house. This house had been bought, and in a legal contract, it had been arranged that Youth with a Mission would pay for the house over a period of several years. The man sold the house because he was returning to his native country in Europe. As soon as he would arrive, he was going to inform Youth with a Mission of his address and bank account number. It was a somewhat peculiar arrangement, but it was all in writing. However, nobody ever heard anything from the previous owner. He had disappeared from the face of the earth. The base leaders of Youth with a Mission, Kalafi Moala and Tom Hallas, made enquiries but could not find anything, except to learn that the man was sought by the police and had probably fled the country. Perhaps that was the reason for the peculiar arrangement. The team sometimes thought that maybe the house was a gift from God. But now, suddenly, about five years later, the former owner showed up. He was angry because he had never received any money. When I confronted him with the fact that we had never received his address or bank account number, he could not give a clear answer. Something was clearly wrong. He rightly demanded his money, but he also demanded money for the years we had made use of the house. He threatened to go to the police and take us to court, but nothing happened. He was simply trying to intimidate us.

In a telephone conversation with Loren Cunningham, the international leader of Youth with a Mission, it was decided to hand the house back to its owner.

The increase of the value of the house over those years was sufficient to cover the compensation claim for the use of the house. And this solved the issue. Also the remaining team members left Papua New Guinea. For a period of five years, teams had gone out from this house to evangelise. This house has been a place of worship and intense intercession. In this house, many, especially young people met the Lord Jesus.

It was a place where the Holy Spirit of the Lord has done amazing things. Now we only had the responsibility for the growing fellowship, and we could give this our full attention. Years later, Youth with a Mission opened a new base in the second largest city of Lae, and that happened just before we were going to leave Papua New Guinea.

In the growing fellowship, we began to teach about repentance. It led to many deep encounters with God. It was in that time that I led a university student to the Lord. When he accepted the Lord, he spontaneously prayed, 'Lord Jesus, forgive me because my father is a witch doctor.' I immediately realised what he was doing: he repented of the wrong aspects of his culture. A few years later, he was able to lead his father to Jesus.

A children's camp was held. A great conviction of sin came upon the children, and deep conversions and encounters with God took place. When the children came back from the camp, that movement also began to spread among the students and adults. Sins were confessed, sometimes sins that had been hidden for a long time. Wrong attitudes were confessed. People dealt seriously with bitterness and unwillingness to forgive. Right choices were made, and wrong relationships were ended. Powerful things happened, and this led to more conversions. We regularly heard of people who had come to Jesus because of what they saw happening in the lives of other family members.

We began to teach about praise and worship and how to put it in practice. It led to even more praise and worship. It often happened in the Sunday evening meetings that nuns in their white habits, and sometimes even priests, danced before the Lord together with the Papua New Guinean believers and sang in new tongues with hands lifted high. We learned so much in that time and enjoyed the blessing of the Lord.

We needed help and asked Hank and Lenie to leave Kavieng and join us in Port Moresby. Hans and Dorothy van der Wal had worked for a while on the Duke of York Islands, a group of islands between Rabaul and New Ireland. They took over the responsibility of the work in Kavieng. Again, Hank and Lenie and we were together. They came to live in one of the three units, so we became neighbours.

George Brown Island, where an early Methodist missionary had come, was the most important place on the Duke of York Islands. That was about a hundred years ago. It took then eight years before the first person became a Christian on these islands, where witchcraft and cruelty were a daily reality. After that, many more people became Christians. But that was three generations ago. The present generation was Christian in name, but much darkness had again taken a hold on the population of the islands.

One day Hans met with a man who was clearly demon possessed. Hans addressed the manifesting demon and demanded that it give its name. A voice spoke through the mouth of the man and said, 'I am light.' Very wisely Hans answered, 'Jesus is light. Are you Jesus?' Silence followed. The demon was silent. Hans commanded the misleading demon to leave. Another demon announced its presence, and again Hans demanded the name of the demon. 'I am love,' was the answer. Hans answered, 'God is love. Are you God?' Again silence. That demon was also commanded to leave the man in the name of the Lord Jesus.

After that, several more demons came out, and the man was freed. These demons called themselves 'light' and 'love' and misled the people they inhabited to think that they were in the light and had love. The words of Jesus, 'If therefore the light that is in you is darkness, how great is that darkness!' became very clear through this event and revealed the true state of many Christians on the Duke of York Islands.

Later an evangelistic team from Rabaul and Port Moresby went to the Duke of York Islands. They were physically abused, and a young man was tied to a tree and beaten with a chain. He survived but will be crippled the rest of his life if a miracle does not take place. Mission in those countries can sound very romantic, but it can also be really tough.

The charismatic movement in traditional churches was flourishing. Regularly we heard of missionaries and church leaders who were filled with the Holy Spirit, and often we made contact with them and enjoyed precious fellowship.

A need for good charismatic books in the country was increasing. There was a small Christian bookshop, but the manager was very anti-Pentecostal and anti-charismatic. Because of the great influence of the charismatic movement, believers often went there to look for well-known charismatic books. Unfortunately, they usually received a fiery sermon against everything Pentecostal and charismatic.

Hank and Lenie developed a vision for what we called the Charismatic Service Centre. This served to provide the body of Christ in Papua New Guinea with material for evangelism and personal growth. It also opened two bookshops, one in Port Moresby and one in Bougainville. They were able to start a tape-lending library. From Brisbane, we received a great number of tapes by well-known speakers. The tapes of Derek Prince were by far the most popular. His clear and systematic exegesis in somewhat slowly spoken English was what the people could handle well. Hank supervised all of this, and it sure kept him very busy.

One day we heard that in the Roman Catholic convent of the Carmelite sisters, just outside of Port Moresby, an outpouring of the Holy Spirit had taken place. The Carmelite order is a prayer order, and with the exception of a short period each day in which the sisters can converse with one another, the rest of the time is spent in silence and prayer.

We made contact with them and were invited to visit them. There were about fifteen sisters in the order, several from overseas, and several Papua New Guinean nuns. They told us how they heard of the charismatic movement and began to pray for the Holy Spirit. Most of them had an experience with the Holy Spirit, spoke in tongues, prophesied, and had visions and deep personal encounters with the Holy Spirit. It was moving and heart-warming to hear. As long as we were in Port Moresby, we went to the convent once a fortnight to pray. Often, these were deep and powerful times of prayer. Whenever we had activities, conferences, or crusades, we would call the convent; and the nuns would pray for us.

One day after prayer, we were chatting, and I asked one of the American Carmelite nuns what she did before she had joined the convent. I am still surprised about her answer. In the Second World War, she had been one of the first female fighter pilots! Other nuns had finished courses at university, but they had all felt the call to dedicate their lives to prayer.

Years later, during one of my visits to the country, I visited them; and they asked how our sons, Mark, Stephen, and Daniel, were doing. I told them. The Mother Superior of the group of nuns told me that they had been praying for John and Coby, Mark, Stephen, and Daniel every day for twenty years. That touched me deeply! Without a doubt, that was one of the reasons that God worked in such wonderful ways in our family. They asked us how Tambitha was doing. She was the girl we had looked after for a year. She was in Barcelona at that moment for an evangelism outreach with Youth with a Mission. She was the first Papua New Guinea Christian to join this type of overseas outreach. They also prayed for her every day!

During my last visit some years ago, the eldest nun, who was eighty-seven then and who had been in the convent for over fifty years, said to me, 'The church leaders in our church have built wind tunnels for years and maybe even centuries, through which they think the Holy Spirit must blow. But the Holy Spirit works and blows the way He wants, and that is often not through these tunnels!' How true!

The growing fellowship in Port Moresby consisted, with the exception of three families, of young single people, mainly university students. When we announced a youth service, it actually meant that the three married couples could not come. Hank and Lenie and Coby and I then prayed, 'Lord, give us more couples in the congregation.' If we ever prayed a prayer that the Lord answered, it was this prayer. Very soon we had marriage ceremony after marriage ceremony after marriage ceremony. Within a year, the next phenomenon started: dedicating baby after baby after baby to the Lord. I really can't remember how many babies we dedicated, but it was dozens and in the course of the years maybe a few hundred.

Two young men who had come to the Lord as students had given up their study and became part of the team of Youth with a Mission: Bob Lutu and Lenden Butuna. Both had been helping missionaries in other places, like Hilding and Ingrid in Mount Hagen. Both came back to Port Moresby and became part of the leadership of the fellowship.

In Rabaul, during an Osborn film evening that Kari Harri held, a young man from the Pangia area in the Highlands had a powerful conversion experience. When he prayed the sinner's prayer, he felt a hand lovingly touch him. It was the hand of Jesus Himself. This somewhat quiet and almost shy young man worked at the post office, but shortly after his conversion, he was transferred to Port Moresby. Kari had told us about him, and straightaway he came to us and did not miss a single meeting. His name was Charles Lapa. Charles was a dear, dedicated Christian but did not stand out at first. Actually, he seemed a very ordinary young man. There was no indication whatsoever that God would use him mightily years later and that his name would be known in the entire country.

We felt challenged about our vision. What did we want to accomplish in this country? We fervently sought the Lord. After much prayer and meditation, I came to one conclusion. The assignment of Jesus was more than clear: 'Make disciples of nations.' How to make an individual a disciple of Jesus was clear to us. But how do you make nations disciples of Jesus? The longer we prayed and thought about it, the clearer it became. You make a nation disciples of Jesus by reaching leaders or upcoming leaders; they have to become disciples of Jesus.

The country was under Australian government jurisdiction, but there was much talk about independence. It was clear that it would not take decades before independence was granted – a few years at the most. The present government leaders were Australians, but then it would be people from Papua New Guinea. Where do you get such capable leaders? It was clear: the university students and students at higher educational institutions would be the leaders of the country in several years' time. God had placed us within walking distance from the university. The message was obvious.

Though I always tried to have men, mainly young men, around me to train them in discipleship, I had an idea; and I put it into practice. Just like Jesus, I chose young men to spend time with, as a group. There were ten of them. I began to spend at least one evening a week with them. We also were together sometimes on a Saturday, and we went away several weekends. Sometimes we prayed together or studied together. Often, I shared my heart with them and told them about the lessons I had learned through the working and dealings of God in my life. I think there was only one part of my life I did not share with them: my marriage to Coby, because that belongs to the two of us. Apart from that, I gave myself to them and shared my life with them, and they began to do the same.

I taught them how to play Monopoly and Scrabble. Sometimes we just had lots of fun. Other times we would eat together, Papua New Guinea style. Then there were times when we prayed for long periods to seek the Lord God for our future. I called them 'my Timothy group'. I had never heard about a missionary or pastor who did this. Cell groups, home groups, and G12 groups were unknown to me in 1974.

We journeyed together like that for three years. In the group were Bob Lutu, Lenden Butuna, David Muap, Gabriel Pepson, Jo Gabut, Francis Houji, Edward Oki, Charles Lapa, Konroy, and Simeon Rassia. Some of the names I mention here have become leaders in this country. Only, I did not know that then. Now, when I go to Papua New

Guinea, we always try to meet. That friendship between us has never disappeared. Some of them I count as my best friends to this day. Sadly, some have passed away and are no longer with us.

After this group, I led another group for a period, and from that group also several came to prominent positions.

I have sometimes been criticised by other Pentecostal missionaries because I gave so much time to ten young men, while the Lord had used me so much in evangelism. The criticism was not pleasant, but I had heard from the Lord to do what I was doing. After we had worked in Port Moresby for over six years and left the country, the Pentecostal missionary who had uttered this criticism came to say goodbye. He said very openly, 'I have strongly criticised you a few times, but now I would like to exchange my leaders for yours.' I thanked him for this genuine compliment.

Edward Oki, who had developed into an extraordinary praise and worship leader, as well as national youth leader, preached years later in a big youth rally in Lae. Many young people came forward to give their lives to Jesus. Just when he was about to pray for them, he did not feel well and asked Charles Lapa to take over. Several hours later, Edward passed away. Years later, when we were back in the Netherlands, I received the phone call. I was upset for days and even contemplated flying to Papua New Guinea to attend his funeral. But timewise I would not make it. Edward Oki left behind his precious wife, Ann, and six children. Edward was a wantok (i.e. a person from the same tribe) of Charles Lapa. Charles led the funeral, the hardest thing he ever had to do, he told me. To me Edward was also a wantok, but even more than a wantok: a son.

Around the time that we came to Port Moresby, a conflict took place in our home church in the Netherlands. Besides other problems, several people were following a somewhat extreme Pentecostal teaching and left the congregation. This affected the financial situation. It broke the heart of the father and patriarch of the congregation. Not long afterwards, he died at quite an old age, and another pastor came who was a good friend of mine. However, he did not correctly discern the conflict in the congregation; and after a while, the problems were of such proportion that the congregation fell apart and ceased to exist.

We did receive financial help from Australia for special things, like the down payment for the housing units, but the major part to meet daily needs still came from the Netherlands and some from the Dutch migrant fellowships. It was a strange experience to suddenly not have a real spiritual home in the Netherlands anymore, neither to receive regular income. Individual friends and acquaintances blessed us with gifts from time to time, but that was not enough for our daily needs. We really asked ourselves if our time as missionaries was over. We would not even have enough money to buy a ticket back to the Netherlands. But the work we did was the work of the Lord, and like the famous George Muller once said, 'God's work done in God's way will have God's support.'

The well-known New Zealand pastor Bob Midgley had come to Brisbane to help Pastor Trevor Chandler in the growing church. This gentle, compassionate, and wise man has made a substantial impact on my personal life and ministry. Trevor Chandler and Bob Midgley heard of our situation through Hank and Lenie and almost immediately booked their flights to be with us for a few days. We shared with them the whole situation, and they offered us to be connected with their church as missionaries. They then took the responsibility to support us in our daily needs. They already supported Hank and Lenie as they came from their church. Officially the work was still called Full Gospel Movement Streams of Power, though we no longer used Streams of Power but only Full Gospel Movement.

Pastor Chandler and Pastor Midgley proposed to change the name of the entire work to Christian Life Centre Papua New Guinea, which we would show our connection with them, but also with the movement of the Holy Spirit in Australia and New Zealand. Many churches born out of the charismatic movement had names like Christian Life Centre, New Life Centre, Life Ministry Centre, Life Outreach Ministry, or Christian Outreach. We followed this advice and became closely connected to Australia in the years following. The name of the fellowship in Port Moresby became Christian Life Centre. Of course we had a close relationship with family, friends, and acquaintances in the Netherlands; but we had become part of an Australian work – a connection that would lead to much blessing.

After our time in Papua New Guinea, we were on leave in the Netherlands for a year. From there we were going to Japan as missionaries, where we were again largely supported from the Netherlands, but the spiritual bond with Australia remained. Also during a difficult period in Japan, when Coby was twice in the hospital, we were wonderfully supported and helped by the churches in Australia. All of this has shown us the importance and value of a good home church for missionaries. We experienced this ourselves.

Unfortunately, the problem with burglary and peeping Toms in Port Moresby was growing. Nearly every day there were burglaries in the town. We also had thieves checking out our three home units and experienced attempts at burglary. But something happened at Hank and Lenie's place that was a cause of much laughter.

In the middle of the night, Hank woke up; he just could not sleep. Lenie was asleep, so Hank got out of bed and went to the living room to pray for a while. Hank wears glasses; but without his glasses on, he stumbled into the living room, plopped down in a chair, and began to pray out loud in new tongues. According to Hank, he was in the living room for about an hour until he returned to the bedroom. But in the dark, without his glasses, he had felt that a shadow in the corner of the room resembled that of a man; but it was more a feeling than seeing and had not paid further attention to it.

The next morning Hank and Lenie saw how the flywire of the window had been cut open and that several louvres (horizontal strips of glass) had been removed. From the window, muddy footsteps went to the corner of the room where Hank had thought he saw a shadow, and there were muddy footsteps from that corner back to the window. The footsteps had not gone any further into the room.

There was only one conclusion we could make. A man had entered through the window; and when he was inside, Hank stumbled into the room, plopped down in the dark in a chair, and began to speak out loud in a peculiar, strange language. The burglar must have been frozen with fear and stood dead quiet in the corner. When Hank left the living room, the burglar went away immediately. We wondered if Hank had spoken the language of the burglar's tribe when he spoke in new tongues. If that were true, what did this man hear? This event caused some amusement amongst us. We could well imagine what had possibly happened. Imagine! A Papua New Guinean burglar frozen with fear, standing dead quiet in the corner for an entire hour while an expatriate spoke his language.

Just outside Port Moresby near the coast, an entire new village had come into being. People from Daru and the province had come to the 'big city' to find their luck or work. They had built their own houses, often very basic and simple. It actually became a district of the capital and was then called Horsecamp. In the early colonial days, it had apparently been a place for horses.

We began to have meetings there. In that village were people who had been present at those first meetings I held on Daru and who had seen the miracles. Most of the others had heard about it and therefore knew who we were. Later they named this village Joyce Bay. To this day, there is a congregation which has been led by Henry for years. He was one of the four boys who went with me to Kiwai Island.

Horsecamp was not an easy place to work. Among the people from that province were those who had very low moral standards. For example, there was a young man who really wanted to follow the Lord. The family had arranged a bride for him, but he wanted to go the way of the Lord. The family took the girl and undressed her. The other family took the young man and undressed him. They were locked up together for one night in which the girl tried everything to seduce the young man.

There was also a lot of witchcraft among the people. When a young woman wanted to lure a young man, she would practice witchcraft. 'Love magic' it was called. The young woman would let the desired young man know that she had practised 'love magic'. This could then totally numb the young man. Often, it led to him following her like a lamb, and they would sleep together.

These were problems that the congregation in Horsecamp had to deal with regularly. What a task! But we saw people coming to Jesus and being delivered from this. Especially when shortly after we had arrived in Port Moresby, the Holy Spirit released a movement of deliverance from evil spirits, which washed over the churches in Port Moresby.

Coby was pregnant again, and all was going well. We really looked forward to our third child. Just before her due date, I was invited to a few special meetings in Australia. At that time, we were just making plans to start a training centre in Port Moresby. The meetings in Australia could present an opportunity to raise financial support for the training centre and provide funds enabling us to begin the centre. Coby and I agreed that I should go. According to our calculation, the baby would arrive two weeks after I returned. Both Mark and Stephen had been born a little late, so this baby would quite likely be late also.

I had closed the last meeting in Australia and was having some coffee and talking with the pastor and some others, when one of the leaders, who had already gone home, came back in again. He walked towards me and said, 'Congratulations.' I looked surprised. Again he said, 'Congratulations, congratulations.'

For a moment I thought that he was referring to the meetings, because we did have some very good and blessed meetings. 'But it's not my birthday,' I said without thinking. 'Why are you congratulating me?'

'You have a son!'

'Yes, I know. I have two sons, to be precise.'

'No, you now have three sons. We just received a phone call. Coby gave birth to a healthy boy early in the evening.' For a brief moment I thought he was joking because everybody knew that Coby's due date was in two weeks' time. But then it hit me: I was the father of three sons.

I tried to get back to Port Moresby straightaway, but the first flight I could get was three days later. When I arrived in Port Moresby, Coby was waiting at the airport with a healthy baby with red hair in her arms and welcomed me home. On the way home, while still in the car, Coby asked, 'What are we going to call him?'

'We had agreed that if it were a boy we would name him Daniel.'

'Okay,' Coby said, 'his name is Daniel.' And that's his name. So we had three boys: Mark, Stephen, and Daniel.

Rose Stephen, the widow of one of the elders, worked at our office. She took care of the Bible correspondence course. At one particular time, we had 5,000 people who participated in that course. One of Rose's daughters did not go to school and was just sitting at home, doing nothing. We took her under our wing, and she helped Coby in the house and with the children. She was very good with children. However, this girl, who was sixteen years old, became pregnant and gave birth to a boy, whom she also named Stephen. We went to the hospital to congratulate her and admire the baby. Mark and Stephen were with us. We said to Stephen, 'This baby is also named Stephen. Say to the baby, "Hello, Stephen."' Stephen looked confused. A baby named Stephen? That was not possible. After thinking for a while, he said, 'Hello me.'

In the meantime, we were also caring for a child whose parents had gone to a Bible school in Australia. The circumstances did not allow them to take the child with them. During the day, we had five small children in our home. Mark at four and a half was the eldest. We also had a dog and a cat which had belonged to Hank and Lenie and which they had given to us when they returned to Australia. I once said, jokingly, 'I am going to hang a sign on the door which says, "Beware of slow-moving traffic."' During the day, Rose's daughter helped Coby, but how Coby coped with all the work was amazing. I admire her and have deep respect for her as my wife, but also as the mother of our three sons and the carer of the other little children whom she often looked after.

Not long ago there was a broadcast on Dutch television from our congregation in Rotterdam. The director had been to Papua New Guinea to interview people who had known us. One of the people who shared something was Rose's daughter. It was very moving to see her face on Dutch television. She spoke about the children but also how she really came to know Jesus through us and that we had taught her English.

Also concerning our marriage and our relationship, I learned a big lesson. Coby contracted glandular fever. It was not easy; she had hardly any energy but had to take care of the children. Of course this also had consequences for our intimacy. One Sunday morning, an English woman came into the Sunday service. She was single, and a doctor, who had been transferred to our town. She was about our age or maybe a bit younger. I looked at her and realised I felt attracted to her. I did not keep this to myself, but that evening I immediately shared it with Coby. The moment I told her about it, the feeling left me. I never felt it again. But imagine if I had kept it to myself . . . Someone happily married can fall in love with someone else. This happens and is not unusual. But it's all about how you handle this feeling. Imagine if I had not told Coby. What is hidden is darkness. And darkness that you try to hide becomes greater darkness. Darkness can only leave in one way: by switching on the light!

Shortly after we came to Port Moresby, another Pentecostal mission came to our town. It was the Australian Pentecostal movement Christian Revival Crusade, commonly called CRC. The founder was Pastor Leo Harris, at the time well known because of his books. The missionary who was put in charge had for many years been assigned to the Foursquare Mission in the Highlands. We knew the couple well and had even been guests at their mission station. They were supported by a number of churches in Australia. Within a short period, they had been able to build a very nice church building and several houses. Because there was hardly any public transport, and what was there was unreliable, CRC modified a number of trucks to carry people. They picked up people for the meetings and afterwards took them home. We had, with great difficulty, been able to buy one and later a second truck. We had great difficulty in making ends meet and to do everything that needed to be done. At CRC, it looked like they could do everything they desired. As a result, they grew quickly; and within a short period, they had outgrown us. They were also located in close proximity to us, while Port Moresby was growing substantially. I found this difficult to take. One day I told the Lord, 'Lord, we have prayed, fasted, conducted spiritual warfare, and worked very hard. They have come much later to work in this city. They have located close to our neighbourhood and have outgrown us. I don't think this is right.' I really meant what I told the Lord. Suddenly I discerned that the Lord asked me a question, 'Are you glad that I bless them?' I could not and dared not answer. After a long time I said, 'Lord, please give me time. I cannot answer you now.'

Three days I fought. I could not answer the Lord. I knew that if I said, 'No, I am not happy,' that would be unacceptable, and I could not and should not say that. If I were to say, 'Lord, I am happy,' then I would be lying, and you can't lie to God. Finally, after three days, I said to the Lord, 'Lord, I choose to be happy, but I am not as yet.' Something inside me broke, and I began to thank the Lord that He was blessing them, and I prayed much blessing on them.

From that moment on, we also began to grow and were doing better financially as well. I learned a tough lesson: God wants us to build His kingdom and not to be focused on our own thing. In the years following, the work of Christian Life Centre became known as a work that was very inter-denominational and open to the larger church. The assignment of the Lord Jesus is clear: make disciples of all nations, seek My kingdom above all, and then He will fulfil the promise He gave, 'I will build My church.' That means that the Lord builds His church and not us!

There had been much talk about 'independence', and on the 16th of September 1975, it became a fact. The evening before, the Australian flag was taken down for the last time. During the independence ceremony, I was about ten metres away from the big stage. The first governor stepped up to the microphone, and while thousands of people were listening, he solemnly declared that Papua New Guinea was now a sovereign state. The beautiful Papua New Guinean flag was raised for the first time, and for the first time the new national anthem was played. A competition for the design of the flag had been won by a young schoolgirl. A diagonal line separates one black and one red side. On one side is a yellow bird of paradise, and on the other side are white stars representing the Southern Cross, which is so clearly visible in Papua New Guinea. Australia and New Zealand also have the constellation of the Southern Cross on their flags.

It was impressive, and I felt and understood Paul's words that he spoke in Athens, 'And He has made from one blood every nation of men to dwell on all the face of the earth, and has determined their pre-appointed times and the boundaries of their dwellings, so that they should seek the Lord, in the hope that they might reach out for Him, though he be not far from each one of us' (Acts 17:26–27).

God determines the times and boundaries of a nation. When the first governor read the declaration of independence, and the flag was raised, something changed in the spiritual realm. No longer was Australia responsible for this country, but this country was now its own nation under God. It was very impressive to attend this ceremony, but what happened spiritually was even more impressive.

It is written in the constitution of Papua New Guinea that the nation shall be a Christian nation under God. Papua New Guinea, though it is a small and insignificant country according to the world's standard, is one of the most pro-Israel countries in the world. This is because the Bible declares that God had chosen this people; and from this people, the Lord Jesus, the promised Messiah, was born.

Michael Somare became the first prime minister, and in the first few years after independence, he became the father of the nation.

During the time of self-government, independence was discussed. A member of parliament, from a remote and little developed area, stood up and moved a motion saying, 'I find this discussion about independence very interesting. I now move a motion that my wife and children and I also get "independence".' Not everybody in the country, not even everyone in parliament at that time, understood what independence meant.

After independence, some things started to change. One of the new rules was that expatriates who worked in the country had to be qualified. This was to get the many non-qualified expatriates out of the country. I did not have any official qualifications. I could not show a diploma or degree of any educational institution. The Pentecostal movement Assemblies of God in New Zealand heard about my situation, and I received an 'honorary diploma of theology'. I filled out my papers with pride: a diploma in theology of Zion Bible College in Auckland, New Zealand. I received my further residence and work permits without a problem. In Australia, I later received an honorary 'diploma in ministry' from the Assemblies of God as an acknowledgement of the work we had done.

At the beginning of our time in Port Moresby, we experienced extraordinary things. At the university, we held a Bible study about the baptism in the Holy Spirit. About twelve students had not yet received the Holy Spirit. We prayed for them and laid hands on them. They began to speak in new tongues. Suddenly a student who had been filled with the Holy Spirit exclaimed, 'He speaks my language! He speaks my language!' One of the students who was speaking in new tongues spoke his tribal language. 'What is he saying?' I asked out of curiosity. 'He's uttering words of praise and speaks about how great the Lord is.' Stunned, the students listened for several minutes to the language in tongues that was being uttered. Then the language in tongues changed, and he could no longer understand it. This student was beside himself; he had heard someone, who did not know his language at all, speak his language in new tongues. The miracle of the day of Pentecost happened again.

Another recently graduated university student had quite a spectacular deliverance from demons. Shortly after, during a Sunday evening meeting, he was touched by the Holy Ghost; and he was completely 'drunk'. The service had ended, but he was totally 'lost' in the Spirit. Finally we carried him to the spare bedroom in our house and laid him on the bed. The next morning he was back to normal. He became one of the most prominent civil engineers in the country.

Another student who came to Jesus had graduated and obtained a good job, but spiritually he was wrestling with something in his life. He made an appointment to talk and pray with me. We shared and prayed for two hours, but nothing obvious happened. He had to go, so we said goodbye. The look in his eyes showed that he was deeply disappointed. I, the man who served God, had not been able to help him. I also was disappointed. I had tried so hard to help him and watched him drive away.

The following Sunday I saw him: he was beaming. 'What happened to you?' was my immediate question. He told me how disappointed he had been when he drove off. He had so hoped that I could help him, but I had not been able to. Suddenly there was an amazing presence of the Lord in his car, and he was deeply touched. He began to cry. 'Lord, what is happening?' was his question. 'I had so expected that Pastor John would be able to help me, but he could not.'

'The Holy Spirit is touching you right now because I am praying for you before the Father,' he heard the Lord say. 'I am your High Priest.' I was deeply moved when he told me this. The biblical truth that the Lord Jesus is our High Priest and that He pleads for us day and night before the Father became a great reality for us.

Because of his story, I began to understand Hebrews 7:25, and it became an especially beloved verse: 'Therefore He is also able to save to the uttermost those who come to God by Him, since He always lives to make intercession for them.'

When I get up, the Lord Jesus is praying for me. When I go to bed at night, the Lord Jesus prays for me. Day and night He pleads and prays for us. No doubt one of the main things He prays for is that all He accomplished on the cross will become reality in all of us. What a high priest! I needed such a high priest really badly!

After this student graduated, he followed the Lord and was, together with his wife, a blessing to many people and a pillar in the congregation. Sadly, several years ago rascals broke into his house, and he was murdered. He is now with Jesus, but his testimony about the Lord Jesus as his High Priest is something we will never forget.

CHAPTER 28

'In My Name shall They Cast Out Evil Spirits'

THE CONGREGATION IN Port Moresby was doing well. There was evident blessing. Almost every week people came to the Lord Jesus. Miracles and healings were happening. The Lord was clearly present in the meetings. Regularly there were powerful testimonies. The people began to understand praise and worship more and more and put it into practice. There were meetings which you wished that they would not end. God was in our midst. After the teaching about David's tabernacle, people were longing for this to become reality not only in their own lives but also in the fellowship. Several praise and worship leaders began to stand out for their leading. Things were just going well but still . . . We saw the joy of the Lord Jesus in the eyes and on the faces of the people. We saw how people were beginning to worship the Lord more and more. But from time to time we would see a sudden dark shadow over a face or we saw someone who normally had no problem worshipping unexpectedly having trouble with it. Some also told us that sometimes it was just a real struggle to be a Christian. We saw Christians who were doing well, but when they sometimes met with family, they felt quite a lot of spiritual pressure and resistance and sometimes had to fight a sense of being drawn back to their 'old life'.

It began to dawn on us more and more that we were dealing with demons, or as they are also called, evil spirits. But what could we do? I did have an experience in which a young woman was delivered from an evil spirit in Sydney, Australia. Also on the Solomon Islands there had been various cases of deliverance from evil spirits, but that happened while the Holy Spirit was powerfully at work, then demons began to manifest, and we only needed to give a short command for them to leave. But now we saw Christians who had to really fight from time to time to keep their head above water, spiritually.

When there were sick people, we laid hands on them, just as the Lord Jesus had commanded. We had been able to lead many people into the baptism of the Holy Spirit. But casting out evil spirits, as the Lord told us to, we had done on a couple of occasions, but only when demons actually manifested.

In the discovery of 'repentance', we had seen that repentance closes doors which were open for demons. In the discovery of 'blessing and curse', we had seen the power of confessing the sins of the forefathers. Also in such moments we had seen and heard evil spirits leave. But here we were dealing with Christians who from time to time were really struggling.

I began to study the Bible about deliverance from evil spirits. Soon it was obvious that the Lord Jesus spent quite a large part of His ministry in casting out evil spirits. He also spent a lot of time healing the sick. The latter, laying hands on the sick, is something we did often. Actually the whole work in Papua New Guinea had started with healings. But I could not say that we were deliberately spending time casting out evil spirits. How do you do that? How do you start?

In our search, we heard that Derek Prince had released a series of six tapes about the subject. We ordered them via the United States, and after several weeks they arrived in the mail. We listened to them very attentively, several times. We made notes and studied every verse that Derek Prince quoted. The final tape was the recording of a deliverance meeting where he taught about deliverance from evil spirits. Following this, he led the people who needed deliverance, from the platform, in a prayer of repentance and forgiveness. Derek Prince constantly pointed people to their own responsibility. They should not think that the evil spirits were to blame for everything. Then he began, from the platform, to command evil spirits to go out in the name of the Lord Jesus.

From the moment that he commanded the evil spirits to go out, you heard the screaming and screeching of evil spirits as they were going out. Derek Prince calmly continued and called various evil spirits by their names: spirits of fear, unclean spirits, spirits of diseases, spirits of gossip and slander, and many more. After a while, it became quiet in the meeting, and Derek Prince gave a few instructions to the people who had experienced deliverance from evil spirits. We were deeply impressed. A special meeting to cast out evil spirits! We had never heard of this before, let alone experienced it. But why not? We held meetings especially for healing and for people to receive the baptism in the Holy Spirit and to speak in new tongues. Why not a meeting especially for casting out evil spirits? The desire to do this began to grow in the fellowship in Port Moresby.

I listened to that sixth tape a number of times and wrote the message out word for word. I practically knew this tape by heart.

Hank and Lenie were on a short leave in Australia, but Bob Lutu and Lenden Butuna were with us. We let them listen to the tapes and gave them instructions for the meeting we were going to have. Though it is a long time ago, now almost forty years, I am sure that we also fasted. I announced in the fellowship that I would teach the following Sunday evening about casting out of demons, and we would pray that evening for people who needed this.

That Sunday evening arrived, and I was quite nervous. This was totally new for me, but it was biblical. The worship was good. The people worshipped the Lord with their whole hearts. Then I began to teach. I had the message of Derek Prince in front of me, completely written down, but I hardly looked at it. I actually already knew it by heart. I explained things one step at a time. The ministry of the Lord Jesus while He was on earth and His command for us to cast out evil spirits. How demons enter our lives. What are demons? The importance of our own responsibility. The absolute necessity of repentance and forgiving others who have hurt us. The people listened very attentively. I sensed great authority while I was preaching.

The teaching was over. Until now things were going well. Then the invitation: 'Whoever feels that he or she needs deliverance from evil spirits, come forward.' There were about 150 people in the meeting. I expected a handful of them to come forward, about ten or so. But to my surprise and shock, about sixty people came forward. And there were only four of us: Coby, Bob, Lenden, and myself. *Lord, help!* I cried out in silence.

What did Derek Prince do when the people had come forward? He led them in a prayer of repentance, with the people taking responsibility for their sins and forgiving others. I had the prayer before me on the small lectern. I spoke the words, and the people earnestly prayed with me. I made the prayer a bit longer, because after that, I had to do something I had never done before: in public commanding evil spirits to go out in the name of the Lord Jesus.

I took a deep breath. *Lord, help me!* I began to do what Derek Prince did. I commanded the evil spirits, who were inside the people who stood in front of me, to go out in the name of the Lord Jesus. At that moment, total chaos broke out, truly, utter chaos. If there had been a button which I could push to open a trap door to allow me to disappear, I would have pushed that button in no time. But that button did not exist, and I was on the small platform behind the microphone, and in front of me chaos had broken out. What did Derek Prince do? He remained calm and continued ordering various spirits to leave.

In front of me, a university student shot, as it were, into the air. He crashed onto the concrete floor with a loud bang and slid underneath a few rows of chairs and screamed extremely loud as the evil spirit cried out its own name. This turned out to be the name of the ruling spirit of his tribe. The student was lying still on the floor and began to magnify the Lord Jesus.

Others bent over as if they had to throw up and grabbed their stomachs. With others, the evil spirits came out with various screams. Others had fallen to the floor and were kicking and hitting with their hands. Others were foaming at the mouth. Coby, Bob, Lenden, and I were busy, very busy! We moved from one to the other, and slowly things settled down. It was clear that many evil spirits had gone out.

After about an hour, all became calm and quiet in the meeting. Soaked from perspiration, I walked back to the small platform and looked around me. Some were still lying on the floor, completely under the power of the Holy Spirit; others had gone back to their seats. Still others were crying or sitting quietly in their seats, enjoying the very strong presence of the Lord. It was beautiful, but when I looked further, I froze and became frightened. In the dark, around the building, there were people standing. It seemed like there were two or three rows of people. They were neighbours and people from the area who had come to see what this terrible noise was all about. How was I going to explain this?

The meeting had lasted a long time, much longer than usual. But clearly a lot had happened. The faces of some people were beaming. We closed the meeting, and slowly the people left. Also the people who had been standing around the building went home. That evening we talked for a long time after the meeting. We all had experienced that as soon as we called on the name of the Lord Jesus, the evil spirits came out. It was a totally new experience for us, and we were deeply impressed by the power of God.

All four of us needed a shower. I could think of nothing else apart from what had happened that evening. I realised that we had discovered an important key of the kingdom of God. We could not realise then how much that key would become a part of our continuing ministry. I fell asleep that night with an enormous sense of victory.

The next day I visited several neighbours and asked them if they understood what had happened the night before. They understood it very well. 'Yes, you were casting out evil spirits, and they went out.' It was a similar response like with Jesus received. The people then too were surprised and said, 'With authority He commanded evil spirits to go out and they went out.' A number of neighbours came to the Lord after this.

The following week several people came for more prayer, and with the limited knowledge we had then, we prayed for them. They were set free. When I think back now, I realise how little we knew and understood then; and yet there were such miracles, sometimes great miracles, of deliverance. I can only come to one conclusion: the Lord blessed the fact that we were stepping out in faith. He saw our lack of knowledge and experience, but He also saw our obedience. We have discovered throughout the years how true this discovery is. God does not necessarily bless knowledge, but He does bless faith and boldness. And there was another reason why so many deep deliverances happened: there was and had been deep repentance among the people.

The Sunday after that, in the morning service, someone came in who had been set free the week before, in quite a powerful way. Coby and I looked at him and said, 'Is it him or not?' It was him. His entire face and appearance had changed. He was not the only one. Throughout the years, we saw that people can change in their appearance after deliverance. We asked for testimonies, and we were breathless as we listened to what had happened in people's lives. What happened on that Sunday evening had changed dozens of people's lives. If the testimonies proved anything, it was that deliverance from evil spirits is an absolute necessity.

The following Sunday evening, we held another special deliverance meeting. When we prayed, it was quieter than the week before. But this time more people were set free.

Bob and Lenden wanted us to pray for them too. What right do we have to pray for other people for deliverance if we are not prepared to take a close look at our own lives? 'Who says we don't need this ourselves?' was their argument. What a beautiful attitude.

Shortly after that, Hank and Lenie returned, and they heard all about what had happened, and they too became quite involved in the casting out of evil spirits. We also spent an evening with the four of us praying for each other. We prayed for quite some time, but we did not feel as if much happened, but that night I went to bed with a very deep feeling of peace and purity. I always felt that the Lord really blessed our willingness to let others pray for us and that we did not put ourselves above the people we ministered to.

From that moment on, we regularly prayed for Christians who came to us because they needed deliverance. We spent many hours and evenings, sometimes until late in the night, praying. Now, years later, we know that when evil spirits do not come out quickly, it usually means one of two things: a lack of revelation about what is going on or the doors through which evil spirits came in have not been closed. If not, then the grounds on which they could stay in a person have not been fully dealt with. We also learned quickly that deliverance can be achieved in a much quieter way.

An English professor who worked at the university had come to the Lord and attended the meetings. He had a formal Anglican background. He enjoyed the meetings, but in the times of worship, he froze. He could not lift his hands and felt an inner resistance to worship. But he genuinely loved the Lord.

One day he came to talk with me, and he told me about his problem and inner struggle. 'I have heard you speak about deliverance from evil spirits. Could my problem have anything to do with that?' he asked. My answer was confirming; but he did find it difficult to accept this, because he was a professor, someone who was well educated. I proposed, 'Let's have a time of prayer, and if there is nothing, then nothing can come out. If there is something, then you will be set free.' It seemed a good idea to him. We made an appointment. Hank and I would pray for him together.

The afternoon of the appointment arrived. After some instructions, Hank and I began to pray for our brother, the professor. Suddenly his belly began to vibrate very fast. The professor looked at his belly, pointed at it, and said, stuttering, 'What is this? What is happening to me? Are these demons?'

'Yes, I think so,' was my answer.

'But that can't be, can it? I cannot have demons. I studied at university, and I am even a professor.' But the unbelievably fast vibrating of his belly continued.

We calmed the professor down and made a proposal. 'You have been very sceptical towards deliverance. We are sure that you need deliverance. Fast for three days in preparation, then we will pray.'

Poor professor. We really felt sorry for him. I think he had never fasted before in all his life. Yet it was good that he was going to fast in preparation for his deliverance. For a long time I thought that I, the one who prayed for deliverance, had to fast also. Of course this is true because the Lord Jesus said this clearly. But if we had to fast in those days for everyone who came for deliverance, then I would not have eaten at all. Fasting is also an act of repentance and humility. After three days of fasting, he came at the time we had arranged. He dragged himself out of his Volkswagen. We started praying, and almost immediately there were obvious and strong manifestations, but the demons were not coming out. We prayed for quite a while. There were only strong manifestations but no deliverance. We stopped and commanded the demons to retreat, and we talked. There was something that was really blocking the process. Almost immediately he told us that he had worked at a university in an African country. There he became interested in images of native gods and collected them. He had taken them with him to Papua New Guinea and were in his house.

He was attached to them and thought it was a precious collection of primitive art. Without a doubt that was a great barrier, if not the barrier. He went home to collect the idols and a while later returned with a cardboard box filled with wooden idols. It was not difficult to see that this was not just tourist material; these sculptures had been used as real idols. He asked the Lord for forgiveness, because the Bible is so clear on this matter. We were going to burn them in the back of the garden.

We prepared everything: wood, paper, branches, and on top of that the idols. Then we poured petrol over it all, and the professor lit the fire. Everything burned except the idols which had been carved out of soft wood. Strange! We again poured petrol over it all, but again the petrol burned up, but not the idols. Then we began to pray and break the power of the demons that were connected to these idols. The Bible teaches us that an idol is nothing but that they are powerful because of the demons connected with them (Deuteronomy 32:16–17 – which Paul quotes in 1 Corinthians 10:19–20). Slowly but surely the idols began to burn. We waited until there were only ashes left. When we went back inside and prayed for deliverance, the demons came out within a few moments, and our brother professor was free.

After this event, God often used him in deliverance. I have heard him say in beautiful 'Queen's English' in the meeting, 'In the name of our Lord Jesus Christ, I command this demon to come out.' It was always wonderful to hear, a professor from England casting out demons from the people among whom he worked.

Our brother the professor was just one of the many people, expatriates, and Papua New Guineans who were set free; and his story contains so many lessons.

There was another deliverance that made a deep impression on me. A married man in his twenties had come to the Lord. His wife was pregnant, but when her body started to show it clearly, he beat her up. She lost her baby. He was filled with remorse and did not know why he had done it. Something had forced him to do so. Then his neighbour's wife became pregnant. When that was clearly visible, he beat her up as well. She also lost her baby. The neighbour reported it to the police. Our brother had serious problems.

He was in a complete panic and immediately came to us. When he saw me, he grabbed both my hands. 'You have to help me. You have to help me.' He was desperate. I was just about to go to an appointment that I could not cancel. We prayed together, and then the next evening, we prayed for him. There were four of us. Demon after demon came out while manifesting and sometimes with a lot of noise. There was one demon which was strongly resisting. I commanded the demon to say its name, and it screamed, 'Wantok sistem!' 'Wantok' is someone from the same language and tribe, which usually is a positive thing, but it can also become a destructive bondage. We commanded the demon to come out in the name of the Lord Jesus. Screaming, the demon came out. Then the man fell to the floor, lifted up his hands, and began to sing a prophetic melody in new tongues. I had never heard someone sing so beautifully in tongues before. Heaven came down. The four of us sat around him on the floor for quite some time, lost in the presence of the Lord.

Later he told us that he loved his grandfather very much and had spent much time with him as a child. He was his grandfather's favourite grandson. But his grandfather had cursed him and said that he would always have problems with pregnant women. His grandfather had also beaten up pregnant women and had done even worse things. When he was at the technical school, one afternoon he was standing on the balcony of the first floor looking down over the balustrade. Suddenly something came over him, and he jumped off the balcony of the first floor. Luckily he landed in a bush and got away with just a few scratches. It was around three o'clock in the afternoon when this happened. Several days later, he heard that on the same afternoon, around three o'clock, his grandfather had passed away. It was obvious. The spirit that had lived in his grandfather had entered him. But now he was free.

This young man founded in the years that followed a number of fellowships in his home area and was used by God in exceptional ways. Several years later, he became the leader of the province and supervised nearly fifty village churches as well as a good-sized church in the main city of the province. Years later, he unfortunately had an affair with a prostitute, whom he made pregnant. He had to let go of his ministry. However, he did openly confess his guilt before the believers and begged for forgiveness.

When we visited Papua New Guinea some years later, we heard his story. I offered to pray for deliverance but only in public because he had been a well-known leader. He and his wife agreed to this. In the meeting, I called him forward. I said, 'You all know who this brother is and what has happened. In this place he has confessed his sins and asked you all for forgiveness. You gave him that. But when a leader in God's kingdom sins and has an affair, it is as far as I know impossible that no demons entered him. Because he was a public leader, I will cast out these demons in public.' He stood before me, and I commanded the demons to leave him. His body bent forward, and a voice shouted out, 'This is our house! This is our house!' The Lord gave me the name of the demon which was manifesting, and I commanded it to go out. The demon screamed and said that it would not go out because it was its house. I heard myself say to the demons that they had ten seconds to come out or God would send an army of angels to deal with them. I counted from ten to zero.

The former pastor was standing bent over before me, and the voice kept shouting, 'This is our house! This is our house!' Then I asked the Lord to send His mighty army of angels. Suddenly from a corner of the building, a sound came. The sound came down over the bent-over former pastor who fell down, and then the sound went to the other side of the building and vanished. I can best describe the sound as a gust of wind that whistled over him and left. The entire event took place around eight o'clock in the evening. When the meeting finished, they had to bring him home because he was under the power of the Holy Spirit. The next morning around seven o'clock, he came to himself. He came to the airport with his wife the morning we left. I asked him how he was doing. The only thing he could say was 'Perfect.' He could not say anything more because he was still under the power of God's Spirit.

For years now, he has been working again as a carpenter. He and his wife and children are following Jesus, and he has chosen not to go back into ministry, which is a wise decision. In his culture, even after showing real humility and deep genuine repentance, this would be unacceptable. A younger man took over his position and is leading the work in that province.

Not all deliverances were dramatic or spectacular. Some were relatively calm, some a little noisier. We were learning much. Many times I have heard the demons cry out, 'All those angels around us, all those angels around us. We have to go past them, and we will not survive.' The first time we heard that I thought, *Whatever*. It's our task to cast out demons so they go out in the name of the Lord Jesus. But when we heard it more often, we began to realise that angels are very closely involved with deliverance. Satan is a liar, and in the Bible, several cases are mentioned in which the demons came face to face with the Lord, and they could only speak the truth in His presence. So when demons spoke about angels, they were speaking the truth.

From Derek Prince we learned that you could demand a demon to give its name. We would do that when there was no revelation. Every now and then we would hear strange words that I did not understand. I then demanded more information like 'What is your work? What are you doing in this person?' Usually we received answers like 'I am a spirit of fear, lies, etc.' Slowly we began to realise that demons have names too, like angels. When we asked the demon for his name, a strange word could well be the name of the demon. In our experience, this proved to be true.

A student who was almost ready to graduate came to talk with me. He knew the Lord Jesus, was filled with the Holy Spirit, and was baptised in water; but he was sure that there were demons in him. When he told me a little about his family, I could understand his conclusion. He said that he had thought to have heard from the Lord to fast for twenty-one days, and then I would pray for him. Because he was studying, we agreed that he would fast; but if he encountered problems, and I asked him to stop, then he would stop immediately. But the twenty-one days went by without problems. The evening to pray for deliverance arrived. Several demons came out, but when I commanded a certain demon to come out, I was shocked. His entire face changed. His eyes began to bulge out; and his face was like a wooden mask, a depiction of an evil spirit, as the Papua New Guinean people carve them out of wood and use them in idol worship. It wasn't a pleasant sight. When the evil spirit left, his face became normal again. After his deliverance, he had a beautiful, open, and friendly face. Several weeks later in a Sunday evening meeting, he became completely 'drunk' in the Spirit. We carried him to our home and laid him on the bed in the guest room. The next morning he woke up. Every time we visit Papua New Guinea, we meet with him, and the warmth and the love between us is strong.

Miracles happened, and people's lives were totally changed. Christians who needed to fight to keep their heads above water, spiritually, now considered it to be easy to be a Christian and follow Jesus. Shy or timid Christians became very bold and outgoing, and married women who were infertile became pregnant.

Among the Pentecostal missionaries, it soon became known that we were conducting deliverance meetings and regularly prayed for Christians to be set free from evil spirits. Most of them were happy and had a positive attitude about this. There were, however, also missionaries who did not accept this at all. They believed that children of God could not have demons. Evil spirits should be cast out of non-believers, but as far as I know, I never heard about them doing that. One missionary was very critical towards us, though we had only shaken hands once at the yearly meeting of Pentecostal missionaries in the Highlands.

Later, at one of those yearly conferences, he sat down at our table during a meal. He wanted to share something with us. 'You know that I have been very critical about you and was absolutely sure that you were doing the wrong thing.' He continued, 'Several weeks ago something happened. Several Christians from a village church not far from our mission station came to my house in total panic, pleading with me to come with them immediately, because a female church member had suddenly lost her mind, and seven men were needed to keep her under control. She wanted to kill people. I went with them, and in the village I saw the woman. I knew her well. She had accepted the Lord and had been baptised in water. The Sunday before she had been in the service. Now seven men were needed to hold her down! She was wild and very strong. The people who were with her said that she had seen an evil spirit and had become possessed.'

We listened attentively. On Bougainville we had experienced something like this. A young woman had been in the meeting in the morning, and then she had gone to work in the gardens. There she had seen the spirit of a dead woman and had instantly gone crazy. At least five men were needed to hold her down. We prayed for a while, and the demons came out in the name of the Lord. It did not sound unfamiliar to us.

The missionary realised that he was dealing with demons, and trembling he began to pray. He had never experienced this before. Suddenly a deep male voice came out of the woman's mouth and said, 'You cannot get me out. You have to get John Pasterkamp from Port Moresby. He is able to get me out.' The missionary was really scared by this voice and what the voice said. He knew that I had never been to that area, and it was impossible for the woman to have known my name. The missionary deeply repented from his criticism and wrong attitude and his erroneous theological position. With several Christians, they prayed for some time for this woman, and she became calm. Later, after a time of fasting, they prayed for the woman again, and she was set free from evil spirits.

After the missionary shared this story, he asked for forgiveness for his criticism and attitude towards us. He was clearly deeply impacted by the event. It had shown him the reality of the spiritual world.

Years later, back in the Netherlands, we also experienced a similar event. A demon spoke through the mouth of a woman and mentioned my name. Also once in Japan a Japanese woman who did not know me, nor spoke English, suddenly walked onto the platform where I was preaching. A voice began to speak through her to me in English and mentioned my name. When we do what Jesus commands us to do, the enemy will definitely know who we are.

In Port Moresby, we once read an article in the newspaper. Doctors did not understand a certain medical problem. There were expatriates who suffered from severe depression, nightmares, and intense stress. Most of them had to go back to their country of origin to recover. Some would suffer from these things for years without improvement. What stood out, however, was that these symptoms only occurred with those who worked as missionaries in Papua New Guinea.

We are not doctors, but when we read it, we understood what was going on. Missionaries who did not believe in the reality of the spiritual world and the possible influence of demons were attacked or, to use a better word, overpowered by demons who destroyed their lives. Throughout the years, we prayed for missionaries who needed deliverance. We know that some of them were set free. Two Pentecostal ministers in Australia whose ministries are well known can bear witness to this. Deliverance changed their lives and renewed their ministry.

Throughout the years, we held quite a few deliverance meetings. Derek Prince was our example. Years later, we came to know Derek Prince personally; and on several occasions, I was the support speaker in conferences in which he was the main speaker. Apart from the deliverance meetings, we have, throughout the years, been able to pray for hundreds of people personally. The Lord Jesus did it often, and we endeavour to follow His example.

Deliverance was not the answer to all problems. We were not able to help everyone. There were situations to which we found no answer, and we could do nothing else but to continue in prayer. However, we saw every time that the greatest weapon against the enemy is genuine conversion.

We also regularly saw that people were set free from demons during water baptism and then were immediately after that filled with the Holy Spirit. While they were still standing in the water, they began speaking in new tongues. Usually they fell in the Spirit and had to be carried out of the water and laid down on the grass. In and through the baptism in water the enemy, the demons, lose every right to that life. When we years later worked as a couple pastoring in Australia, and after that in the Netherlands, we always longed to see that again. We keep reaching out to the Lord and often say to Him, 'Lord, do it again by Your Spirit.'

CHAPTER 29

Rascals

'RASCAL' IS AN English word meaning a person of disrepute, a villain. The word has no positive meaning.

But the word is sometimes used in a playful way, for example, when an older person says to a cheeky child, 'You little rascal.' But in Papua New Guinea, this is certainly not the common meaning of the word.

In Papua New Guinea, the word refers to the many unruly and criminal young people, whom they call rascals, and these rascals were becoming a serious problem. You would hear more and more about burglaries, violence, raids, rape, robberies on the road, stolen cars, and people being terrorised and even murdered. We unfortunately experienced this ourselves. Not so much when we lived in our small white unit in Boroko, but mainly when we had moved and lived in our new house next to the church. That house had a two-metre-high fence surrounding it. Bougainvillea bushes grew against the fence. Bougainvillea is a bush that has big sharp thorns. We also had a good watchdog inside the fence. Still, we were burgled nine times. Once our house was under siege by a small gang of rascals in the middle of the night. Our two eldest boys still remember that well. They were very frightened and were hiding underneath the table. We phoned the police, but their answer was 'Sir, there is so much going on tonight. Maybe we can send a car in four hours.' Not very encouraging. Another time the gang members were sitting on our fence ready to jump into the garden, and they shouted, 'We are armed! Go inside or we will shoot at you!'

Once all our clothes were stolen. We had been to a wedding, and I had consecrated the marriage. After the reception, the bride had changed into a dress in our house and had left her wedding gown behind. When we came home later, all our clothes were gone, including the wedding dress. Rascals had broken into our house and simply emptied our closet where we kept our clothes. They had laid everything on the bed, packed it up in the bedcover, and left. We only had the clothes we were wearing, and a bed without a bedcover! We lived in the tropics where it is quite hot, and sometimes we used two sets of clothes in a day. Now we had nothing left.

When we had just moved to Boroko, we decided to get a dog, a dachshund (sometimes jokingly called a 'sausage dog'), who was about three years old. We thought that because he had a good bark, he could warn us. Besides that, he would be fun for the children. However, it turned out the dog was not potty trained, so he had to stay outside. The first night that he was outside, I woke up because of his barking. I went to see what was going on. There was a big frog sitting in front of our house.

A few days later, I woke up again. I heard our dachshund whine softly. *Whatever*, I thought and went back to sleep. The next morning I discovered that our car was gone! We found it back six months later, a total wreck. The demolisher gave me about fifty euros for the parts.

I came home one night, and in front of our gate was the body of a murdered man, an experience I would rather not go through again. Another time a woman from the neighbourhood was grabbed by a group of rascals and raped. Several days later, the wife of one of our missionaries was surrounded by a group of rascals; they wanted to rape her too. Someone saw the situation and drove his car into the group and rescued the woman. Several young rascals were slightly wounded. This incident really shook us.

The problem began to grow worse, especially in the capital, Port Moresby; but soon other cities, like Lae, Goroka, Mount Hagen, and Rabaul also suffered from it. In the smaller towns, the problem was not so bad at first, because everybody knew each other.

A young couple from Port Moresby who worked for the electricity company were transferred to Goroka. One evening they went to the meeting and parked their car right in front of the church building. They left their sleeping baby behind in the car. When, a little later, they went to check to see if everything was okay, the car with the baby was gone. Total panic! Several streets away, the car was found. The baby was still sleeping. When the rascals stole the car and drove away, they apparently noticed that there was a baby sleeping in the back. People from Papua New Guinea, also rascals, respect children. But the situation grew worse and worse. It was estimated that in and around Port Moresby, there were several thousand rascals.

Young men, always two or three, took turns to sleep in the little hall of the church to prevent burglaries and robbery. Otherwise, there would not have been a single chair or anything else left.

When you talked with expatriates who lived in Port Moresby, the conversation would soon be about the rascals. Many of them had experienced them or knew someone in their area or circle of friends who had problems with the rascals. Those conversations usually only made the fear worse.

The newspaper started to keep a record of how many burglaries and raids had taken place in the capital each day. Many expatriates, but later also more highly educated Papua New Guinean people (and therefore well-to-do), slept with weapons by their bed, something we absolutely refused to do. But in Port Moresby, our sleep was not very relaxed. At the slightest sound we would wake up and wonder what was going on. We often got out of bed to see what it was that woke us up. Therefore, it was not unusual for expatriates, who had experienced a visit by the rascals, to feel unsafe and to leave the country.

Who and what were rascals? What drove them to behave the way they did?

Most of them were young men who had left their villages and had come to the city to try their luck or simply to get away from village life. We heard of young men who had behaved badly in their village, who in former days would be dealt with by the village itself. Because of the social structure and pressure to conform, wrong behaviour was not very common in the villages. In the city, you could easily walk away and disappear into the crowd; there was no social pressure or control. It was also easy to find a wantok in the city, someone from your tribe and language, and you could move in with him.

There were also young men who were school dropouts. They had attended school for a while, but their grades had not been good enough to continue. They had learned too much to go back to the simple life in their village. They had tasted a different style of life at secondary school and sometimes even at university.

Others saw that expatriates and rich Papua New Guinean people had more than they had and that burglary and violence were an easy way to get what they wanted. We had wondered where all the stolen stereos, radios, and other expensive equipment ended up. It was traded somewhere but where? According to rumours, there were Chinese traders who bought everything and shipped it elsewhere; but this, as far as we know, has never been proven. The rumour that people from the government were involved with some of these gangs was true. We later discovered this for ourselves.

Modern movies have also played a part in the problem, particularly those that glorify violence and immorality. Furthermore, the behaviour of women as shown in those films caused many men to get totally wrong ideas about women, which caused more problems. Rascals who were converted told us about the influence such films had been on them.

Above all, the problem of the rascals is a by-product of a third world country developing too fast. It was also a result of the introduction of an educational system that was more orientated towards Western values rather than their own culture. This, in turn, caused a quick demise of their own traditional, cultural values and family ties. The opinions about the cause of the rascal problem differ greatly. That's why the opinions of how the problem should be handled are also very different.

After the first elections, a woman entered parliament. She was very articulate and had attained a high level of education. She was part of the opposition and regularly attacked the government for their lack of initiative and action in solving the problem with the rascals. When she converted several years later, she openly confessed that she had been the driving force behind a gang in order to attack the government and destabilise it.

That demonic forces also had much to do with this problem was clear to us. Spiritually speaking it was total war! I often thought that the demons, who had been the driving force behind the tribal wars, were now the driving force behind the various gangs.

As a result, a fear came over the city, especially in the evenings; and that fear was something you could sense and feel. One night I dreamt that one of our children was murdered in a horrible way. It took me days to shake off the feeling and impressions of that dream. I did not tell Coby about this until years later.

One night I woke up. Two hands held me around my throat, and I could not breathe. All air was blocked, and the grip grew stronger. I was gasping for air. But there was nobody! Coby was lying next to me peacefully asleep, while I was nearly choking. I understood and felt that it was demonic. With all the power I had, and I mean *all* the power I had, I began to call upon the name of the Lord Jesus. I could not manage to get out more than a whisper, but it was the name of the Lord Jesus. The grip weakened a little. Again and again and again I called upon the name of the Lord Jesus, and the hands increasingly released their grip. I could breathe again and kept calling on the name of the Lord Jesus until I was able to do so freely. Finally the hands let go of me, and that terrible, evil presence vanished. I was wide awake and quite shocked. I knew that this was not an ordinary demon. This was a principality of the kingdom of darkness; and I was, and am still, convinced that it was the demonic prince over the city of Port Moresby. Actually I was somewhat angry with Coby; while I had to fight for my life, she had continued to sleep peacefully. I did not understand how she could do that. But she really had not been aware of anything. The next morning I told her what had happened. I was quite shocked but also very impressed with the power and authority that is in the name of the Lord Jesus. The entire event reminded me of what had happened that evening in Rabaul, when I had seen the living mask outside the window. That had also been a confrontation with a demonic principality, the ruler over that tribe and area. I shared the experience with the entire team. We started to realise that the devil was extremely angry with us and was trying to stop us. I once heard someone say, 'If the devil always leaves you alone, you should ask yourself what you're doing wrong. You are clearly not a threat to him.' How true! The devil was not leaving us alone. In some way we were doing something that threatened him, and later we found out how true that was.

In those days I was away a lot, sometimes for several weeks. I went to Bougainville, Rabaul, Kavieng, and West Irian and also abroad to speak at conferences. Coby would then be home by herself, with the boys. We lived on the compound next to the church together with other workers and Bible school students. That in itself provided a feeling of safety, because if it had become known that a white woman was home alone, Coby would not have been safe. She had discovered a tactic that was apparently working. As soon as she heard a noise or suspected something, she ran through the house, turned on all the lights, and slammed doors. By doing that, she gave the impression that there were more people in the house. Apart from that, it was agreed that if she screamed, the others would come straightaway.

We often showed movies, because they attracted people. We had our own copy of the famous movie *The Cross and the Switchblade* and showed it regularly. The book was very popular for a long time, and it sold well in our bookshop. Because of the movie, many people came to Jesus. And we also discovered that the rascals were drawn to this movie, because in it, they saw their own kind and were proud of that, but they also saw the power of God which was able to change them.

In the fellowship, things went well. In the meetings, there was an obvious presence of the Holy Spirit. There was also a powerful intercessory group that was led for a long time by our Australian secretary Glenys. They prayed for hours every Friday evening. There was much prayer for the city and for God to work among the rascals. The passion and compassion with which the Papua New Guineans prayed for their own country and people has always impacted us deeply.

One day we came together for prayer, which we had been doing for quite some time, with several missionaries and local leaders of the various churches in the city. The week before, things had been quite bad again in the city, and also at our place there had been another burglary. I was irritated and angry and complained about the lack of action from the police, and the weak manner in which the police were handling the problem. 'We need more and better police,' I grumbled.

A Lutheran missionary who was quite charismatic and who always came to these times of prayer said to me, 'John, we do not need more or better police. This city needs a David Wilkerson.' His words struck me deep in my heart. I realised he was right. In my frustration and anger, I was looking for a natural solution, but the real solution was a spiritual one. I had heard from God.

I kept thinking about it for days and decided to preach about it the following Sunday to challenge the people. I took the verse from Matthew 11:19. Jesus was a friend of sinners and tax collectors. He loved them. He was not afraid of them. On the contrary, he was with them often, not to approve their behaviour but to show them true love.

I preached from my heart and shared what the Lutheran missionary had said, 'John, we do not need more or better police. This city needs a David Wilkerson.' All the Christians who were there knew what that meant. I challenged them. 'Who is going to be this David Wilkerson in Port Moresby and Papua New Guinea? Go and pray about it.' It looked like no one responded, but three years later I found out that a young man had heard the call and prayed in silence, 'Lord, let me be the David Wilkerson in this city.'

Nobody knew that morning that he had prayed that prayer. I definitely did not know, but God heard that prayer. It would take about three years before the answer to that prayer became evident, and the rascals came to know about it! Actually the whole of Papua New Guinea came to know about this young man who had prayed that prayer. His name? Charles Lapa.

CHAPTER 30

The Bible School

FOR YEARS WE had a dream: to have a training centre where for a year we could train especially young people, for the work of the Lord. In Kavieng, we had built a small building on our land behind the house to start a training centre; but apart from several courses and training on weekends, a full-time training centre never came into being.

On Bougainville, we had the opportunity of establishing a Bible school at village level, and that became the Haari Bible school. But the dream of a training centre for young people who had a calling of God on their lives and who had also gone through higher education, especially tertiary education, remained a dream.

But now we were in Port Moresby, and the Lord sent us many educated young people. The dream could become a reality here. These young people would serve all over the country after their education was completed. The dream grew stronger and stronger, and we knew that it wasn't just a dream: the Lord was speaking about what we should do. There were several problems though. Where could some fifteen to twenty students live for a year, and who was going to lead the school? We prayed even more intensely. The Lord needed to guide us and provide for us.

The first miracle happened rather soon. An Australian, who was a member of a fellowship that we knew in Australia, was the owner of a large rubber plantation in the mountains behind Port Moresby, an hour away from the city. On that plantation he built a large house, which was in a beautiful location, where he had lived with his family. Because of the children's education, the family had returned to Australia. Therefore, a Papua New Guinean supervisor was appointed. The owner visited regularly to organise things for the business, but the large house was vacant! He came to visit us because he had heard about us in Australia and offered us to make use of his large house at the plantation. Wow, wow, wow! The first miracle. We now had accommodation. The road to the plantation was an unpaved road that in the rainy season could be difficult to negotiate. We would therefore need a four-wheel-drive vehicle. The Lord would also provide in that matter, that was for sure! Now we only needed a principal for the school. It was clear that we had to look to Australia for that.

Of all the Bible schools and training centres we knew, there was one that had really made an impression on us: Pastor Hal Oxley's Bible school in Melbourne. The school provided two years of full-time training. The students lived together, and they were part of the congregation. In that way the students experienced for two years of church life in a flourishing congregation, which was in the middle of a movement of God's Spirit. I was bold and wrote a letter to Pastor Oxley and explained the situation to him. Was there someone in his congregation or someone on his team who could come to Papua New Guinea for several years to build a training centre similar to theirs? Someone who could at the same time train Papua New Guineans, who eventually could lead the training centre? In my letter, I mentioned about twelve points that conveyed the vision for the Bible school. We sent the letter, prayed, and anxiously awaited the reply. How would Pastor Oxley respond? We were asking quite a lot.

One of the pastors in Pastor Oxley's congregation was Terry Boyle. He was second in charge of the congregation. In a time of prayer and seeking God's face, he felt the Lord had spoken to him and given him a plan to set up and lead a training centre outside Australia, in a country that needed to be evangelised. Terry had written down eight or nine points and let his wife, Caroline, read them. Her reaction was 'Throw that away in the bin! That will never happen!' But Terry did not throw it in the bin; he put it in the drawer of his desk. Deep in his heart, Terry knew that this was not just a pipe dream. He knew that God had spoken to him. We had written a letter to Pastor Oxley, and Terry had put the paper with what he had written down, in the drawer of his desk.

Pastor Oxley went overseas for a conference. He handed over the responsibility for the congregation and the Bible school to Terry. He also asked Terry to open his mail, which was quite odd because Pastor Oxley never let anyone open his mail. Pastor Oxley had lost his wife years before, and as a widower, he and no one else opened his mail. But now he had asked Terry to open his mail, while he was absent, and Terry did what he was asked.

Several days later, Terry opened a letter from Papua New Guinea. Our letter. Terry was flabbergasted. The eight or nine points that he had written down and put in his drawer were all mentioned in our letter. This was no coincidence. His wife, Caroline, was also very surprised and admitted this was no coincidence.

When Pastor Oxley returned, Terry told him what had happened. If Pastor Oxley himself had opened the letter, he would probably have thought 'impossible' and then written a friendly but clear letter back. Terry later said, 'I wonder if he would ever have shown the letter to the elders.' Even Pastor Oxley had to admit that this was indeed very special and could not be put aside. After some deliberation, Terry decided to visit Papua New Guinea to see things for himself. He contacted us and came.

Terry's visit was wonderful. We got along really well. We felt like we had known each other for years. Terry preached in the church. Not every visitor from overseas comes across well in another culture, but Terry did a great job. The people enjoyed him. His dream and our dream for a training centre were identical. That makes one suspect that we both heard from the right source. However, Terry did not think too highly of Port Moresby as a city and as a place to live. It had not rained in months; everything was dry and dusty. But in that place in the mountains, at the rubber plantation and the large house, there it had rained and everything was green. Terry was convinced. This was what he wanted. We were overjoyed.

Pastor Oxley's congregation already had quite a large evangelism and missionary programme in Australia and overseas. To maintain another family was not possible. But Pastor Chandler's church was willing to do so, and in that way Terry and Caroline and their three children would be supported from Brisbane. It is truly remarkable what Pastor Chandler's church has done for the work in Papua New Guinea.

Everything seemed ready, and Terry and Caroline were preparing to come so that we could start the training centre in the New Year. And the first students had already applied.

We lived next to the church. Tom Kuipers was with us to help us. He was the son of the Dutch couple that for a while had led the work on Daru, and now was pioneering in the province of Milne Bay in the east of Papua New Guinea. Tom had learned the building trade from his father. Though he was only nineteen years old, he had built our house and was now working on expanding the main meeting hall. Tom could do it all; he worked with concrete, laid bricks, worked with wood, built simple furniture, installed a sewerage system, and so on. In the Old Testament, God had two men, Bezalel and Aholiab, who were very specially anointed by His Spirit to build the tabernacle. Tom also had an anointing and a God-given ability to build, although he was young. Nobody doubted that. He also was a good guitar player and became part of the music team. Later he would even marry a lovely Papua New Guinean girl and move to Australia. A number of years ago, we heard that Tom had suddenly passed away. He was fifty years old. We have very precious memories of him.

Concerning the Bible school or training centre, we received confirmation after confirmation. Hank van der Steen had been to Australia and was on a plane to fly back to Port Moresby. Next to him was an empty seat. It was announced that they were going to wait just a little bit longer for a passenger who had come on another flight that was delayed. Out of breath, the man entered the plane and took his allocated seat next to Hank. Then the plane left. Hank and this man got talking. He was the owner of the rubber plantation where the Bible school was going to be! Hank had never met him before. A meeting like that gives one the feeling that God was at work.

In the meantime, Hank and Lenie were asked to return to Australia to take up the position of church administrator which entails the whole business and organisational side of the church. In many larger congregations, this is a full-time job. Hank and Lenie accepted the offer. They had been in Port Moresby for three years. It was hard to say goodbye to them. Between Hank and Lenie and Coby and me had grown a deep friendship, a friendship that is still strong today. In the years since, we have met several times in Australia and also in the Netherlands where Hank and Lenie still have family. Every time we meet, all four of us experience that strong feeling of friendship and bond between us.

Then something happened that nobody had counted on. Out of the blue, the government claimed all the plantations that belonged to foreigners, and the owners were forced to sell their property to the government, often for a low price. The plantations were then given to cooperatives in the villages so that a village could run the plantation. The rubber plantation of this brother was also claimed, just when all the plans and preparations for the school were nearly finished. Students had already applied, and some of them had paid the tuition fees in advance. We prayed and prayed, and there was only one solution: to build a simple accommodation block for the students on the land next to the church. In the meantime, a young couple from Holland had joined us: Stefan and Ans de Boer. Stefan was quite handy, and he and Ans helped us with the practical things. With great speed, a dormitory was designed in the style of our house, and we received the permit to build. Then Tom and Stefan started building with all the help they could get. It was an adventure of faith because we did not have the money. But the money came, sometimes just in time.

One morning we needed building materials, but there was no more money. We prayed. Right after the prayer meeting, a Swiss man who had come to know the Lord came to bring a cheque for $1,500. God had spoken to him that morning. We continued building. This happened a number of times. But the accommodation would not be ready in time. We prayed again because the date to start was coming close. About fifteen kilometres away from Port Moresby was a very basic and somewhat primitive Boy Scout camp. We negotiated and for a low price were able to rent it for a few months. Lenden Butuna, the dean, would live with the students at the camp. However, Terry and Caroline had no place to live. We could not rent a house, but there were expatriates who would go on leave and wanted people to live in their house to prevent burglary. And so Terry and Caroline and their three children lived temporarily in a leave house.

When the school dormitory was finished, Tom and the others would immediately start building a house for Terry and Caroline. And that is indeed how it happened.

Two months after the school had started, the dormitory was finished, and the students came to live next to the church. Several months later, the house for the Boyle family was finished, and we became neighbours. Bob and Ruth Lutu and their little girl also lived next to the church. All the houses and buildings were built in the same simple but attractive style. Lenden Butuna, the first dean of the school, lived in one of the rooms of the building.

We started out with twenty students. Among them were several couples. They had to live together in a small room. We never heard a complaint! Sometimes there were even small children with them. It all went well.

We were one big happy family: five Pasterkamps, five Boyles, three Lutus, Lenden Butuna, and twenty students. The atmosphere was amazing. The children played with each other and were having a great time. Among the students were Piniari Sialis and his wife, Eloi, who would become a leader in the work, and Charles Lapa and his wife, Lucille (Charles became possibly the most well-known evangelist in Papua New Guinea, as the media once called him 'a prophet to his own nation'). Another couple was Gabriel and Cecilia Pepson. Gabriel became a public servant and served for seven years as ambassador of Papua New Guinea in Brussels, Belgium. Later he became the secretary general of the Foreign Affairs Department.

Every morning the students spent half an hour, sometimes much longer, in prayer and worship. After that, they studied and received training. They cooked their own meals. In the afternoon, they often had open-air evangelism, evangelism in neighbourhood schools, children's services, or they worked in the garden of the Bible school. The students became part of the core of the congregation, and in a short time, they were a great inspiration to the congregation and other young people. The spiritual level of the congregation went up because of the Bible school which became a part of the church. It was the best thing we have ever done. Terry and Caroline were great and had really found the right place for themselves. Terry often said, 'The Lord enthused me with the plantation and the large house in the mountains, because I did not like Port Moresby at all. But it was only His bait. Port Moresby was the right place for the school.' Terry and Caroline and their children would stay in the country and lead the Bible school for six years.

Although we always spoke about a training centre in the beginning, the name 'Bible school' stuck, and that is how it remained. Everyone was talking about 'the Bible school'.

In June 2007, Terry and Caroline were in Amsterdam for an evening as part of a trip through Europe. We had not seen each other for fifteen years. When we were having dinner together, Terry and Caroline said it again, 'Our six years in Papua New Guinea were the best and greatest years of our lives.'

I once heard Brother Andrew (who became famous through smuggling Bibles behind the Iron Curtain and later into China) say, 'When you spend two years at Bible school in harmony with your roommate, then you deserve a diploma.' How true. At our Bible school, young people from different tribes and backgrounds lived together and learned how to be a fellowship together. In those years, deep friendships were born which have remained to this day. The Bible school also led to a few happy marriages, but that could have been expected. In Australia, Bible schools were sometimes nicknamed 'bridal schools'.

In the meantime, Glen McDonald from Christian Life Centre had arrived to help us as secretary and children's worker. But Glen was also a great prayer warrior, and that's how a weekly intercession night was born. Those evenings were very powerful. The love, passion, and compassion with which the students prayed for their own country was moving. We sometimes sang a beautiful song: 'Lord, I ask you for

Papua New Guinea.' Quite a few people from the congregation came to these evenings of prayer, and I often heard them sing this at the prayer meeting, while the tears ran down their faces. They passionately loved their own country. It was a time of much intense intercession. I myself had an experience with the Lord in that time, which is too intimate and personal to share, but which I will never forget. Some things you experience with the Lord are good to share with others, but some other things are between you and the Lord, and that has to stay that way. There also was a consciousness of the holiness of God. Charles Lapa was always present on those Friday nights, and he prayed passionately for the rascals. He was the one who prayed to become the David Wilkerson for the city and his country. We did not know about that yet, but God heard his prayer.

I was often away, within the country itself, to visit workers and missionaries, or on patrol, but at times also in Australia or New Zealand for missionary conferences. In one way or another, the work of Christian Life Centre in Papua New Guinea had become known, especially our training programme and the discipleship group which I had begun as well as the freedom we gave to our Papua New Guinean workers. Because of this, I was later given the opportunity to also speak in quite a lot of conferences in Asia and Egypt.

When I was at home, I often taught the entire week, and sometimes two weeks continuously. I would, for example, teach on the book of Romans, Ephesians, the gifts of the Holy Spirit, or the six foundations of our faith, as mentioned in Hebrews 6. Glen handled all the organisational work; Peter Singut, a Papua New Guinean, did all the practical work like picking up people from the airport, driving people around, and maintaining our vehicles. I could therefore focus completely on the spiritual side of the work. They were our best years, with much blessing and a lot of fruit. There had been missionaries before us in Papua New Guinea who had hardly seen any harvest or fruit from their work. They sowed, and we were allowed to harvest.

Something happened when we started the Bible school that would have a great effect on the Bible school and the way we thought about training and equipping.

After the country had become independent and the first government was installed, I had to go to Rabaul to visit the workers there. On the plane that could carry about thirty-five passengers, I was assigned a seat next to a Papua New Guinean man, and I immediately recognised him from pictures in the newspaper. He was one of the ministers of the new government. He introduced himself. He asked me if I was a tourist, and I told him that I had been living in the country for about ten years. He wanted to know what I did. I told him I was a missionary. He wanted to know everything and asked where I worked and lived. I became a little cautious because you never know where someone you do not know is coming from. I told him that I lived and worked in that part of Port Moresby called Waigani. 'Oh,' he said, 'I also live in Waigani.' *I have to watch my tongue*, I thought. There were two churches in Waigani, and he asked me in which church I worked. So I answered that I worked in Christian Life Centre. 'That church next to the small fire brigade building?' he asked.

'Yes, that one,' I hesitantly replied. We love to sing, praise, and worship, and in the tropics all the windows are open, so the entire neighbourhood would hear us sing. And in Papua New Guinea they do not sing quietly!

'So you are that church that sings so beautifully. My wife and I live just behind the church, and on Sunday evening we often sit on our balcony to listen to your singing.' I sighed with relief. He continued, 'You are that church that believes in the Holy Spirit, aren't you?'

I answered, 'Yes, that is us all right. We believe in the Holy Spirit. Just like the first disciples of Jesus were filled with the Holy Spirit at Pentecost and spoke in new tongues.'

The minister told me that he had attended an Anglican missionary school and that he called himself a Christian. 'But,' he said, 'I want to know more about the Holy Spirit. When you are back in Port Moresby, you have to make an appointment with me to talk about this together.' And that is how it happened. When after a week I came home, I made an appointment with his secretary and visited him in his office in the government building.

He had reserved an hour for me. It was a pleasant conversation. I could speak freely about the baptism in the Holy Spirit. Though he had attended a Christian school, this was new for him. He listened attentively. The hour was almost over, and then he said, 'I still have another question. I am part of the first government since my country has become independent. What advice can you as a missionary give to me as a government minister?'

I had never been asked a question like that, and I knew of no course or teaching programme at Bible schools that covered this topic, 'How do I advise a government leader?' Inwardly I prayed, *Lord, wisdom, now, and lots of it*. A thought crossed my mind, and I realised it was the Holy Spirit who gave it to me. I answered, 'Sir, you know the stories from the Bible from the Old and the New Testament, isn't that right?'

'Yes, I know them,' was his answer.

I continued, 'Have you noticed that most of the great men of God in the Bible, especially in the Old Testament, were political leaders? Joseph was minister of agriculture. Moses gave the people the law. Joshua was the leader of the army and later the political leader of the people. David and Solomon were kings. Daniel was an important political leader. Nehemiah was a supervisor of the city, and there are many more.'

The minister looked surprised, and after a while, he answered, 'No, I have never really thought about that, but it is true.' He was clearly surprised.

I continued, 'They were great because they had learned to be dependent on the wisdom that God gives.'

The minister was touched by the answer that the Lord gave me, and it made him think deeply. 'Will you pray for me that I will have that wisdom as well?' he asked. I received permission from him to lay hands on him. It does not happen every day that I get the opportunity to lay hands on a government leader, I thought to myself. We prayed, and then the hour was over. I said goodbye, and he thanked me for our time together.

I walked through the corridor of the government building to go outside. I was actually very pleased with myself, especially how I had given that answer. I could have patted myself on the back. I took the handle of the door that led outside, and the Holy Spirit spoke to my heart, 'What are you going to do with this knowledge?' From that moment on, I realised that we should not only train young people for the work of the Lord, such as evangelists, pastors, youth and children workers, etc. We also have to train young people who have a calling and destiny to work in society and hold important positions there. We adjusted the training programme. The teachings from the Sermon on the Mount became the backbone of our training programme. The Sermon on the Mount is the inner life of a radical disciple of Jesus, whether he leads a church or is a politician or a leader in the world of business.

Many of our students entered the work of the Lord, and some became prominent leaders. Several students were appointed to high positions in government and in politics. One of the students, Gabriel Pepson, initially was assistant secretary of the Finance Department, then he became the ambassador of Papua New Guinea in Europe for seven years and lived in Brussels with his family. After that, he became the secretary general of foreign affairs. His desire is to go into politics.

When I asked him once which teaching had made the most impact on him, he answered without hesitating, 'The Sermon on the Mount and your teaching about law and grace.'

Jo Gabut, who as a student had prayed during the sinner's prayer, 'Lord, will you forgive me because my father is a witch doctor,' was the secretary general of the Department of Mines, Oil, and Energy for a good number of years. Once, when he travelled back home via Brussels after a visit to Canada, we met him; and I also asked him the question as to which teaching had made the most impact on him. His answer was also 'The Sermon on the Mount.'

One of the students became undersecretary of finances, and another became undersecretary of health. Some served for a time in the government after the elections. But also in other areas students received prominent positions. They became lawyers, solicitors, engineers, and business people and held positions in the area of finance. Our deepest desire and commission of the Lord was, and still is, to flavour society with radical disciples of Jesus.

CHAPTER 31

Much Blessing, Many Miracles, and Breakthroughs

WHEN THE LORD Jesus was filled with the Holy Spirit, the heavens were opened and He served and lived under an open heaven. That is what it was like during those last years in Port Moresby. The heavens were open, and there was much blessing. The atmosphere in the fellowship and at the Bible school was fantastic. The students, workers and missionaries, the children, and those who lived around the church building were one big happy family. Truly, the heavens were open.

There was much prayer, much passionate intercession, but also much praise and worship. It was all new and one big adventure. We had first experienced singing in tongues and free worship at the camp in Sydney. During our visits to Australia and New Zealand, we also experienced various aspects of worship and learned from it. In our own church, an unusual development began to take place.

Very early at the beginning of our time in Port Moresby, we experienced that on one Sunday morning, during the praise and worship, quite a number of people began to clap rhythmically. Within moments, everybody joined in. I did not know what this was and had never experienced it before. For a moment I thought that it was something cultural which was trying to disturb the worship. I wanted to stop it, but the Holy Spirit spoke very clearly within me: 'This is of Me. I am teaching My people how to wage spiritual warfare in praise.' I did not do anything but was surprised about what the Lord had spoken so clearly. After about ten minutes, the clapping slowly ceased, and it became quiet. I told the congregation what God had just spoken to me. After that meeting, the rhythmical clapping happened regularly, not every Sunday, but when there was a special moving of God's Spirit. I began to recognise it and began to discern spiritual warfare in praise that exalts the Lord. I also saw examples of this in the Bible. It was clearly different than the usual praise.

Edward Oki had a real anointing to lead the singing and especially in exuberant praise. When a meeting began, and it was somewhat heavy going, he was able, under the anointing, to release something in the people that after one or two songs there would be freedom. Very often people danced and with enthusiasm were able to exalt the Lord without hindrance.

One Sunday morning, Edward began to lead; but after one song, I could not see him anymore. Then suddenly, I saw him. He was lying stretched out on the stage behind the pulpit, in total worship to the Lord. There was such a presence of the Lord, such holiness. Within moments, everyone was either lying on the floor or kneeling down and remained in that attitude during the entire service. For two hours there was this total engagement in complete worship of the Lord, sometimes with singing, other times in free worship, but also with long periods of silence in which no one dared to speak, because God was in our midst. I was not able to preach that morning, neither did I want to.

On another Sunday, Edward went up to the microphone and said, 'The Lord has spoken to my heart that we should not have our praise and worship in this building today, but outside, as we walk through our neighbourhood.' Before I fully realised what he had said, Edward walked out of the church. The musicians followed him and then the entire congregation. In the weeks after that, we saw people from the neighbourhood coming to our church and accepting Jesus. Every service was an adventure: how would the Holy Spirit lead us this time?

Edward Oki had a special ability to lead praise, one of the other singers in spiritual warfare and again another singer in prophetic worship. If one of them was leading, the others were usually on the platform as singers. We experienced times when the Holy Spirit began to move in a certain way and then the worship leader would take a step back, and one of the others take his place, because he had an anointing to lead in that aspect of worship. Since leaving Papua New Guinea, I have not experienced that again. We still feel a longing for these times. We saw the reality of David's tabernacle in our midst.

The heavens were opened, and often you did not want the meeting to end, because God was there. We have felt: one more step and we are in heaven!

Monday evening was the time of practice for the worship leaders and musicians. We could hear them from our home. One Monday evening our boys were already in bed, and Coby and I sat next to each other on the couch in the living room. We heard the singing and music, and suddenly wave after wave of the presence of the Lord spread from the church over all the surrounding area. Though we lived some fifty metres from the church, the waves of the presence of the Lord entered our house as well. We sat on the couch for a long time and allowed His presence to wash over us. It was so powerful and so precious.

One Sunday afternoon I was walking to the church. I heard somebody play the mouth organ (harmonica). It was the melody of a worship song. I walked to some bushes, and there underneath one of the bushes was Edward Oki playing the harmonica. I did not even know that he could play that instrument. But before I reached Edward, the presence of the Lord washed over me. I stood there for quite some time. I did not want to leave. Edward did not notice my presence. We really discovered the reality of David's tabernacle. God lives and is enthroned in the praises of His children.

Many miracles, even outstanding miracles, happened. A young couple, graduates from university, had their first child, a girl. They gave her the name Suau. After several months it was clear that something was not right. Her head began to swell on one side. Everybody saw it. The doctor in the hospital sent them to Australia for further research. In Australia, they examined her and found a tumour in her head. In the laboratory, a small part they had taken from the tumour was examined. It was malignant, and it was a fast-growing tumour. She was nine months old but would not live much longer. We had already prayed for her several times, but there was no sign of healing.

One Sunday morning, just before we celebrated communion, Terry Boyle leaned over to me and whispered in my ear, 'The Lord says that we have to pray for little Suau and to anoint her with oil.' I responded immediately, took the microphone, and shared what the Lord had said to Terry. We called the parents to come to the front with Suau, anointed her with oil, and prayed for her. Suau was healed from that moment on. The last time I heard about her, she was nineteen years old.

A young couple from Mount Hagen was expecting their second child. They already had a boy of about two years old, a very lively little boy. I had nicknamed him 'bulldozer' because this solid little boy did not stop for anything once he started running.

After about six months of pregnancy, the contractions started and did not stop. They immediately took the mother, named Anne, to the hospital, and there the child, a girl, was born; she was dead.

The premature and lifeless baby was wrapped in a green cloth and put to the side. The medical staff helped the mother with the afterbirth and then were going to take her to the ward. Anne realised that she would go to the ward without her baby and the following day would go home without her baby. She looked at the green bundle and asked the doctor if she could hold her baby for a moment. When she held the baby, she loudly cried out, 'Lord Jesus, You have done so many miracles. I ask You for a miracle for my baby!' She watched the little green bundle and could only see a tiny foot, and then she saw the foot move. 'Doctor, Doctor, her foot just moved!' she cried out. The doctor was afraid that she was hallucinating. But Anne looked again at the baby and saw the foot move. 'Doctor, please look!' The doctor looked, and he too saw the foot move. They took the baby from the cloth and saw how the body began to gain colour from the feet up. Then the baby started to cry. All the people in the delivery room were beside themselves. It was about half an hour ago that the baby was born dead, and now it was alive.

The baby was immediately put in an incubator. After two weeks, the child was strong enough to go home. Anne and her husband were thrilled, and the story of the miracle of their baby spread like wildfire among the people they knew.

Several weeks later, the baby was dedicated. The parents had given her the name Miracle. I had the honour of dedicating little Miracle to the Lord. God was thanked and praised that morning.

When Coby and I visited Mount Hagen several years ago, to conduct a series of meetings, a young woman came up to us after the service and said, 'Do you know who I am?' No, we didn't. Then I recognised the woman standing behind her. It was Anne, Miracle's mother. The woman in her twenties standing before us was Miracle. We were deeply moved. Miracle was recently married and had given birth to a baby. Miracle is a healthy woman, and she follows Jesus. She knows the story of her birth and tells it often.

This was the account of just two miracles from that period. But they show what it was like: heaven was open. Many more miracles happened, but these two are engraved in our memories. But that did not mean that everyone was healed or experienced a miracle in that time. During this amazing time, a young couple from the fellowship lost their recently born child. We prayed for them in church, and the way in which the Lord touched and comforted them was also totally supernatural.

From time to time the Lord sent men and women whose ministry was to build up the churches in Papua New Guinea. Two sisters of the German Lutheran order of the Sisters of Mary were especially used by God. It was remarkable to see a sister in a white habit preaching, and then demons shouting at her through the mouth of a young man, challenging her. She calmly walked towards this young man and cast out the demons in the name of the Lord Jesus.

Pastor Trevor Chandler visited several times. During one of his visits, we took him to a camp in the mountains behind Port Moresby. There was no electricity in the meetings, just kerosene lamps. Many insects swarmed around those lamps and around Pastor Trevor. Suddenly Pastor Trevor stopped. An insect had flown into his mouth, and before he knew it, he had swallowed it. He stopped, and everybody began to laugh. In the churches in the villages, this happens often. Pastor Trevor recovered and said, 'Anyway, his mother will be glad that her son is in the ministry.' People burst into laughter and could hardly regain their composure. We even saw two people fall to the floor because they were laughing so much.

Later I sent this little story to the Asian edition of *Reader's Digest*. It was published in the 'humour' column, and I received eighty American dollars. In any case, it does portray something of the atmosphere that was present. God was working, and there was a lot of fun too. We discovered that those two go together.

From time to time the Lord sent more people with unique ministries, to strengthen the work in Papua New Guinea. A special visit was that of Pastor Frank Houston, whose ministry in 1969 had such an impact upon our lives.

I had accepted an invitation to speak at a missionary conference of the Assemblies of God in Auckland, New Zealand. The other speaker was Pastor Brian Bailey. Originally he was from England, but at the time he was living in the United States. We often met people who were prophetic, but only a few times did we meet a real prophet. Brian Bailey was a real prophet. During the conference, he promised to come to Papua New Guinea, which he did several times. The following happened during one of his visits.

One of the Siwai men had left the work with a small group of Christians and had started something himself. He called himself an apostle, which was causing confusion. Several believers knew him well and wanted to remain loyal to him. But we did not quite know what to do about it. Then Brian Bailey arrived. Brian and his wife, Audrey, arrived late in the afternoon; and we did not have much time to talk. That same evening, the first meeting of the conference would be held. Brian began to preach. His topic? How do you handle people who call themselves apostles but who are not apostles? We were listening very intently. He gave the answers that we needed, and in the weeks following, we were able to act. Eventually nearly all the believers came back into the work.

David Muap, who came from New Ireland and was the dean of the Bible school, went to Rabaul and Kavieng at the invitation of the Uniting Church. He had phenomenal meetings. Demons were cast out, the sick were healed, and believers were powerfully filled with the Holy Spirit. The word went out to all the islands that God was moving.

At various locations in the Highlands, movements of God's Spirit erupted. One of the workers from Port Moresby was in one place able to lead many people to the Lord and baptised 387 people in the freezing cold water of a river which flowed down from the mountains. There were more people to be baptised, but those doing the baptising were half frozen from the cold and became unable to move. Several days later, they resumed and baptised the remaining new believers.

The tuition fees for the children of Terry and Caroline and our children became more and more expensive. Our children could only go to the international school. The church in Brisbane which was supporting us had reached their limit of support for missionaries and could do no more. We asked ourselves how we could continue. We did not doubt that the Lord would provide and lead us, but the question was how.

Again I was invited for the yearly missionary conference of the Assemblies of God in Auckland. The other speaker was again Pastor Brian Bailey. I had given a message on Sunday evening from Revelation 12, which proclaims that believers overcome Satan by the blood of the Lamb, the word of their testimony, and by not loving their lives even unto the death. That means that if necessary, and when the Lord asks it of us, believers are willing to give their lives for Jesus. After the message, I led the 2,500 people present in a song of worship that we had just learned. The worship lasted for an hour. It was unforgettable. In the middle of that time of worship, the Holy Spirit spoke to my heart: 'Your next assignment is Japan.' I was stunned and overwhelmed. After the service, I shared it with Pastor Bailey. He too had heard from God about our calling to Japan. I then knew that our time in Papua New Guinea was coming to an end. It was not easy to tell Coby about this when I got home, but she also felt that this was a word from the Lord. By then we had been in Papua New Guinea for thirteen years and lived in the tropics, and physically we were beginning to feel the effects. We were in Papua New Guinea for another year and then left for a year's leave to the Netherlands and then to Japan.

In many places in Papua New Guinea, there was an unmistakeable moving of God's Spirit. We all felt it. It became more and more powerful. There was intense prayer and much worship. The third year of the Bible school had begun. The students were on fire for God. We organised a workers' conference in the capital and invited Pastor Peter Morrow from New Zealand to be the main speaker. We knew Peter and his wife, Anne. I had preached a few times in their church in Christchurch. God was using Peter in a unique way, especially among the Pentecostals but also in the charismatic movement. Peter Morrow was very prophetic and was seen by many as a prophet.

One morning during the workers' conference, God spoke to my heart that the missionaries and leaders should wash the feet of the Papua New Guinean workers. I shared this with Peter, and with tears in his eyes, he confirmed this. Peter had never experienced a feet-washing ceremony before. It was gripping to see the missionaries kneeling on the floor and washing the sometimes rough, hardened, dark feet covered with callouses. Many tears were shed that morning by the national workers and by the missionaries. Later the national workers spontaneously washed the feet of the missionaries. There are some meetings one will never forget. This was one of them.

Peter had made jokes about the fact that he was so skinny. He sure was skinny and was sometimes called, by way of a joke, 'New Zealand's skinniest preacher'. He himself said in jest that there were books about how to lose weight for people who were overweight, but that as far as he knew, there were no books for skinny people about how to gain weight. 'But,' he said, 'someone has told me that it helps to eat a lot of bananas.' I heard that and had an idea. We spread the message that everyone was to bring a banana on Sunday morning and keep it out of sight. We then would take a love offering of bananas and give it to Pastor Peter.

In the meeting, I spoke about the special ministry Peter had, how we were blessed by it and how God had used him. But we were also very concerned for him because he was so skinny, and therefore, we would take up a special offering. At a certain signal, workers with plastic baby bathtubs came into the meeting, and everyone put their banana in the tubs. We gave Peter three baby bathtubs filled with bananas. It was hilarious. Peter often said that never before had anybody played a trick him as well as we did that time. All this shows the joyous, relaxed, and lovely atmosphere that was present. There was indeed much joy and happiness in our meetings.

Then it happened. The meeting on Saturday evening, during the visit of Peter Morrow, came. Again there was much joy and a lot of laughter. Peter himself joined in heartily. We had not yet heard about the Toronto blessing; that came years later. But after an hour and a half, I wondered if it would not be time to become more serious. Did my Dutch conservatism rear its head? I asked Pina Sialis to come and to lead us in worship. My actual thought was that in this way we could regain some order in the meeting. Pina began to lead. Immediately there was powerful spiritual warfare in praise. It was different from other times. Then all of a sudden the heavens tore open. In the spirit, I saw it and how everywhere demons were fleeing in total panic because God's Spirit had come. Even now, while I write this, I find it hard to describe what happened. The comment 'the heavens were torn open' is probably what comes closest to it. The praise and worship that evening was in a higher dimension. We had never experienced praise like this. Peter Morrow also had never experienced anything like this before. The meeting lasted until late that evening.

Towards midnight, we received a phone call from America. The well-known street evangelist Arthur Blessitt, pastor of the Sunset Strip, had heard from God to come to Papua New Guinea and would arrive the following afternoon on a flight from Hawaii. I knew the book in which he tells how he received from God the plan to walk, carrying a big wooden cross and evangelising from place to place. Wherever people gathered, he would stop and testify or preach.

The following morning, in the Sunday meeting, I told everybody that Arthur Blessitt would arrive in the afternoon, and asked for all the believers to go to the airport to welcome him. That is all we knew. We did not even know what he looked like.

That afternoon 300 believers from the fellowship came to the airport. All kinds of people came out of the arrival lounge, but we did not recognise anyone until a man, with somewhat long hair and carrying a life-size folded wooden cross, came out of the arrival hall. You could not miss him. International travellers do not usually carry a big wooden cross.

The believers cheered and lifted Arthur on their shoulders and carried him around the airport. When Arthur was back on his feet, he gestured to everyone to be seated, and he began to speak. It caused chaos because it became difficult for other passengers to go from the arrival lounge to the parking lot.

Arthur spoke, testified, and prayed. Together with the believers, he prayed for his time in Papua New Guinea. He told them how he had received a letter from someone in Papua New Guinea who had read his book and how God had spoken to him. The week after that, he was invited to speak at a breakfast meeting with the president of America, but he had cancelled that and taken the first available flight to Papua New Guinea. God had clearly sent him. Right there at the airport, he asked if anyone wanted to accept Jesus, and three people went forward to do so.

It seemed like the meeting that evening was filled with godly electricity. Peter Morrow and Arthur Blessitt both preached. There was something going on in the spirit realm, something very special. The entire meeting was a dimension higher or deeper, whatever you want to call it.

On Monday, Arthur began to walk through the city carrying the big wooden cross. We asked the Bible school students to join him. We changed our whole program, God had clearly arranged something else.

That same afternoon Charles Lapa called us from the bookshop. He had just led a gang leader called Jo to Jesus. The gang leader had asked if he could bring his gang to the church that evening and have a meeting. 'Of course,' was our response. 'What time are they coming?' Charles did not know. We told Arthur about it when he came back, and he was enthusiastic. A gang wanted a meeting! I asked Charles how he knew that gang leader. He somewhat sheepishly told me that he had tried for several years to connect with the youth gangs, because he had heard me challenge people one Sunday morning, when I said that this city needed a David Wilkerson. He had prayed that morning and asked

God if he could be that person, and from that moment, he had started visiting the gangs, to try to gain their trust and friendship.

That evening we prepared everything. We had no idea how many gang members would show up. We only had a few lights on because gangs do not like much light. A little after nine they arrived, about sixty gang members, or 'rascals' as they were known. We gave them something to drink, and we had some snacks. Charles shared a little, and Arthur gave his testimony. Around half past eleven, nearly sixty gang members were on their knees, several with tears in their eyes. They prayed to Jesus for forgiveness and cleansing. After twelve o'clock, sixty deeply touched men, mainly young men, went home. We were thrilled and stunned. What was happening?

Among the gang members who had come was the leader of another gang. He asked Charles if we could have a meeting the following evening for his gang. He asked specifically if Arthur and Charles could be there. He told us how Charles had often visited them and had spent time with them. They trusted him. He never knew that Charles had prayed, 'Lord, let me be the David Wilkerson of this city.' That evening also about sixty rascals arrived. Arthur testified and Charles testified. With the exception of three rascals, they all went down on their knees and prayed the sinner's prayer: 'Lord Jesus, I come to You. Thank You that You love me and have always known me. I repent of my sins and ask You to wash me clean with Your blood of all my sins, etc.'

More rascals showed up on Wednesday evening when we held another meeting with Arthur and Charles, about fifty of them. Later that night, they all went down on their knees. It was amazing.

On Thursday, another group of rascals arrived. They all went down on their knees and prayed to accept Jesus. Friday evening it happened again. We just stood there and watched it happen.

In the meantime, the police had heard that rascals were coming to our church, and they blocked the street. When the police left later that evening, they thought no one had shown up, but then the rascals came to church. All of them accepted Jesus.

Saturday evening another group of rascals came, and again the Holy Spirit moved. There was great joy in heaven.

On Sunday morning, several rascals came to the meeting. Usually the rascals did things when it was dark, but now a few of them came openly, in the light. The first rascals who had repented were baptised, among them Jo who was the first one Charles had led to Jesus. Some were already filled with the Holy Spirit, while others received the Holy Spirit that morning.

The Sunday evening after that, more rascals came to the meeting, and a good number came to the Lord Jesus.

Jo was sought by the police, and he asked me to come with him to the police station. He wanted to turn himself in. I went with him on Monday morning. A Papua New Guinean police officer at the counter asked what he could do for Jo. 'I am Jo whom you are looking for, and I came to turn myself in.' The police officer was so surprised he nearly fainted and quickly went to get the commander. I confirmed that this was indeed Jo. Jo was eventually sentenced to two years in prison, but he was released earlier because he testified so much in prison and led many fellow prisoners to Jesus. He had committed quite a few crimes, but even the court saw the change in his life. Jo is now a pastor of a Pentecostal church.

Nearly every evening there were meetings with the rascals. Charles and Arthur were busy, very busy. But it was so good. It was as if we were living in a dream world. We slept little those months, but that did not matter. I once said to our team, 'I would rather die in the midst of a revival than sleep through it!' I am still of the same opinion.

During the day, Arthur Blessitt went into town with his cross, and some Christians joined him. One morning, the first place where he stopped was in front of the bank. Several boys, among them our eight-year-old son, Mark, held up the cross; and Arthur began to preach. I was there as well.

Suddenly a young Papua New Guinean woman came out of the building crying. She walked up to Arthur and said she wanted to accept Jesus. Then she told him that she had a dream that night. In her dream, she was in the office and looked outside and saw a life-size wooden cross and a man who preached about Jesus. The man prayed with her and led her to Jesus. She was deeply moved by the dream, and when she arrived at work that morning, she told her colleagues about it. They looked at her and thought she had flipped. An hour later, she looked outside, and there was a life-size wooden cross and a man who was preaching. More staff members of the bank went outside, stunned. Arthur was able to pray with some of them.

It was December and just before Christmas when all this happened. In one of the small supermarkets was a dark-skinned Santa Claus who sat at the window and handed out candy to children and shook their hands. Then Arthur stopped in front of the window with his big wooden cross and began to preach. Soon after Santa came outside and, being very emotional, asked if Arthur could pray for him. Santa came to repent. The children had to wait for a while before Santa returned to hand out sweets.

A few days later, Arthur was on the other side of town. On the hill was a squatters' area, a place where people had built shacks to live in. The news had preceded his arrival: 'The man of God with the cross is coming.' A father took his crippled little son and carried him down. He walked straight up to Arthur and said, 'Man of God, pray for my boy.' Arthur prayed for the boy and put him on his feet, and the boy began to walk. The father was astonished. He cried, shouted, and just didn't know what to do, because he was so happy. The Lord Jesus had healed his son. A large group of people came, and Arthur began to preach. Many people gave their lives to Jesus that morning. They had seen the power and love of Jesus!

After two weeks in Port Moresby, Arthur went to Mount Hagen in the Highlands and walked from Mount Hagen to Lae, which took a few weeks. Charles and several others joined him. Arthur carried the large cross. Where people gathered they stopped, testified, and preached while Charles would often interpret.

Near a small village, an old man walked up to them. Trembling, he touched the cross. He said, 'Now I have seen the cross of Jesus and touched it. Now I believe.' Arthur later told me that he did not have the courage to tell this man that this was not the real cross of Jesus.

After several weeks, Arthur came back to Port Moresby, completely exhausted. We booked him into a hotel where we think he would have slept for most of three days.

Just before he left, he was with the Bible school students one morning and told them about his life and the price it costs to be used by God. The words 'it was impressive and unforgettable' are too weak to describe that morning.

Arthur's flight back to America departed at midnight. In the meantime, my parents had come from the Netherlands and were with us for three months. Especially my father was deeply impressed by him. When Arthur had checked in, he said, 'We will thank the Lord for this time.' He had been in Papua New Guinea for over two months. In the middle of the airport, near the departure hall, we knelt down with a group of Christians to thank the Lord and to say goodbye. My father was there too, and while the other travellers were watching, he also knelt down. He never forgot that moment.

The work among the rascals continued. In a short period, several hundred had come to the Lord Jesus.

A news headline in the paper said, 'Crime in the capital decreased because of good police work.' The converted rascals did not accept that and wrote a letter to the editor saying, 'We have found Jesus and have repented and are now having Bible studies. It has nothing to do with the police.'

Soon articles appeared in the newspaper: 'Converted rascals are having Bible studies.' More and more attention was given to it. One day the national newspaper published two pages with testimonies of converted rascals and Charles's testimony. This exploded like fireworks. Everyone noticed that something had happened.

The minister of youth affairs invited Charles and his team to come and talk with him. They led him to Jesus in his office.

The minister of justice also invited us to come and talk with him. I was at that meeting. He had attended a missionary school and said that he believed in Jesus, and he asked us to pray for him. 'You have achieved more than we could ever have done with the police' was his conclusion.

Charles and his team were invited to visit the minister of police, a naturalised Australian man. He was deeply impressed by everything that was happening. He asked Charles and his team to organise an evangelistic campaign. All rascals could come, and police would not act. Again he stated that though several rascals were sought by the police, the police would not arrest them. The campaign was at the expense of the police department and took place just after we had left Papua New Guinea.

The meetings were charged with the presence of the Lord. Quite a number of converted rascals came to the meetings, while they also formed their own groups. Charles was their leader. They trusted him. Charles himself could never have imagined that all this would happen. Because most of the converted rascals did not speak English, Charles and his wife, Lucille, decided to start a Pidgin English–speaking congregation in the area of Morata, near Waigani. Now there is a church, several refuge homes for rascals, workplaces, gardens, where they grow their food, and accommodation. Recently, in a supernatural way, they became the owners of a very large piece of land just outside the city, and most of the work will move to that place in the future.

It also spread to other areas. In the Highlands, a murderer came to Jesus. He turned himself in. He was sentenced to twenty-one years in prison. After two years, they released him. Within the prison, he had led many to Jesus. The judge said, 'You are of more use outside of prison than inside.' And he was released on probation. As far as we know, he was never again in trouble with the police.

Our departure was approaching. Caroline and Terry were expecting their fourth child, so we decided that they would move into our house. One of the Papua New Guinean workers moved into their house, and we lived for those last two months in a leave house.

In one of the last meetings, the Holy Spirit fell again. Several people with demons began to manifest, but the next moment they were free. The spirit of prophecy fell, and the most shy and withdrawn believers were prophesying, one after the other. We had not experienced this before either. I realised this was 'the spirit of prophecy,' as mentioned in Revelation 19:10.

Our farewell was one big celebration. A huge 'mumu', a traditional meal, was made. And then the last Sunday arrived.

In the morning I ordained, with the laying on of hands, the team of ministries that would lead the work in the nation. Six men in total. There were over thirty churches and three Bible schools, in Siwai, Port Moresby, and recently also in Goroka. The Lord gave me prophetic words for everyone individually, and finally I blessed Terry because we had all felt that he was to lead the team for a period. I laid hands on him and prophesied over him. Then I sat down and had an amazing experience. I said to Coby who was sitting next to me, 'I do not have it anymore. Terry has it now.' I felt that I no longer had the anointing and authority to lead the work. Through the laying on of hands, I had given it to Terry. He told me after the service, 'From the moment that you laid hands on me, I had something that I did not have before.' Terry led the work for two more years. When he left, the leadership was given to one of the national leaders, who took it for a couple of years.

That evening was our big farewell. Hundreds of people had come. We hugged. There was a lot of crying. We received gifts, and we thanked the Lord together and committed each other to the Lord.

The following afternoon, our flight departed. First we went to Australia for a week, and then we had a ten-day holiday in Singapore, and from there to the Netherlands. When we left Papua New Guinea, hundreds of people had come to the airport. When all passengers were on board, there were many people behind the fence who were waving and cheering. A fellow passenger asked surprised, 'Are all those people there for you?' When we answered that they were, he said, 'Then you must be an important government official or something like that.' When I told him that we were missionaries who were saying goodbye, he was stunned. 'Has the gospel made such an impression then?' Yes, the gospel had really made a deep and lasting impression.

When the plane taxied to the runway, Coby was crying. The three boys were quiet. I did not know what to do with myself. We left and would certainly come back for visits, but our fourteen years of being missionaries in Papua New Guinea were over.

When we departed, I was thirty-seven years old. However, our life is still closely connected with this country and its people, and especially the believers. The Lord has allowed us to do more than just to work in Papua New Guinea, and looking back, Papua New Guinea was a most precious time. It was our 'school of the Spirit'.

During one of my farewell visits, I flew to Kerema in the Gulf Province. I spoke briefly with the Australian captain of the flight. I asked him how long he had been in the country. He answered that he had lived and flown here for some years and had gone back to Australia, but he had returned. Then he looked at me and said, 'You may not understand this. You can leave Papua New Guinea, but Papua New Guinea does not leave you.' I knew exactly what he meant!

Before we left, some leaders said to me, 'You are not a Dutchman but a white Papua New Guinean. We have reserved a spot on the church grounds, and we want you to be buried there when your time has come.' It was a great compliment.

Twenty years earlier, a prophetic word was spoken over my life: 'At a young age I will call you, and at a young age you will serve Me.'

CPSIA information can be obtained
at www.ICGtesting.com
Printed in the USA
LVHW110900140223
739388LV00008B/387/J